A

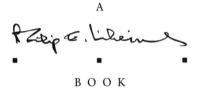

B O O K

The Philip E. Lilienthal imprint
honors special books
in commemoration of a man whose work
at University of California Press from 1954 to 1979
was marked by dedication to young authors
and to high standards in the field of Asian Studies.
Friends, family, authors, and foundations have together
endowed the Lilienthal Fund, which enables UC Press
to publish under this imprint selected books
in a way that reflects the taste and judgment
of a great and beloved editor.

The publisher and the University of California Press Foundation gratefully acknowledge the generous support of the Philip E. Lilienthal Imprint in Asian Studies, established by a major gift from Sally Lilienthal.

Global East Asia

THE GL●BAL SQU■RE

Edited by
Matthew Gutmann, Brown University
Jeffrey Lesser, Emory University

The Global Square series features edited volumes focused on how regions and countries interact with the rest of the contemporary world. Each volume analyzes the tensions, inequalities, challenges, and achievements inherent in global relationships. Drawing on work by journalists, artists, and academics from a range of disciplines—from the humanities to the sciences, from public health to literature—The Global Square showcases essays on the histories, cultures, and societies of countries and regions as they develop in conjunction with and contradiction to other geographic centers.

Each volume in The Global Square series aims to escape simplistic truisms about global villages and to provide examples and analysis of the magnitude, messiness, and complexity of connections. Anchoring each book in a particular region or country, contributors provoke readers to examine the global and local implications of economic and political transformations.

1. *Global Latin America: Into the Twenty-First Century*, edited by Matthew Gutmann and Jeffrey Lesser

2. *Global Africa: Into the Twenty-First Century*, edited by Dorothy L. Hodgson and Judith A. Byfield

3. *Global Middle East: Into the Twenty-First Century*, edited by Asef Bayat and Linda A. Herrera

4. *Global East Asia: Into the Twenty-First Century*, edited by Frank N. Pieke and Koichi Iwabuchi

Global East Asia

INTO THE TWENTY-FIRST CENTURY

*Edited by Frank N. Pieke
and Koichi Iwabuchi*

UNIVERSITY OF CALIFORNIA PRESS

University of California Press
Oakland, California

© 2021 by The Regents of the University of California

Library of Congress Cataloging-in-Publication Data

Names: Pieke, Frank N., editor. | Iwabuchi, Kōichi, editor.
Title: Global East Asia : into the twenty-first century / edited by
    Frank N. Pieke and Koichi Iwabuchi.
Other titles: Global square ; 4.
Description: Oakland, California : University of California Press, [2021] |
    Series: Global square ; 4 | Includes bibliographical references and index.
Identifiers: LCCN 2020048860 (print) | LCCN 2020048861 (ebook) |
    ISBN 9780520299863 (hardback) | ISBN 9780520299870 (paperback) |
    ISBN 9780520971424 (ebook)
Subjects: LCSH: Globalization—East Asia—21st century. |
    East Asia—21st century.
Classification: LCC HN720.5.Z9 G565 2021 (print) | LCC HN720.5.Z9 (ebook) |
    DDC 303.48/2095—dc23
LC record available at https://lccn.loc.gov/2020048860
LC ebook record available at https://lccn.loc.gov/2020048861

Manufactured in the United States of America

25 24 23 22 21
10 9 8 7 6 5 4 3 2 1

CONTENTS

Introduction

THE MANY FACES OF GLOBAL EAST ASIA

Frank N. Pieke and Koichi Iwabuchi

GLOBAL EAST ASIA IS MUCH more than a handful of powerful countries and rich multinational companies. East Asian globalization is built on a dizzying combination: a very strong and very deep civilizational self-consciousness fused with hypermodernity, wealth, influence, and power. With its focus on global East Asia, this book will view the global square from the perspective of this rapidly rising global center.

Its civilizational status and spectacular modernity enable global East Asia to cater to and merge with the full range of global tastes and styles—from haute couture to soap operas, and from traditional art to Pokémon. East Asian foods have blended into the world's cuisines. East Asian popular culture (television, movies, gaming, music) has become ubiquitous not only elsewhere in Asia but also in the West, as have East Asian religions and ways of thinking. As East Asia has become richer, the movement of East Asians across the world has evolved far beyond the old diasporas of Japanese, Koreans, and Chinese. Global East Asia has become a center of innovation in science and technology, rivaling and in certain areas even surpassing the West. While no match for the United States yet, Chinese military power reaches far beyond the region into the Indo-Pacific. East Asian—and especially Chinese—power and influence also stretch beyond the conventional military and civilian domains into the cyberspace and outer space.

East Asia's position as a global core strikes many people as something new and sudden—used, as we are, to seeing the West as the center of the world. Yet East Asia's global impact has a long and complex history. Some of this history is intertwined with Western expansion, colonialism, and imperialism, while other aspects have emerged independently from and sometimes even earlier than the rise of the West. Japan's economic and military power dates from the Meiji Restoration of 1868. China's dominance goes back even further: until the late eighteenth century, China was by far the largest and most developed society and economy in the world. In fact, Western expansionism in the sixteenth and seventeenth centuries was in large part driven by the desire to tap into the wealth of China and competition for trade with this then-uncontested center of gravity of the world economic system.

Like any other region, East Asia is an imaginary unit with unclear and seemingly arbitrary boundaries. Undisputedly, Japan, China and Korea are at its core, not only geographically, but also as powers, economies, and cultures. Mongolia and Taiwan are usually also included. Japan, Korea, and China all self-consciously pride themselves on a long history of political unity and independence, a deep civilization, and a strong common and unifying culture. More than perhaps anywhere else in the world, these countries' people see their unity as self-evident, unquestionable, and eternal. This unity is vested not only in the imported notion of the nation but also, and more importantly, follows from the long history of unitary states that shape, represent, rule, expand and defend a country and its people and culture.

The history of these three great nations is connected through war, conquest, migration, trade, piracy, travel, and especially culture and religion. Chinese Confucianism has grown deep roots in Korea and Japan, as has the Buddhism that came to these two countries through China. In Japan and Korea, Chinese writing, literature, and arts have been adopted and perfected to such an extent that they often surpass the Chinese originals.

The nature and the limits of the current boundaries of the East Asian region were informed by the history of imperial expansion and competition before the twentieth century. The last dynasty in China, the Qing Dynasty (1646–1912), was a product of invasion and conquest by a non-Chinese people, the Manchus, whose origin lies in what is now China's Northeast (Manchuria), which borders Korea to the south and Russia to the north. Their empire included not only all of historical China but also large tracts of non-Chinese territories to the north, west, east and south, such as Taiwan, Xinjiang, or Mongolia, which were incorporated into the empire through conquest, trade, settlement, and acculturation. However, elsewhere Qing expansionism ran up against spirited resistance, particularly in Burma (Myanmar), Vietnam, Tibet, and Korea. To the north, the Qing faced direct competition from another, equally aggressive and expansionist empire: Tsarist Russia.

This history continues to mark both the national borders of contemporary China and the boundaries of the region of what we call East Asia. East Asia as we imagine it today therefore does not include the Russian Far East and the territories beyond the Qing Empire in Central and Southeast Asia. Tibet remains an interesting liminal case. As a contemporary part of the People's Republic of China, it should be included in East Asia. However, because of its long history of independence from the Qing, it is often seen as a part of South Asia or even Central Asia rather than East Asia.

More recently, conflict and warfare in the twentieth century have done more to sever than to reinforce the connections between East Asian countries. The rise of Japan toward the end of the nineteenth century soon led to conflict and open warfare with the great regional powers of the day: the Qing and Russian Empires. Japan's open aspiration to create an empire for itself in East Asia—and later also in Southeast Asia and the Pacific—was justified with an imaginary constellation of Asian or East Asian connections that went together with lofty names like "Pan-Asianism" and the "Greater East Asia Co-Prosperity Sphere." Yet Japan envisioned empire in a very different manner from the way the Manchus had three centuries earlier when they conquered China and established the Qing dynasty. In the twentieth century, China was no longer the cultural, economic, and political center that empire builders aspired to conquer, control, and make their own; it was instead a peripheral object of colonial ambition of new and more powerful centers. A similar colonial ambition applied to other parts of the Japanese empire in East and Southeast Asia. Unlike the Qing, the Japanese did not bring disparate peoples and cultures together into a unified political imperial structure in their conquest; rather, they enhanced their fragmentation and division by fueling anti-imperial and anticolonial aspirations for independence and nationhood across Asia. When the Second World War was over, the final result was a postcolonial collection of independent nation-states built from the rubble of Japanese and Western colonial empires.

The aftermath of the war also created the new division between Communism and the self-proclaimed capitalist and democratic "Free World." Not Europe, but East and Southeast Asia became the main theater in which the Cold War turned into open hostility and even acute armed conflict across a "Bamboo Curtain" that ran straight through the East Asian region and even individual nations. In Asia, the hot battles of the Cold War separated China from Taiwan, North Korea from South Korea, and North Vietnam from South Vietnam.

The history of the Second World War, postwar nation building, and Cold War division still informs the political reality of East Asia. Despite the strong cultural continuities that remain and the many more recent and unparalleled connections forged by investment, trade, exchange, travel, migration, popular culture, and fashion, it is hard to imagine East Asia as a unit, both for the people in the region itself and elsewhere. China and Korea continue to make political hay from the lack of Japanese guilt about the atrocities of the Second World War. North Korea has not only survived the end of the Cold War but has now added a nuclear dimension to its art of brinkmanship. Japan, South Korea, Taiwan, and even Hong Kong continue to be part of the capitalist and democratic world focused on the United States as a superpower, security umbrella, and cultural and political center, as demonstrated again by the protests and demonstrations in Hong Kong in 2019 and 2020.

Meanwhile, China is fast becoming a superpower in its own right. To China, the United States seems intent on resurrecting the old Bamboo Curtain in East Asia, no longer to thwart communism but simply in order to contain the ambitions of an equal and a rival. As China self-consciously seeks space to grow and expand, it has therefore not been able to turn east but has been compelled to venture farther afield to the west and south to Central Asia, Southeast Asia, Africa, Latin America, and increasingly also to Australia and Europe.

Since we started working on this book in 2017, the depth of the cleavage between China and the United States has increased remarkably, to the point that globalization itself is under siege. A growth of nationalism, protectionism, and identity politics, coupled with a general distrust of elites, big business, and government has been building up not just in North America and Europe but in Asia as well. When this movement merged with hardline neocon forces in the Trump administration in the United States, events started to escalate rapidly with no end in sight at the time of writing (May 2020).

The China-US trade war is not principally about unfair trade practices, jobs, or immigration. It is perceived on both sides of the Pacific as a struggle for hegemony, and it is increasingly openly so. The United States is trying to repatriate the global supply chains of its businesses, erect trade barriers, punish Chinese companies, and in general to limit its strategic exposure to China. In Europe, terms like "industrial policy" and "systemic rivalry" have suddenly entered the political debate on China, while the robustness of the alliance with a no-longer-trusted United States is explicitly questioned. China, in turn, has awakened to its strategic vulnerability caused by a dependence on American and European high-tech products, science and technology, and even food; in response, it is increasingly seeking to turn its

Belt and Road Initiative into a sphere of influence and even control. It is highly unlikely that a genuine disentanglement and deglobalization are still possible, even if, like the Trump administration, one is unconcerned about the price tag. However, globalization is without a doubt on the backfoot and antiglobalization can no longer be dismissed as the product of a lunatic fringe: it has become thoroughly mainstream.

With the benefit of hindsight we can now see that the high tide of globalization in the 1990s and 2000s could only happen because, for a brief period after the end of the Cold War, the United States was the sole superpower. Globalization was therefore not, as is often thought, a remedy against conflict between great powers; it was rather a consequence of its (temporary) absence. In a unipolar world, globalization processes could grow relatively unencumbered by geostrategic vulnerabilities that come with realist, zero-sum competition between rivals and enemies. This is not meant to say that in this period globalization was fully uncontested, but rather that geopolitical considerations played only a minor role in assessments of its merits or demerits. In this sense, the current wave of antiglobalization is not a temporary setback but a return to more normal times with competing nation-states as the dominant players once again.

China's state-led globalization and emerging superpower status are fundamentally changing the nature and impact of globalization (or at least contributing materially to such a change). China benefited enormously from the high tide of globalization in the 1990s and 2000s, but its deliberate and selective use of globalization as part of its strategy of strengthening its power has now reached the point that across the world the dangers associated with unfettered globalization are deemed to have become too great.

Free trade is being replaced by trade war. An emphasis on the need for the free flow of data and information are giving way to cyber sovereignty. Global cultural flows are enlisted even more openly to strategies of nation branding, soft power, and influencing. The free flow of people—always the most controversial and restricted aspect of globalization—is deteriorating into demographic contestation: states direct the burden of asylum seekers, refugees, and unskilled migrants to others, while selectively attracting the students, skilled migrants, and tourists that they think they need. What remains are the big global challenges of climate change, environmental degradation, and global health. But, as has been starkly demonstrated by the coronavirus crisis in 2020 and 2021, here too state power and superpower competition come increasingly to the fore as countries try to pick and choose what they do and what they don't do together: a kind of *globalization à la carte* that is a direct threat to the global commons.

EAST ASIAN NATIONS AND MEDIA FLOWS UNDER CULTURAL GLOBALIZATION

In this book, we will give ample space to these historical and strategic realities; paradoxically, this is a book on globalization, written in what have become antiglobalizing times. Yet there is much more to globalization than international relations and trade; indeed, this was the very reason for embarking on this book and the *Global Square* series of which it is a part. Even the most quotidian global processes are informed by the fact that, all over the world, East Asia has become a beacon of modernity, independence, and wealth, and is often seen as an alternative to the West. As this book will show, although the East Asian region itself remains politically divided, at the level of their economy, society, and culture, as well as in their patterns of globalization, there is much that East Asian countries share.

The rise of East Asian media culture and its regional spread are indicative of a de-Westernizing trend in cultural globalization; here South Korea and Japan, rather than China, are at the forefront. Especially since the mid-1990s, media culture from South Korea and Japan has spread and found unprecedented reception in and beyond the East Asian region. However, it should be noted that the development of cross-border media cultural exchange in East Asia has been advanced in the context of an uneven globalization process. The logic of media corporations has structured the production, circulation, and consumption of media culture. Simultaneously, the governments' opportunist use of media culture for political and economic national interests has also intensified. Rather than enhancing global or regional connections and flows, such forces tend to discourage the development of cross-border dialogue. Reigniting nationalism, they foster diversity in a tight nation-to-nation framework instead of inclusive engagement with diversity within national borders.

The global cultural influence of the US media industry is still the most powerful, but the configuration of global cultural power nevertheless has become much more complicated, decentralized, and interpenetrating. The expansion of East Asian cultural exports to regional and global markets has been promoted by the integration of markets and capital. Transnational media industries have taken advantage of the revolutionary development of media communications technology and the global expansion of media markets. Although the United States is still at the core, transnational partnerships and cooperation among media and cultural corporations heavily involve East Asian countries as well. The spread of Japanese anime and video games throughout the world, for example, has been enabled by mergers, partnerships, and other forms of cooperation among multinational media corporations based in the United States and other developed countries. American distribution networks have enabled the worldwide spread of Pokémon (distributed by Warner Bros.) and the anime films of Hayao Miyazaki (distributed by Disney). The Pokémon anime series and movies were even deliberately "glocalized" and, eventually. "Americanized" to make them more acceptable to global consumers outside Asia.

East Asia itself is not free from this trend, as global media giants have successfully entered East Asian regional media markets as well. Hollywood studios have not only actively recruited talented directors and actors from East Asia. They have also embarked on remakes of Japanese and Korean films and coproductions with East Asian companies. The activation of regional media flows has also been engendered by the development of and collaboration among the main hubs in the region itself (Japan, Korea, Hong Kong, Taiwan, China), whose major media corporations have forged transnational partnerships to facilitate the mutual promotion, coproduction, and remaking of their products.

The expansion of market-driven globalization of media culture has prompted governments to enact policies to encourage and facilitate the growth of the cultural market, as the media and information sectors have become a sizeable part of the national economies. Furthermore, increasing international rivalry requires policy initiatives that promote soft power: creative industries or content businesses with the aim of exporting more cultural commodities and enhancing the brand images of the nation. As the counterpart to "hard" military or economic power, the term "soft power" was originally developed in the United States in the post-Cold War context, and it has been widely adopted by governments that seek to exploit the economic and political usefulness of culture, media, consumer products, education, and so forth to enhance the international image and attractiveness of their nation.

"Cool Britannia" was one of the pioneering policies outside the United States that aimed at media and culture production as part of promoting the national interest. Governments in East Asia have also begun to actively pursue this approach in the new millennium. The most notable case, in terms of media culture, has been South Korea since the late 1990s, with the international promotion of South Korean media culture, a phenomenon called the Korean Wave. Korea's success encouraged other Asian governments also to enhance their nation's soft power. Japan has been promoting "Cool Japan" as well, while China has embarked on an ambitious initiative to rebrand its language and traditional culture in order to build up its influence abroad, the Confucius Institutes being the best-known example of this. The widespread adoption of soft power has accompanied the alteration of its original purpose of advancing foreign policy aims to more generally establishing appealing images of the nation, smoothing international political negotiations, and boosting the economy.

Whether the export of media culture actually improves a country's national image and promotes its national interests is debatable. Yet, what is more important is that a politically pragmatic cultural policy tends to discourage discussions about the impact of culture in the service of wider public interests. A national or even nationalist cultural policy discussion does obscure worrying trends regarding the independence, diversity, and fairness caused by the globalization of the media cultural industry, such as the high concentration of media ownership and intellectual property rights in the hands of a few global companies or the exploitation of creative workers by hierarchical international outsourcing systems.

Furthermore, while soft power and nation branding aim at the international projection of national images, it should be noted that these things in equal measure serve internally oriented governance. Collaboration between the state and media culture industry serves to reproduce the idea of the nation as an organic cultural entity. The image of the nation in these branded narrations may be highly commercialized, dehistoricized and incoherent, but it very effectively reinforces an essentialized national culture and an exclusive national cultural ownership and belonging. This provides the basis for the expression of national cultural distinctiveness, and it organizes an international interface for the perception of the nation in its global cultural encounters.

CROSS-BORDER DIALOGUE AND TRANS-ASIAN ANTAGONISM

As media cultures have been caught in unprecedented trans-Asian circulation and reception, the mutual referencing of modern experiences has also become a normal practice among people in East Asia. Mutual consumption of media cultures like television dramas, films, and popular music does not just deepen people's understanding of other societies and cultures. It also encourages people to perceive the spatial-temporal distance and closeness to other Asian modernities. Sympathetic watching of Japanese or South Korean television dramas has, for example, encouraged audiences in various countries in East Asia to take a fresh view of gender relations, the lives of the youth, and the practice of justice in their own societies through the lens of the modernities elsewhere in East Asia.

While images from other Asian countries might evoke an orientalist nostalgia caused by temporal distance, they also promote a sense of coevalness beyond differences in development or wealth. Mutual referencing in East Asian media cultures encourages people to critically and self-reflexively reconsider their own life, society, and culture as well as their sociohistorically constituted relations and perceptions of others. Furthermore, mundane media consumption is often accompanied by virtual interactions via web-based discussion sites and social media. Eventually, many people visit other East Asian countries as well, where they meet new people, join transnational fan communities, and might even learn local languages. These postmedia and posttext activities further promote cross-border mediated connections, and interactions in East Asia.

However, cross-boundary dialogues forged by East Asian media cultures are never free from disparity, othering, and marginalization. Apart from the disparity in the material accessibility of media culture, the rise of soft power competition has added fuel to the flames of antagonistic nationalism in East Asia. The regional circulation of Japanese media culture encounters the negative legacy of Japanese colonialism. Historical dramas from South Korea present Chinese viewers with historical claims and Korean national ownership of traditional culture that clash with their own understanding of the facts. The blockbuster historical drama series *Jumong* (2006–7), for instance, depicted the heroic military feats of the Goguryeo Kingdom (37 BC–668 AD) against the Chinese in the northern parts of the Korean peninsula just a few years after the Chinese government had depicted that same kingdom as a suzerain state of the Chinese empire. The rise of the Korean Wave has sparked adverse reactions in Japan, Taiwan, and China against a perceived cultural invasion from Korean media culture. The media output of countries that are less developed are also often mocked as "cheap imitations" of American or Japanese media culture. Japanese mass media, for example, keenly and repeatedly reported on a replica theme park in China that it claimed has many "cheap copies" of popular characters such as Mickey Mouse and Doraemon. This feeds into the stereotype of the uncivilized vulgarity of Chinese modernity as exemplified by copyright violations, food contamination, and the rudeness of Chinese tourists, which clearly disqualifies China as a genuinely first-rate, developed nation.

CONCLUSION

East Asia is home to a rapidly rising superpower and the two largest economies in the world after the United States; its global impact, therefore, is qualitatively different from that of all other regions outside the Western world. However, global East Asia is much more than these truisms of international politics and global political economy suggest it is. Many aspects of global East Asia are less obvious or apparent, yet they are equally important, and many questions remain. This book will delve into these issues to show that global East Asia is also a region like any of the other covered in this series. East Asian people, cultures, religions and even ideologies have woven themselves into the tapestry of our global square—sometimes thanks to but quite often regardless of the region's prominence.

However, we also recognize that the age of unfettered globalization is well and truly over, and that in many ways we are going back to the future of competition and conflict between great powers. Here East Asia, and more precisely China, is leading the way, which why this book will end with a section specifically dedicated to its rise. In these final chapters, we will show that globalization is still very prominent but is increasingly informed by the competition between China, the United States, and other great powers. Although globalization might not be dead, it has by now certainly lost its innocence.

PART ONE

Global East Asia

PAST AND PRESENT

Frank N. Pieke

AS HAS ALREADY BEEN STATED in the introduction to this book, East Asia's global impact did not start with the current "age of globalization" at the end of the Cold War in the late 1980s; in fact, East Asia already was very much central to the first age of globalization between the fifteenth and eighteenth centuries. Since China was one of the cores of the then emerging world trade system, the bounties of its trade were among the main prizes that Western explorers and mercantilist trading companies were after. In what is sometimes called the second "age of globalization," during the second half of the nineteenth and the first half of the twentieth century, East Asia was both the agent and the victim of the colonial and imperial ambitions that dominated the era. After the Meiji Restoration in 1868, Japan developed into a conqueror and colonizer of other countries in East and Southeast Asia, with Korea, Taiwan, and China among the main victims of its imperialist drive.

Eventually, Japan's grand ambitions led to its downfall at the end of the Pacific War in 1945. In chapter 1, "Reluctant Keystone: The Nexus of War, Memory, and Geopolitics in Okinawa," Jeff Kingston presents one telling case about how the scars and memories of that war still affect the geopolitics of our current day and age. To the United States, their military base in Okinawa at the crossroads of the Pacific is the foundation of its strategic relationships with Japan, China, and the Koreas. To Okinawans, the US military base is a constant reminder of their suffering during the closing stages of the war. Anti-base sentiments express the anger about what can go wrong when Okinawans get caught in conflicts over which they have no control, including the current possibility of US-China conflict.

From the end of the First Opium War in 1842 until the start of the war with Japan in 1937, China was subjugated by several imperial powers, including Britain, France, Germany, the United States, and Japan, but it was never fully colonized by any one of them. China's treaty ports could therefore become unique sites where global flows of goods, culture, trade, money, and people—all of which were associated with not one but multiple imperial powers—met, hybridized, and moved away again to other parts of Asia or the cosmopolitan centers of Europe and North America. The role of China's treaty ports' as cosmopolitan cores in what was then a peripheral part of the world system is well-illustrated in chapter 2, "From Jazz Men to Jasmine: Transnational Nightlife Cultures in Shanghai from the 1920s to the 2010s." The authors Andrew Field and James Farrer's discussion of jazz music in Shanghai illustrates that the city's role as a global hub continued even during the war years and into the socialist period, and that it bloomed again after the post-1970s reforms. Recently, Shanghai, together with other global cities like Hong Kong, New York, Singapore, and Tokyo, has taken on a fully global dimension, the city adding its own unique sound and flavor to the flows of the world's jazz music.

After the Second World War, the battle lines of the Cold War made free exchange between the capitalist First World and the Communist Second World impossible. Not all traffic came to a halt, but flows of goods, people, money, and especially ideas were much more politically and strategically charged than ever before or after. Julia Lovell's chapter 3, "Maoism as a Global Force," turns to an almost forgotten but still hugely impactful East Asian vector of such global influence from the Communist world: Maoism. At the height of the Cold War and beyond, Mao and his revolutionary ideas appealed to left-wing rebels and civil rights and antiracism campaigners in Western countries. Across the developing Third World, Maoist politics inspired postcolonial movements and nations with ideals like self-reliance, peasant rebellion, and the power of the revolutionary will. Lovell concludes the chapter with an assessment of China's current partial Maoist revival and its significance for China's international relations.

Linked heavily to state power, foreign policy, and international institutions, development aid is not commonly included in discussions of globalization. On the basis of their analysis of the unique nature of Japanese development aid, in chapter 4, "Japanese Development Aid and Global Power," Hiroshi Kan Sato and Akiko Sasaki make a powerful case that it should. Development aid is an important field of interaction and hybridization of the distinct national approaches and philosophies underpinning the concept and practice of development. Initially in the 1950s and 1960s, Japanese overseas development assistance was strongly rooted in Japan's own culture and historical experiences, but that has changed over the years. At first, Japan gradually started to converge with dominant Western approaches, but more recently the influence of the Chinese approach has also become apparent. The aid paradigms shaped by the OECD countries emphasize the noncommercial aid that comes with the political conditions of good governance, democracy, and human rights but that does not have ties to business interests in the donor country. China's aid policies are driven by commercial or strategic interests and are predominantly based on interest-bearing and conditional loans. As the center of gravity of the world economy shifts from West to East, development aid is also affected. New styles of aid associated with emerging donors like China, and increasingly with South Korea and India as well, will become more prominent in the twenty-first century, leaving their imprint also on the approaches of other donor countries.

Finally, in Lindsay Black's chapter 5, "Conflict and Cooperation in Global East Asia," we move to the complexities of intraregional relations in East Asia, the most immediate theater in which the impact of Japan's previous and China's current global rise is felt. Since the Second World War, the United States has always dominated East Asian affairs. Its unpredictable stance under President Trump presented East Asian states with great challenges. Black argues that the relational and flexible nature of intraregional cooperation in East Asia might be more suited to deal with this than the institutionalized and rule-based approaches that tend to dominate in Europe. Although this makes relations less predictable, it simultaneously provides actors with room to maneuver the volatile and shifting relations between China, Japan, the two Koreas, and Taiwan.

ONE

Reluctant Keystone

THE NEXUS OF WAR, MEMORY, AND
GEOPOLITICS IN OKINAWA

Jeff Kingston

OKINAWA, CAUGHT BETWEEN TOKYO, WASHINGTON, AND BEIJING,
is yet again navigating the riptide of regional geopolitics. Contemporary
Okinawan perceptions inevitably draw on the collective trauma of the US
invasion and Japanese betrayal in 1945. Now these foes are allies, but a rising
China and a threatening North Korea are again thrusting Okinawa into the
crosshairs of geostrategic maneuvering. US policymakers often refer to
Okinawa as the keystone of the Pacific owing to its location at the crossroads
of competing claims in the East China Sea and sitting, as it does, astride
China's naval gateway to the Pacific. There is a widespread awareness about the
costs of being this keystone, an awareness based on wartime memories and
current discontent about how the US-Japan alliance shifts so much of the bur-
dens onto Okinawans without their consent.

SIX BETRAYALS

A profound sense of betrayal permeates Okinawan discourse about the war
and contemporary battles over base hosting. At the Okinawa Prefectural
Peace Museum, wartime Okinawa is depicted as a "breakwater" for the
nation, a place where the US "Typhoon of Steel" was to be kept at bay. In a
war that was already lost, it was a desperate gamble on a strategy to fight a
decisive and sufficiently bloody battle against the Americans in order to sof-
ten the terms of surrender. Contesting the central government's narrative,
the museum highlights the senseless carnage and wasted lives, sacrificed for
Japan's main islands and the Showa Emperor's (Hirohito's) war. Based on
eyewitness reports, visitors also confront the story of group suicides by

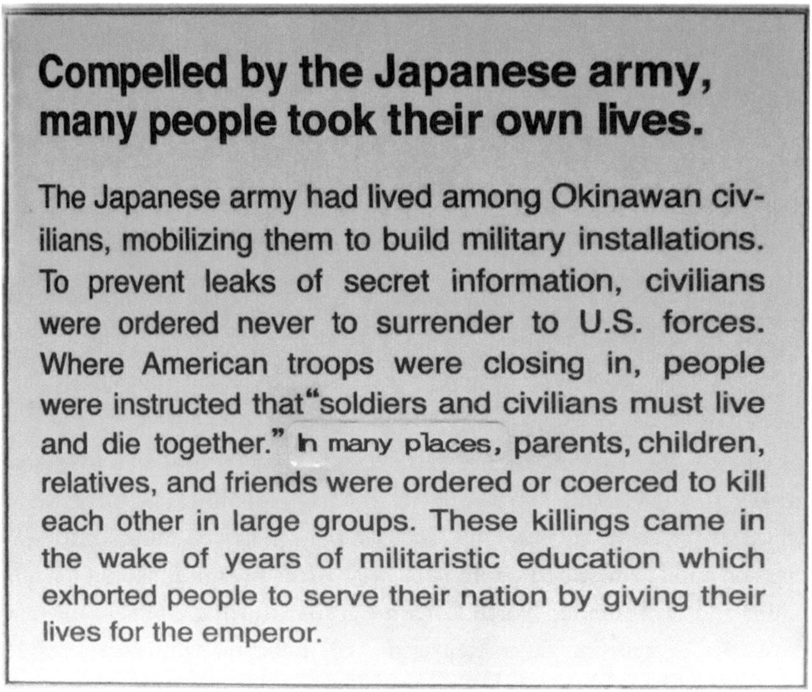

> # Compelled by the Japanese army, many people took their own lives.
>
> The Japanese army had lived among Okinawan civilians, mobilizing them to build military installations. To prevent leaks of secret information, civilians were ordered never to surrender to U.S. forces. Where American troops were closing in, people were instructed that "soldiers and civilians must live and die together." In many places, parents, children, relatives, and friends were ordered or coerced to kill each other in large groups. These killings came in the wake of years of militaristic education which exhorted people to serve their nation by giving their lives for the emperor.

FIGURE 1.1. Group suicides, Okinawan Prefectural Peace Museum.

Okinawan civilians instigated by Japanese soldiers who distributed grenades and urged the islanders to kill themselves.

Not far from the museum at Yomitan there are two caves where those hiding suffered different fates. In the Shimuka Gama cave there were some one thousand survivors who were saved from mass suicide by two local men who had worked in Hawaii. Arguing against using the hand grenades distributed by the Imperial Japanese Army, they asserted the Americans were not bloodthirsty barbarians. By contrast, those at the Chibichiri cave in the same village resisted the Americans with bamboo staves; the majority of them, urged on by a hardcore military veteran, died.

The inescapable conclusion to draw from the prefectural museum is that Tokyo thrust Okinawans into the cauldron of war because it could not accept defeat and was putting off the inevitable surrender. This is the core betrayal: being used as sacrificial pawns to buy time for wartime leaders to shed their delusions. Adjacent to the museum is the Peace Memorial Park, a site frequented by school groups and relatives of those who died. As one surveys the phalanxes of granite walls engraved with the names of all the

FIGURE 1.2. Okinawan wall of death, Peace Memorial Park.

soldiers, conscripts, and civilians who died in the Battle of Okinawa, including Allied soldiers, one sees how the devastating folly of war is grimly conveyed. This history is not forgotten and is a trauma at the heart of Okinawan's collective identity, one barely acknowledged in the rest of Japan, and therefore resented all the more bitterly.

The second betrayal came in 1952 when Tokyo regained sovereignty, putting an end to the US occupation in exchange for allowing the United States to retain administrative control over Okinawa and maintain military bases there. This trade was made on April 28 of that year and is now commemorated by Okinawans as the Day of Humiliation. An elderly intellectual who worked for the US administration during that time and who is now an anti-base activist contends that Okinawans were eager to see the back of the Japanese military and hopeful about the Americans that many welcomed as liberators.[1] But, as the US military abandoned democratic values and suppressed the pro-reversion movement (reverting to Japanese administrative control), it sparked an anti-American backlash. Then as now, crimes committed by US personnel periodically ignited the dry kindling of discontent.

The third betrayal was the forced evictions in the aftermath of the Second World War that made room for the bases. The "bayonets and bulldozers" approach to land grabs remain central to local perceptions about the illegitimacy of the US presence. These legitimate grievances are largely ignored by the Japanese media, which mainly focuses on the "blackmail" angle, portraying Okinawans as shakedown artists looking for a payoff who ratchet up protests as a negotiating tactic.

According to my octogenarian interlocutor, the fourth betrayal that exposed the United States as hypocrites was the ouster of a pro-reversion, anti-base politician in 1956. Senaga Kamejiro (1907–2001) had previously been jailed for two years in 1954 for "harboring blacklisted communist activists from Amami island."[2] Apparently, that was a crime under military rule on what Chalmers Johnson dubbed the Cold War island.[3]

After Senaga won the 1956 Naha mayoral election, the Americans called him the "red mayor," and he became a target of US Cold War era pressures. The US Civil Administration (USCA) military government that controlled Okinawa froze the city's assets, withheld US subsidies, and even turned off the water, finally pressuring the assembly into dismissing Senaga. The US military authorities then prevented him from seeking reelection by barring anyone with a criminal record from running for office. These strong-arm tactics proved counterproductive, transforming Senaga into a martyr while boosting anti-American sentiments.

In 2017, a documentary titled *Beigun ga Mottomo Osoreta Otoko: Sono Na wa Kamejiro* (Kamejiro: The man most feared by the US military) was shown nationwide at movie theaters. Senaga was feared because of his charismatic speaking style and his fearlessness in denouncing the American presence. I was struck on a visit to Henoko in 2018 by the number of Okinawans and demonstrators from elsewhere in Japan who invoked his memory in explaining the origins of anti-base sentiments, attesting to the influence of the documentary.

Senaga was also a prominent advocate of reversion to Japanese administration. On April 28, 1960, the anniversary of the Treaty of San Francisco, local unions and the teachers' association group launched the Okinawan Prefecture Council for Reversion to the Home Islands.[4] Their goal was an end to the US occupation of Okinawa, and it was finally achieved in 1972. This movement gained momentum as the United States shifted its troops to Okinawa from the main islands. Ambassador Edwin Reischauer (1961–66) argued in favor of this shift, since he worried that the American military presence was at risk of becoming overly politicized in Japan and would be politically less problematic if concentrated in distant Okinawa where the Japanese needed travel permission during the period of US control. As a result, the ratio of Japan-based US troops stationed outside and inside Okinawa went from nine to one in 1952 to one to three in 1972.[5] This helped insulate most Japanese from the US military presence, ensuring it never developed into an electoral issue in Hondo (the rest of Japan) elections, just as the ruling Liberal Democratic Party (LDP) preferred.

The Status of Forces Agreement (SOFA) represents the fifth betrayal, since Okinawans think it is overly protective of the rights of US servicemen and enables them to evade accountability for the crimes they commit in Japan. A 2016 poll found that 79 percent want to revise or abolish the SOFA.[6] The Japan SOFA concluded in 1960 has been revised slightly since a 1995 gang rape incident to allow local interrogation and prosecution in serious crimes, but US military court martials are the rule. Thus, there is some accountability, but Okinawans bristle at the persistence of extraterritoriality. Compared to other nations where the United States has SOFA, such as Japan's wartime allies Italy and Germany, the terms are decidedly less accommodating. In Europe, US soldiers are subject to local laws and courts. There are strictly enforced rules on flights by American planes, while local control is far more extensive than in Japan.

Terrence Terashima, an Okinawan journalist, recalls the anger stirred by the 2004 crash of a helicopter at Okinawa International University adjacent to the United States Marine Corps Air Station Futenma in Ginowan City.[7] It was an accident waiting to happen, as the base is located in a densely populated residential area. Terashima says that after the crash Japanese policemen and onlookers were chased from the scene by US MPs at gunpoint as they secured the area for their investigation, a brazen encroachment on national sovereignty that is a microcosm of the larger base presence.

Reversion was realized in 1972, but for many Okinawans it was a diplomatic deceit that constitutes the sixth betrayal, since the continuing base presence meant that they only regained a semblance of sovereignty. My octogenarian interlocuter said he was "skeptical that it ever really meant anything." According to him, the disappointments have mounted. as the transfer to Japanese governance provided few tangible benefits. As a result, anger was redirected at Tokyo for not doing more to stick up for Okinawans. Tiago Sesoko, a diaspora Okinawan with a Brazilian passport, says that this continued presence keeps the war experience alive, as his relatives in Okinawa "unanimously agree that the memories of the war will not die until the American bases are moved out of Okinawa, and the areas occupied by the bases are returned to our people."[8]

The dilapidated downtown of Henoko shows signs of the "halcyon days," as one can still make out the faded signs for honky-tonks that catered to bustling crowds of soldiers during the Vietnam War era. The Sea View, Pink Diamond, Ace of Clubs and other bars and love hotels catered to soldiers on R and R. Henoko is no longer so lively; as in the rest of Japan the proportion of the elderly population is growing, while signs of affluence are scarce.

Activists from around Japan stay at Cushion, a dormitory in central Henoko where a futon and breakfast in shared accommodation runs two thousand yen a night. Inside is a communal space with photos of past protests, a few computers, and a T-shirt stand for those looking for activist fashions. It is next door to a Christian outreach center that shares the premises with Whiskey Dick's and Zero Tatoo, catercorner from Shiva's Indian restaurant and bar. These establishments stand out for being brightly painted in a monochrome townscape, but business at them is slow. From Cushion it is a five-minute walk in one direction to the Camp Schwab gates, where demonstrators gather to block access; and it is a bit further in the opposite direction to access the Henoko Tent Village on the waterfront where one can board boats to view the installed embankments or paddle kayaks a kilometer or so to the construction site in Oura Bay. Here there is a beach fronting Camp Schwab's long fence that is colorfully festooned with anti-Henoko posters. Rent-a-cops patrol the inside perimeter, taking photos of anyone approaching the fence in a lame attempt to intimidate them. On the day I visited, eighty-five kayaks (including some university students) set off, but only paddlers who pass a test are allowed to join the protest, a precaution against drowning or some other mishap. The students told me that this was a club activity and that they had been before. They wanted to raise the awareness of fellow students back in Kobe by sharing their experiences and attracting new recruits.

At noon on April 25, 2018, the protestors at the Camp Schwab gates were taking a lunch break in the shelters up the hill and across the road, but spotters alerted them to an approaching convoy of trucks. Suddenly, several hundred people dashed to take their positions blocking the gates. An elderly gentleman in a wheelchair was at the vanguard, flinging himself into the ranks of police that were gathered there to keep protestors at bay. As the police tried to push him away from the other demonstrators, some with canes pushed in even though the previous day the police had detained some elderly

FIGURE 1.3. Anti-base protests in front of Camp Schwab.

protestors and kept them in an unshaded cage under the blistering sun for several hours, spitefully denying them toilet access. As the scene unfolded, it looked almost choreographed--as though everyone knew their roles and played them well. The police on this day were menacing but restrained, careful not to harm anyone. In the end, the seven-truck convoy was blocked; the mission was accomplished.

The government decided in 1996 to build a replacement facility for the US Marine Corp Air Station Futenma at Henoko so that it could be closed, since operations there endangered surrounding residents. The government plan is to build a V-shaped runway on reclaimed land in Oura Bay (Henoko) on top of a coral reef in pristine waters. Okinawa islanders oppose this plan because it's not immediately obvious why reducing the US military footprint requires building an additional military facility in the prefecture rather than somewhere else. Okinawa's political leaders have tried various means to block the project but so far have had no success.

Terashima, the Okinawan journalist, explains that locals understand that Henoko is a done deal but still deem the protests crucial because, if they quietly concede, this will reduce the chances of limiting the US military presence elsewhere in the prefecture. He argues that Okinawans' sentiments changed after the US withdrawal from Clark and Subic bases in the Philippines in the early 1990s, making Okinawans less tolerant and more willing to protest the lingering US presence, especially because in Japan the US military is concentrated disproportionately on their islands.

Islanders also feel a sense of betrayal by the Democratic Party of Japan's (DPJ) president Hatoyama Yukio, who promised in 2009, as the then prime minister, to relocate Henoko outside Okinawa but failed in this quest. He raised the Okinawans' hopes, but then discovered it didn't make a difference as the pro-US alliance establishment rallied to sabotage his plans.[9] It is this loss of hope that convinces some locals that they might as well take the money on offer from the central government.

SHARED VALUES?

Democracy is ostensibly one of the core common values of the alliance, but Prime Minister Abe's machinations in Okinawa resembled the Liberal Democratic Party's (LDP) old-school, Chicago-style politics where satchels of moola are delivered in smoke-filled rooms. The Abe-dozer running roughshod over Okinawans and democracy on behalf of the alliance exposed the emptiness of shared values that Washington has been happy to go along with, all the while averting its eyes from the unpleasant spectacle.

Okinawa's governors have long opposed the Henoko base project, and public opinion polls indicate that Okinawans are also opposed to it, but the democratic will of the islanders has been subordinated to the alliance. In a 2017 poll, the *Ryukyu Shimpo* found that 74 percent of islanders oppose the Henoko relocation plan.[10] Their views are politically awkward and therefore ignored because the base must be built no matter what. Invoking the nostrum of shared values in public discourse provides background music as Washington pressures Tokyo to dance to its tune.

Onaga Takeshi won the prefecture's gubernatorial election in 2014 owing to his predecessor Nakaima Hirokazu 's 2013 betrayal, granting the Abe government permission for proceeding with the Henoko project in exchange for over US$20 billion over eight years. This deal was unexpected, since Nakaima won elections in 2006 and 2010 by staunchly opposing the planned base. Onaga tried to block the Henoko reclamation by rescinding his predecessor's approval but after extensive legal maneuvering, the central government prevailed in this David-versus-Goliath battle. Onaga died of pancreatic cancer in 2018 as Tokyo proceeded with the reclamation phase, dumping rocks and sand into the bay and, in so doing, killing the coral and degrading the environment needed for marine life in the area. In the "Keystone of the Pacific," this is the deeply flawed bedrock of the alliance where considerations of expediency trump shared values. The *Ryuku Shimpo* fumed: "The Japanese government has trampled the will of the people of Okinawa with an iron fist in order to build a base for the US military."[11]

Denny Tamaki won a thumping landslide victory in the 2018 gubernatorial elections by promising to continue the fight against Henoko; this was yet another embarrassing setback for the Abe government. The Abe government was further displeased by Tamaki holding an island-wide referendum in February 2019 in which 72 percent of Okinawan voters gave the thumbs down to the Henoko relocation plan. Subsequently, in a nationwide poll conducted in March 2019, 69 percent said the central government should respect the results of the referendum while only 19 percent said there was no need to.[12] Even so, the Abe cabinet dismissed the results and is proceeding against the democratic voice of the people. It has also barred *Tokyo Shimbun's* Isoko Mochizuki from the prime minister's office press conferences. This journalist is known for asking tough questions that Abe's chief cabinet secretary, Suga Yoshihide, found irritating and awkward, but what prompted her ban was her role in exposing the environmental damage being done to Oura Bay owing to landfill work at Henoko. Although the contract calls for using gravel, the local contractor has cut costs by using cheaper, iron-laden, red earth that is harmful to marine life, another black eye for the troubled Henoko project.

For many Okinawans, the problem goes beyond crime and noise pollution. The environment matters, and in our image-sensitive world, destroying a coral reef while threatening the habitat of the endangered dugong (a manatee) is a hard sell, especially for a base that almost nobody wants and many actively oppose. Incidentally, the geology of Oura Bay is unsuitable for the runway project, as a government survey in 2016 found the sea bottom has the consistency of mayonnaise, raising construction costs considerably and further delaying the project. The least bad temporary solution still appears to be shifting Futenma's operations to the massive Kadena Air Base, but intraservice rivalry is blocking this. In 2011, Senators Carl Levin, Jim Webb, and John McCain backed that plan, dismissing Henoko as "unrealistic, unworkable and unaffordable."[13]

In terms of the anti-base movement, Terashima believes there is a sizeable pro-base contingent, especially among younger Okinawans, who don't share their elders' experiences and perspectives, and who tend to focus on the cool factor of the US presence and the employment opportunities it affords. Okinawa has the highest unemployment and lowest per capita income in Japan, so the somewhat higher wages (two hundred to three hundred yen higher per hour) on the bases are appreciated. The chance to use English, American cultural influences, and opportunities to leverage these to work in the entertainment industry appeal to younger Okinawans. This generational divide is often overlooked.

For example, Akiko Urasaki, a popular rapper who performs as Awich, has a positive take on the US presence, drawing on childhood memories raised in the vicinity of US bases. Urasaki, whose late husband was American, is raising a mixed-race daughter. In an interview for *CNN*, she said that she "took English classes after school and experienced a world full of super-sized ice creams, hip hop and opportunity. Without realizing it, US culture became part of an identity that she's now proud of."[14] "We see the base as another space of life," she added, "not a space for preparing for war—we don't see that part. She believes that Okinawans should not cling to an identity of victimization and instead tap into "the benefits of the base presence." "Being able to speak English opened up so many doors for me. If all the kids in Okinawa could do that, we wouldn't be poor. If it were up to me, everyone on this island would be bilingual by now", Urasaki says. In her opinion, "If it's a political strategy for us to develop an emotional attachment to the bases so that they'll stay here long, they are successful, because we do."

This is an unfathomable view for those Okinawans who worry that youth is uninterested in politics and overly complacent about the militarization of their homeland. It is also a minority view, as polls indicate that the vast majority of Okinawans are opposed to the US military presence; indeed, support for the US Marines' withdrawal is at an all-time high of 53 percent.[15] While a recent East-West Center study finds relatively more positive attitudes among younger Okinawans, it also shows that they express strong resentment about the disproportionate base-hosting burden. The study concludes that "the construction of a replacement base at Cape Henoko is widely regarded as a betrayal of Okinawa to broader Japanese interests and prejudices."[16]

Chinen Namie, a fortysomething Okinawan social worker, told me she had elementary school teachers who survived the Battle of Okinawa and grew weary of hearing their war stories. But over time, "the meaning of horrific stories sank in and started making sense to me. I suppose that the fact that military bases are in Okinawa means we are allowing wars to continue to happen. Anti-base activity is a demonstration to let the world know that we refuse to be part of militaristic activities, we are against any war in any part of the world, and we are trying to minimize any militaristic activities."[17] She adds that these sentiments are widespread because, "every single family in Okinawa was affected by the battle. We all have someone to mourn for on the Irei no Hi [June 23, the day the battle ended]."

Sesoko also disagrees with Urasaki, saying, "Okinawans believe that the US bases make them a target and are afraid they will once again get caught in a major war. Also, some Okinawans believe that Chinese are becoming more aggressive and might even target Okinawa because of the American bases."

Across the generations there is a shared resentment about discrimination against Okinawans. Chinen has reservations about the emphasis on cultural assimilation that prevailed when she was in school in the 1980s: "I became a perfect native Japanese speaker but didn't develop Okinawan in me. I see now it was a wrong kind of efforts that my parents' generation made, but they worked hard to be part of Japan and now they feel bitterly betrayed."

In 2016, Osaka police dispatched to cope with anti-base protestors angered locals by screaming Doujin (aborigine) at them. This scornful expression of prejudice reinforces resentment among Okinawans, who have endured a century of cultural oppression that denies they are Japanese.

SIDELINING DISSENT

The Japanese government jailed Okinawan anti-US base activist Yamashiro Hiroji from October 2016 to March 2017 on trivial charges, keeping him in solitary confinement. Yamashiro heads the Okinawa Peace Movement Center and it is obvious why he was targeted. He is the Senaga Kamejiro in twenty-first century Okinawa, a charismatic speaker who revs up crowds with his fiery rhetoric and inspires them with his fearlessness. In a situation many deem hopeless he gives hope. As Lawrence Repeta argues, "The extended detention of Hiroji Yamashiro is a shocking display of raw government power. . . . It appears that Japan's government will put aside the most basic human rights protections in order to crush protesters like Yamashiro."[18] He adds, "Arbitrary detention is a standard tool used by authoritarian governments to silence critics throughout the world." It is hard to reconcile what is going on in Okinawa with the alleged "shared values" that are frequently invoked by American and Japanese leaders as the cornerstone of the alliance.

The CIA thinks that propaganda can help alter Okinawan public opinion about the US military presence, suggesting that it would be counterproductive to focus on military and strategic benefits owing to local memories and anxieties.[19] Instead, the CIA has suggested that Americans should focus on the economic benefits for Okinawa and invoke the bases' potential for humanitarian disaster and other relief activities around the region. But no amount of spin-doctoring can overcome anger about crimes committed by US soldiers against Okinawans.

UNWELCOME GUESTS

One of the many crimes committed by American personnel in Okinawa involved the 2016 rape and murder of a twenty-year-old local woman by a US contractor (a former marine) employed at the US Kadena Airbase. Sadly, this horrific crime fits into a larger pattern of sexual violence that has become all too familiar to Okinawans and has inflamed local antipathy toward the US military bases.

Some sixty-five thousand people turned out to mourn her killing and to protest an alliance that shifts a disproportionate hosting burden onto Okinawa. It was a grim ceremony commemorating the dangers of having so many soldiers stationed in Okinawa that stir resentments against both Tokyo and the United States. It highlights the continuing arc of indignity that stretches from the original sin of the Battle of Okinawa, to the 1952 abandonment of the prefecture to US administration until 1972, the heavy-handed suppression of the anti-base movement during that era, and the rapes and killings that have ensued since reversion. Okinawa's governor, Onaga, apologized to the deceased woman for failing to protect her, recalling the horrific 1995 gang rape of a twelve-year-old girl by three American servicemen. This incident forced the United States and Japan to commit to a reduction of the US military presence in Okinawa as outlined in the 2006 roadmap.

The vast majority of Okinawans are opposed to hosting the US bases, yet despite this long-standing opposition, Okinawa still hosts 70 percent of the US military presence in Japan with thirty-one bases occupying about 15 percent of the main island's land mass. How has it been possible to sustain the US military presence over the decades given this inhospitable situation? Ignoring the will of the people is one compelling answer. Sarah Kovner argues that Tokyo and Washington try to insulate Japanese society from the negative impact of US bases, including literally soundproofing nearby homes and schools and otherwise discrediting and marginalizing anti-base protests and grievances.[20] And most mainland Japanese enjoy the soundproofing of distance, ensuring that Okinawa's burden is out of earshot and out of sight.

While Kovner takes other scholars to task for ignoring various aspects of anti-base protests and sentiments, she overlooks the powerful legacy of the wartime horrors suffered by Okinawan civilians who died during the US invasion. This history can't be silenced, as it reverberates loudly among a traumatized people whose memories are consecrated in museums, monuments, rites of collective commemoration, and family lore.[21]

The largest twenty-first-century protest in Okinawa attracted one hundred thousand participants in 2007 to condemn the Ministry of Education's directive to secondary school textbook publishers, requiring them to refrain from suggesting that Japanese military forces instigated Okinawan group suicides in 1945. This revisionist whitewashing during Abe's first stint as prime minister disregarded eyewitness testimony by survivors. It smacked of Tokyo trying to erase a memory that is part of islanders' collective identity, stoking seething resentments toward the mainland.

Robert Eldridge, an academic who served from 2009–15 as an advisor to the US Marines, was a prominent advocate for the bases who has since recanted.[22] He was fired in 2015 for an unauthorized leak of security camera footage of anti-Henoko protests.[23] In the past he branded Okinawa protests "hate speech" and dismissed them as "mob rule." Now, however, he argues that the 2006 roadmap actually heightened recriminations and undermined trust because it "ignored the complicated social, political, and economic dynamics within Okinawa, focusing on the military, and the US military in particular."[24] He also condemns the Henoko base relocation project because it "does not meet the requirements of a 21st century alliance or even a modern-day relationship with local citizens." His apostasy on the bases provides a damning indictment by an insider sympathetic to the US presence.

CONCLUSION

The US military presence in Japan has lasted seventy-five years; it is an encroachment that remains the unfinished business of the Second World War and is a constant reminder to Okinawans of their shared nightmare in 1945. During this prolonged occupation, no amount of soundproofing can quell the high-decibel reality of subjugation and discrimination that serves as a counterpoint to the "shared values" of the alliance and that explains why Okinawa is the reluctant keystone.

Contemporary pacifism and anti-base sentiments draw on local rancor about what can go wrong when Okinawans get caught between larger and distant forces pursuing agendas at odds with their own interests. Now that tensions with China are ratcheting up, this may gain a whole new dimension, and many islanders feel as though they are being put in harm's way once again.

The economic inducements of base hosting are needed by Japan's poorest prefecture, but this dependency also rankles. Given the ongoing tourism boom and Japan's rapidly aging population, accelerating the reduction in military bases could open attractive opportunities for a Florida scenario of resorts, golf courses, and retirement communities. This would be more appealing to locals and probably would generate greater economic benefits. Yet prospects for such a transformation appear remote, since both Tokyo and Washington still regard Okinawa as an indispensable platform for projecting military might, and policymakers remain deaf to the democratic voice of Okinawans.

NOTES

1. Interview April 2018; the subject prefers to remain anonymous.
2. Tani 2007.
3. Johnson 1999.
4. Tani 2007, 83.
5. Philip Brasor, "No One Else Wants Okinawa's U.S. Bases." *Japan Times*, September 2, 2017, https://www.japantimes.co.jp/news/2017/09/02/national/media-national/no-one-else-wants-okinawas-u-s-bases/.
6. SOFA (Status of Forces Agreements) are negotiated with governments hosting US forces to establish the legal framework for handling any crimes they commit along with other ground rules covering local operations.
7. Interview April 2018.

8. Interview May 2018.

9. Penn 2017.

10. "Okinawa Poll Reveals More Than 74 Percent Oppose Henoko Relocation, 70 Percent Consider Base Concentration Unjust," *Ryuku Shimpo*, May 9, 2017.

11. "Editorial: The Japanese Government Suing to Allow Land Filling Is a Reckless Trampling of Democracy," *Ryuku Shimpo*, October 18, 2018.

12. "Abe Support Rate Falls; 69% Want Okinawa Vote on Base Issue Respected," *Japan Times*, March 10, 2019.

13. "Integration of Futenma with Kadena is a Challenge to Okinawans," *Japan Press Weekly*, May 13, 2011, http://www.japan-press.co.jp/s/news/index.php?id=1841.

14. Emiko Jozuka, "Beaches, Bases, Battles: The Seven-Decade Fight for Okinawa," *CNN*, June 17, 2018. https://edition.cnn.com/2018/06/16/asia/japan-okinawa-bases-new-battle-intl/index.html.

15. "Over 40 Percent of Okinawans Want Bases Withdrawn and 53 Percent Want Marines Withdrawn," *Ryuku Shimpo*, June 3, 2016; "Okinawa Poll Reveals More Than 74 Percent Oppose Henoko Relocation," *Ryuku Shimpo*, May 9, 2017.

16. Morrison and Chinen 2019, 4.

17. Interview May 2018.

18. Lawrence Repeta, "The Silencing of an Anti-U.S. Base Protester in Okinawa," *Japan Times*, January 4, 2017.

19. Mitchell 2018.

20. Kovner 2016.

21. John Junkerman, *Okinawa: The Afterburn* (New York: First Run Features, 2016), http://www.cine.co.jp/english/works/e_urizun/.

22. Robert Eldridge, "The Four Mottainai in Okinawan Affairs," *Japan Times*, February 13, 2018.

23. Jon Mitchell, "U.S. Marines Official Dismissed over Okinawa Protest Video Leak," *Japan Times*, March 23, 2015.

24. Eldridge, "Four Mottainai."

REFERENCES AND FURTHER READING

Johnson, Chalmers, ed. 1999. *Okinawa: Cold War Island*. Cardiff, CA: Japan Policy Research Institute.

Junkerman, John, dir. 2016. *Okinawa: The Afterburn*. New York: First Run Features. http://www.cine.co.jp/english/works/e_urizun/.

Kovner, Sarah. 2016. "The Soundproofed Superpower: American Bases and Japanese Communities, 1945–1972." *Journal of Asian Studies* 75, no. 1 (February): 87–109.

Lummis, Douglas. 2019. "It Ain't Over Till It's Over: Reflections on the Okinawan Anti-Base Resistance." *Asia-Pacific Journal* 17, no. 1 (January): 1–5.

Mitchell, Jon. 2018. "CIA: How to Shape Okinawan Public Opinion on the U.S. Military Presence." *Asia-Pacific Journal* 16, no. 5 (July): 1–10.

Morrison, Charles E., and Daniel Chinen. 2019. *Millennial+ Voices in Okinawa: An Inquiry into the Attitudes of Young Okinawan Adults toward the Presence of U.S. Bases*. Honolulu, HI: East-West Center.

Penn, Michael. 2017. "The Hatoyama Administration and the Outing of the Establishment Media." In *Press Freedom in Japan*, edited by Jeff Kingston, 56–63. Abingdon: Routledge.

Tani, Miyume. 2007. *Myth, Protest and Struggle in Okinawa*. Abingdon: Routledge.

From Jazz Men to Jasmine

TRANSNATIONAL NIGHTLIFE CULTURES IN SHANGHAI FROM THE 1920S TO THE 2010S

Andrew David Field and James Farrer

IN THE 1920S, SHANGHAI BECAME A CRUCIBLE of modern, urban, nighttime entertainment in Asia. Even in the darkest days of the war during the 1940s and the Mao era of the 1950s and 1960s, we can trace influences in and out of Shanghai to neighboring Japan, Taipei, Singapore, and Hong Kong—cultural flows that greatly increased again with the opening up of China in the 1980s. Shanghai's legacy as a nightlife metropolis also has a global dimension, as represented in the 2018 film *Crazy Rich Asians,* featuring performances and a soundtrack by the Shanghai diva Jasmine Chen.

JAZZING SHANGHAI IN THE 1920S AND 1930S

Between the 1920s and 1930s, Shanghai earned a global reputation as a city of jazz and nightlife. Around the world, the new concept of "nightlife" had become associated with an American culture of transgressive speakeasies, flapper girls, gangsters, African American jazz men, and above all, energetic and sexualized dancing.[1] Entranced by Hollywood films and American music, the so-called Shanghailanders—the small yet influential population of Europeans and Americans who inhabited the city's two foreign settlements—also began to set up hotel ballrooms and nightclubs featuring jazz musicians from America, Russia, and the Philippines.

One of the early musicians to grace the city was a Danish American named Whitey Smith. Arriving in 1922 from San Francisco, he led a jazz orchestra composed of other white Americans. They played in the fanciest ballrooms of the era, such as the Astor House and later the Majestic Hotel, where he claims in his memoir that he "taught China to dance" by blending Chinese

FIGURE 2.1. Valaida Snow in Shanghai.
Source: *China Press*, July 3, 1927.

folk sounds and melodies into the band's repertoire of American hit tunes.[2] This fusion of Chinese musical elements into Western jazz and vice versa turned out to be the formula that launched a new era of Chinese pop music and got the entire city (or at least a good portion of it) fox-trotting and jitterbugging in the city's jazz cabarets.

Meanwhile, other musicians from America were arriving in the city to take up the jazz standard and carry it not just into China but all over the Asia Pacific. Among them was an African American drummer and bandleader named Jack Carter, who had already played in Tokyo and Manila by the time he arrived in Shanghai in 1925. The following year, he returned to America and brought back other African American jazz musicians to Shanghai, including trumpeter and singer Valaida Snow and her sister Lavada (whom he eventually married) and the now legendary jazz pianist Teddy Weatherford, who had played in a band at the Vendome Theater in Chicago with a young Louis Armstrong.[3] For a year or more starting in 1926, Jack Carter's orchestra played on the rooftop of the Plaza Hotel in Shanghai's French Concession with a view of the Huangpu River; they were touted as the best jazz band in Asia. Jack Carter went on to perform in many other port cities in the Asia-Pacific, including Singapore and Batavia (now Jakarta), before returning to the United States in 1928 with Valaida and Lavada Snow. Meanwhile, Teddy Weatherford remained in Shanghai and eventually took up a gig with another orchestra performing at the new Canidrome Hotel in

FIGURE 2.2. Filipino musicians made up the jazz orchestra that played at the Paradise Ballroom, a large ballroom and taxi-dance hall located in the Sun Company Department store on the corner of Thibet Road and Nanjing Road, which catered to a mainly middle-class Chinese clientele. Source: This set of images is from a volume published by the Sun Company to celebrate the opening of their new ballroom in 1936 (first author's personal collection).

the heart of the French Concession, where he kept the city's elites dancing with his powerful stride piano style. Weatherford would later gain fame for spreading jazz in India; he truly was one of the great transnational musical influencers of the era.

Meanwhile, a Chinese musician named Li Jinhui was composing China's first "native" jazz song. At that time, Li was organizing a song and dance troupe of young women that included his own daughter Minghui. The group toured Southeast Asia, where their tunes became standards. Li's song "Drizzle" (Maomaoyu), first recorded in 1927 with Minghui singing in Mandarin Chinese, was a sexy, sultry song about two lovers, and soon it became a hit in the Chinese jazz cabarets. Li Jinhui became a leading composer of modern Chinese pop music, which blended American jazz and European music with more traditional and folksy Chinese sounds. His most famous pupil, Zhou Xuan, became a leading lady in many films produced in

Shanghai in the 1930s, and she is arguably the most important singing star of the age.[4]

In 1934, the African American trumpeter Buck Clayton arrived with his Harlem Gentlemen after being wooed by Teddy himself to sail from Los Angeles to Shanghai. He and his band performed hot jazz at the Canidrome Ballroom. They also spent many nights at the Paramount Ballroom, an ultra-modern ballroom financed by Chinese capitalists that featured American and Russian jazz orchestras and fabulous floor shows. By 1935, after a fracas with an American gangster, Buck Clayton and his Harlem Gentlemen found themselves at the Casanova Ballroom performing the Mandarin Chinese tunes of Li Jinhui and other pop composers of the era.[5] That same year, at the behest of Green Gang boss Du Yuesheng, who thought that China should have its own native jazz bands, Li Jinhui founded a fully Chinese jazz orchestra, the Clear Wind Dance Band (Qingfeng Wuyuedui), which performed a combination of Chinese and American pop tunes at the Yangtze Hotel in the International Settlement.[6]

Most Chinese cabarets featured dance hostesses, who were paid in tickets for each dance by their male customers, or who were paid to chat with them at tables on the edge of the dance floor. This culture of taxi dancing was a global one, and it was prevalent at hundreds of clubs in American cities such as Chicago.[7] While Russian women fleeing the 1917 revolution had launched this industry in Shanghai in the 1920s, and many Japanese women danced in Shanghai cabarets in the early years as well, by the 1930s this industry was dominated by young Chinese women who flocked to the city's dance halls from the nearby hinterlands to earn money as dance hostesses. By the 1930s, tens of thousands of these women worked the city's dance halls. These establishments earned a reputation in the city's print and film media for turning young Cinderellas into movie stars or wives and concubines of powerful and wealthy men, even if this only happened to a small number of them. Like the Filipino musicians who played the two-minute tunes to which they danced, the vast majority of these young Chinese women toiled on in obscurity as they struggled to survive in the big city.[8]

SHANGHAI AND INTER-ASIAN CULTURAL FLOWS

Western musicians may have been the stars of the city's jazz scene in the 1920s and 1930s, but it was the Filipino bands that made up the majority of the city's jazz men; they played American jazz or its Chinese counterpart in most of the city's cabarets, especially those that catered to a largely Chinese clientele. This was true not only in Shanghai but all over the Asia-Pacific. They worked the shipboard orchestras that traveled between port cities in Asia, with Shanghai serving as a hub for finding new jobs. The wartime occupation by the Japanese from 1941 to 1945 may have been a heyday for Filipino musicians, who now did not have to compete with Westerners in the city.

Another Shanghai-centered nightlife network involved the Japanese jazz men who came to Shanghai to learn from Shanghai jazz greats. Unable to afford visiting the homeland (*honba*) of jazz in the United States, Japanese musicians began coming to Shanghai in the early 1920s to learn from the foreign players in the city. By 1926, the Japanese had opened their first jazz club in the city on Sichuan Road, one of the main commercial streets in Hongkou's "Japantown." These clubs, such as the Blue Bird, Tiger, and Lion offered Japanese musicians lucrative wages, and a "band man" who brought a female dancer with him from Japan could even receive an advance on his salary. Thus, the presence of Japanese dance hostesses in these clubs was directly tied to the migration of Japanese jazz musicians. These dancers, in turn, were an attraction for male customers from around the city.

One of the Japanese jazz greats who earned his chops in Shanghai's club scene was Nanri Fumio. In 1929 he came to Shanghai, where he organized practice sessions with American jazz legend Teddy Weatherford. Nanri would later travel to San Francisco. He played in the northeastern Chinese city of Dalian during the early years of the Second World War, and in the immediate postwar era he would become famous in Japan for his Dixieland jazz and bebop.[9]

During the war, Japanese continued working in Shanghai clubs, as similar establishments were being closed in Japan. Some collaborated with Chinese and other Shanghai-based musicians. Hattori Ryoichi, a saxophonist and composer, spent the later war years in Shanghai, composing music for Japanese films and organizing concerts for the propaganda arm of the Japanese occupiers. Hattori later said he was inspired by Chinese pop styles in his creation of a "Japanized" jazz pop music. After the war, he wrote movie scores for the Shaw Brothers Studio in Hong Kong. Another Asian transnational talent whose career intersected with Japan's wartime occupation of China was Yamaguchi Yoshiko. To her Chinese audiences, most of whom thought she was Chinese, she was Li Xianglan. Many of her songs became standards throughout Asia and are still part of the repertoire of Asian jazz singers, including contemporary Shanghai jazz diva Jasmine Chen, who, like Li Xianglan, spent her childhood in the northeast region of China before coming to Shanghai to make a name for herself.

Under the new Communist regime starting in 1949, social dance flourished for a while in Communist Youth League-organized parties. But the foreign musicians were sent away, and the cabarets were closed down by 1954. By 1957, Westernized music and social dance were banned altogether as bourgeois evils. For the next two decades, the Shanghai commercial nightscape went dark. As China underwent the travails of the Great Leap Forward and the Cultural Revolution, Shanghai's musical diaspora became influential in other Asian cities, including Singapore, which also attracted some of Shanghai's famed dancers. These women worked in that city's dance halls in the 1950s. Many of these cabarets were named after Shanghai amusement halls, such as the Great World and the New World. In 1953, the Singapore Dance Hostesses' Association even held a five-night dance to raise money for the founding of Nanyang University, the Chinese university in the city.[10] Elsewhere, in Malaysia and in Taiwan, the dance hall culture and musical pop culture forged in Shanghai's cabarets continued to develop, and it eventually produced postwar Asia's first pop megastar, Teresa Teng (Deng Lijun), who became famous for her renditions of Old Shanghai pop songs. Between Taipei and Hong Kong, a pantheon of pop divas carried the torch of Shanghai singers like Zhou Xuan and Li Xianglan and created the Gangtai style of contemporary pop music in greater China.[11]

THE RETURN OF GLOBAL NIGHTLIFE

Between the 1950s and 1970s, Hong Kong was emerging as a nightlife hub in Asia. The British colony attracted many nightlife refugees from Shanghai, some of whom performed in the city's dance halls and nightclubs. In the 1970s, Hong Kong was caught up in the disco revolution, which had been brought there partly by African American GIs. By the 1980s, the city was exporting DJs to other Asian cities, including some of the hottest clubs in the Roppongi nightlife district in Tokyo. The rise of clubbing districts like Wan Chai and Lam Kwai Fong, still booming today, made Hong Kong the new international nightlife metropolis for East Asia.

In the late 1980s, this new form of clubbing culture came to Shanghai. Shanghai's own nightlife was undergoing a revival, albeit a choppy one owing to both national and local politics. When the first Hong Kong DJs began spinning at Shanghai's two preeminent international hotels in 1987 and 1988, there already were hundreds of dance venues in the city, most of which featured the type of band music tunes and partnered social dance that had been popular in the late 1940s and into the early Mao years. *Di-si-ke* (disco), however, would be the youth soundtrack of the 1990s, with DJs from Hong Kong manning the booths at many of the biggest "disco plazas" in the city. The chatty, personal style of the Hong Kong DJ would spread throughout mainland China during this period, usually accompanied by sexy "dance leaders," who taught the crowd the right moves.

Meanwhile, other Shanghai clubbing pioneers were learning their nightlife lessons in Tokyo. One of these was Shanghainese Gary Wang, who lived in Tokyo from 1993 to 1999. Wang returned to Shanghai, bringing his knowledge of hip-hop with him. He first DJed in 1999 at DKD Club, one of the premier clubbing venues on the rowdy nightlife street of Maoming South Road. In 2007, he opened his own club called Shelter in a former bomb shelter on the quiet and leafy Yongfu Road near Fuxing Road. Like Maoming South Road, this quickly became a flourishing nightlife and bar street. Shelter attracted DJs from around China and Asia, including many top acts from Japan. Although hip-hop remained a mainstay, the club introduced many genres of music to the city, from jazz to electronica.

Hong Kong entrepreneurs would also be instrumental in bringing to Shanghai the VIP style of clubbing that now dominates the biggest nightlife spaces in the city. One of the earliest and arguably most influential of these clubs was Park 97, which was named in celebration of the handover of Hong Kong to China in 1997, the year the club opened in Shanghai's Fuxing Park. A group of entrepreneurs that had helped establish the bar and club district of Lam Kwai Fong in Hong Kong took charge of the new Park 97. In 2001, the venue saw the addition of a small dance club called California Club, and thereby attracted an international crowd.

The club's floor manager was Hong Konger Thomas Yeung. He built up a network of wealthy, young, and beautiful people who occupied the most expensive tables. Chris Lee, a Mauritian whose father had studied in Shanghai before moving to Taiwan and amassing a fortune through blue jean dyeing factories, served as DJ. Thomas Yeung went on to help found the highly successful club chain, Muse, before starting a new more exclusive club called King of Party.

By the 2010s, a new "caste" of people known as the fu'erdai or "second-generation rich"—the globetrotting children of big-time entrepreneurs and

FIGURE 2.3. Jasmine Chen performing at the Wooden Box jazz club in Shanghai in 2012. Source: Video still image by Andrew Field.

powerful officials—were stepping out to party in the city's VIP clubs, ordering up trains of iced champagne served in buckets decorated with sparklers. The record sum charged for one night of fun was achieved not in Shanghai but in Beijing by Wang Sicong, son of tycoon Wang Jianlin, who lavished around US$400,000 on his circle of friends.[12]

While the fu'erdai partied in VIP spaces and private clubs, others enjoyed the resurgence of the city's international jazz scene in clubs such as the JZ Club. This club started in 2004 and has changed locations twice since then; it has also spawned several other venues in its stable. One of the regular performers at JZ's venues is Jasmine Chen. Chen started out as a classical pianist in her home province of Liaoning. While studying music at the University of Leeds, she switched from classical piano to jazz vocals. Since 2004, she has sung in Shanghai's clubs and elsewhere around the world. Her repertoire includes a wide range of songs—from 1930s Shanghai pop tunes to American and Latin jazz standards.

Recently, Jasmine has taken her local fame to new global heights after recording three songs for the soundtrack to the film *Crazy Rich Asians* (2018). Those songs—"Waiting For Your Return" (Huayang nianhua), "Give Me a Kiss" (Gei wo yige wen), and "I Want Your Love" (Wo yao ni de ai)—are all romantic diva pop songs from 1930s–1940s Shanghai and 1950s Hong Kong; they connect the "crazy rich" Chinese of today to the legacy of Shanghai's Jazz Age.

From transnational jazz men to globe-trotting Jasmine Chen, Shanghai has been a centrifuge of music, dance, and design elements, blending them and then spinning them back out to other cities in the Asia-Pacific region and beyond. Shanghai has had particularly close ties to Hong Kong as a city of music culture, but these ties are now increasingly in competition with flows to other global cities from New York to Singapore and Tokyo. Shanghai adds its own distinct tones to this global mix. As Jasmine Chen's global career illustrates, Shanghai musical nostalgia has a cachet that even Hollywood—and certainly Chen's many fans throughout Southeast Asia—can appreciate.

NOTES

This essay is based largely on Farrer and Field 2015.

1. The term "speakeasy" was used for underground clubs that served alcohol during the Prohibition era in America, when alcohol was officially banned. "Flapper girls" was a term used in the 1920s for fashionable young women who frequented nightspots, liked to dance, and were sexually open and available.

2. Smith (1956) 2017.

3. Moller 1976.

4. Jones 2001.

5. See Clayton 1986 for the story of his two years in Shanghai, which he claims in his memoir were "the best two years of my life."

6. Jones 2001, 101–2. The Green Gang (qingbang) was the leading crime syndicate in Shanghai during the 1920s and 1930s.

7. Cressey (1931) 2008.

8. Field 2010.

9. Atkins 2001.

10. "Cabaret Asssists [sic] Colony Education," *Singapore Free Press*, May 8, 1953, 8; also the exhibit at the Chinese Heritage Centre, Nanyang Technical University (seen February 20, 2016).

11. Moscowitz 2009.

12. Field and Farrer 2018.

REFERENCES AND FURTHER READING

Atkins, Taylor E. 2015. *Blue Nippon: Authenticating Jazz in Japan.* Durham, NC: Duke University Press, 2001.

Clayton, Buck. 1986. *Buck Clayton's Jazz World.* London. Palgrave Macmillan.

Cressey, Paul. (1931) 2008[. *The Taxi-Dance Hall: A Sociological Study in Commercialized Recreation and City Life*. Chicago: University of Chicago Press.

Farrer, James, and Andrew David Field. 2015. *Shanghai Nightscapes: A Nocturnal Biography of a Global City*. Chicago: University of Chicago Press.

Field, Andrew David. 2010. *Shanghai's Dancing World: Cabaret Culture and Urban Politics, 1919–1954*. Hong Kong: Chinese University Press.

Field, Andrew David, and James Farrer. 2018. "China's Party Kings: Shanghai Club Cultures and Status Consumption, 1920s-2010s." In *Polarized Cities: Portraits of the Rich and Poor in Urban China*, edited by Dorothy Solinger, 127–48. Lexington, MD: Rowman & Littlefield.

Jones, Andrew F. 2001. *Yellow Music: Media Culture and Colonial Modernity in the Chinese Jazz Age*. Durham, NC: Duke University Press.

Moller, Allard J. 1976. "A Jazz Odyssey: Jack Carter's Orchestra." *Storyville* (February–March): 97–103.

Moscowitz, Mark. 2009. *Cries of Joy, Songs of Sorrow: Chinese Pop Music and Its Cultural Connotations*. Honolulu: University of Hawaii Press.

Smith, Whitey. (1956) 2017. *I Didn't Make a Million*. Manila: Philippine Education Company. Reprint Hong Kong: Earnshaw Books.

THREE

Maoism as a Global Force

Julia Lovell

ON MARCH 11, 2018, CHINA'S ANNUAL PARLIAMENT—the National People's Congress—voted overwhelmingly in favor of abolishing the constitution's restriction limiting any one president to two terms in office. "The 64-year-old Mr. Xi [Jinping] essentially became a president for life," concluded the *Washington Post,* "in a return to personal dictatorship that China has not seen since Mao Zedong. Forgetting the lessons of Mao's often disastrous reign, Mr. Xi is attempting to construct a 21st-century model of totalitarianism and offer it as an example to the rest of the world."[1] Although the amendment did not surprise many China-watchers, nonspecialist Anglophone commentators seemed wrong-footed. From the tone of their coverage, it appeared that many such analysts had long assumed that, as China turned commercial and capitalist after the death of Mao, the country would become "more like us"; that Mao and Chinese Communism were history. The opposite has happened. Xi Jinping—son of one of Mao's own revolutionary comrades—has renormalized aspects of Maoist political culture. Criticism/self-criticism sessions, Mao's strategy of the "mass line," and the personality cult remain central to the legitimacy and functioning of China's Communist government.

This essay will argue that Maoism has long been underestimated by Western analysts. After briefly defining "Maoism," it will seek to recenter Mao's ideas and experiences as major forces that have shaped China, as well as the world, since the Second World War. The essay will conclude by assessing China's current partial Maoist revival and its significance for China's self-positioning in the world. In a clear break with post-Mao China's reserved approach to foreign affairs, Xi Jinping and his closest advisors have re-asserted the PRC's global ambitions and relevance with an energy and confidence unseen since Mao's Chinese Communist Party (CCP) proclaimed China the center of the world revolution. An exploration of the CCP's history of global interventions under Mao can provide clues to its contemporary repertoire and its ambitions for international relations, and illuminate regional conflicts and tensions originating in the dissemination of Mao's revolutionary strategies during the Cold War.

In 1935, Mao maneuvered his way into a position of leadership in the CCP. Within ten years—a decade that saw the country scourged by floods, famine, and Japanese invasion—Communist Party membership had surged to 1.2 million and its armies had increased to more than nine hundred thousand.[2] After another four years, the Chinese Communists under Mao Zedong had expelled their rivals for control of China, the Nationalists under Chiang Kai-shek, from the mainland to Taiwan. Since its founding in 1949, the People's Republic of China (PRC) has managed to survive longer than any of the revolutionary regimes that preceded it in China—despite the convulsions of a vast man-made famine (the Great Leap Forward between 1958 and 1961, which caused at least 30 million deaths), and a civil war manufactured by Mao (the Cultural Revolution between 1966 and 1969) that disrupted the lives of tens of millions of Chinese people. Born of an era in which China was often treated with scorn by the international system, Mao assembled a practical and theoretical toolkit for turning a fractious, failing empire into a global power. He created a language that intellectuals and peasants, and men and women could understand; a system of propaganda and thought control that has been described as "one of the most ambitious attempts at human manipulation in history"; and a disciplined, effective army.[3]

Maoism is a body of contradictory ideas that has distinguished itself from earlier versions of Marxism in several important ways; some are differences in degree, others in kind. Giving center stage to a non-Western, anticolonial agenda, Mao declared to radicals in developing countries that Russian-style Communism should be retooled to suit local, national conditions. Breaking with the Soviet emphasis on the industrial proletariat, he told revolutionaries to take their struggle out of the cities and to fight protracted, guerrilla war from base areas deep within the countryside. Although Mao was determined, like both Lenin and Stalin, to build a one-party state with military discipline, later in life he also championed an anarchic democracy, telling the Chinese people that "rebellion is justified": that when "there is great chaos under Heaven, the situation is excellent."[4] He preached the doctrine of voluntarism: that by sheer audacity of belief the Chinese—and any other people with the necessary strength of will—could transform their country; revolutionary zeal, not weaponry or material reality, was the decisive factor. Mao also declared that "women can hold up half the sky." Although his own womanizing practice fell far short of his rhetoric, none of his global peers voiced such an egalitarian agenda.

The term "Maoism" has been used both admiringly and pejoratively for several decades to signify a spectrum of political behavior ranging from mass democracy to Machiavellian brutality against political enemies. The English terms "Maoist" and "Maoism" gained currency in Anglo-American Cold War analyses of China, and they were intended to categorize and stereotype a "Red China" that was the essence of an alien threat. After Mao's death, they became catch-all words for dismissing what was perceived as the unitary repressive madness of China from 1949 to 1976. Here the term is not understood in this petrified form. "Maoism" in this essay is an umbrella word for the wide range of theory and practice attributed to Mao and his influence over the past eighty years. In other words, this term is useful only if we accept that the ideas and experiences it describes are living and changing, have been translated and mistranslated, both during and after Mao's lifetime, and on their journeys within and without China.

Before Mao and his lieutenants had even founded the People's Republic, Mao was already eager to take a leadership role in the world revolution. In early 1949, almost a year before consolidating his control of the mainland, he was keen to build an "Asian Cominform" in China to direct the revolution on that continent. At the end of July 1949, Mao's Marxism-Leninism Academy opened, hosting Asian Communist leaders on a one-year course in Mao's revolution. In November 1949, Mao's second-in-command Liu Shaoqi (endorsed by Stalin) declared that armed struggle "is the road of Mao Zedong [and an] inevitable path toward the liberation of other people in the colonial and semicolonial countries." The following year, Liu remade the point more explicitly:

> After the victory of the revolution, the CCP should use all means to help the Communist parties and people among the oppressed peoples of Asia to fight for liberation . . . to consolidate the victory of the Chinese Revolution worldwide. . . . We should provide fraternal assistance and warm hospitality to the Communist parties and revolutionaries from all countries . . . introduce them to details of the experiences of the Chinese Revolution [and] answer their questions carefully.[5]

In 1950, some four hundred trainees gathered at the academy in Beijing to begin their apprenticeships in insurgency before being sent back to lead the revolution in their respective Asian countries. That year, the CCP took another important step in organizing the world revolution by setting up the International Liaison Department, which was responsible for coordinating interactions with other Communist parties and insurgencies.[6] The first cohort of trainees came from Vietnam, Thailand, the Philippines, Indonesia, Burma, Malaya, and India, and it included men like Mohit Sen, who in subsequent decades would become a lynchpin Indian Communist leader. The curriculum was dominated by the theoretical study of Mao's essays and by observation of the ongoing Chinese revolution.

This early program of outreach influenced the course of one of the earliest post-Second World War anticolonial revolts and hot conflicts of the Cold War: the Malayan Emergency. Chin Peng, the young leader of the Malayan Communist Party (MCP), had first been attracted to Mao's ideas as a teenager in the late 1930s. Relative to the CCP's assistance to Ho Chi Minh's coterminous rebellion against French colonial armies in Vietnam, Chinese material aid to the MCP was very limited. Nevertheless, the MCP relied heavily on moral and strategic support from Mao and his lieutenants. Senior members of the MCP attended the Marxism-Leninism Academy and in 1951 MCP propaganda began to underline Mao's unique theoretical contributions to Communist revolution. By the middle of the 1950s, British colonial operatives had intercepted MCP-CCP courier lines; these communications indicated extensive contact between the two parties. Two members (of a total of four) of the MCP politburo were in China, regularly dispatching CCP directives back for adoption in Malaya. However, in the mid-1950s, the PRC bid for leadership of the Afro-Asian Solidarity Movement, which led to a softening of public utterances about the worldwide "victory of the Chinese revolution." It was from Beijing that the MCP received the orders to "fold up the flags and silence the drums": to stop the armed struggle and negotiate with the British in 1956.[7]

By the end of the 1950s, Mao's international ambitions had returned to militancy. Between 1960 and 1964, Mao commissioned a series of polemical articles that denounced Soviet "peaceful coexistence" with the capitalist world as "revisionism," and that proclaimed Mao's strategy of "protracted war" as the key to unlocking world revolution. In 1965, Minister of Defense Lin Biao theorized and encouraged the export of Maoist revolution in his paean to global Maoism, "Long Live the Victory of People's War":

Mao Zedong's thought is a common asset of the revolutionary people of the whole world. This is the great international significance of the thought of Mao Zedong. . . . Hold aloft the just banner of people's war. . . . Victory will certainly go to the people of the world![8]

Upping his rhetoric in 1966, Lin Biao described the Little Red Book—of which more than a billion copies were printed, in dozens of languages, between 1966 and 1971—as a "spiritual atom bomb of infinite power."[9] Through the 1960s, Mao's CCP launched a charm offensive to win over the world beyond China. Mao assiduously portrayed himself in public as the friend of those oppressed by US and Soviet imperialism: of Black Americans, of the Vietcong, of struggling Communist insurgencies everywhere. The CCP welcomed a continuing stream of "Third World" visitors; it bombarded Asia, Africa, and Latin America with broadcast and print propaganda in local languages; it pledged generous aid packages when it could ill afford them.

Many of the consequences of Maoism's international travels were unintended. Indonesia after 1963 became a test case in China's post-Soviet foreign policy for exporting the wisdom of the Maoist model of radical, anticolonial confrontation. Leading Indonesian Communists were inspired by the militant rhetoric of Mao's revolution in the early 1960s. This enthusiasm encouraged and inspired some of them to confront their main political rival, the Indonesian military, culminating in the killing of six generals on October 1, 1965. This decision in turn gave the army a pretext to trigger a nationwide purge of real and alleged "Communists" in the ensuing months, in which at least five hundred thousand Indonesians—many of whom were ethnic Chinese—were murdered.

In the three regions into which Mao's China sank most material aid—Africa, Vietnam and Cambodia, and North Korea—these programs of outreach won the CCP very little political traction. In Africa, aid budgets were received by pragmatic state builders with, for the most part, little interest in implementing Maoist politics. Mao-era China in Africa arguably had its deepest influence on the guerrilla struggle of the Zimbabwe African National Union (ZANU) against white-minority rule in Southern Rhodesia. Nonetheless, this impact was restricted primarily to military strategy in the civil war of the 1960s and 1970s; the transmission of political models after ZANU took power in 1980 has been very limited. Huge CCP investment in the Communist parties of Vietnam, Cambodia, and North Korea, meanwhile, actually fueled anti-Chinese nationalism in those states between the late 1940s and the 1970s, even as their Communist movements were undoubtedly influenced by Mao-era Chinese theory and practice.

Contrary to Marxist and Maoist theory, the people most attracted to Mao's ideas in the industrialized West in the 1960s and 1970s were not workers or farmers but students. After 1966, and climaxing with student protests in 1968, students and intellectuals in the United States and Western Europe enthusiastically embraced Mao's denunciations of US imperialism in Vietnam. Militants saw his apparent encouragement of youthful rebellion against the political establishment in the Cultural Revolution as "a successful, world-changing version of [protests] in Paris, Berkeley, West Berlin."[10]

This Mao fever had some unexpected outcomes. Protestors ignored Mao's profoundly autocratic leanings and claimed him instead as a symbol of playful rebellion for the countercultural lifestyle. The radicalism inspired by the Cultural Revolution bled into the terrorism of groups such as the Red Army Faction in West Germany and the Red Brigades in Italy, both of which posed serious threats to the stability of the states within which they operated. The Red Brigades saw themselves expressing Mao's mass line through violence perpetrated "in the name of the masses," even as they translated Mao's injunction toward "self-reliance" into a clandestine existence that isolated them from ordinary Italians.

The influence of Maoism on South Asia and Latin America was also unpredictable. There, the CCP's practical outreach was limited to inviting delegations (some of whom were offered political and military training) and to distributing "external propaganda" preaching the virtues of China under Mao. And yet, in these regions, Mao's ideas had arguably their greatest "hard-power" impact outside China.

In India, a far-left Sinophile wing of the Communist Party broke off from the main party during the Sino-Soviet split to found a pro-China grouping. In 1967, a rural rebellion against police brutality that started in the village of Naxalbari in rural West Bengal merged with student protests in nearby cities to drive an insurrection inspired by Mao and his ideas. Encouraged by the Chinese media, the "Naxalite" insurgency spread from the border with Nepal, down to Kerala in the south. While that earlier conflagration was for the most part extinguished by a brutal state response in the early 1970s, splinters of the original movement continued to fight and organize. Since the early 2000s, the Maoists have gained further traction by linking their cause to environmental protests. In 2003, the Indian government—ambitious to increase taxation revenues—began granting lucrative mining contracts to

FIGURE 3.1. Communist Pantheon in Naxalbari. Source: Julia Lovell.

multinational corporations, especially in mineral-rich Chhattisgarh and Jharkhand. Maoist insurgents based in these states organized locals into resisting government and corporate efforts to evict people from their land in order to prepare it for industrial development. In 2004, several parts of the Indian Maoist movement reunited within a new organization and army: the Communist Party of India (Maoist) and its People's Liberation Guerrilla Army. In 2006, the country's prime minister identified the Maoist insurgency as the "biggest internal security threat to the Indian state."[11] The Indian government claims that twenty of the country's twenty-eight states are affected; in reality, the Maoist operation is centered on central-eastern India.

In Nepal, admiration for Mao and his revolution percolated deep into left-wing politics from the 1950s onward. After decades of political organization in the far west of the country, in 1996 Nepali Maoists (under the newly formed Communist Party of Nepal—Maoist, CPNM) declared a "People's War" against the state. A decade later, the CPNM had fought their way to a position of decisive political power. Their People's Liberation Army had grown from a few dozen to ten thousand-strong and had wrested 80 percent of Nepal's territory from state control. Their armed rebellion was the principal reason for the collapse of the monarchy and the establishment of a federal republic in Nepal after 2006. Between 2006 and 2016, two leaders of the CPNM served as prime minister of Nepal across a total of three terms; many other leaders have served in successive governments. Although the CPNM did not achieve its original ambition—state capture resulting in unchallenged control of the country in the manner of the CCP in 1949—Nepal is now the only country in the world where you can meet self-avowed Maoists in power. Nepal's Maoist conflict—breaking out five years after the collapse of the Soviet Union, at a time when China under CCP rule was moving toward a model focused on private economic growth—at first glance resembles an exotic anachronism. It becomes comprehensible only through remembering the history of global Maoism, and the ideology of "people's war" sown by China's radical outreach of the 1960s and 1970s. The same can be said for the Communist Party of Peru-Shining Path insurgency of 1980–91, led by Abimael Guzmán, a philosophy professor inspired by Mao's militancy during the Sino-Soviet split who received political and military training in China in 1965 and 1967.

Mao's theory and practice were publicly marginalized in China shortly after his death and the purge of his closest Cultural Revolution lieutenants, the so-called "Gang of Four." But although the Chinese Communist Party has long abandoned the utopian turmoil of Cultural Revolution-era Maoism in favor of an authoritarian capitalism that prizes prosperity and stability, the Great Helmsman has left a heavy mark. The CCP's official 1981 judgment on the Mao era contained only mild criticism of two of its most disruptive and destructive campaigns, the Great Leap Forward and the Cultural Revolution. Mao's portrait still hangs in Tiananmen Square in the center of the capital. In the middle of the square, his embalmed body lies in state. "Mao's invisible hand" (as one recent book puts it) remains present in China's party-state—for example, in the deep politicization of its judiciary; the supremacy of the party over other interests; the intolerance of dissident voices; and an adaptive "guerrilla style" of policy-making.[12]

In 2011, markers of Mao-style politics began to return to the mainstream of Chinese public life. That year, for the first time since the death of Mao in 1976, China experienced both an official and a popular revival of Maoist culture with Bo Xilai's experiment in neo-Maoist government in Chongqing, West China. A year later, Bo was in prison, his career ended by a huge political scandal that included the poisoning of a British businessman ordered by Bo's wife. But Xi Jinping, Bo's main rival and China's new president since 2012, quickly adopted features of Bo's Maoist project. In high Maoist style, Xi has intensified Party control alongside cultivating personal power.[13] He has reinstated the Party as the disciplined, monolithic, solely legitimate representative of China, its people, and its national interest. To achieve this, Xi has invoked distinctly Maoist language and techniques. Just five months into his tenure, he launched the Mass Line Campaign—a conscious throwback to Mao's original, pre-1949 concept. The campaign had three steps: listening to the opinions of the masses; responding by criticizing officials; and correcting their "style of work." Xi has freely deployed the term "rectification," with strong echoes of Mao and his first mass movement, the 1942 campaign in Yan'an whereby Mao and his supporters created a unified party ideology.

Xi's China is of course very different from Mao's: tied into global finance; its stability and political legitimacy bound to economic performance rather than ideological purity; its media too diversified for a single official message to convince its increasingly well-traveled, ambitious (and tax-paying) citizens. Xi's revival of the Maoist political repertoire, moreover, is opportunistically partial. An authoritarian party-builder, Xi is happy to invoke Mao's historical prestige—as founder of the CCP-in-power and of the PRC—to enhance his own prestige and push forward his own objectives (disciplining the party, removing opposition to his rule). But he has buried memory of the Cultural Revolution's mass mobilization of society and revolutionary destruction of the state and party apparatuses.

These large discrepancies between Mao's and Xi's China notwithstanding, what Xi has done is calculate that there is now enough temporal distance between the current moment and the memories of excesses under Mao for it to be safe to deploy the father-of-the-nation symbolism of Mao. Xi's big project is the "Chinese Dream": the restoration of China to its old, pre-nineteenth-century place in the sun, but under CCP rule. Like Mao, and unlike Xi's immediate predecessors, Xi and his people have reached for an emotional political message to bolster the CCP's legitimacy. How the PRC will weather the contrasts between the CCP's Maoist heritage and the hybrid, globalized nature of contemporary China is one of the key domestic challenges the country faces.

What does this partial revival of Maoist practice mean for China's relationship with the world beyond its borders? Xi Jinping has pushed harder on foreign policy than any of his predecessors since Mao. He and his close advisors are the first leaders since Mao to talk confidently of the international relevance of the Chinese/CCP model.[14] The surging economic, political, and military might of the country suggests that the projects of Xi and his CCP—inflected as they are by their Maoist heritage and emerging at a time when China is far more globally powerful than it was under Mao—will have a growing impact on international politics and institutions.

NOTES

1. "A New Form of Totalitarianism Takes Root in China," *Washington Post*, February 25, 2018.

2. Spence 2013, 430.

3. Goldman 1987, 223.

4. Although there is no clear written source for the "chaos" quotation (widely attributed to Mao), it is highly plausible, given his other utterances at the start of the Cultural Revolution. See, for example, MacFarquhar and Schoenhals 2009, 52.

5. Shen and Xia 2014, 202–3, 208.

6. Shen and Xia 2014, 205–6.

7. Chin 2003, 367.

8. Lin Biao, "Long Live the Victory of People's War!" marxists.org, September 3, 1965, https://www.marxists.org/reference/archive/lin-biao/1965/09/peoples_war/index.htm.

9. Lin Biao, "Foreword to the Second Edition of Quotations of Chairman Mao Tse-tung," marxists.org, December 16, 1966, https://www.marxists.org/reference/archive/lin-biao/1966/12/16.htm.

10. Ethan Young, interview, March 24, 2015, New York.

11. Sundar 2016, 13.

12. Heilmann and Perry 2011.

13. Li 2017.

14. See, for example, Wang Xiaohong, "'2018 Liang Hui—gaige xin zhengcheng' xinxing zhengdang zhidu wei shijie zhengdang zhengzhi fazhan gongxian zhongguo zhihui" ["Two Conferences—a new journey in reform": the new style party system contributes Chinese wisdom to the global development of political parties], China Plus, accessed March 15, 2018, http://news.cri.cn/20180308/962b9850–3a41–45ac-57c0-a4afdaa2d9e4.html.

REFERENCES AND FURTHER READING

Adhikari, Aditya. 2014. *The Bullet and the Ballot Box: The Story of Nepal's Maoist Revolution*. London: Verso.

Chin, Peng. 2003. *Alias Chin Peng—My Side of History: Recollections of a Revolutionary Leader*. Singapore: Media Masters.

Cook, Alexander C., ed. 2014. *Mao's Little Red Book: A Global History*. Cambridge: Cambridge University Press.

Friedman, Jeremy. 2015. *Shadow Cold War: The Sino-Soviet Competition for the Third World*. Chapel Hill: University of North Carolina Press.

Goldman, Merle. 1987. "The Party and Intellectuals." In *The Cambridge History of China*. Vol. 14, *The People's Republic, Part I: The Emergence of Revolutionary*

China, edited by Roderick MacFarquhar and John K. Fairbank, 218–58. Cambridge: Cambridge University Press.

Heilmann, Sebastian, and Elizabeth Perry, eds. 2011. *Mao's Invisible Hand: The Political Foundations of Adaptive Governance in China*. Cambridge, MA: Harvard University Press.

Li, Sangkuk. 2017. "An Institutional Analysis of Xi Jinping's Centralization of Power." *Journal of Contemporary China* 26, no. 105 (January): 325–36.

Lovell, Julia. 2019. *Maoism: A Global History*. London: Bodley Head.

MacFarquhar, Roderick, and Michael Schoenhals. 2009. *Mao's Last Revolution*. Cambridge, MA: Harvard University Press.

Mertha, Andrew. 2014. *Brothers in Arms: Chinese Aid to the Khmer Rouge, 1975–1979*. Ithaca, NY: Cornell University Press.

Rothwell, Matthew. 2013. *Transpacific Revolutionaries: The Chinese Revolution in Latin America*. New York: Routledge.

Shah, Alpa. 2018. *Nightmarch: Among India's Revolutionary Guerrillas*. London: Hurst.

Shen, Zhihua, and Yafeng Xia. 2014. "Leadership Transfer in the Asian Revolution: Mao Zedong and the Asian Cominform." *Cold War History* 14, no. 2 (May): 195–213.

Spence, Jonathan. 2013. *The Search for Modern China*. New York: W. W. Norton.

Sundar, Nandini. 2016. *The Burning Forest: India's War in Bastar*. Delhi: Juggernaut.

Zhou, Taomo. 2019. *Migration in the Time of Revolution: China, Indonesia and the Cold War*. Ithaca, NY: Cornell University Press.

FOUR

Japanese Development Aid and Global Power

Hiroshi Kan Sato and Akiko Hiratsuka-Sasaki

INTERNATIONAL DEVELOPMENT AID STARTED with the famous "Point Four Program" in US President Truman's inaugural speech in 1949. For Truman, sharing US technical knowledge with underdeveloped areas of the world would be fundamentally different from the old imperialism and colonialism, which amounted to "exploitation for foreign profit." Instead, such assistance would be inclusive and universal in its aspirations: "All countries, including our own, will greatly benefit from a constructive program for the better use of the world's human and natural resources."[1]

Japan, as the first non-Western country to join the circle of donor countries, has struggled to come to terms with such Western universal values as the underpinning of development aid that ultimately derives from Christian ethics. This chapter explores the history of Japanese development aid to clarify the Japanese Official Development Assistance (ODA), which emerged differently from Western development experiences. Specifically, we will look into the unique approaches of Japan's own development experiences, *kaizen*, by focusing on the Livelihood Improvement Program (LIP) and the One Village One Product (OVOP), both of which emphasize the utilization of existing resources and self-reliance.

AID AND CHARITY IN JAPANESE CULTURE

In countries with a Christian background, development aid is rooted in charitable activities. In Japan, though the charity movement was spread by philanthropists, big merchants, and prominent Christians after the Meiji Restoration in 1868, it remained restricted to people of a certain social status.

Japanese development aid has different ethical roots. We would like to elaborate this in three points. First, the Japanese philosophical view toward charity affects public behavior. For instance, the Confucian concept of *intoku* (hidden virtue) might have caused a reluctance to accept charity as a public activity. The concept encourages people to help others but not to practice *intoku* openly: donating to or helping others is not done in order to gain recognition.[2] In addition, the Japanese saying, "if you help others, the good will be paid forward and it returns to yourself in the long run," has strong currency among people. Development aid might be repaid when one finds oneself in dire need. When a dreadful earthquake with a magnitude of 9.0 hit Japan in 2011, many developing countries that had received aid from Japan previously supplied emergency assistance. In all, Japan received approximately US$1.5 billion, making it the biggest aid-receiving country that year.[3]

The second aspect of the uniqueness of Japanese aid culture is the country's own earlier experience of receiving aid during the period after the Second World War. The defeated country received a tremendous amount of relief supplies from its conquerors, saving the lives of thousands of starving people. In total, the United States contributed around US$1.8 billion between 1946 and 1951 through two funds, GARIOA (Government Aid for Relief in Occupied Areas) and EROA (Economic Rehabilitation in Occupied Areas). Of the total, US$1.3 billion were in grants.[4]

The US aid supplies were much appreciated by the people of Japan, but they felt ashamed at the same time. This consciousness was related to a third feature—namely, the mindset of "self-reliance," which evolved over the course of modernization in the late nineteenth century. During the Meiji period, the government hired Western experts to bring new knowledge and expertise about modern infrastructure, industrialization, the legal system, and state building. The salary for those experts was paid by the Japanese government, leaving a deep culture of self-reliant development over the years.[5] This experience has partly shaped the core of Japan's foreign aid philosophy.[6]

OVERVIEW OF JAPANESE ODA

The history of Japan as a donor started shortly after the Second World War, despite the fact that the country was one of the largest aid recipients at the time. Along with war reparations and economic cooperation, Japan started development aid by joining the Colombo Plan in 1954 and offering technical

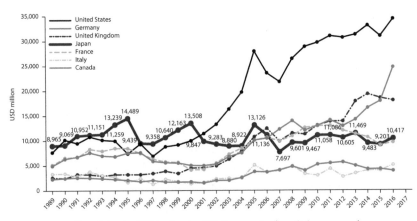

FIGURE 4.1. Trends in the ODA of major DAC countries (net disbursements).

cooperation to countries damaged by Japan during the war.[7] War reparations—mainly to countries in Southeast Asia—continued until 1976 and were provided in tandem with economic cooperation.[8] Although still suffering from poverty, the Japanese government found in economic cooperation a solution to improve Japan's reputation in the eyes of both Asian and Western countries and a way to restart healthy trade activities.[9]

Although such cooperation was meant to atone for the war and to spur the development of receiving countries, Japan also intended to gain market entrance for trade and investments.[10] Looking back on the history of Japanese ODA, the Ministry of Foreign Affairs (MOFA) explains that "the historical background of Japan's financial assistance ... combined with the basic policy of placing emphasis on providing cooperation for Asian countries having close links with Japan, became the model for the subsequent Asia focus of Japan's ODA."[11]

Besides technical and economic cooperation, the Japan Overseas Cooperation Volunteers program has been dispatching young generations to developing countries to help in fields like agriculture, public health, and education since 1985.[12] In the 1970s, Japan's ODA focused on Southeast Asia, mainly in order to serve the promotion of trade. In 1987, the then Ministry of International Trade and Industry (MITI) combined investment, trade, and ODA into a "Trinity Model"[13] to support Japanese companies in the foreign expansion of their business, especially in Asia. Under this strategy, Japanese ODA continued to expand throughout the 1980s and 1990s.

In the late 1980s, however, international criticism of Japan's trade surplus reached a peak. To meet this criticism, the government decided to restrict the use of ODA exclusively to serve Japanese interests, and it doubled the amount

TABLE 4.1 Revision of ODA Charter of Japan

	Principles
1st ODA Charter (1992)	Humanitarian viewpoint Recognition of interdependence among nations Environmental conservation Support of self-help efforts aimed at economic take-off in developing countries
2nd ODA Charter (2003)	Supporting self-help efforts of developing countries Perspective of "Human Security" Assurance of fairness Utilization of Japanese experience and expertise Partnership and collaboration with the international community
3rd ODA Charter (2015)	Contributing to peace and prosperity through cooperation for nonmilitary purposes Promoting human security Cooperation aimed at self-reliant development through assistance for self-help efforts as well as dialogue and collaboration based on Japan's experience and expertise

NOTE: Principles of the first Charter are from Japan's ODA White Paper of 2006.
SOURCE: The Ministry of Foreign Affairs of Japan 2003, 2006, and 2015.

of ODA within ten years. This resulted in Japan becoming the largest ODA donor in the world between 1991 and 2000 (see fig. 4.1).[14]

The Japanese shift away from promoting its own interests concurred with a global trend focusing on social development, which started with the *Human Development Report* of the United Nations Development Program (UNDP) in 1990 and the World Summit for Social Development in Copenhagen in 1995. Furthermore, Japanese industries had become competitive enough to no longer need ODA to support their businesses abroad.

Reflecting on the trends in development aid and the domestic economic situation, Japan published its first ODA Charter in 1992, which has been revised twice since then (see table 4.1). The first Japanese ODA Charter claimed that development aid was necessary for "mutual dependency"—that is, the notion that helping others will serve one's own interest in the long term. Japanese aid policy also emphasizes humanitarian reasons and the promotion of self-help as well as the autonomy of recipient countries. This philosophy reflects Japan's historical experience as an aid recipient and a developing country, and in this respect it differs from the aid policies of Western donors, which rather value the promotion of universal values, such as freedom and democracy.[15]

Following the global trends, the Charter was revised in 2003 and shifted the focus to poverty reduction and antiterrorism. After the 9/11 attacks in

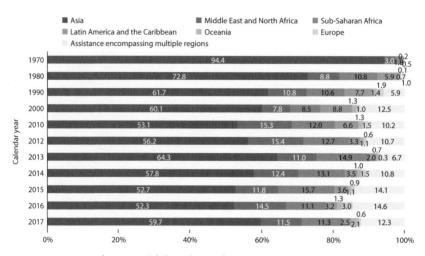

FIGURE 4.2. Trends in Japan's bilateral ODA by region.

2001, the United States increased the use of ODA as an instrument in the fight against terrorism. Just one year earlier, the leaders of 189 countries at the United Nations Millennium Summit pledged to meet the Millennium Development Goals (MDGs) and to eradicate poverty in 2000. Nevertheless, in the 2003 revision, the national interest also continued to have a prominent place owing to the stagnation of the Japanese economy and the contraction of the domestic market in Japan.

After Japan lost its position as the world's top donor in 2001, the ODA budget started shrinking along with the Japanese government's budget deficit. In the revised Charter of 2015, Japan's self-interest again became more apparent, although this tendency was also seen among Western donor countries.[16] The ODA budget was further reduced; as a result, Japan dropped to number four on the list of donors in the world in 2017. Under the Third Charter, Africa instead of Asia became the main recipient of aid in order to eliminate poverty. As shown in figure 4.2, while over 90 percent of bilateral ODA went to Asia in 1970, this dropped to 50 percent in 2015. However, Asia is still preferred by the business sector, even though some former recipients of Japanese aid in Southeast Asia have been rapidly developed and are therefore in less need of aid. The Keidanren (Japan Business Federation) has released several policy proposals regarding the strategic promotion of the infrastructure system since 2013, emphasizing a focus on emerging economies in Asia as a part of their requests.

Under the influence of global trends and the pressure from industry, Japanese ODA policy has changed over the years. Although the emphasis on self-reliance continues to be the core value underlying its aid philosophy, Japan shifted to more self-interested, infrastructure-oriented ODA in 1960s and 1970s. In the 1990s and 2000s, Japan followed a global trend to meet the MDGs. In recent years, Japan's self-interest has come to the fore once more, but this is now in line with the global trend among both established Western donors and emerging donors, such as China and India.

DEVELOPMENT EXPERIENCES OF JAPAN: *KAIZEN* AND ONE VILLAGE ONE PRODUCT

The mindset of self-reliance is rooted in Japanese aid culture. How does this reflect the experience of development of Japan itself? To answer this question, let us take a closer look at two prominent examples: the Livelihood Improvement Program (LIP), as an example of *kaizen,* and the One Village One Product (OVOP).

Kaizen means improvement in Japanese. This approach thus far has been widely implemented in various fields both inside and outside Japan: manufacturing, community development, hospital management, and so on. The most famous *kaizen* approach is from the Toyota car factory management, spreading globally in the manufacturing sector. The core value of *kaizen* is "creating the attitude shared among all members of an organization to consistently pursue advanced levels of quality and productivity, and not just applying the organization's management method."[17]

This concept is famous among industrial sectors, yet it is not limited to industry and manufacture. It was also adapted in rural development activities to alleviate poverty before the rapid economic growth of the 1960s and 1970s, which was called the Livelihood Improvement Program[18] (LIP), or *seikatsu kaizen* in Japanese. For both the industrial and rural development sectors, the common idea is a "bottom-up, participatory approach of continuous improvement of work."[19]

The LIP mobilized agricultural extensionists under the Ministry of Agriculture. Starting from improvements to the cooking stove, they proceeded with other aspects of rural life, such as sanitation, nutrition, and clothing, by working together with rural residents, especially women. By the middle of the 1960s, the LIP had contributed to uplifting the living standards and the escape from poverty in most Japanese rural areas. It has also contributed to women's empowerment.

FIGURE 4.3. Cooking seminar in Aishima, Yamaguchi Prefecture in Japan, ca. 1960. Photograph by Akiko Honma.

Generally, economic growth widens the income disparity between the urban and rural population in developing countries. In the Japanese case, however, most of the rural areas have also benefited from rapid economic growth, keeping the urban-rural gap relatively small. The benefits of economic development have spread widely across the country; even in the rural areas, education, public health, and infrastructure have become universal. Livelihood Improvement activities have played an important role. They have accustomed villagers to the need to improve their living environment by themselves and to adapt to change. Not only macroeconomic growth and development but also the improvement of everyday life through LIP activities at the microlevel have enabled Japan to reach the status of a developed country.[20]

Another example of Japan's development experience is One Village One Product (OVOP). It was started in a small mountain town called Oyama in Oita prefecture in 1961 with a movement of planting plums and chestnuts. At that time, rice officially was the main pillar of Japanese agriculture, and it was a big risk for the local government to disregard this fundamental national policy. In this region, however, plums and chestnuts were more suitable to the local climate and landscape, so an increase of income was expected from changing the main agricultural products.[21] Besides such a transition in agriculture, the local government and agricultural cooperative, together with local residents, worked on improving efficiency and modernization of agriculture, income generation, and the capacity building of residents themselves through learning, sometimes from abroad in order to enrich village life.[22]

TABLE 4.2 Comparison of a conventional development method
and "kaizen" method

	Conventional development method	Kaizen method
Purpose	To improve life	To improve life
Starting point	Start from "things lacking"	Start from "things available"
Core idea	Transplantation, replacement	Creation, adaptation
Important tool	Technology, funds	External information, social capital (helping each other)
Investment	External investment	Investment from local municipalities, self-effort of community
Leader of projects	Experts from outside	Local residents, leaders
Event organization	Sporadic	Sustainable
Core	Productivity, income generation	Comfort, safety, saving
Main interest	As "much" as	As "long" as

SOURCE: Sato 2008

The Oita prefectural governor at the time, Mr. Morihiko Muramatsu, conceptualized the cases of Oyama and other regions as what is now known as the OVOP movement. He developed it into a more general principle for regions to produce their specialized products suited to their unique resources and culture.[23]

One Village One Product and many other successful rural development experiences in Japan are embedded in the idea of endogenous development. Contrary to externally driven development, these development experiences apply a participatory approach to using existing resources and knowledge instead of external aid. Endogenous development puts the initiative of local residents at the core; they decide whether and how to utilize assistance from the outside.

Such experiences have encouraged the Japanese development approach and have influenced aid policies. As shown in table 4.2, conventional aid from the United States and Europe tends to assist the recipients by allowing them to import things that are lacking. By contrast, the *kaizen* approach starts with what is at hand; it tries to utilize local resources, knowledge, or culture as much as possible. Things can be adopted or imported from the outside, but they are not necessarily limited to financial or technical aid. They can involve concepts and ideas as well.

FIGURE 4.4. One Village One Product: Fruit processing group in Kenya. Photograph by Kiyonori Matsushima.

The *kaizen* and OVOP approaches do not require a huge budget or extensive facilities; they make small, but significant improvements and mobilize the initiative and active engagement of residents. A small but successful case can be a pilot project that can be shared and learned from other regions. In such a way, a local Japanese development example can become a development method in international aid as well.[24]

Kaizen projects including LIP have spread widely around the world. The Japan International Cooperation Agency (JICA) has so far provided *kaizen* projects in manufacturing to over thirty countries.[25] LIP has been transferred to rural communities in China, Africa, and Latin America.[26] From Latin American countries alone, 350 local practitioners have participated in courses provided by JICA.[27] Like in Japanese rural areas, residents in those countries discuss how they can improve their lives and start from what they can do themselves—like cleaning the streets, improving their kitchens, healthcare, and so on.

One Village One Product has also spread globally. It was introduced to the local Chinese governments of the Shanghai, Wuhan, and Jiangsu provinces in the late 1980s, to Southeast Asian countries like Malaysia and Indonesia in the 1990s, and to the Philippines and Thailand in the early 2000s.[28] Although the sustainability of projects implemented overseas needs to be further investigated, OVOP has been widely introduced elsewhere in Asia, and in Africa and Latin America as well. There are also shops selling OVOP products from developing countries at Japanese airports and online stores.

In the case of Thailand, the national government has sent delegations to Oita prefecture to develop a Thai version of OVOP. In 2001, the Thai government introduced its scheme as One Tambon One Product (Tambon is a subdistrict in Thailand). Unlike the Japanese case, which started from the bottom up, this was initiated by the central government and then disseminated to the local governments.[29] As the movement gained wide recognition, the government developed certificates, an OTOP product logo, OTOP e-commerce, and an OTOP Product Champion competition.[30]

Sometimes the successful case study of the Japanese development approach is thought of as a magic wand to solve problems instantly and efficiently;[31] officials from developing countries attempt to simply absorb and copy it. However, the approach should be adapted to the local context, as the methodology's origin is different from the recipient's culture. Such a process of localization gradually changes a development methodology to make it sustainable. In other words, localization is the essence of successful cross-cultural development aid.

NEW PARADIGMS OF DEVELOPMENT
AID FROM EAST ASIA

As the center of gravity of the world economy shifts from West to East, development aid is also affected. Emerging donors like South Korea, China, and India are increasingly prominent in the twenty-first century with new styles of aid.

The aid paradigms shaped by the OECD countries emphasize noncommercial aid without ties to business interests in the donor country. When the Chinese came to the scene of development aid, however, they implemented aid policies in their own way. Some researchers point out that Chinese aid is in fact rather similar to Japanese aid in the 1960s and 1970s: it is driven by commercial or other interests and predominantly based on interest-bearing and conditional loans.

However, owing to the impact of China's rise, the current global trend is changing the landscape of development aid again.[32] OECD countries themselves gradually follow similar, interest-oriented approaches because of domestic pressures. As was discussed earlier, Japan follows this trend as well; the revised Charter in 2015 reflects the same spirit of inviting the private sector as a stakeholder of development intervention.

Another feature of the Asian types of ODA is group training programs. East Asian countries organize many courses for officials from developing countries. The relationships between the Western donors and recipients are frequently made easier by historical connections dating from the era of colonialism. In such cases, recipients and donors share similar legal or administrative systems, facilitating the absorption of development assistance. In the case of aid from East Asia, however, recipients first need to understand the social and administrative systems of donor countries—not necessarily an easy task—to make cross-cultural aid possible and effective. Countries like Japan, South Korea, and China are therefore keen to invite the trainees from developing countries and let them observe and understand what lies behind the success of East Asian economic development. However, owing to financial constraints, this type of training course has recently received criticism in Japan.

As a successor to the MDGs, Sustainable Development Goals (SDGs) were adopted in 2015 to achieve sustainable development by 2030 for all developing and developed countries. SDGs emphasize Public Private Partnerships (PPPs), which encourage the private sector to enter the field of development and poverty alleviation. PPPs seek to answer the classic questions: how to combine public interest with private profit and how to insert redistribution mechanisms into the global market economy.

The conventional standard of development aid theory is based on experiences of advanced countries and claims to universality that are fundamentally Western in origin and signature. This discourse of universality might now face a paradigm shift as new donors are emerging from non-Western and non-Christian worlds that emphasize particularity and local context. Furthermore, development aid in the era of SDGs ought to be consistent with social and environmental sustainability, requiring the transformation from conventional modernization theory based on Western experiences. Development aid from East Asia might be a prominent alternative aid philosophy with global applications. Viewed from this perspective, understanding East Asian experiences of development continues to be relevant for the developed and developing world alike.

NOTES

1. Harry S. Truman, "Inaugural Address," (speech, Washington, DC, January 20, 1949). https://www.trumanlibrary.org/whistlestop/50yr_archive/inagural20jan1949.htm.

2. Uo 2013.

3. "Higashi Nihon Daishinsai heno kaigai karano sien jisseki no rebyu cyosa" [Survey of the result of foreign aid for the Great East Earthquake], International Development Center of Japan (IDCJ), accessed January 30, 2019, https://www.idcj.jp/pdf/idcjr20140304.pdf.

4. "ODA cyotto iihanashi" [A short, good story about ODA], Ministry of Foreign Affairs of Japan, accessed February 24, 2019, https://www.mofa.go.jp/mofaj/gaiko/oda/hanashi/story/1_2.html (hereafter cited as MOFA).

5. Katano 2011.

6. "Japan's Official Development Assistance Charter," Ministry of Foreign Affairs of Japan, June 30, 1992, https://www.mofa.go.jp/policy/oda/summary/1999/ref1.html.

7. The Colombo Plan (the Colombo Plan for Cooperative Economic and Social Development in Asia and the Pacific) is a regional intergovernmental organization aiming for social and economic development of the region that started in 1951, following the Commonwealth Conference on Foreign Affairs held in Colombo in 1950. It was originally limited to the Commonwealth countries, but later non-Commonwealth countries like Japan also joined.

8. "Japan's Official Development Assistance White Paper 2004: Accomplishments and Progress of 50 Years," Ministry of Foreign Affairs of Japan, accessed November 14, 2020, https://www.mofa.go.jp/policy/oda/white/2004/index.html (hereafter cited as "Japan's Official Development Assistance, 2004").

9. Sato 2016; "Japan's Official Development Assistance, 2004."

10. "Keizai Kyoryoku no Genjo to Mondaiten" [The current status and the problems of economic cooperation], Ministry of International Trade and Industry,1958, 15; Sato 2016; "Japan's Official Development Assistance, 2004."

11. "Japan's Official Development Assitance, 2004.".

12. "JICA Kaigaikyoryokutai jigyogaiyo" [JICA overview of Japan Overseas Cooperation Volunteers], Japan International Cooperation Agency, accessed April 21, 2019, https://www.jica.go.jp/volunteer/outline/publication/pamphlet/pdf/gaiyo.pdf (hereafter cited as JICA).

13. "Keizai Kyoryoku no Genjo to Mondaiten" [The current status and the problems of economic cooperation], 1987.

14. "Japan's Official Development Assistance White Paper 2006," Ministry of Foreign Affairs of Japan, accessed August 28, 2018, https://www.mofa.go.jp/policy

/oda/white/2006/index.htm (hereafter cited as "Japan's Official Development Assistance, 2006").

15. MOFA 1991, 19.

16. Hulme 2016. The Charter was renamed from the ODA (Official Development Aid) Charter to the Development Cooperation Charter in the revision in 2015 in order to include nonofficial stakeholders such as the private sector and NGOs.

17. JICA, *Kaizen Handbook* 2018, accessed April 18, 2019, https://www.jica .go.jp/english/news/field/2018/c8hovm000 od1yoh4-att/KaizenHandbook_Main .pdf.

18. Originally, LIP was an external development program brought from the United States and adapted to Japanese rural areas. Agricultural extension systems were transplanted to Japan in 1947 from the United States and they aimed to improve livelihoods and enhance agricultural technology. Although the basic structure was introduced from the United States, each movement was not a copy but was created bottom-up by the local participants (Sato et al. 2011, 82).

19. Shimada 2018, 2.

20. Sato 2001, 147.

21. Matsui 2006.

22. For example, they have sent young generations to Israel since 1969 and absorbed the philosophy and methods from the Kibbutz movement. Matsui 2006; Hideo Ogata, "Hirakareta machidukuri" [Open rural development] (paper, Oyama, Japan, February 17, 1991).

23. Oita OVOP, International Exchange Promotion Committee, accessed August 20, 2018, http://www.ovop.jp/en/.

24. Sato 2008.

25. JICA, *Kaizen Handbook* 2018, accessed April 18, 2019, https://www.jica .go.jp/english/news/field/2018/c8hovm000 od1yoh4-att/KaizenHandbook_Main .pdf.

26. Ota 2019, 162.

27. Ota 2019, 162.

28. Matsui 2006, 146.

29. Natsuda et al. 2012.

30. Natsuda et al. 2012.

31. Matsui 2006, 149.

32. Hulme 2016.

REFERENCES AND SUGGESTED READING

Hulme, David. 2016. *Should Rich Nations Help the Poor?* Cambridge: Polity Press.
Katano, Susumu. 2011. *Meiji Oyatoi gaikokujin to sono deshi tachi* [Hired foreign experts and their disciples during the Meiji era]. Tokyo: Shinjinbutsu ouraisha.
Matsui, Kazuhisa. 2006. "Isson Ippin Undo ha donoyouni tsutaeraretaka." [How was the One Village One Project Movement introduced?] In *Isson Ippin Undo to*

Kaihatsu tojokoku -Nihon no Chiiki Shinko ha dou tsutaeraretaka. [One Village One Project Movement and developing countries: how were lessons from Japan's rural revitalization transferred?], edited by Matsui Kazuhisa and Yamagami Susumu, 145–51. Chiba: IDE-JETRO.

Ministry of Foreign Affairs of Japan. 1991. *Japan's ODA 1990.* Tokyo: Association for Promotion of International Cooperation. https://www.mofa.go.jp/files /000119315.pdf.

———. 2003. "Japan's Official Development Assistance Charter." August 29. https://www.mofa.go.jp/policy/oda/reform/revision0308.pdf.

———. 2015. "Cabinet decision on the Development Cooperation Charter." February 10. https://www.mofa.go.jp/files/000067701.pdf.

Natsuda, Kaoru, Kunio Igusa, Aree Wiboonpongse, and John Thoburn. 2012. "One Village One Product—Rural Development Strategy in Asia: the case of OTOP in Thailand." *Canadian Journal of Development Studies* 33, no. 3 (October): 369–85.

Ota, Miho. 2019. "Cyunanbei ni okeru seikatzu kaizen undo no tenkai" [Development of livelihood improvement approach in Latin America]. In *Sekai ni hirogaru nouson seikatsu kaizen-Nihon kara Cyugoku, Africa, Cyunanbei he-* [Improvement approach for livelihood: toward new rural development from Japan the countryside in China, Africa, and Latin America], edited by Mizuno, Masami, and Tadashi Horiguchi: 162–84. Kyoto: Koyoshobo.

Sato, Hiroshi. 2001. "Sengo Nihon no Seikatsu Kaizen Undo" [Livelihood improvement program in Japan after the Second World War]. In *Kaihatsugaku wo Manabu Hito no tameni* [For the people learning the development study], edited by Kyoko Kikuchi, 144–63. Kyoto: Sekaishisosha-Kyogakusha.

———. 2008. "Noson kaihatsu niokeru 'model' apurouchi no imi" [The meaning of the "model" approach in rural development]. In *Kaihatsu to Noson—Noson Kaihatsuron Saiko* [Development and village—rethinking rural development theory],edited by Hiroshi Sato and Masami Mizuno, 247–73. Chiba: IDE-JETRO.

Sato, Hiroshi, Masami Mizuno, Miho Ota, Kazuko Oguni, and Yoko Fujikake. 2011. "Episode 69: Urgent Resettlement." In *Wisdom of the Livelihood Improvement (KAIZEN) in Post-War Japan: Lessons Learnt from the First Developing Country*, 81–82. Tokyo: Japan International Cooperation Agency, Overseas Cooperation Volunteer Office. https://openjicareport.jica.go.jp/810/810/810_ 000_12066163.html.

Sato, Jin. 2016.*Yaban kara seizon no kaihatsuron* [Development: from the state of barbarians to livelihood]. Kyoto: Minerva.

Shimada, Go. 2018. "Achievements and Further Issues in Kaizen Research for International Development: Deriving Policy Implications from Interdisciplinary Approach." *Journal of International Development Studies* 27, no. 2: 1–11.

Uo, Masataka. 2013. "Japan." In *Global Fundraising: How the World is Changing the Rules of Philanthropy*, edited by Penelope Cagney and Bernard Ross, 43–58. Hoboken, NJ: John Wiley & Sons.

———

Conflict and Cooperation in Global East Asia

Lindsay Black

INTRAREGIONAL RELATIONS IN EAST ASIA are complex, requiring an understanding of East Asian history, globalization, domestic politics, great power politics and the myriad institutions that bind the region together. The result is seldom a clean picture that defines East Asian intraregional relations simply in terms of conflict or cooperation; rather, it is something more uncertain, dynamic, and fluid. This chapter provides an overview of intraregional relations in East Asia in all their messy complexities. It opens with a consideration of historical factors that continue to shape intraregional relations in East Asia today. It moves on to address the forces of globalization to show how economic interconnectivity provides a bedrock for intraregional relations and also an impetus for regional cooperation. Finally, this chapter presents the fluctuating foreign policy of the United States toward East Asia, thereby highlighting the uncertain environment in which East Asian policymakers operate.

INTRAREGIONAL RELATIONS IN EAST ASIAN HISTORY

Historical grievances between East Asian states are a source of tension and continue to inhibit cooperation. More positively, former regional orders also provide East Asian policymakers and thinkers with models for foreign policy today. This is not to say that the history of the region inevitably conditions contemporary international relations. The ravages of the Vietnam War have not prevented warmer US-Vietnam ties from developing, and ASEAN-Japan relations have been cordial for decades, as Southeast Asian leaders have largely forgiven Japan its history of imperialist expansion. It is more a question of how a variety of actors, from leaders to nationalist organizations, have interpreted East Asia's past. Three periods in particular are worth bearing in mind: the Sinocentric world order, Japanese imperialism, and the Cold War.

The Sinocentric world order is one example of a model that Chinese scholars reference to justify China's foreign policy goals today. Zhao Tingyang and Yan Xuetong emphasize how China's regional relations mirror the "benevolent" Sinocentric regional system.[1] According to them, China's rise will be mutually beneficial for those states that embrace it. Unsurprisingly, such one-sided accounts have been challenged for their historical inaccuracies as well as for providing academic support for government policies that are perceived to be assertive and domineering by many in the region. For example, critics point to the July 2010 ASEAN Regional Forum (ARF) meeting in Hanoi where China's then foreign minister Yang Jiechi, angered by ASEAN states' opposition to China's territorial claims in the South China Sea, snapped "China is a big country and other countries are small countries and that is just a fact."[2] Clearly, a hierarchical regional order with China at the center is not always equal and mutually beneficial, and can instead fuel fears of China's rise.

Nonetheless, the Chinese government has persisted in promoting the win-win nature of its relations with regional states, encapsulated in key policies such as its Belt and Road Initiative (BRI). The BRI is of course heavily contested. William Callahan argues that the BRI constitutes not only a regional economic policy but also an ideational strategy to establish norms favorable to China at the heart of intraregional relations.[3] For Tim Summers, on the other hand, the BRI is not distinctively Chinese; rather, it is more of a "spatial fix," a way of linking China's periphery to the broader East Asian economy so that it may benefit from and reproduce the logic of neoliberal globalization.[4] From this perspective, the BRI is not transforming the global political economy but supplementing or even developing it. Indeed, it is hard to see what precisely distinguishes the BRI from Japan's "developmental regionalism," an approach designed to further Japan's regional economic interests through close government to business relations. We should indeed ask just how much China's BRI owes to Japan's approach to development and China's experience of receiving Japanese Official Development Assistance (ODA, see chapter 4 of this volume).[5] Japan consistently failed to gain political recognition for the vast ODA it channeled into East Asian economies, and it still remains to be seen whether China's "win-win" rhetoric will convince regional states.

Japan's past imperialist aggression from the late nineteenth century to the end of the Second World War has also hampered Japanese attempts to present their regional policy as benevolent and engendering cooperation. Neighboring states, particularly China and the Koreas, continue to perceive Japan's failure to adequately apologize for its past aggression as evidence that Japan is unfit to exert regional leadership. A number of Japanese leaders have prevaricated over and sought to nuance their apologies and have visited the controversial Yasukuni Shrine, where Japan's war dead are entombed, in a bid to appeal to nationalist voters and so as not to appear weak on the international stage. However, neighboring governments are hardly innocent either, seeking to stoke nationalism in their country by memorializing historical sites and museums with anti-Japanese rhetoric and content. This was the case in September 2010, when the detention of a Chinese fishing boat captain by the Japan Coast Guard (JCG) for ramming a JCG vessel in waters off the disputed Senkaku or Diaoyu Islands led to massive protests throughout China. For China, the Diaoyu Islands were illegally appropriated during the period of Japanese imperialism. When the Japanese government bought the islands from its private Japanese owner in November 2012, nationalist demonstrations again erupted across China with the acquiescence of the Chinese government. Anti-Japanese sentiment has also had an impact on Japan's regional policy. During the 1980s, for example, the Ministry of Foreign Affairs of Japan (MOFA) refrained from playing too overt a role in the development of two key regional groups, the Asia-Pacific Economic Cooperation (APEC) forum and the ASEAN Regional Forum (ARF), out of a concern that regional states would be wary of Japanese regional leadership. Here again, the past, or rather an interpretation of the past, continues to shape attempts at regional cooperation and at times engenders regional tensions.

The Cold War period has also shaped regional tensions and affected the possibilities for cooperation in East Asian intraregional relations. The bipolar (capitalist versus Communist) structure impeded regional cooperation during the Cold War itself. Key security flashpoints, such as China-Taiwan relations and tensions on the Korean peninsula, date back to the early Cold War period. China-Taiwan relations developed from the end of the Chinese Civil War. Following Communist Party Chairman Mao Zedong's declaration of the establishment of the People's Republic of China on October 1, 1949, Mao's opponents, the nationalist Kuomintang Party, led by Chiang Kai-shek, fled with their remaining forces to Taiwan. Here, Chiang would proceed to establish an economically successful, anti-Communist bastion from which he hoped to retake the mainland. Chiang's hopes of reconquering China would never be fulfilled, but periodic clashes between Taiwan and China, coupled with a determination on both sides to reunite the country, endured throughout the Cold War. These tensions continued into the post-Cold War era, notably with a flare-up of hostilities in 1995 and 1996, known as the Taiwan Strait crisis. The dispatch of the US seventh fleet to the Strait ultimately helped to calm the situation, but China's large-scale display of its military might left the region in no doubt of the Communist Party's preparedness to use force if necessary to retake Taiwan. This stance was formalized in March 2005, when China's National People's Congress passed the antisecession law. On the other hand, China's opening up to the global economy from the late 1970s on, and particularly China's accession to the World Trade Organization in December 2001, resulted in massive Taiwanese investment in mainland China. These economic ties have tempered the extent to which either side would risk conflict, but they have also brought Taiwan further within Beijing's orbit, as mainland China has become the second largest economy in the world.

The division of the Korean peninsula along the 38th parallel was also a result of the Second World War and it became an embedded aspect of East Asian security relations following the Korean War, which lasted from 1950 to 1953. Erupting in the aftermath of the victory of the Chinese Community Party, as well as the Soviet blockade of Berlin, the impression that Communism was on the march shaped the US response to the Korean conflict. George F. Kennan's famous article extolling a targeted and multifaceted approach to containing Communism gave way to a US foreign policy, encapsulated in National Security Council document 68 (NSC 68), and geared to expanding the US defense budget and responding militarily to the threat of Communism across the globe. As North Korean troops marched south toward Pusan in the summer of 1950, the Truman administration decided on a robust military intervention under the auspices of the United Nations to push North Korea back across the 38th parallel. The North, supported by Chinese "volunteers" from the People's Liberation Army (PLA), fought the US-led UN forces to a stalemate, leaving the Korean peninsula divided to this day.

While South Korea, as a US ally, embarked on a rigorous program of economic development, North Korea's economy remained underdeveloped by the end of the Cold War. Partly in order to bargain for much-needed aid in the post-Cold War era, and partly in order to demonstrate its resolve to defend itself against US aggression, North Korea, still led by Kim Il-Sung, threatened to withdraw from the Non-Proliferation Treaty (NPT) in 1993, raising the specter of a nuclear-armed North Korea. This crisis was resolved through the creation of the Korean Energy Development Organization

(KEDO) which provided energy and aid to North Korea in return for denuclearization. This deal unraveled in 2001, with the G. W. Bush administration in the White House. In the context of the 9/11 attacks on New York and Washington and the subsequent "war on terror," President Bush labeled North Korea as part of the axis of evil. Led by Kim Il-Sung's son, Kim Jong-Il, and grandson, Kim Jong-un, North Korea successfully developed its nuclear weapons program. Denuclearizing the Korean Peninsula remains a core regional security concern, but the diverse foreign policy interests of the main actors in this case—notably, the United States, China, Japan, South Korea, and Russia—have rarely aligned to tackle this issue effectively. Recent summits between President Donald Trump and Kim Jong-un have similarly seen little progress on the denuclearization issue.

US unilateralism—that is, the ability of the United States to determine regional affairs through its political, military, and economic power—can also be attributed to Cold War dynamics. Rather than promoting the evolution of regional cooperation in East Asia, the United States built a series of bilateral alliances through which it could dictate terms as the stronger partner. Although US pressure has not always been successful in terms of changing the policies of its allies, Japan, South Korea, Taiwan, and ASEAN states have all had to keep the US position firmly in mind when determining policy. Even after the Cold War, regional cooperation has been impeded by a US government unwilling to cede its dominant position in East Asia—for example, when the George H. W. Bush administration rejected the then Malaysian prime minister Mohamad Mahathir's East Asia Economic Group (EAEG) proposal in 1990.[6] US unilateralism is therefore a structural constraint that all East Asian states have had to contend with since the Cold War.

DEVELOPMENTAL STATES, GLOBALIZATION, AND ECONOMIC INTERCONNECTIVITY

Since the end of the Second World War, East Asian economies have expanded rapidly. Rather than opening their economies to international competition, East Asia's developmental state model sought to channel capital to protect and develop key industries, such as automobiles, steel, and chemicals, until such a time that these industries could emerge as global leaders. This developmental state model was characterized by centrally managed economies and strong links between the bureaucracy and business. Led by Japan's surging economy from the late 1950s, the developmental state model gradually spread through the region, when it was adopted by the "Asian Tigers" (Taiwan, South Korea, Singapore, and Hong Kong) in the 1960s and 1970s.

⌊The development of East Asian states received a further boost with the onset of globalization. The transformation of production and manufacturing, coupled with the revolution in communications technology from the 1970s on, led to dramatic shifts in the political economy of the East Asian region.⌋ As production relocated to the cheapest and most efficient sites, the region became bound by international production networks managed by multinational companies.⌊East Asia's developmental states capitalized on globalization by promoting the efforts of their multinationals.⌋Developing economies in Southeast Asia responded by opening up their economies to foreign investment, and they became key production sites. Over time, international production networks have bound East Asian economies together, driving economic development. The key point here is that any consideration of regional security tensions always needs to keep in mind the underlying focus of East Asian states on maintaining economic growth.

One might think that through these international production networks multinationals are able to exercise not only economic but also political power. While there is a limit to how much domestic and multinational firms can or try to influence the foreign policies of East Asian states, their lobbying power should not be underestimated. For example, Taiwanese businesses have acted as credible communicators who reassure the Chinese government of their long-term commitment to China-Taiwan economic ties during periods of cross-straits tension.[7] In addition, production relations encourage further transnational interactions at the city and prefectural level that involve actors other than national states.

Another way in which globalization has impacted the intraregional relations of East Asian states has been through finance. The 1997 Asian financial crisis proved to be a critical juncture for the region. Lacking the foreign reserves to maintain its peg to the US dollar, the heavily indebted Thai government decided to revalue the Baht in 1997, triggering a loss in investor confidence and rapid capital flight out of the country; this then spread through the region. Malaysian prime minister Mahathir's previously rejected East Asia Economic Group proposal was suddenly resurrected in the form of the ASEAN Plus Three group, which immediately sought to shore up the region's finances. One of the ASEAN Plus Three's most notable achievements was the establishment of the Chiang Mai Initiative, a currency swap agreement between states that would enable them to better defend themselves in the face of future financial crises. Following the 2008 Global Financial Crisis, the Chiang Mai Initiative was further strengthened.[8]

This level of regional cooperation was not uncontested. While China preferred the "closed regional" model for the ASEAN Plus Three, Japan sought a more open regional model involving extraregional actors, notably its alliance partner, the United States. Japan's response, forged during the Koizumi Junichirō administration in the early 2000s, was the East Asia Summit, which the United States joined in 2010. These two overlapping regional groups entered a packed field of multilateral institutions that already included ASEAN, ARF, and APEC. These competing institutions raised the question of whether a survival of the fittest would ensue as institutions lost their relevance and fell by the wayside.[9] However, the jumble of East Asian regional fora continues to endure. For some, this mishmash of institutions constitutes "much ado about nothing" with the real hub of regional cooperation being based around international production networks rather than state-based groups and interstate competition.[10]

On the other hand, the smorgasbord of regional institutions may signal that the dynamics of intraregional relations in East Asia are more nuanced. Amitav Acharya argues that the ASEAN norms of consensus building, non-intervention, nonuse of force, peaceful settlement of disputes, and regional solutions to regional problems guide the behavior of regional actors.[11] For Qin Yaqing, ASEAN is also at the center of intraregional cooperation in East Asia.[12] Qin argues that rather than pooling sovereignty and institutionalizing and legalizing cooperation, as in the European Union, East Asian states prefer to maintain their sovereign independence, cooperating on functional issues of interest, such as in the case of the Chiang Mai Initiative, to induce gradual changes. According to these scholars, the various regional fora enable East Asian states to maintain relations through dialogue and cooperation while keeping in check overly ambitious efforts to formally integrate the region.

THE UNITED STATES AND THE FUTURE OF INTERSTATE RELATIONS IN EAST ASIA

Since the Second World War, the United States has always dominated East Asian affairs; therefore, examining its stance may also provide some instruction as to where the region might be heading. Over the past two decades, US involvement in East Asian affairs has been far from consistent, complicating the foreign policy calculations of regional actors. During the G. W. Bush administration, US attention turned to its wars in Afghanistan and Iraq, as well as the broader "global war on terror." As a result, the United States focused less on East Asian regional affairs, allowing China to gain more influence in the region. As China became more assertive in its relations toward other East Asian states from 2009 onward, so the United States under President Barack Obama looked to "pivot" back to the region. Although the pivot proved to be a rather limited and underwhelming foreign policy strategy, two aspects are worth considering. First, as part of the pivot, the United States adopted a more proactive, and arguably provocative, stance in the South China Sea by dispatching its naval forces on frequent freedom-of-navigation operations. Second, the United States joined the Trans-Pacific Partnership (TPP), a free-trade agreement that looked to establish new standards of trade for the twenty-first century and included Australia, Brunei, Canada, Chile, Japan, Malaysia, Mexico, New Zealand, Peru, Singapore, and Vietnam. China's omission from the TPP was notable. The agreement threatened not only to divert trade away from China but also to leave it behind on key issues like intellectual property and trade dispute resolution. An additional but increasingly important element in this geoeconomic strategy was America and Japan's rejection of China's Belt and Road Initiative.

On entering office in January 2017, President Donald Trump promptly withdrew from the TPP and adopted a more isolationist, but also more combative, strategy. This included threatening trade wars with East Asian partners, including Japan and South Korea, and starting an actual trade war with China. In the case of US allies, Trump even presented security guarantees as negotiable and dependent on better trade relations. Trump's aggressive trade strategy, ambivalent stance on security relations with East Asian allies, and generally maverick foreign policy have demolished the foundations of US-Asia relations. This has encouraged previously cold political relations in East Asia, particularly those between China and Japan, to become warmer. With the uncertainty surrounding Trump's regional policy, the Japanese prime minister, Abe Shinzo, sought to improve relations with Chinese President Xi Jinping, even looking for opportunities for Japanese businesses in the BRI. At the same time as Trump's withdrawal from the TPP, Japan became central to the development of its revised variant, the Comprehensive and Progressive Agreement for Trans-Pacific Partnership. Clearly, Abe is attempting to hedge both against China's rise, through his support for the Trans-Pacific Partnership, and against US abandonment, through his more recent backing of China's BRI. Only time will tell if Japan is able to successfully negotiate this path.

CONCLUSION

Capturing the complexity of intraregional relations in East Asia requires an understanding of a myriad of issues, actors, relations, and processes that either bind the region together or inhibit it from doing so. A combination of historical memory, domestic politics, great power politics, the forces of globalization, and regional institutions all shape intraregional relations in East Asia today. As each of these factors is in flux, so intraregional relations remain quite fluid. The unpredictable stance of the United States under President Trump presents East Asian states with further challenges. In this climate, rather than constructing legalized institutional frameworks that bind the behavior of states, as in the European case, intraregional cooperation in East Asia appears to be more relational and flexible. This can make relations less predictable, engendering interstate tensions, while simultaneously providing actors with room to maneuver as they attempt to resolve these same tensions.

NOTES

1. Zhao 2006; Yan 2011.
2. Yahuda 2012.
3. Callahan 2016.
4. Summers 2016.
5. Söderberg 2011
6. Cumings 2008.
7. Chan 2009.
8. For discussions of the Asian financial crisis, see Beeson 2014; Emmers and Ravenhill 2011.
9. Pempel 2010.
10. Ravenhill 2009.
11. Acharya 2004.
12. Qin 2013.

Acharya, Amitav. 2004. "Will Asia's Past Be Its Future?" *International Security* 28, no. 3 (Winter): 149–64.

Beeson, Mark. 2014. "Crises and Their Consequences." In *Regionalism and Globalization in East Asia—Politics, Security and Economic Development*, 186–203. New York: Palgrave Macmillan.

Callahan, William. 2016. "China's 'Asia Dream': The Belt Road Initiative and the New Regional Order." *Asian Journal of Comparative Politics* 1, no. 3 (May): 1–18.

Chan, Steve. 2009. "Commerce between Rivals: Realism, Liberalism, and Credible Communication across the Taiwan Strait." *International Relations of the Asia-Pacific* 9, no. 3 (March): 435–67.

Cumings, Bruce. 2008. "The History and Practice of Unilateralism in East Asia." In *East Asian Multilateralism—Prospects for Regional Stability*, edited by Kent Calder and Francis Fukuyama, 40–57. Baltimore: Johns Hopkins University Press.

Emmers, Ralf, and John Ravenhill. 2011. "The Asian and Global Financial Crises: Consequences for East Asian Regionalism." *Contemporary Politics* 17, no. 2 (April): 133–49.

Pempel, T. J. 2010. "Soft Balancing, Hedging, and Institutional Darwinism: The Economic-Security Nexus and East Asian Regionalism." *Journal of East Asian Studies* 10, no. 2 (March): 209–38.

Qin, Yaqing. 2013. "East Asian Regionalism: Architecture, Approach and Attributes." In *China and East Asia: After the Wall Street Crisis*, edited by Mu Yang, Yaqing Qin, and Peng Er Lam, 3–22. Singapore: World Scientific.

Ravenhill, John. 2009. "East Asian Regionalism: Much Ado about Nothing?" *Review of International Studies* 35, no. 1 (February): 215–35.

Söderberg, Marie. 2011. "Japan's ODA as Soft Power." In *Japan in Decline: Fact or Fiction?*, edited by Purnendra Jain and Brad Stephens, 35–54. Folkestone: Global Oriental.

Summers, Tim. 2016. "China's 'New Silk Roads': Sub-National Regions and Networks of Global Political Economy." *Third World Quarterly* 37, no. 9 (March): 1628–43.

Yahuda, Michael. 2012. "China's Recent Relations with Maritime Neighbours." *International Spectator* 47, no. 2 (June): 30–44.

Yan, Xuetong. 2011. *Ancient Chinese Thought, Modern Chinese Power*. Princeton, NJ: Princeton University Press.

Zhao, Tingyang. 2006. "Rethinking Empire from a Chinese Concept 'All Under Heaven' (Tian-xia, 天下)." *Social Identities* 12, no. 1 (January): 29–41.

PART TWO

East Asian Global Cultures

Koichi Iwabuchi and Frank N. Pieke

EAST ASIAN MODERNITY CANNOT BE REDUCED to a derivative of a Euro-American original, although the latter's impact is undeniable. Trans-Asian connections in the production, circulation, and reception of media and other forms of culture are highly relevant, yet they remain insufficiently understood. In studies of cultural hybridization, the non-West has long been represented as imitating, appropriating, and mongrelizing the West, over-looking cultural mixing and intertextual reworking within Asia.

Food and foodways provide perhaps the most immediate and visible example. In chapter 6, "Hybridity and Authenticity in Global East Asian Food," Sidney Cheung, from his own experience of living and working in Hong Kong, Japan, and China, discusses how foodways and cuisines in East Asia influence each other and are changed as they move from one East Asian country to the other. Cheung then broadens the scope of his analysis, showing how Japanese and Chinese food have had very distinct and different modalities of globalizing. In each case, migration and travel obviously play important roles, but the Japanese government's promotion of sake, for instance, has given this Japanese rice wine an important place in the representation of Japanese cuisine and culture abroad. Moreover, quality control of Japanese food across the globe conforms to standards set in Japan that are enforced through a network of wholesale and retails agents in Japan. The globalization of Chinese food could not be more different. Food standards set and enforced in China hardly play a role, and Chinese people living abroad have been more flexible in adapting their recipes to local tastes and using foreign ingredients.

East Asian producers of culture increasingly collaborate more across national borders. Successful television dramas and films are frequently remade in other parts of East Asia, while Japanese comic series are often adapted as television dramas and films. A prominent example is *Liuxing huayuan* (Meteor garden), which is both a Taiwanese television drama series and a Japanese comic series. The drama series became very popular in many parts of East and Southeast Asia, so much so that separate Japanese and Korean versions were produced later. Most recently, an unofficial Chinese version was also produced. Another example is the girls' comic series, *Hana yori dango* (Boys over flowers), local adaptations of which are widely read across East Asia.

The transnational circulation of culture interconnects industries and people of East Asia, but it is a Janus-faced process. East Asian cultures encourage transgressive cross-border connection and dialogue. The recent development, in particular, of media culture connections in East Asia has promoted mutual understandings and self-reflexive dialogues. Digital communication technologies have also blurred the boundaries between producer and consumer, diversified cultural expression, and facilitated cross-border connections, including those among marginalized people and activists.

However, much more powerful forces work in the opposite direction. Transnational culture is primarily market-driven, generating new kinds of governance and inequality. The unevenness in transnational cultural flows is intensified by the various kinds of alliances among transnational culture industries in the developed countries, including both Western and non-Western ones. As states in developed countries strengthen their alliance with (multinational) corporations to enhance their national interests, the (re)production of cultural asymmetry and unevenness becomes further institutionalized in a globalized world.

These complexities of transnational cultural flows between East Asia and Western societies come to life in the next two chapters of this part of the book. Jung-sun Park in chapter 7, "Trans-Pacific Flows and US Audiences of Korean Popular Culture," observes that the Korean Wave (*Hallyu*) hardly comes from a global powerhouse. The Korean Wave thus challenges established center-periphery relations, revealing the diversification of cultural influence. Hallyu is part of new cultural reverse flows from the non-West. Local, regional, and global elements are simultaneously and tightly intertwined. At the same time, Hallyu has strongly been influenced by the West, especially the United States, and the emergence of the Korean Wave in Asia is at least in part a creation of Western media industries.

The connection between the state and corporations reinforces a container model of the nation, muffling marginalized voices and obscuring sociocultural diversity within national borders. Cultural internationalism celebrates cultural diversity between nations, but it ignores how national boundaries are discursively drawn. Marginalizing internal sociocultural differences and politically heterodox voices, these boundaries' existence is not considered as constitutive of the nation or as existing for the sake of the nation's image as that image is projected externally.

No country illustrates this better than China. In chapter 8, "Ai Weiwei and the Global Art of Politics," William Callahan traces the evolution of arguably the world's most famous living artist, Ai Weiwei, from a quirky establishment figure in Beijing to a reluctant Chinese dissident to an exiled, global artist-activist. After going into exile in Europe, Ai focused on the global issue of refugees, thereby expanding from a critique of China's domestic oppression to the global problem of refugees without any special reference to the situation in his home country. Although the Chinese Communist Party and its government are no longer his main target, it could be argued that their very invisibility and Ai's silence on domestic issues in China show how his art and activism are still shaped by the global power of the People's Republic of China.

Soft power and nation branding tend to be blind to marginalized groups, even if their voices are expressed and shared in the public space within the nation. This is also—and perhaps especially—true for East Asian countries. For example, in Japan, the "Cool Japan" policy has been quickly and substantially developed, whereas the government has remained stubbornly reluctant to foster cultural diversity and deal with multicultural situations. While the two might not have a direct causal relationship, the reinforcement of national borders (for instance, through the enhancement of border control) and an inadequate attention paid to cultural diversity within the nation at the very least coincide with efforts to step up soft power and nation branding.

It is therefore no coincidence that the promotion of the outflow of cultural products is complemented by the restriction of the inflow of people, and especially of long-term immigrants. Cultural outflows are eagerly promoted by states and the culture industries. Transnational encounters with foreign cultures have multiplied through the production and consumption of cultural commodities, such as foods, films, television, music, or tourism. This trend is shared by all developed countries, including the East Asian ones. However, the vector points in the opposite direction in developing countries: more inflow of culture, including media culture, is accompanied by greater outflows of people, predominantly as labor migrants. International inequality, accompanied by cultural imperialism and border closure, have been newly articulated and enhanced by the advance of cultural globalization.

SIX

Hybridity and Authenticity in East Asian Foodways

Sidney C. H. Cheung

EARLY ANTHROPOLOGICAL STUDIES OF FOOD and eating centered largely on questions of taboo, totems, sacrifice, cast, and communion. They approached food from the angle of cultural symbolism, structuralism, and the relations between humans and the world they live in. However, because of the rapid social change in the global environment caused by immigration and the global sourcing of food ingredients, anthropologists in the last few decades have paid more attention to the dynamic transformation of foodways.

Localization and hybridization of global foodways have created new dishes that do not simply reject traditional or "authentic" elements in food and eating. Having said that, we can easily find hybrid ingredients combining with authentic traditional recipes, authentic regional cooking reemerging in fusion-style foods, authentic local dishes served together with hybrid ones, and so on. Only after careful investigation will we understand the complicated texture of taste that has been constructed through sociopolitical development in different societies. Foodways are an important marker of identity in many globalizing modern societies. They provide insight not only into social changes, cultural nationalism, or traditional values, but also into the political economy of cultural inheritance.

In East Asia, like elsewhere in the world, food plays a dynamic role in the way people think of themselves and others and thus even in politics. An example is provided by dog meat in Korea, which reflects not only traditional eating habits, but also the political relations between South Korea and the United States during the 1980s. For Koreans, *posint'ang*, a stew made with dog meat, had old-fashioned and folksy connotations, but it was abhorrent to American dog lovers and animal-right activists, for whom this was important enough to demand a boycott of the 1988 Olympics in South Korea.[1] Serving as a politicized identity marker between the United States and Korea in the run-up to the Olympics, eating dog meat became much more than just a Korean tradition.

MY FOOD JOURNEY IN EAST ASIA

Growing up in Hong Kong with Cantonese parents from Chaozhou and Shunde, Cantonese food was served at home most of the time; non-Cantonese food was not unfamiliar to me either. With limited knowledge of worldwide foodways, I went to Japan for tertiary education in 1984, when Japanese food was not widely known in Hong Kong except for teppanyaki. The dish featured prominently in a popular movie called *Teppanyaki* directed by Michael Hui in 1984, where the skills of a teppanyaki chef were made fun of. Not knowing the success story of Benihana or cowboy-style grilled steak and seafood in the United States,[2] many Hong Kongers (including myself) just thought that teppanyaki was an authentic way of serving steak and seafood in most of the Japanese restaurants.

My first sashimi (raw fish) meal in Japan was a treat at a set lunch with five or six pieces of red tuna served with rice and miso soup. Around the same time, there was a rapid growth in the number of sushi bars in Japan. These bars featured conveyor belt sushi or sushi-go-round, which had been invented in Osaka in 1958 and had become widely popular in the 1980s. In such a bar, two pieces of the same sushi were put on a conveyor belt mounted on the bar with a plate that had a specific color identifying their price. Customers could pick the ones they liked without having to order in advance. Compared with traditional sushi places, these bars were cheap and customers did not necessarily have to be familiar with the food.

A memorable item during my early days in Japan was cold Chinese oolong tea sold from vending machines. It was a surprise to see cold oolong tea in a plastic bottle. For me, green tea was a hot drink, and the etiquette of a formal tea ceremony was an iconic part of traditional Chinese culture. Nowadays, the Japanese might have similar feelings when they see and taste different kinds of *matcha* (Japanese green tea powder originally used mainly in tea ceremonies) products outside Japan.

Another surprise was Chinese cuisine in Japan. At the time, there were two major kinds of *chuka ryori* (Chinese cooking). The first was fast food offered in small restaurants that served fried rice, fried dumplings, and set meals with meat, vegetables, white rice, and a clear soup. The second, more upscale type was banquet food with dishes from various regions in China, such as Sichuan spicy tofu, Cantonese dim sum, Tianjin omelet, Shanghai dumplings, sweet and sour pork, chili shrimp, Beijing roasted duck, Yangzhou fried rice, almond tofu dessert, and so on. Having all of them together as Chinese cuisine was not something I had seen before going to Japan.

During the 1980s, Chinatowns in Yokohama and Kobe became popular tourist destinations among the Japanese as parts of the "China boom" in Japan. With the tremendous increase in the numbers of Japanese working and traveling abroad for business or tourism, internationalization was not only some kind of national policy but could be observed through changes taking place in individual lifestyles and diets. The popularization of the distinctive and exotic Cantonese dim sum, which started in Yokohama Chinatown, serves as a good example of changing tastes and social values among Japanese consumers.[3]

The longer I stayed in Japan, the more foods I found that had been adapted to Japanese tastes and expectations, such as Japanese curry, pizza on bread, upside-down fried Chinese dumplings, rice burgers, Christmas cake, reciprocal chocolate gifts after Valentine's Day, and even an American hamburger chain.[4] An important factor in the localization of foreign foodways in Japan was television programs and cooking contests, such as *Iron Chef* and many other programs about travel and local and overseas gourmet food in the early 1990s. However, the introduction of Western foodways in Japan goes back much earlier. *Wayo setchu ryori*, or the mixture of Japanese and Western food, and the rise of Western restaurants started already in the early part of the twentieth century. After Japan's defeat in the Second World War, the stationing of US forces triggered an inflow of American popular culture and foods.[5]

When I moved back to Hong Kong in the mid-1990s after having been away for ten years, I encountered many foodways that were new to me. As in Japan, Hong Kong's living standards had steadily improved since the 1970s, and people were able to spend more on dining out. Hong Kong residents also traveled abroad more frequently, creating a demand for foreign food and an exotic eating experience. The new wealth also raised expectations for more refined foods to suit individual tastes. "Nouvelle Cantonese" cuisine, combining a delicate taste, expensive ingredients, and Western-style catering, became popular in upscale Cantonese restaurants located in downtown areas. Different foods, such as American fast-food chains, French fine dining, Italian pasta, Japanese sushi, Korean barbecue, Thai spicy food, Vietnamese,

FIGURE 6.1. Puhn Choi: Traditional puhn choi offered during village festival. Source: Sidney C. H. Cheung.

and regional cuisines from China arrived and significantly influenced Hong Kong society and foodways.

My early research on food culture and changing eating habits in Hong Kong was conducted in 1995 as part of a four-member research team. We examined the relationship of culinary traditions, dietary rules, and consumption trends with changes in the city's cultural identity in the years leading up to the handover to China in 1997. We found that the great variety of both local and imported food in Hong Kong reveals broader social practices and values. In this research project, I interviewed food critics and journalists to collect up-to-date information on the development of the food industry since the 1950s, concentrating particularly on Cantonese restaurants that ranged from inexpensive and "old-fashioned" to middle-class-oriented nouvelle cuisine.

During the project, I was particularly surprised to discover first the rising popularity and subsequent decline of Hakka restaurants.[6] Hakka food became popular in the 1960s and 1970s because people found it tasty and rich in meat, an important consideration for those employed in manual jobs in industry or construction. The decline of Hakka restaurants in the 1980s was related to the dietary revolution mentioned earlier, when Hong Kong people were looking for different ways to represent their new, globally connected status rather than being focused primarily on the economic and nutritional value of food.

Since the late 1990s, developments in local food trends in Hong Kong took a further turn with the emergence of different versions of "country-style cooking," which emphasizes local, domestic, and traditional culinary skills. My first encounter with *puhn choi* (literally "basin food"), a dish from Hong Kong's rural New Territories, happened after a field visit there with some of my students. In puhn choi all ingredients are served together in one pot from which everyone at the table eats together. This dish usually comprises layers of inexpensive, local ingredients such as dried pig skin, dried eel, dried squid, radish, tofu skin, mushroom, and pork stewed in soybean paste. Puhn choi subsequently became fashionable in urban Hong Kong. The dish was promoted in guidebooks, websites, and travel magazines about traditional village settlements and heritage sites in the New Territories. It also became a festive food for the Lunar New Year, Winter Solstice, and Mid-Autumn Festivals and other occasions.[7]

EAST ASIAN FOODWAYS IN THE GLOBAL MARKET

The globalization of East Asian foodways has been in large part the result of other aspects of globalization, such as migration, tourism, or the spread of popular culture. An excellent example is the globalization of Japanese sushi caused by the increasingly cosmopolitan tastes of the urban upper and middles classes in developed countries.

Yet the globalization of East Asian foodways has not happened simply on the back of migration, travel, or the export of popular culture. In the Japanese government-led promotion of tourism from the early 2000s on, for instance, sake, or Japanese rice wine, has been given an important place in the representation of Japanese culture. A range of regional sakes have been promoted overseas at dinners where sake was served together with different cuisines. Sake appreciation has been formalized through the certification of sake professionals and sake sommeliers (wine stewards). As a result of the national policy of promoting Japanese food overseas, Japanese beef, rice, and snacks have found their way to many other countries, some of them in fact even being produced outside Japan.

Japan plays yet another role, one that is much less visible but arguably even more important. The country started buying foodstuffs from many different countries in the last century. Examples of these include prawns from Indonesia and Papua New Guinea, bananas from Taiwan and the Philippines, matsutake from Korea and China, and so on. With the global boom in the

FIGURE 6.2. Japanese sushi and sashimi set offered in Hong Kong highlighting ingredients directly from Japan. Source: Sidney C. H. Cheung.

consumption of Japanese foodstuffs, Japan also acquired a unique position in the redistribution of many of these items, according them a Japanese standard of freshness and quality.[8]

Bestor explains how the rising demand for bluefin tuna due to the popularity of sushi and other Japanese dishes has created a "gold-rush mentality on fishing grounds" worldwide led by the export of the high standards at the

Tsukiji seafood market in Tokyo (which was replaced by the Toyosu seafood market that opened in 2018). The monitoring and quality control of global Japanese food involves a network of wholesale and retails agents in Japan, even though many of the ingredients may in fact be sourced from many different places across the globe.[9]

In contrast to the Japanese mode of globalization, China has been playing a very different role indeed. Chinese traders have a long history of importing dried products from many countries, such as sea cucumber from Southeast Asia, abalone from Japan and America, and nuts and fruits from the Middle East. The way such imports have been handled is different from the Japanese practices. Foodstuffs can only be imported in Japan if they conformed to very strict standards. Japanese food requires Japanese-made ingredients, such as soy sauce, sushi vinegar, or wasabi, and imported ingredients that have been subjected to strict Japanese standards, such as bluefin tuna, prawn, or crab. Chinese people put less emphasis on food standards, and Chinese cooks are more flexible and adaptive in using foreign ingredients while maintaining their conventional culinary techniques.

As a result, Chinese foods and foodstuffs sold in foreign markets have also not been subject to strict China-originated authenticity norms and reveal a much greater variety. The impact of Chinese food across the globe greatly predates and exceeds Japan's, both in terms of its spread and its impact across the entire socioeconomic spectrum. Japanese food was exported as a refined culinary tradition catering to the globalizing tastes of the world's growing urban middle classes. The main vector of the spread of Chinese food, however, was labor migrants, most of whom came from rural areas. Japanese global foodways claim authenticity and aspire to maintain Japanese standards. Chinese food, wherever it went, was rapidly adapted to local tastes, standards of living, and available ingredients.

A few examples further demonstrate this point. *Chifa* in Peru is a culinary tradition based on Cantonese cuisine combined with Peruvian ingredients and cooking practices. Cantonese Chinese migrants going to Peru in the late nineteenth and early twentieth centuries were mainly working-class people; they brought with them their skills of daily cooking instead of professional culinary techniques. Making use of local ingredients was necessary for reasons of cost and availability. Therefore, chifa consists of simple items such as fried rice and noodles, as well as basic dishes commonly found in South China, but with local favors and additions. Chifa originated in Peru, where it is still a popular type of food; there are thousands of chifa restaurants across the country. From Peru, chifa has spread to neighboring countries in South America, such as Ecuador and Bolivia.[10]

Other examples that demonstrate the character of globalized Chinese foodways are Macanese cuisine in Macao and *Peranakan* or *Nyonya* cuisine in Indonesia and Malaysia. Macanese cuisine is unique to Macau and consists of a blend of Portuguese, African (Mozambique), Indian (Goa), Southeast Asian (Malacca), and Cantonese culinary traditions and ingredients. Many dishes were the unique invention of the families that moved all the way from Europe to Asia with their experiences of different periods of stay in various countries over the course of the last few centuries, and it is still impossible to find a common set of recipes for all Macanese cuisine. Since Macau was the final destination of these families, Cantonese culinary techniques commonly serve as the major cooking method of combining ingredients from across the world in Macanese cuisine.

Peranakan or Nyonya cuisine originated with Chinese migrants who settled in Malaya and Indonesia between the seventeenth and nineteenth centuries. They intermarried with Malays, with Chinese from other parts of China, and sometimes with Europeans. The dishes they developed gradually became commercialized, and they have spread to restaurants in other Asian countries, including Japan and Hong Kong, as well as Europe by way of the Netherlands, the former colonial power in Indonesia.

In more recent decades, global Chinese food has also started to spread in ways that are similar to Japanese food, especially in North America and Europe. Globalization has shifted the class basis of Chinese food. Travel, tourism, and even the residence of foreigners in China, as well as the presence of ever-larger numbers of upper- and middle-class Chinese migrants, students, and tourists abroad have raised the demand for authentic and more exclusive Chinese foods among the more discerning types. Although Cantonese cuisine remains the major Chinese cooking style in many countries, other Chinese culinary traditions, such as Sichuanese, Hunanese, or Yunnanese cuisines, have become increasingly popular as well.[11]

A WORLD OF CHOICES

Different models and networks support the globalization of Japanese and Chinese food that reflect the ways that quality and authenticity are understood and maintained in these countries themselves. Japan plays a strong role as the center in monitoring and standardizing Japanese cooking skills and ingredients. China plays a much weaker role in safeguarding the standards and quality of Chinese food. Japanese food puts a strong emphasis on the authenticity of the ingredients, such as fish imported directly from Tokyo's seafood market. Traditionally trained Japanese sushi and tempura chefs are in high demand, although new forms of Japanese fusion with sake pairing are also getting more popular. The globalization of Chinese food has been carried by Chinese migrants, who had little knowledge of or interest in highbrow notions of authenticity or quality, to different countries. Catering chiefly for a lower- or middle-class clientele, their cooking was quickly adapted to local tastes, budgets, and ingredients. Only relatively recently has China's mode of globalization changed. Rural labor migrants are gradually being superseded by urban Chinese students, investors, professionals, and tourists. Across the world, authentic Chinese cuisines have taken their place among the world's many cuisines in cities across the globe. The older, hybrid Chinese cuisines that are a true token of centuries of globalization might gradually disappear, only to be replaced by "genuine" Chinese cuisines that, ironically, are pretty much the same the world over. The cosmopolitan elites might have much more choice of authentic and high-quality foods, but that choice will be the same wherever they go.

NOTES

1. Janelli and Yim 1993, 186.
2. See "History of Benihana," Benihana, accessed February 18, 2019, http://www.benihana.sk/en/about-us/history.
3. Cheung 2002.
4. Watson 1997.
5. Cwiertka 1999.
6. Hakkas are a Chinese ethnic group in southeastern China with a distinctive language and culture that sets them apart from the Cantonese or other majority populations.
7. Cheung 2005.
8. Rath and Assmann 2010.
9. Bestor 2000 and Bestor 2004.
10. See Wikipedia, s.v. "Chifa," last modified November 9, 2020, https://en.wikipedia.org/wiki/Chifa.
11. Liu 2015; Arnold, Tunç, and Chong 2018.

Arnold, Bruce Makoto, Tanfer Emin Tunç, and Raymond Douglas Chong, eds. 2018. *Choy Suey and Sushi from Sea to Shining Sea: Chinese and Japanese Restaurants in the United States.* Fayetteville: University of Arkansas Press.

Bestor, Theodore C. 2000. "How Sushi Went Global." *Foreign Policy* 121 (November–December): 54–63.

————. 2004. *Tsukiji: The Fish Market at the Center of the World.* Berkeley: University of California Press.

Cheung, Sidney C. H. 2002. "The Invention of Delicacy: Cantonese Food in Yokohama Chinatown." In *The Globalization of Chinese Food*, edited by David Y. H. Wu and Sidney C. H. Cheung, 170–82. New York: Routledge.

————. 2005. "Consuming 'Low' Cuisine after Hong Kong's Handover: Village Banquets and Private Kitchens." *Asian Studies Review* 29, no. 3 (September): 259–73.

Cwiertka, Katarzyna J. 1999. "The Making of Modern Culinary Tradition in Japan." PhD diss., Leiden University.

Janelli, Roger, and Dawnhee Yim. 1993. *Making Capitalism: The Social and Cultural Construction of a South Korean Conglomerate.* Stanford, CA: Stanford University Press.

Liu, Haiming. 2015. *From Canton Restaurant to Panda express: A History of Chinese Food in the United States.* New Brunswick, NJ: Rutgers University Press.

Rath, Eric C., and Stephanie Assmann, eds. 2010. *Japanese Foodways: Past & Present.* Urbana: University of Illinois Press.

Watson, James L., ed. 1997. *Golden Arches East: McDonald's in East Asia.* Stanford, CA: Stanford University Press.

SEVEN

Trans-Pacific Flows and US Audiences of Korean Popular Culture

Jung-Sun Park

THE KOREAN WAVE (*hallyu* in Korean), or the transnational popularity of Korean popular culture, has from its inception been viewed in a variety of often contradictory ways. Hallyu is not from a country that is a traditional economic, political, or cultural powerhouse. The South Korean economy is strong enough, but the country is not a world leader like the United States, Japan, or the European Union. The division of the two Koreas and the complex geopolitics in Northeast Asia often situate the country on the receiving end of influence rather than the other way around. Additionally, South Korea was not known for its cultural influence even in Asia before the sudden rise of the Korean Wave. The Korean Wave thus challenges the established center-periphery relations in global cultural flows, exemplifying the diversification of the routes and the directions of cultural influence.[1]

The Korean Wave is part of new cultural "contra" or "subaltern" flows from the non-West.[2] At the same time, Korean popular culture has been strongly influenced by the West, especially the United States. Contradictory aspects coexist in the Korean Wave. Nationalism and transnationality are juxtaposed. Local, regional, and global elements are simultaneously and tightly intertwined. The emergence of the Korean Wave in Asia is partly owing to Western media industries' creation of regional media markets.[3] The *K* in the Korean Wave has become highly contested as its transnational hybridization and cross-fertilization progress. In more recent years, intensifying digitalization has also profoundly transformed the nature and scope of the Korean Wave; this is sometimes labeled the Korean Wave 2.0.[4]

The complexities of the Korean Wave are also reflected in variations in its local reception.[5] The expansion of the Korean Wave beyond East and

Southeast Asia has further complicated these trajectories. In the US context, the reception of Korean popular culture is interrelated with factors such as transnationalism, race, and ethnicity. In order to understand this, I will compare three groups: Korean Americans, other Asian Americans, and non-Asian Americans.[6] The recognition and popularity of Korean popular culture in the United States culminated in the recent success of BTS (Bangtan Boys). But long before its current integration, Korean popular culture has been part of the culture of Korean American communities.[7] Beyond the Korean American communities, the reception of Korean popular culture by Asian Americans more generally is grounded in their positionality and experiences as racial others. Moreover, transnational connections with their countries of origin add another layer to both Korean Americans' and other Asian Americans' consumption of Korean popular culture, which distinguishes their experience from that of non-Asian Americans.

HALLYU AND KOREAN AMERICANS

By and large, the basic reasons that Korean Americans like Korean popular culture are similar to those shared by other ethnic and racial groups. They all like the good looks of their favorite stars, the interesting story lines taken from television dramas or movies, and the powerful dance moves and catchy tunes of K-pop music. What separates them from others is that their transnational and ethnic links with Korea have widely exposed them to Korean popular culture in their daily lives, especially in metropolitan areas. This has contributed to them taking on the roles of creators and distributors, as well as consumers, in the Korean Wave.

Korean immigration to the United States dates back to the early twentieth century, but the majority of Korean immigrants came after 1965, when the amended US immigration laws opened a door to people from most parts of the world.[8] Not long after their immigration, Korean Americans in metropolitan areas established ethnic media, which provided both connections with Korea (hence, emotional comfort) and information necessary for the immigrants' survival and adjustment in their new homeland. While Korean language newspapers require proficiency in Korean, programs aired on Korean television channels, especially those with English subtitles, were more accessible to non-Koreans. Thus, already in the 1970s, Korean television dramas and news reached non-Koreans, although it must be noted that their number remained small because of the limited number of programs with English subtitles and the latter's often inferior quality.[9]

Much diversity exists within the Korean American community. Korean Americans' take on Korean popular culture varies according to generation, gender, place of living, sense of identity, family composition, and so on. Generally speaking, until the beginning of the 2000s, the first-generation and some 1.5-generation Korean Americans were the main audience and consumers of Korean pop cultural products, especially Korean television dramas. For the first-generation Korean Americans, in particular, watching Korean television dramas, movies, and variety shows has long been their number one pastime. In the 1980s and 1990s, Korean video rental stores flourished in Koreatowns. With the advent of the digital era, people shifted to streaming services and social media services, although few DVD rental stores still serve certain ethnic Korean audiences, especially the first-generation elderly population.

Until the 2000s, the majority of younger-generation Korean Americans did not pay much attention to Korean popular culture. Language and cultural barriers and a lack of interest in or bias toward their heritage culture distanced the younger generation from Korean popular culture. However, the phenomenal success of the Korean Wave in Asia that began in the late 1990s piqued the younger generation's interest. Those who were drawn to Korean popular culture did so for a range of reasons. Some found an alternative role model in Korean pop stars, while others felt proud of the new status of Korean popular culture and with it all things Korean. As the presence and popularity of Korean popular culture have grown, its positive impact has become more far-reaching. A twenty-something Korean American who is not even a big fan of Korean popular culture told me that she was "proud" of the global success of Korean popular culture, implying a degree of "ethnic ownership" by virtue of being Korean American. Yet, Korean popular culture is not a source of pride or identity for all younger Korean Americans. As David Oh's research illustrates, likes and dislikes of Korean popular culture coexist, and factors such as gender and peer group affect the acceptance of Korean popular culture among younger-generation Korean Americans.[10]

Korean Americans have also become more actively involved in the making and dissemination of the Korean Wave as entertainers, distributors, and producers, a trend that has become more noticeable over the years. This was encouraged by Korean management companies, which sought to incorporate talented young people (both Korean and non-Korean) from overseas to serve foreign markets.[12] With an eye on the United States and encouraged by their success in Asia, major management companies actively began to recruit Korean American talent to become the next hallyu stars. Aspiring Korean American talents, motivated by the limited opportunities that Asian American entertainers have in the United States, also sought to pursue careers in Korea.[13] To name just a few, Korean American stars include actress Yunjin Kim and idol stars such as Jessica (a former member of Girls' Generation), Krystal (f(x)), and Taecyeon Ok (2PM). In the K-pop scene, the influence and presence of Korean American stars are most visible. In fact, some Korean Americans played a pivotal role in introducing and populariz-ing certain music genres and styles such as R&B and hip-hop in Korea, and many popular K-pop idol groups have at least one Korean American member. Korean Americans have also contributed to the growth of the Korean Wave as distributors. For example, the first legitimate streaming service for Korean television dramas, DramaFever.com, was founded by two Korean Americans.[14]

If we also include temporary migrants and *yuhaksaeng* (students studying abroad) from Korea, the contribution of Korean Americans is even greater. Psy, the YouTube record-breaking Korean musician, and Soo Man Lee, the founder and CEO of SM Entertainment, one of the "big three" management companies in South Korea, belong to this category. Jin-Young Park, the CEO of JYP, another big three management company, also spent a few years in the United States when he was young.

The significant role of Korean Americans and Korean American com-munities in hallyu's trans-Pacific travels will be further strengthened by the proposed building of US hubs by two major Korean entertainment compa-nies, SM and YG, in the greater Los Angeles area.[15] They are designed to become multifunctional entertainment buildings that will include recording studios, practice rooms, and restaurants.

Korean American consumption of Korean popular culture is inseparable from their immigration history and transnational connections. Korean Americans also assume multiple roles in the transnational flows of Korean popular culture as consumers, creators, and distributors. This multilayered involvement distinguishes Korean Americans' relations with the Korean Wave from that of other Asian Americans and non-Asians in the United States.

Asian Americans are usually drawn to Korean popular culture because of its attractive content and entertainers. Yet their experiences are also more specific to their Asian ethnicity. When Korean popular culture began to circulate beyond Korean American communities, other Asian American populations enthusiastically accepted it. Many of them were already aware of the amazing success of Korean popular culture in the Asian region. Their interest in Korean popular culture genres and programs was often first raised through their transnational ties to family and friends in their countries of origin where Korean popular culture had already become popular.[16] Korean television dramas, subtitled or dubbed into several Asian languages, expanded Korean popular culture's reach into Asian American communities. Younger Asian Americans were more inclined to K-pop.

Pan-Asian ethnicity is observed on both sides of the Pacific in conjunction with the Korean Wave. In Asia, many intra-Asian collaborations have taken place, such as coproduction, inclusion of various Asian members in K-pop groups, format renting, and borrowing. Some even would like to see the Korean Wave move toward a hybridized "Asian Wave," hoping that this will expand the market and increase profits for the involved parties.

In the United States, pan-Asian ethnicity is often articulated with identity construction and a sense of community and belonging, especially among youths. Young Asian Americans often lack fellow Asian role models in the US media. For them, globally famous and successful Korean stars are attractive and easy to identify with because of their similar look and ethnic background. The alternative model that Korean pop stars or culture can provide, based on a pan-Asian element, is illustrated by Anita, a college student who identified herself as Cambodian (she also has Chinese and Thai background). Anita told me that she loved Korean popular culture, particularly television dramas. She said that she could relate to the stories and easily imagine herself in the characters' position because they looked like her. She would have liked to watch Cambodian television dramas, but the country did not produce quality television dramas, so she watched Korean dramas instead, claiming that she learned about her heritage through them. Owing to the trauma caused by the Khmer Rouge, her parents had not talked much about Cambodia or its traditions. Korean television dramas provided her with an understanding of Asian cultural values and traditions, such as the significance of family.

Pan-Asian ethnicity is also found in the overlapping fandom of Asian popular culture. This is typically noticeable in European and US contexts, where Asia is often viewed without much attention to its internal diversity. Someone might be a fan of both Korean and Japanese popular culture without at first being too much aware of the differences between the two.[17] In other cases, someone might actually be looking for something Asian rather than specifically Korean or Japanese. Similar tendencies are found among Asian Americans. For example, a Filipino American student, Lucy, told me that she first encountered K-pop music when she was searching for J-pop music. Initially, she thought that the song she listened to was J-pop. Others I spoke to mentioned that they learned about K-pop through Japanese anime fan sites.

Panethnicity works in different ways in Asian Americans' consumption and reception of Korean popular culture. Combined factors, such as shared experiences as marginalized others, internalized Orientalism, or even loosely interrelated cultural traditions, may connect Asian Americans with Korean popular culture. At times, the shared taste and references in popular culture generate an imagined panethnic camaraderie or provide a means for identity construction that connects them to each other.

SPREAD OF HALLYU AMONG NON-ASIAN AMERICAN AUDIENCES

Over the years, the fan base of Korean popular culture in the United States has expanded to include non-Asian populations. Even among the general public, familiarity with Korean popular culture is increasing. Korean popular culture has entered people's pop cultural landscape, especially among the youth. In the earlier years, the novelty probably attracted fans. Then, when Korean popular culture, especially music and television dramas, became more popular, keeping up with the trend also became a factor.

Specific alluring points of Korean popular culture differ depending on the genre. The particular musical and performance styles of K-pop attract audiences who like K-pop's beat, melodies, variety of genres, well-choreographed powerful dance moves, charisma of performers, sexiness, and fashion styles. Well-made music videos with creative, interesting storylines, and nice visual images add to the attraction of K-pop music. According to my interviewee

Jennifer, "when you listen to Korean pop, you want to listen to the music and know the choreography. It creates the fans to be active whether it's attending a concert or being part of a fan base."[18] "Cover dances" are quite popular among K-pop fans: mimicking the highly disciplined choreography is challenging yet satisfying.[19] K-pop also touches the audience's emotional chords. Comments, such as "I feel empowered" and "it gave me hope and strength," indicate the emotional boost that my interviewees received from the music. But the emotional connections can also be calmer and more introspective, even nostalgic. A not-so-young fan of K-pop who responded to my online survey wrote:

> K-pop taps into a 90s sense of style and sound. I love how listening to K-pop evokes the same feelings I get when I listen to a classic Nsync song. It takes me back to when I was a child. K-pop can be extremely successful if it maintains its 90s sound.[20]

The physical attraction of individual performers also plays a part. Multimember boy bands and girl bands provide, as a college student, Cindy, put it, "the option of choosing who your ideal type is."[21] The members in a group are usually given a "character" or a "persona" that they act out, especially in their interaction with fans. The group members often play their role in public and on their SNS (Social Networking Sites) as part of their fan service. This adds room for audiences to create their own stories, including the "pairing" of different members. This is similar to what Japanese manga and anime fans do with animation and manga characters. Fans create new relations (including love relations) between characters from anime and manga and reshape the stories. The construction of K-pop group members' relationships includes designating family roles like mother, father, and daughter to each member. This playful and interactive aspect of K-pop fandom connects the fans and their favorite stars in a special way and maintains the fans' devotion.

Fans pointed out that one of the reasons they really like Korean entertainers is because they care about their fans. Unlike Hollywood stars, Korean stars are much more personable and approachable. They also communicate with their fans through various social media, and they regularly send caring, sweet messages, which give an illusion that the stars pay personal attention to the individual fans. Some of the stars even call their fans their "family." The sense of closeness, community, and special attention and care are part of the magic behind hallyu fandom in the United States.

As I mentioned earlier, local receptions of Korean popular culture vary. Musicians popular in Korea or elsewhere in Asia are not necessarily popular in the United States. For example, groups with hip-hop elements and unique, bold fashion styles like 2NE1 and Big Bang were popular both in Korea and the United States, but Wonder Girls and BoA were not successful on the other side of the Pacific despite their huge success in Korea and elsewhere in Asia. The management of concerts by Korean musicians is unique and helps to reach broader audiences. K-pop concerts in the United States often include several groups that all are managed by the same company. This is an effective way to attract the audience, which gets to see groups that are unlikely to perform together under other circumstances, to new groups.

Korean television drama is another popular genre, and its fans are also diverse. In Los Angeles I encountered many Latina fans. Interestingly, many of them do not seem to feel that cultural differences are a hurdle to enjoying Korean television dramas. Carmen, a college student, told me that she actually did not have any problem understanding Korean television dramas and the situations portrayed in them. Many of my Latina sources are familiar with Latin American telenovelas that make it easier for them to relate to Korean television dramas' often convoluted story lines. Compared to music, language is a more serious issue for television drama consumption. In the earlier days, the availability of free downloading, together with fan-subtitled versions of Korean television dramas, lessened this problem. Nowadays, Korean television dramas with high quality subtitles are widely available through various streaming sites.

As with Japanese anime and manga, online fan communities play a significant role in the popularity of Korean popular culture.[22] Those sites are not simply a place where hallyu fans get information about their favorite stars, music, and shows; they are also a community where they share their lives and concerns with fellow fans across borders. A student named Jane described her experience with an online K-pop community as follows:

> We not only talk about K-pop but we also talk about our personal lives, our hopes, and dreams as well as our disappointments. I have met a lot of people from different countries through K-pop. I met people from Europe, America, South America, Asia, Australia. and we all could talk to each other.

So, K-pop consumption is not merely about love for an entertainer and his or her music; it is also about constructing one's identity and building cross-cultural communities and affective connections.

Despite its unmistakable success, hallyu's future prospects remain unclear. In music, the trend in the United States is not necessarily conducive to the further success of Korean bands: multimember boy or girl bands are already passé.[23] On the other hand, considering the recent success of BTS, it is also possible that K-pop might be able to carve out its niche in areas without strong local competitors. Another barrier is language. Unless the musician or actor is fluent in English, it is difficult to connect to the general public. Although fans might not mind the Korean lyrics, these might limit the reach of K-pop among the general public. One source even mentioned "America's nationalism" as a limiting factor for K-pop's future. Moreover, racial stereotyping has long restricted Asian Americans' opportunities in the media.[24] The situation in the film industry may have improved a little over the years, but the visibility of Asians is still limited and their roles are often marginal. In the music industry, Asian Americans with national fame are almost nonexistent.

In addition, different aesthetics regarding what is considered physically attractive may affect Korean entertainers' popularity. For instance, the "pretty boy" style, which is very popular in Asia, does not necessarily fit the general US public's notion of male attractiveness. Such images may appeal to certain subgroups, such as young Asian American female fans, but they look "too feminine" to the general public. Some argue that the "pretty" looks and gentle manners of Korean male entertainers may suggest new gender aesthetics and standards to the Western audiences, but, even so, it will take a long time to shatter existing gender images and ideals.[25] The supposedly "sexy" Asian female stars are also not straightforwardly accepted, as the notion of "sexiness" varies and is, to some extent, culturally bound.[26] Female "cuteness," a reliable selling point in Asia, does not work in the same way in the United States. Bridging the cultural gap without losing one's identity and distinctive style will be a challenging task for those aspiring Korean entertainers interested in the US market.

Then there is the ongoing issue of the Orientalist gaze. Many non-Asian fans are drawn to Korean popular culture because of its "exotic" character, which is drawn from a "mysterious Orient" that they do not know well. The irony here is that contemporary Korean popular culture is a hybrid that has taken many of its forms and styles from the West. So, in a way, those who are drawn to Korean popular culture with a kind of Orientalist expectation may eventually be won over because of its familiarity. K-pop, which has adapted various Western music styles and genres and which also includes many pieces produced by Western composers, probably best exemplifies this case.

CONCLUSION

Over the years, Korean popular culture has accomplished something no one had imagined twenty years ago—reaching out into the world and becoming accepted and loved by people across cultures, generations, and backgrounds. This has been a remarkable achievement for a country that has not been a dominant force in the political and economic domains. This success illustrates the changing cultural and power relations between the East and the West, the multiplying routes of cultural influence, and the intensifying and complex hybridity of contemporary popular culture.

As I have argued, the recent increasing visibility and acceptance of Korean popular culture in the United States is closely intertwined with the rise of the Korean Wave itself, but its own local context and roots can be traced back to the post-1965 Korean immigration to the country. In fact, Korean Americans and Korean American ethnic media paved the way for Korean popular culture's smooth trans-Pacific travels long before even a remote possibility of such things was fathomable.

Since popular culture is in constant flux, we cannot know for sure what future awaits the Korean Wave. It might eventually fade away or, alternatively, be localized to become a part of various local cultures. If hallyu is to extend its lifespan as a distinctive phenomenon in non-Asian regions, it will have to continue to find ways to cater to the tastes and preferences of local audiences while maintaining the uniqueness, creativity, and energy that are the source of hallyu's identity and vitality.

NOTES

1. Park 2014.
2. Thussu 2007, 23.
3. See Morley and Robins 1995.
4. Jin 2016.
5. See Park 2006.
6. Part of the data utilized in the paper was drawn from my long-term research on transnational flows of Korean popular culture, which began in Chicago in the

mid-1990s. But most of the quotations and case studies are based on an online survey conducted in spring 2016 as well as on interviews and participant observation data collected in Los Angeles since the early 2010s. I received 163 responses to the online survey, approximately 53 percent of which were fully answered. About 49 to 51 percent of the respondents provided personal background information, including race/ethnicity, age, and occupation. Among 80 people who identified their race/ethnicity, 35 were Asian/Asian American (including 6 Korean Americans); 29 were Hispanic (including 17 Mexican Americans); 9 were Caucasian Americans, one was African American; and 6 were multiple-heritage Americans. In terms of age, out of 83 respondents, 23 were teenagers; 38 were in their early 20s (20–23); 13 were in their in mid-20s (24–27); 3 were in their late 20s; 4 were in their early 30s, one person was in their early 40s, and one was in their late 60s. In terms of occupation, the majority were students (57 out of 80 respondents). The other occupations included cashier, ESL teacher, English teacher, filmmaker, high school coach, independent living instructor, mental health worker, office manager, realtor, veterinary technician, web content coordinator, and publicist.

7. See Park 2004.

8. See John Lie's chapter in this book for more details.

9. In Los Angeles, imported Korean dramas, entertainment programs and news were aired through rented ethnic channels as early as 1975. The first independent Korean television station was founded in 1983 in the US cable network system. See Lee 2015, 173.

10. Oh 2015.

11. See Park 2014; Lee 2015.

12. Recruitment is not limited to people from a Korean background. Ethnic Chinese entertainers, for example, are now part of the Korean Wave. One of SM Entertainment's idol groups, EXO, used to have two separate units, EXO-K and EXO-M. The latter consisted of multiple Chinese members in order to reach the Chinese market.

13. See Xing 1998; Park 2014.

14. Lee 2015. DramaFever.com was later sold to Softbank and then to Warner Brothers. It stopped its streaming service on October 16, 2018.

15. In 2013, SM Entertainment announced its plan to create the SMTOWN Museum in the heart of Los Angeles's Koreatown (see Brown 2013). In 2014, YG Entertainment's plan to establish the "YG Land" in Orange County in California was reported (see Hong 2014).

16. Before Korean popular culture got traction in the United States, the information from their countries of origin had a greater significance for Asian Americans' exposure to and selection of Korean popular culture, particularly among the first generation of Asian Americans. With the growing recognition and popularity of Korean pop culture in the United States in recent years, together with intensifying digitalization, nowadays Asian Americans are more likely to learn about Korean popular culture domestically than before.

17. See Hong 2013. This type of panethnic tendency is intertwined with Orientalism. As an individual develops a further liking and understanding of a

particular Asian country's popular culture, more focused attention may be given to that particular culture. However, most casual fans tend to simply enjoy Asian culture rather than Korean or Japanese culture, specifically.

18. Interview with a college student.

19. "Cover dances" refer to the audiences' imitation of the choreography of K-pop music.

20. This is a comment written by a respondent who participated in my online survey in 2016.

21. This is a comment that a student made in our classroom discussion on K-pop.

22. Kelts 2006; Hong 2013.

23. This is a point made by my survey respondents.

24. See Xing 1998.

25. See Hong 2013; Jung 2011.

26. See Jung 2013.

REFERENCES AND FURTHER READING

Brown, August. 2013. "K-Pop Museum to Open in Koreatown." *Los Angeles Times.* August 8, 2013. https://www.latimes.com/entertainment/music/la-xpm-2013-aug-08-la-et-ms-kpop-museum-koreatown-20130808-story.html.

Hong, Grace Danbi, 2014. "YG Entertainment to Establish YG Land in California." Yahoo! Style. March 7, 2014. https://sg.style.yahoo.com/news/yg-entertainment-to-build-yg-land-in-california-055555950.html.

Hong, Seok-Kyeong. 2013. *Segyehwawa dijiteol munhwa sidaeui hallyu: Pulhauseu, gangnamseutail, geurigo geu ihu* [The Korean Wave in the era of globalization and digital culture: full house, Gangnam Style and after]. Paju: Hanul Akademi.

Jin, Dal Yong. 2016. *New Korean Wave: Transnational Cultural Power in the Age of Social Media.* Champaign: University of Illinois Press.

Jung, Eun-Young. 2013. "K-pop Female Idols in the West: Racial Imaginations and Erotic Fantasies." In *The Korean Wave: Korean Media Go Global*, edited by Youna Kim, 106–19. London: Routledge.

Jung, Sun. 2011. *Korean Masculinities and Transcultural Consumption: Yonsama, Rain, Oldboy, K-pop Idols.* Hong Kong: Hong Kong University Press.

Kelts, Roland. 2006. *Japanamerica: How Japanese Popular culture Has Invaded the U.S.* New York: Palgrave Macmillan.Lee, Sangjoon. 2015. "From Diaspora TV to Social Media: Korean TV Dramas in America." In *Hallyu 2.0: The Korean Wave in the Age of Social Media*, edited by Sangjoon Lee and Abé Mark Nornes, 171–91. Ann Arbor: University of Michigan Press.

Morley, David, and Kevin Robins. 1995. *Spaces of Identity: Global Media, Electronic Landscapes and Cultural Boundaries.* New York: Routledge.

Oh, David. 2015. *Second-Generation Korean Americans and Transnational Media: Diasporic Identifications.* Lanham, MD: Lexington Books.

Park, Jung-Sun. 2004. "Korean American Youth and Transnational Flows of Popular Culture Across the Pacific." *Amerasia Journal* 30, no. 1: 147–69.

———. 2006. "The Korean Wave: Transnational Cultural Flows in East Asia." In *Korea at the Center: Dynamics of Regionalism in Northeast Asia*, edited by Charles Armstrong, Gilbert Rozman, Samuel Kim, and Stephen Kotkin, 244–56. Armonk, NY: M. E. Sharpe.

———. 2014. "American Youths and the Korean Wave: A Case Study." Paper presented at the Global Top 5 Conference, Ewha Womans University. Seoul, Korea. May 30–31, 2014.

Thussu, Daya Kishan. 2007. "Mapping Global Media Flow and Contra-Flow." In *Media on the Move: Global Flow and Contra-Flow*, edited by Daya Kishan Thussu, 11–32. London: Routledge.

Xing, Jun. 1998. *Asian America Through the Lens*. Walnut Creek, CA: Altamira Press.

EIGHT

Ai Weiwei and the Global Art of Politics

William A. Callahan

IN THE PAST DECADE, Ai Weiwei has burst out from his limited role of a Chinese artist to become an artist-activist who has "gone global." Ai first gained international fame as the consultant for Beijing's "Bird's Nest" Olympic stadium, which was designed by the Swiss architectural firm Herzog and de Meuron. Just before the 2008 Olympics, however, Ai became infamous for denouncing the stadium as China's "fake smile" to the world. In October 2010, Ai fascinated the art world with his *Sunflower Seeds* exhibit at London's Tate Modern art gallery; before the exhibit closed in May 2011, Ai became a global political figure when he was illegally detained by the Chinese government for eighty-one days. After years of postdetention harassment by China's party-state, in 2015 Ai moved into self-imposed exile first in Germany and subsequently in the United Kingdom, where he continues to produce compelling art—and activism.

This chapter charts Ai's transition from being a "Chinese" artist to being a global artist. In China, Ai worked as a patriotic Chinese dissident to criticize the illegitimate power of the corrupt Communist party-state. After he went into exile in Europe, Ai refocused on the global issue of refugees, especially in his film *Human Flow* (2017). In this way, he expanded from a critique of China's domestic oppression to creatively address the global problem of refugees. Strangely, though, one of the main beneficiaries of the Ai Weiwei's own globalization has been China's party-state: for whatever reason, it is no longer the main target of his art-activism.

Ai Weiwei is famous for crossing boundaries, especially the boundary between art and politics. His activities explore the limits of what is acceptable in China both in terms of political action and aesthetic taste: in 2000 he coorganized an exhibit in Shanghai called *Fuck Off,* and more recently his nude photos were denounced as pornography both by the police and in the court of public opinion. He thus is a polarizing figure among both artistic and nonartistic audiences who delights in making people—both friends and enemies—feel uncomfortable.

However, Ai's work as an activist-artist is not noteworthy because it is "new." His critique of China's politics and society is actually part of a broad and ongoing debate about the moral crisis that China faces after four decades of economic reform and opening. Ai's contribution to this debate is straightforward: he feels that the People's Republic of China (PRC) is a corrupt authoritarian state and that the country can only be saved if the government respects freedom of expression and the rule of law.[1] Here Ai conceives of politics as a Manichean struggle of good versus evil, wherein the heroic dissident fights the cruel state. He thus shares many political values with Nobel laureate Liu Xiaobo, who also questioned Beijing's authoritarian rule. Yet Ai's style and tactics are quite different. Liu acted as a classic dissident. The Charter 08 manifesto, which landed Liu in jail for "state subversion," reads like a five-year plan for rational democratic reform in China. Ai, however, takes a different approach to resistance that blurs art, life, politics, and activism. Rather than writing earnest essays that demand rational governance, Ai appeals to people's outrage, mocks the government, and works primarily through the internet to witness and expose the party-state's oppression in new and interesting ways.

This often takes the form of an ideological campaign for government transparency and accountability that is expressed through visual art. Although Ai has always been political in the sense of demanding freedom of expression, he was moved to intervene more directly in politics by China's Wenchuan earthquake in 2008. Noticing that public schools often suffered more damage than surrounding buildings, many people felt that the schools collapsed because of substandard construction stemming from official corruption. After the government refused to investigate, Ai enlisted hundreds of volunteers in what he called a "Public Citizen Investigation Project" to expose the combination of state and private corruption that had produced this tragedy.

Eventually the citizens' investigation compiled and published a list of the names of the 5,212 children who were killed in the earthquake. Again jamming the line between art and politics, Ai turned this tragedy into visual art. The *Wall of Names*, which lists in Chinese and English the name, gender, age, and school of each of the victims was exhibited as an artwork. Ai's massive mosaic *Remembering* (2009), exhibited at Munich's Haus der Kunst, lined up nine thousand school bags to spell out one mother's reaction to her daughter's death: "She lived happily on this earth for seven years." Ai thus uses art to highlight the party-state's lack of accountability; this includes the literal counting of dead children.

Ai Weiwei's eighty-one-day illegal detention also provoked activist art that targeted China's party-state. *S.A.C.R.E.D.* is a six-part installation of half-scale dioramas in iron boxes; it uses the themes of *supper, accusers, cleansing, ritual, entropy*, and *doubt* to reproduce the scene of Ai's illegal detention in a cheap hotel room.[2] This art work exemplifies both the invisibility of being held in secret detention and the hypervisibility of being under constant surveillance by a team of guards. It also addresses issues of transparency at a structural level: in the art gallery, people can only see into *S.A.C.R.E.D.*'s six boxes through small, awkwardly placed holes; hence viewers are turned into voyeurs who are complicit with China's party-state.

ART, EXILE, AND GLOBAL WITNESSING

Up until his illegal detention in 2011, Ai's work focused almost entirely on China. His art, as we saw above, aimed to expose the oppression of the party-state. Ai's art generally exhibits Chinese things to the world—one hundred million ceramic sunflower seeds in London, or thousands of children's backpacks in Munich. However, after 2009, Ai more or less disappeared from the mainland's Chinese-language media, which was restricted by the censorship regime from even criticizing his work. At the same time, Ai received support and praise from the artistic and activist communities outside China. After his release from detention, Ai was named one of *Foreign Policy*'s "100 Top Global Thinkers of 2011," and he made the shortlist for *Time* magazine's "Person of the Year 2011." Still, even after his release in 2011, Ai was worn down by the strain of four years of quasi-house arrest, artistic and political censorship, and threats against his family.

This combination of push-and-pull factors finally motivated Ai to accept Germany's offer to set up a studio in Berlin. Once the government returned his passport in 2015, Ai moved into self-imposed exile. But this European exile was not a totally new experience. Actually, Ai has spent most of his life like that. Soon after Ai was born in 1957, his family was sent into internal exile on the harsh borderlands of the PRC because Ai's father, the famous Communist poet Ai Qing, had criticized Mao and the Communist Party. The family only returned to Beijing in 1976, as the Maoist period drew to a close.

After living for five years in Beijing, Ai was frustrated by the restrictions on artistic expression in China, and in 1981 he went to study in the United States. After dropping out of art school, Ai bummed around New York as an illegal alien: he did odd jobs and hung out with visiting Chinese artists, film-makers, and poets, all the while shooting over ten thousand photographs.[3] He returned to Beijing in 1993 to see his sick father, and was based in China until 2015. Hence, Ai has only spent seventeen of his sixty-odd years not in exile.

It is not strange, then, that Ai Weiwei made *Human Flow* (2017), a film about the current global crisis of the world's sixty-five million refugees. Like with Ai's art-activism in China, the message of *Human Flow* is extremely clear: we need to look beyond national borders and national interests to appreciate the refugee problem as a global issue of humanity that demands a global solution. Ai's goal in this film is not simply to inform people about the inhumane conditions of refugees but also to provoke a new global activist community that would creatively do something to help refugees.

To understand the global artistry of *Human Flow* it is helpful to see how it addresses the fluid situation of transnational migrants through the inter-play of the local, the national, and the global, as well as the individual and the collective. *Human Flow* not only criticizes nationalism and territorial bor-ders; it also aims to efface such borders in its presentation. Although people in the film are categorized according to their citizenship for bureaucratic reasons, *Human Flow* forces viewers to appreciate less national and more global identities, spaces, and experiences. While national police certainly are shown guarding national borders, most of the film presents the plight of migrants who are often a multinational or transnational group of travelers. Likewise, most of the expert testimony offered in the film is from people who work for the United Nations and transnational aid groups. Ai questions national boundaries by juxtaposing different geographical scales through the journey to twenty-three countries and over forty refugee camps: "At times

FIGURE 8.1. Selfie of Ai Weiwei offering tea and a blanket to a refugee, "Human Flow" (2017).

during the film, the viewer may be disoriented, [and] not know which country or camp he or she is in. Yet this sensation is integral to the film."[4]

Even so, the film risks reproducing the hackneyed logic of a package holiday that overwhelms the audience. One reviewer felt that the film's "patchwork construction can make it hard to determine exactly which particular crisis you're in at any given moment. The colors of land, skin and sky are often all you have to go on . . ."[5] In other words, *Human Flow* is like a grand tour of suffering that merges many horrible experiences in ways that risk reaffirming the hierarchical division of a safe "here" in Euro-America from a dangerous "there" in refugee camps. Interestingly, because of its appeal to global humanity, there is not a clear Other or enemy in this film. It is certainly critical of European (and Western) policing, apathy, and complicity. But since the West is the target audience, it is not constructed as the Other to the refugee self. Indeed, Ai's new country of residence—Germany, which let in over one million refugees in 2015 alone—comes off as a welcoming place.

Human Flow also addresses these artistic-activist issues through an individual and collective dynamic. The film starts off with an image of a boat rocking gently in the deep blue sea. Filmed from a drone far above and accompanied by evocative music, the scene is more beautiful than agonizing: the bright orange dots (that we later recognize as people in life jackets) look cute against the aquamarine canvas. It is only when the drone descends that we see the precarious position of the people in this overloaded boat. A police boat comes up alongside the refugee-filled vessel, and the refugees come ashore on the Greek island of Lesbos. At this point, Ai Weiwei appears, filming the scene with his smartphone. Next, we witness Ai offering hot tea and a reflector blanket to a tired and wet man who has come from Iraq (see fig. 1).

The cinematography of this opening scene is repeated numerous times in the film to visually depict a mixture of collectives and individuals, who are both general and specific, on the one hand, and abstract and material, on the other (see fig. 2). It is common in documentary films to choose an individual and follow that person on a journey, either to show his or her unique idiosyncrasies or to represent the general experience of a collective. Ai, however, explains that he didn't want to choose between the faceless mass of the collective and the unique experience of the individual; his purpose was to "get more knowledge on a global scale. Not making a film about one family or one person, but global scale to see the humanity, the human flow." [6]

This appeal to the collective has echoes in Ai's earlier artistic work: in the one hundred million porcelain *Sunflower Seeds* (London, 2010–11); in the 5,212 names on the *Wall of Names* of the Wenchuan earthquake victims (London, 2015); and in the more than forty camps in twenty-three countries depicted in *Human Flow*. Many of the film's sections begin with a drone's-eye view, establishing a shot that shows wide landscapes and seascapes. Again, as the drone descends, the view shifts from the abstract to the material, from the aesthetic to the social, and from the collective to the individual. One scene starts far above an abstract pattern that evokes Islamic geometric designs; as it descends, a refugee camp of orderly tents in the desert takes shape; then we see things moving around like ants; finally, we see these things emerge as people, including young children, who cheer on the drone as it hovers just above them. The transition from collective to individual, however, is incomplete: since the images are captured from above, we don't clearly see specific people's faces.

After these establishing shots, which highlight the shared experience of global humanity, the film offers a series of images of individuals. In addition to depicting how people encounter challenging situations, the film also shows them doing things in everyday life: cooking food; checking and charging

FIGURE 8.2. Drone's-eye-view of a refugee camp, "Human Flow" (2017).

mobile phones; and playing. The film thus employs a humanizing strategy that presents refugees not just in life-or-death crises but also as ordinary people who do ordinary things in daily life. Everyday life is also where Ai again enters *Human Flow* as a character: we see him grilling meat, getting a haircut, giving a haircut, and taking selfies with refugees. Here we are shown that refugees are just like "us" in Euro-America—and indeed could be us. In one scene, Ai offers to exchange passports and homes with a Syrian man in a camp: "Next time you are Ai Weiwei. Exchange tent for studio in Berlin.... I respect you." For some, however, the film is problematic. Although Ai says that the purpose of the film is not to follow one family or one person, the film actually does follow Ai on his own personal journey of discovery. Whereas in his earlier work, Ai positioned himself as the rebel of Chinese art, he now presents himself as the Chinese savior of humanity.[7] Sometimes this presentation is compelling, but at other times it is like Marie Antoinette's performance as a milkmaid at the Versailles dairy. Ai was criticized for an earlier refugee-themed photograph, whereby he appropriated the image of the toddler, Alan Kurdi, who was found dead on a Turkish beach in the summer of 2015, by lying down on the beach in a similar way. While it is common to criticize Euro-Americans for appropriating the experience of people of color, here we have an example of the Chinese savior mentality, also known as the "Yellow Man's Burden."[8] Although the lingering gaze of the camera can "humanize" suffering people, it also risks becoming a "colonial gaze" that exploits them. And, as mentioned above, the colossal scale of the film risks morphing the experience into a Grand Tour of dark travel.

Lastly, it seems odd that China is invisible in a film about the global refugee crisis. On the one hand, China is a major source of refugees in the world; on the other hand, China is one of the most antirefugee places in the world. According to an online poll, 97 percent of the Chinese public opposes receiving any refugees at all.[9] Beijing is commonly criticized both for sending North Koreans back across the border to face certain punishment and for not allowing dissidents, Uyghurs and Tibetans, to leave the PRC. Ai actually mentions North Korea in one of the interviews promoting his film, but he does so only to criticize a "Western mentality": "I've seen people who escape North Korea and cannot accept the Western lifestyle. Don't take the Western lifestyle as the natural, absolute condition."[10] Interestingly, this criticism of Western hypocrisy chimes with the message promoted by the Chinese

Communist Party's Propaganda Department. This is not a one-off: in exile, Ai focuses his activism on global issues rather than on the Chinese party-state. For example, although he lived in Xinjiang for over twenty years, Ai has been relatively quiet about the PRC's mass "reeducation" camps. Ai's global resistance activities in exile are therefore still shaped by the party-state back in China. And, as mentioned above, Germany, Ai's new home, also comes off looking pretty good.

Human Flow thus shows how Ai Weiwei has followed the lead of China's state-owned enterprises to "go global." While many political dissidents become irrelevant in exile because they still focus on the authoritarian state back home, Ai has successfully recast both his art and his activism to adapt to his new European exile experience. Rather than being simply an individual artist creating individual works, Ai has expanded to work as a director who orchestrates artistic and cinematic works on an epic scale. The film is interesting because it works hard to provide objective facts for rational discussion at the same time as it provokes collective emotional experiences. Indeed, one of my students explains that seeing *Human Flow* in 2017 "changed his life"; it showed the power of artistic documentary films, and it inspired him to study filmmaking as a mode of global political activism.

CONCLUSION

As a Chinese artist struggling against a Communist party-state, Ai Weiwei seems like an idiosyncratic case that does not explain much else. But Ai is interesting for a number of reasons. Living and working in China, America, Europe, and refugee camps has allowed him to creatively combine these experiences for art and activism that is truly global. As a long-time exile who has felt the sharp boot of the party-state on his own body, Ai doesn't simply represent other people's suffering: his art demonstrates how his own oppression is also a collective experience shared by many inside and outside China. Ai's concern with accountability raises the important issue of how one can speak truth to power in an authoritarian state. Lastly, his film *Human Flow* shows that Ai is not simply a "Chinese artist": this creative juxtaposition of his personal refugee experience with those of a range of other refugees is an indication of his working hard to provide information about the horrible situation migrants face while at the same time provoking a global form of resistance. Still, Ai's shift from a very visible resistance to the Chinese party-state to a global activism in which China is largely invisible shows how his resistance is still shaped by the global power of the People's Republic of China.

NOTES

1. Ai Weiwei, interview with the author in Beijing, May 27, 2013.

2. See Marlow and Tancock 2015.

3. Ai Weiwei 2011.

4. Andrew Cohen, the "Final Press Notes" to *Human Flow* (2017), accessed May 23, 2018, https://www.humanflow.com/press-kit/.

5. Robbie Collin, "Human Flow Review: Ai Weiwei's Refugee Documentary Weighs on Your Heart Like a Cannonball," *Daily Telegraph*, December 8, 2017, https://www.telegraph.co.uk/films/0/human-flow-review-ai-weiweis-refugee-documentary-weighs-heart/.

6. Ai Weiwei to John Snow, *Human Flow*," extras section.

7. See Callahan 2014.

8. See Nyiri 2006.

9. Li Ruohan, "97% of Chinese Would Reject Receiving Refugees: Online Poll," *Global Times*, June 20, 2018, http://www.globaltimes.cn/content/1107731.shtml.

10. Ai Weiwei, "Nationality and Borders are Barriers to Our Intelligence and Imagination," interview with Ai Weiwei, *New Perspectives Quarterly* 34, no. 4 (October 2017): 39.

REFERENCES AND FURTHER READING

Ai Weiwei. 2011. *Niuyue 1983–1993 / New York 1983–1993*. Berlin: DISTANZ Verlag.

Ai Weiwei. 2017. *Human Flow* Final Press Notes. Online at https://www.humanflow.com/press-kit/, last accessed May 23, 2018.

Callahan, William A. 2014. "Citizen Ai: Warrior, Jester, and Middleman." *Journal of Asian Studies* 73, no. 4 (November): 899–920.

Kraus, Richard Curt. 2004. *The Party and the Arty in China: The New Politics of Culture*. Lanham, MD: Rowman & Littlefield.

Marlow, Tim, and John Tancock, ed. 2015. *Ai Weiwei*. London: Royal Academy of Arts.

Nyri, Pal. 2006. "Yellow Man's Burden: Chinese Immigrants on a Civilizing Mission." *China Journal* 56 (July): 83–106.

Osnos, Evan. 2010. "It's Not Beautiful: An Artist Takes on the System." *New Yorker*, May 24, 54–63.

Rojas, Carlos. 2014. "Collective Creation and the Politics of Visibility. In North Korea from South Korea, North Korea from South Korea." In *Ai Weiwei: Living Art on the Edge*, edited by Hans Werner Holzwarth, 333–39. Berlin: Taschen.

Shambaugh, David. 2013. *China Goes Global: The Partial Power*. New York: Oxford University Press.

Sorace, Christian. 2014. "China's Last Communist: Ai Weiwei." *Critical Inquiry* 40, no. 2 (Winter): 396–419.

Strafella, Giorgio, and Daria Berg. 2015. "Twitter Bodhisattva": Ai Weiwei's Media Politics." *Asian Studies Review* 39, no. 1 (January): 138–57.

PART THREE

Education, Science, and Technology

Frank N. Pieke

EAST ASIAN SOCIETIES HAVE TRADITIONALLY been highly literate. In the Confucian tradition shared by China, Korea, and Japan, education and literacy are valued as the chief, if not the sole, way to become a civilized person and a full member of society. Entry into the ruling elite, at least in theory, required education, literacy, and civilization. Nowadays, a strong educational ethos and aspiration is still present across all of East Asia, including China, despite more than twenty-five years of Maoist valuation of "red" ordinary workers and peasants and suspicion of the "expert" elite after the establishment of the People's Republic of China in 1949.

East Asia's global footprint is also strongly shaped by education, science, and technology. The number of foreign students in all East Asian countries is high and rising, caused by a combination of often low costs relative to the United States, concessionary admission criteria for foreign students, and the quality of the education on offer. However, what is more visible is the large number of East Asian students abroad. Chinese students alone now make up more than 15 percent of all foreign students in the world. Many universities in the developed world have come to rely on them, both financially and because of the talent that they bring.

In this section we discuss how China, Japan, and South Korea have responded to challenges from global competition through the internationalization of their national higher education and research systems in recent years. In chapter 9, "China, Japan, and the Rise of Global Competition in Higher Education and Research," Futao Huang looks at the changes in the internationalization strategies for higher education in Japan and China. This includes recent national-level projects to improve the global competitiveness of their national higher education systems, changes in international mobility, and ways in which individual universities strive for academic excellence and make efforts to become international brands. Huang concludes that the institutions of higher education in both China and Japan have accepted standards of international competition and have focused on the production of graduates with global perspectives and competencies. China has also begun to export its educational services through jointly operated institutions and programs with foreign partners. In China, striving for excellence and international branding is an important part of making the country a global center of learning and research. In Japan, the main objective has been to recruit inbound international students and to produce graduates with a global outlook and competencies for the local labor market.

In South Korea, a foreign education is valued so much that many students embark on study abroad principally to improve their chances of gaining admission to one of Korea's notoriously competitive universities later on. In Taiwan, studying abroad—in particular, in the United States—is so common that it is actually quite hard to meet members of the educated elite there who have not done it. For Chinese parents, sending their children to universities, secondary, or even primary schools abroad is often part of a deliberate transnational family strategy of gaining a foothold in a developed country, usually without wishing to give up their life, business, or careers in China.

In chapter 10, "The Educational Exodus from South Korea," Adrienne Lo and Leejin Choi focus on early study abroad in order to discuss the shape and consequences of this singular focus on international educational achievement. In South Korea, study abroad has become a very divisive issue. The large number of youths leaving to study and work abroad is either viewed as a reflection of the insufficiencies of South Korea, or, alternatively, as proof that the country has become a fully advanced society whose citizens confidently operate on the global stage. Yet other voices present education migration as just one more vehicle of class reproduction through which the South Korean elite ensure the brightest of futures for their own children.

Beyond education and training, research in East Asia is also fully connected with global science and technology. China in particular, but also South Korea, Japan, and Taiwan, have well-funded national strategies in place to make their research institutions competitive with those of Western countries. They must develop the technologies and products of the future that will enable their economies to lead rather than to follow.

Until only a few decades ago, the notion of Western science was hardly questioned. Although East Asia was trying to emulate the West in the popular imagination, it was thought unlikely that the East Asian latecomers would catch up, and it was taken for granted that the West defined the rules of good science. In chapter 11, "From Wild East to Global Pioneers: Life Science Developments in East Asia," Margaret Sleeboom-Faulkner, using the example of regenerative medicine, shows how the tables are being turned. Regenerative medicine draws on molecular biology and tissue engineering to develop therapeutic applications by replacing, engineering, or regenerating human cells, tissues, and organs. In stem cell science, the "Wild East" has become a leading region with a major influence on how the research field develops. To understand this shift, we need to adjust our perception of scientific advancement. Rather than individual researchers or research institutions, the competition between nation-states shapes the development of the field, particularly through political and regulatory moves. The development of stem cell science in East Asia and the world does not simply reflect the growth of scientific capacity in East Asia; it also reveals the increased scientific ambition of the countries in this region in the world.

Transnational links are important here, and many of the top researchers or leaders of high-end tech firms have often spent a considerable amount of time in the United States, Europe, Japan, or Australia as students, visiting scholars, or even as resident researchers and entrepreneurs. However, since 2018 it has become increasingly difficult to mesh transnational links with strategies for national competitiveness. The increasingly open rivalry with China has tempted the United States to weaponize scientific links in order to hurt China in its ambition to become the world's leading nation in science and technology. US-based researchers with active links to China, particularly if they are ethnic Chinese, run the risk of criminal investigation, revocation of funding, or even the loss of their job. In science, too, the age of global innocence seems to be well and truly over.

East Asia's global footprint as a powerhouse of science, technology, and education also includes approaches based on its own traditions. In chapter 12, "A Concise History of Worldling Chinese Medicine," Mei Zhan discusses some of the key events and features in the making of traditional Chinese medicine through translocal encounters and entanglements. In the 1960s and 1970s, when China fashioned itself as the champion of the postcolonial proletariat, traditional Chinese medicine was exported from China to Third World countries as the perfect preventive medicine for the rural poor. Since the 1980s, however, Chinese medicine has been reworlded as a new kind of preventive medicine for the holistic wellbeing of the cosmopolitan middle class. Most recently, the worlding of Chinese medicine not only involves spreading it outside China; acupuncturists and other healers from North America, Europe, and Japan are also invited back to China. They teach Chinese students and practitioners new techniques, new business models, and new naturalistic and countercultural understandings of health and medicine that have been grafted onto Chinese medicine in their own part of the world.

_____

NINE

China, Japan, and the Rise of Global Competition in Higher Education and Research

Futao Huang

SINCE THE LATE 1990S, East Asia has been part of the growing international competition in higher education and research. As is the case with other countries, the East Asian objective is to enhance the quality, reputation, and attractiveness of higher education and research. China, in particular, has boosted the mobility of both inbound international students coming to Chinese campuses and outbound Chinese students going abroad. At the same time, Chinese universities have risen rapidly in the main international university rankings.

Major changes have occurred in the internationalization of higher education in China and Japan. As compared to earlier phrases, a number of similarities can be identified in the goals and practices of internationalization between the two countries. Nevertheless, important differences in their efforts to achieve excellence also exist. Excellence and internationalization are both broad concepts with varying interpretations across national contexts, and they do not necessarily mean or imply the same things in China and Japan.

STRATEGIES AND PRACTICES

China

The meaning of the internationalization of higher education has shifted gear in China since the latter part of the 1990s. Internationalization has included English-language courses and teaching materials; instruction in English; international dimensions to university teaching and learning; and even fully foreign educational programs or campuses.

The first national-level strategy for academic excellence in China was the so-called Project 211 in 1995. The aim of the project was to develop around one hundred "well-known" research universities in China. As a follow-up to the project, in May 1998 the Chinese government launched the new national Project 985 with the purpose of establishing several "world-class" universities. The thirty-nine universities included in this project were expected to become world-class by the middle of the twenty-first century. In September 2017, the Chinese government launched the Double World-Class Project. This project includes building world-class universities with Chinese characteristics and establishing disciplines that are first class globally. In a manner that is similar to Project 985 but much more ambitious, it aims for China to have forty-two world-class universities and approximately 456 world-class disciplines in ninety-five universities by the middle of the twenty-first century.

However, the primary goal of the project is not only limited to the development of world-class universities and disciplines but includes the overall improvement of Chinese higher education. According to the Chinese ministry of education, the ultimate goal is to make China a center of learning worldwide and to boost China's international competitiveness and soft power.

Compared to the two projects in the 1990s, a much clearer and more ambitious strategy and road map have been laid out. Three main steps will be taken. By 2020, several Chinese universities and some disciplines must be ranked world-class. Several of these disciplines must be approaching the top end among those deemed to be world-class. By 2030, more universities and disciplines will have to be labeled world-class and be at the top end of those considered world-class. The overall quality of national higher education will have to be substantially improved. By 2050, the number of Chinese world-class universities and disciplines will have to be greatly increased, and China will have to have a strong overall higher education system.

An important aspect of China's drive to upgrade its research infrastructure has been to bring top researchers to China. Already starting in the early 1990s, the Chinese government embarked on national projects to attract and hire high-level "talents" and scientists from abroad. The main projects include the following: the One Hundred Talents Project of 1994, the Chang Jiang Scholars Program of 1998, the Thousand Talents Plan of 2008, the Recruitment Program of Young Global Experts of 2011, and the Ten Thousand Talents Plan of 2012.

Although China strives to boost the global reputation and impact of its universities and disciplines in accordance with international standards, there is also a very strong emphasis on Chinese characteristics and the Chinese national context. For example, a basic principle is that the universities and disciplines involved are rooted in China to solve Chinese problems and to produce graduates dedicated to socialist construction.

Strengthening research and education, of course, not only happens for reasons of national prestige and academic excellence but is embedded in a long-term strategy to upgrade the Chinese economy, thereby ensuring long-term sustained growth. A centerpiece is the ambitious Made in China 2025 industrial strategy that started in 2015. This strategy entails large-scale state and private investment in research and innovation in ten core, future-oriented industrial sectors. The goals of the strategy are to enable both state and private Chinese companies to become global leaders in these core industries by 2025, and for China to be a global technological superpower by 2049.[1]

Japan

The first national-level strategy for the internationalization of higher education in Japan was the 100,000 Plan, which was developed in 1983. This plan intended to have one hundred thousand international students studying in Japan by the year 2000. However, the main goal of the plan was not to participate in global competition and enhance the quality and international competitiveness of Japan's higher education and research. The 100,000 Plan puts more emphasis on Japan's academic contribution to the international community by accepting international students, especially those from developing countries in the region.

In the 1990s, however, this had changed. New policies and strategies emphasized the need to improvement of international aspects of higher education institutions and to strengthen their ability to compete at an international level. The Global Human Resource Development Project was implemented in 2004. This strategy originated with Japan's large enterprises, which were facing increased global economic competition. Global companies need people who can think independently and work in an international environment. In order to foster such global human resources, partnerships were forged between universities, enterprises, and society. In 2012, the Japanese government embarked on the Global Human Resources Project. This project requires selected universities to play a leading role in enhancing the globalization of other Japanese universities.[2]

In 2008, the government launched the Global 30 Program; this aims to enroll three hundred thousand foreign students by 2020. Thirteen universities were selected to achieve this target. With additional funding from the central government, these universities are required to accept more international students and to develop new English-medium degree programs.

In 2014, the Japanese government issued the Top Global University Project. This project aims to enhance the international compatibility and competitiveness of higher education in Japan. It provides intensive financial support for selected universities that are expected to press forward with comprehensive internationalization and university reform. Japan's top thirteen "world-class" universities have the potential to be ranked in the top one hundred of global university rankings. A further twenty-four "innovative" universities will have to continue to lead the internationalization of Japanese society, based on a continuous improvement of their current internationalization efforts. It was reported that the central government would allocate 7.7 billion yen annually to the project for the next ten years.[3]

Finally, in 2017 the Japanese government launched the Designated National University Project. In a manner that was similar to the previous strategies, this project focused on enhancing the autonomy, the efficiency, and the effectiveness of universities, as well as on closer collaboration with industry, business, and foreign partners. As of 2019, only six from among eighty-six national universities have been selected as Designated National Universities: the universities of Tohoku, Kyoto, Tokyo, Nagoya, and Osaka, and the Tokyo Institute of Technology. The Japanese government strongly expects these universities to strive for global excellence. For example, the home page of Tohoku University states the following: "as a Designated National University, we will have the means to further internationalize our education, reinforce our research capabilities and push ahead with structural reforms to make us even more competitive."[4]

OUTCOMES AND CHALLENGES

There is little doubt that remarkable progress has been made in both China and Japan in internationalizing higher education and research and in raising their quality and international competitiveness.

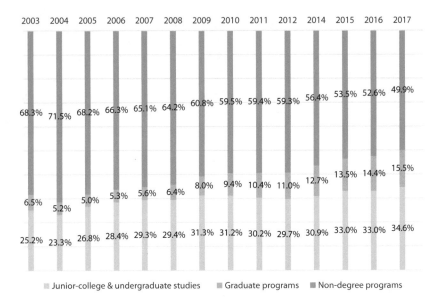

68.3% 71.5% 68.2% 66.3% 65.1% 64.2% 60.8% 59.5% 59.4% 59.3% 56.4% 53.5% 52.6% 49.9%

13.5% 14.4% 15.5%

6.5% 5.2% 5.0% 5.3% 5.6% 6.4% 8.0% 9.4% 10.4% 11.0% 12.7%

25.2% 23.3% 26.8% 28.4% 29.3% 29.4% 31.3% 31.2% 30.2% 29.7% 30.9% 33.0% 33.0% 34.6%

■ Junior-college & undergraduate studies ■ Graduate programs ■ Non-degree programs

FIGURE 9.1. International students in China by type of students. Source: Ministry of Education (China). *Laihua liuxuesheng jianming tongji* [A brief statistics of inbound international students coming to China]. Beijing: Ministry of Education, 2019.

China

Chinese campuses have witnessed a steady and quick growth in the number of international students. As of 2018, Chinese universities have accommodated approximately five hundred thousand, up from just a little over one hundred thousand in 2004.[5] More importantly, as shown in figure 9.1, the number of those pursuing degrees increased, while those enrolled in nondegree programs dropped from 68 percent in 2003 to 50 percent in 2017. The percentage of those at junior colleges and involved in undergraduate studies expanded from 25 percent in 2003 to 35 percent in 2017; and those in graduate programs increased from 7 percent in 2003 to 16 percent in 2017.

Since 2005, the Chinese government has increased both the number of young scholars and graduate students dispatched and funded by the China Scholarship Council and their affiliations to world-famous universities. In 2016, that number reached 107,005. Of those, 44,814 were visiting scholars and 62,191 were doctoral, master, or undergraduate students. Of these scholars and students, 93,865 (88 percent) went to the United States, the United Kingdom, Canada, and other developed English-speaking countries. They are concentrated in the sciences (15.4 percent), engineering (36.6 percent), agriculture (3.17 percent), and medical sciences (6.68 percent), while only 38.1 percent work in the humanities or social sciences.[6] Nevertheless, the vast majority of Chinese students abroad are either self-funded or are funded by non-Chinese sources and in manner that is beyond government strategizing. According to the data by the Chinese Ministry of Education, in 2017 there were 540,000 private students abroad, accounting for more than 90 percent of the total Chinese students going abroad.[7]

The internationalization of Chinese academic teaching and research is by no means limited to student mobility. As early as the mid-1990s, internationally collaborative institutions and programs began to be set up in China. National data shows that by early 2002, sixty-seven international institutions and seventy-two international programs had been approved with the authority to award foreign degrees or degrees from Hong Kong universities. The Chinese government has encouraged both Chinese universities and foreign institutions to establish internationally collaborative universities, and degree (including double and joint degree) or nondegree programs at various levels over the past few decades. In 2018, the number of such programs and institutions had reached 2,342. Among these, 1,090 institutions and programs are authorized to confer bachelor's and master's degrees.[8]

Chinese universities have also made efforts to establish their own international branch campuses, particularly in South-East Asian countries. These campuses mainly provide academic programs in the Chinese language, as well as in Chinese cultural history and heritage. Although they are as yet few in number, they show that China is leveraging its existing soft power through the export of higher education in South East Asia.[9]

Explicit and targeted government policy and funding have facilitated the rise of Chinese universities in the international rankings. In fact, the first such global university ranking, the *Academic Ranking of World Universities,* was created by Shanghai Jiaotong University in 2003. Although there are no Chinese universities as yet ranked in the top twenty, since 2015 two Chinese universities (Tsinghua and Peking University) have been listed in the top one hundred; these were joined by one more (Zhejiang University) in 2018. Although there is still a long way to go, it is very likely that this is only the beginning as Chinese universities raise their global academic quality and prestige and become more globally competitive in the future.

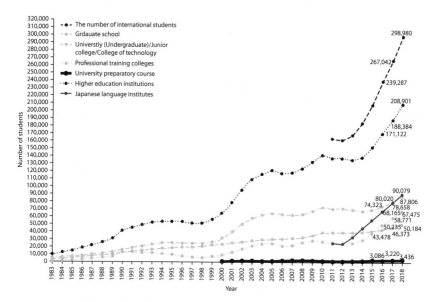

FIGURE 9.2. Inbound international students to Japan. Source: Japan Student Services Organization (JASSO). International Students in Japan 2018, 2019. https://www.jasso.go.jp /en/about/statistics/intl_student/data2018.html.

Japan

Raising the number of inbound international students is a key component of the Japanese government's strategy to internationalize higher education. This strategy has been very successful. As demonstrated by figure 9.2, more than 298,000 inbound international students studied at Japanese campuses in 2018.

Regarding the developing global human resources, the 2014 national survey of deans of Japanese universities showed that a large number of faculties have native English teachers and invite guest lecturers from companies to promote students' active learning, and to provide students' internship in domestic companies.[10] As for changes in the numbers of English-medium-only degree programs, by 2015 the number of universities providing English-medium undergraduate degree programs rose to forty, accounting for 5 percent of the total number of degree programs. The number of faculties with English-medium-only undergraduate degree programs increased to seventy-three. Further, the number of universities providing English-medium-only graduate degree programs increased to 126, making up 20 percent of the total. Finally, the number of graduate schools with English-medium-only degree programs increased to 247.[11]

There has, however, been a decline not only in the number of Japanese universities that were listed in the top one hundred in the *Academic Ranking of World Class Universities*, which went down from six in 2006 to three in 2018. In 2017, Japan also lost its single university (Tokyo University) ranked in the top twenty. This indicates that there has been a relative decline in the global prestige or excellence in Japanese universities in the last decades, especially when compared to the quick progress made by Chinese universities.

CONCLUDING REMARKS

The desire for prestige and excellence has been an important driver of internationalization in both China and Japan. Policies and institutional practices in the internationalization of higher education and research in both Japan and China have concentrated on enhancing teaching, learning, and research, accepting international standards and participating in international competition.

The two countries share numerous similarities in this pursuit. They include strong and direct leadership, strategy and funding by the central government, a focus on a few selected top institutions, a clear-cut and comprehensive road map for carrying out all relevant national strategies, and so on. However, compared to Japan, it appears that China has made more effort to export educational services and to allow jointly operated institutions and programs with foreign partners. In Japan, more endeavors have been undertaken at local campuses to recruit international students and to produce graduates with a global outlook and competencies. Further, more emphasis has been put on the enhancement of international competitiveness of Japanese educational activities through a close partnership between universities and government, industry, and business.

NOTES

1. Zenglein and Holzmann 2019.
2. "Project for Promotion of Global Human Resource Development," Ministry of Education, Culture, Sports, Science and Technology-Japan, accessed May 27, 2019, http://www.mext.go.jp/en/policy/education/highered/title02/detail02/sdetail02/1373895.htm.

3. "Top Global University Project," Ministry of Education, Culture, Sports, Science and Technology-Japan, accessed July 29, 2019, http://www.mext.go.jp/en /policy/education/highered/title02/detail02/sdetail02/1395420.htm.

4. "A New Future for Tohoku," Tohoku University, accessed June 3, 2019, https://www.tohoku.ac.jp/en/about/designated_national_university.html.

5. Ministry of Education (China), *Zhongguo jiaoyu nianjian* [Yearbook of education in China 2019]. Beijing: Ministry of Education, 2019.

6. "2016 chuguo liuxue shuju: zongshu 54 wan ren, 7 cheng gongdu benke yishang xueli" [2016 data of outbound students: total 54,000, 70 percent pursuing undergraduate or higher degrees], Ministry of Education (China), March 1, 2017, http://www.sohu.com/a/127589550_112831.

7. "2017 nian chuguo liuxue renshu po 60 wan, tongbi zeng 11.74%" [Over six hundred thousand Chinese students going abroad, a year-on-year increase of 11.74 percent]), Ministry of Education (China), March 3, 2018, http://news.cctv .com/2018/03/30/ARTIUmNsfjeXP5bP4uZu110w180330.shtml.

8. Huang 2018.

9. He and Wilkins 2018.

10. Futao Huang, "Globally-Oriented and Locally-Based? Strategies and Practice of Producing Global Human Resource in Japan" (paper presented at the Fifth Annual UW-PKU Workshop on Higher Education, Peking University, Beijing, China, May 25, 2019).

11. "Heisei 27 nendo no daigaku niokeru kyouiku naiyou do no kaikaku jyoukyou nitsuite (gaiyou)" [Situation of reforms on university education in 2015: a summary], Ministry of Education, Culture, Sports, Science, and Technology (Japan), accessed July 29, 2019, http://www.mext.go.jp/a_menu/koutou/daigaku /04052801/__icsFiles/afieldfile/2019/05/28/1398426_001.pdf..

REFERENCES AND FURTHER READING

Altbach, Philip. G., and V. Selvaratnam, eds. 1989. *From Dependence to Autonomy: The Development of Asian Universities*. Dordrecht: Kluwer Academic Publishers.

Ebuchi, Kazuhiro. 1997. *Daigaku kokusaika no kenkyu* [Research on internationalization of universities]. Tokyo: Tamagawa Press.

Grunzweig, Walter, and Nana Rinehart, eds. 2002. *Rockin' in Red Square: Critical Approaches to International Education in the Age of Cyberculture*. Münster: Lit Verlag.

Hayhoe, Ruth. 1996. *China's Universities, 1895–1995: A Century of Cultural Conflict*. London: Routledge.

He, Lan, and Stephen Wilkins. 2018. "The Return of China's Soft power in South East Asia: An Analysis of the International Branch Campuses Established by Three Chinese Universities." *Higher Education Policy*. https://doi: 10.1057 /s41307–018–0084-x

Horie, Miki. 2002. "The Internationalisation of Higher Education in Japan in the 1990s: A Reconsideration." *Higher Education* 43, no. 1: 65–84.

Huang, Futao. 2017. "Double World-Class Project Has More Ambitious Aims." *University World News.* September 29, 2017. https://www.universityworldnews.com/post.php?story=2017092913334471.

———. 2018. "What Do the International HE Programme Closures Mean?" *University World News.* August 24, 2018. https://www.universityworldnews.com/post.php?story=20180822101208887.

Knight, John. 2002. "The Impact of GATS and Trade Liberalisation on Higher Education." In *Globalisation and the Market in Higher Education: Quality, Accreditation and Qualifications,* edited by Stamenka Uvalic-Trumbic, 191–209. Paris: UNESCO.

Ministry of Education (China). 2019. *Zhongguo jiaoyu nianjian* [Yearbook of education in China 2019]. Beijing: Ministry of Education.

Ministry of Education (Japan). 1992. *Gakusei hyakunijyuunenshi* [History of 120-year school system]. Tokyo: Kabushiki kaisya gyousei.

Pepper, Suzanne. 1996. *Radicalism and Education Reform in Twentieth-Century China: The Search for an Ideal Development Model.* Cambridge: Cambridge University Press.

Tsuchimochi, Gary. H. 1996. *Shinsei daigaku no tanjyou* [The emergence of newly-established universities]. Tokyo: Tamagawa Publishing House.

Umakoshi, Taoru. 1997. "Internationalisation of Japanese Higher Education in the 1980s and 1990s." *Higher Education* 34, no. 2: 259–73.

Zenglein, Max, and Anna Holzmann. 2019. *Evolving Made in China 2025: China's Industrial Policy in the Quest for Global Tech Leadership.* Berlin: Mercator Institute for China Studies.

TEN

The Educational Exodus
from South Korea

Adrienne Lo and Lee Jin Choi

SOUTH KOREANS OFTEN SPEAK about the present as a time of dizzying change. Whether comparing the poverty of the postwar years to the technologically sophisticated lifestyle of contemporary Seoul or contrasting the politically repressive twentieth century against the public protests of today, one frequently used narrative trope frames the present as starkly different from the past. Expressions of nostalgia for a simpler time mingle with pride in the nation's progress. In personal narratives about the course of one's own life as well as in narratives about the nation, the pace of change is described as sudden and disorienting, through frameworks that deemphasize personal agency.

International migration is often presented along these lines. While South Korea, like all nations, has never been homogenous, it is common to speak of migration as radically transforming an ethnically and linguistically pure population. Newspapers are awash with tales of the dramatic rise in foreign students, primarily from China, who attend South Korean universities; the travails of female migrants, mostly from China and Vietnam, who marry poor rural men; and the growth of the foreign resident population in South Korea, from 0.5 percent of the population in 1990 to more than 4 percent today. At the same time, the fact that an increasing number of South Korean youth and young adults leave to study and work abroad is viewed as evidence of a national crisis, a dispiriting reflection of the insufficiencies of South Korea, or, conversely, as proof that the country has at last made it, as its confident citizens surge forward on the global stage.

In this chapter, we look at one node in this interconnected web of migratory flows: Early Study Abroad (ESA), or the short-term migration of preuniversity youth and children. What is unique about the South Korean phenomenon is the extent to which migration, and the transformation of the self that it promises, has come to be seen as a necessary part of the South Korean life course across the class spectrum.[1] First, we provide a brief overview of the phenomenon and discuss its economic underpinnings. We examine the demographics and images of personhood associated with ESA. Last, we review how state efforts to stem the outflow of education migrants reveal tensions about the neoliberalization of education and the risks and rewards of globalization.

LEAVING KOREA

Elite Koreans have been leaving the country in pursuit of education for a long time. They migrated to Beijing in the centuries when Korea was part of the sphere of Chinese influence and to Tokyo during Japanese colonization (1910–45). Education migration to the United States was encouraged under the US military government (1945–48) and also after the Korean war (1950–53) when South Korean military, government, and academic leaders were sent to the United States for training. Today, the United States is the leading destination for South Korean education migrants of all ages (see fig. 10.1). This is in large part because of the institutionalization of English in South Korea, since evaluations of English proficiency are important for university entrance and professional employment.[2]

Leaving the country is one way that South Koreans attempt to secure their children's futures in a time of precarity, given the high costs of housing, the rise of part-time and contract work, and an unemployment rate of over 20 percent among university graduates in recent years. Cautionary tales about those who fail to gain access to a top-tier university and the stable employment it promises abound: young adults who leave for working holidays in Australia or Canada, barely getting by in menial jobs; others who drop out, forsaking unfulfilling professional lives in Seoul for an economically marginal existence on Jeju Island. ESA is often described by its participants not as an exciting quest or a fun adventure but as a resigned journey to obtain social capital thought to be unavailable in South Korea: "real" English; a neoliberal flowering of the self that would be stifled back home; access to experiences that instill in the child the wherewithal to develop into a world citizen. It is parental anxieties about their children's futures, fueled by alarmist tales of youth gone awry, that drive ESA.

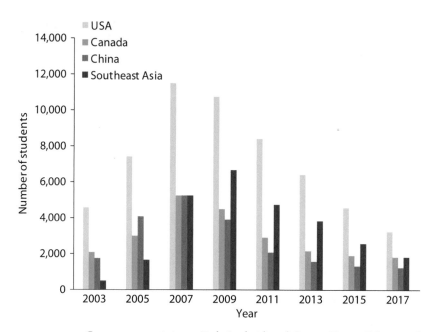

FIGURE 10.1. Government statistics on Early Study Abroad. Source: Korean Educational Statistics Service. Statistics on [early] study-abroad students. https://kess.kedi.re.kr/mobile /stats/school?menuCd=0101&cd=4218&survSeq=2018&itemCode=01&menuId=m_0101 05&uppCd1=010105&uppCd2=010105&flag=A.

TRENDS IN ESA

ESA is a somewhat difficult phenomenon to quantify. It is usually framed as having taken off in the 2000s as a result of the globalization efforts begun by President Kim Young Sam in the 1990s and the neoliberalization of the education system. As private afterschool preparatory institutes burgeoned and the number of South Koreans studying abroad at the postsecondary level expanded from 24,315 in 1980 to 190,364 in 2006, those participating in ESA also grew, from 1,562 in 1998 to 29,511 in 2006 (see fig. 10.2). At first, middle and high school students were the primary participants, but primary school students have been the largest constituency since 2003. Since 2006, official ESA numbers have declined steadily, with only 8,238 students recorded in 2017. However, this decline is more apparent than real, as we will discuss shortly below.

ESA is understood by its participants as driven by the belief that children need to live abroad while young in order to acquire fluency in foreign languages and the ease of feeling at home in the world. The temporal narrative of

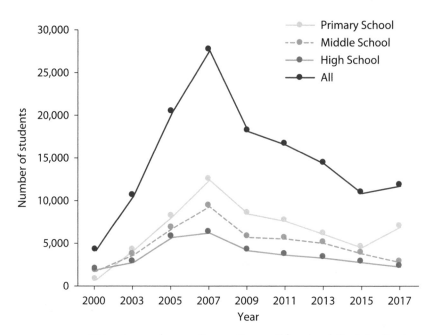

FIGURE 10.2. ESA migrants by age. Source: Korean Educational Statistics Service. Statistics on [early] study-abroad students. https://kess.kedi.re.kr/mobile/stats/school?menu Cd=0101&cd=4218&survSeq=2018&itemCode=01&menuId=m_010105&uppCd1=0101 05&uppCd2=010105&flag=A.

ESA lays the groundwork for the development of a confident, multilingual adult whose interactions with foreigners will be smooth and stress-free. This narrative is built on a modernist contrast with the figure of the insecure, awkward South Korean of an older generation. ESA is usually distinguished from permanent migration because it culminates in a planned return to South Korea in childhood or early adulthood. This return, and the professional career that draws on those qualities obtained abroad, are hallmarks of stories about ESA "success." What counts as ESA varies from short-term summer programs to decades abroad with stays of a year or more being the norm.

While official government statistics show a peak in 2006 and declining numbers since then, such figures are widely viewed as undercounts. Government definitions of "pure ESA" exclude many who plan stays in foreign countries through job postings abroad, self-employment, or as students or researchers. Students who enroll in international schools either domestically or abroad are also not counted, even though they are motivated by much the same desires as those who engage in "pure ESA." From our perspective, the decline in official statistics is partly demographic, as the school aged population has shrunk, but it is also evidence that families have found other ways of pursuing migration. Surveys reveal aspirations across the board for education migration even if only a few have the funds to pull it off. The decline in ESA numbers reflects shifts in form, not waning desires, as official ESA students often find themselves abroad alongside those who are not.[3]

ESA is a stratified form of migration. Most of those who can afford to go are wealthy—a recent survey of Seoul school districts revealed a twentyfold gap in the number of ESA students in wealthy versus poor districts. For the elite, ESA is usually part of a lifelong set of envisioned stints away from home and back again—English-language private kindergartens, ESA, elite domestic high schools followed by undergraduate or graduate studies abroad. Elite students often go to top destinations like the United States or Canada and attend private schools while abroad, while nonelite students attend public schools and go to less desirable locations, such as New Zealand or the Philippines.

ESA can also be a way for weaker students to circumvent South Korea's highly selective education system. Although most students gain entry to top-ranked domestic universities via a nationwide entrance exam, those who have studied outside the country for a certain number of years can apply instead through a special, less competitive admissions process. Or ESA can lay the groundwork for acceptance to a well-regarded foreign university. The image of the ESA student is thus highly bifurcated. Some, derisively labeled as engaging in *topi yuhak* or "escape study abroad," are imagined as losers who leave because they cannot make it back home, while others are seen as exemplary global citizens. These images are gendered, such that girls and women are more likely to be seen as susceptible to moral corruption during their time away.[4]

The United States is the top destination for students of all ages. In recent years, China, the Philippines, and Singapore have grown more popular. For some, these are stepping-stones, sheltered crucibles to bolster children for the harsher climate of the West when they are older. For others, they are valued because of their relatively short distance from South Korea, cheaper living costs, and greater opportunities to learn Chinese as well as English.[5]

Experiences of ESA vary greatly by destination. Families of more modest means often find themselves trapped once they are abroad. Privileged ESA students in Singapore can, for example, attend more forgiving international schools, where they will get higher grades and not be subject to the highly selective public education system. Such students can also salvage educational trajectories gone astray by moving to a third country or switching schools, options not usually available to working-class students.[6] Studies of ESA students in North America have focused on how school experiences are shaped by students' racialization, especially in high school.[7] An extensive body of work examines how ESA exposes rifts in globalization—conflicts between essentializing versus flexible ideologies of language and identity; local versus South Korean understandings of what forms of capital are most valued; aligning with versus escaping from the cultivation of the neoliberal self.[8] Lastly, in keeping with the South Korean understanding of ESA as a difficult endeavor, descriptions of the so-called "wild goose family" have tended to highlight the figure of the bereft and lonely father, left behind in South Korea, and the overwhelmed mother, unable to manage her children effectively abroad.

GLOBALIZATION AND MIGRATION

In this section, we examine how ESA has been received, both in South Korea and in the countries to which students have journeyed. For the most part, this wave of Korean migration has not drawn much attention in North America. In contrast with the alarmist stories about astronaut families from Hong Kong in Vancouver or Los Angeles in the 1990s, the appearance of South Korean migrant children and youth has garnered remarkably little attention in either the American or the Canadian press. Researchers have detailed the challenges that educational institutions have faced in coping with South Korean high school students who are subject to lax supervision in their boarding houses; practices around the sharing of assignments and study guides that some schools frame as academic integrity violations; and managing the expectations of parents who may have unrealistic aspirations for academic success. Other scholars have examined how this form of migration can profoundly affect families' and children's psychological well-being. In some university departments, applications for admission from South Korean female applicants are regarded as students whose primary goal is not the degree per se but bringing one's children to live overseas and attending public school without having to pay the hefty fees often charged to nonresidents. Such students can, as one professor noted, be less interested in finishing their degrees in a timely manner and more interested in prolonging their stay as much as possible to see their children through successful college applications. Yet these concerns have remained largely local, as ESA students and their parents are not always recognized as distinct from immigrant Korean Americans.

How are we to understand this erasure? There has been a great deal of anxiety around Chinese educational migration and birth migration in American and Canadian media outlets in recent years. In this outpouring of coverage, Chinese students are cast in moralizing terms, as Communist patsies who are manipulated by secretive forces from the embassy; cheats who have gotten in courtesy of their high-priced consultants, shady transcripts, and dubious test scores; or interlopers taking the rightful places of domestic students. Sometimes, Chinese students are cast as welcome cash cows, a much-needed source of revenue for universities and local economies in the age of declining state funding for education.

In this sense, the relative invisibility of South Koreans is perhaps not altogether unwelcome, given the ways that Korean Americans were made hypervisible as violent and racist in the US media in the 1990s. In that era, scenes of Korean American merchants wielding guns on rooftops as they guarded their businesses during the 1992 uprisings in Los Angeles were widespread, as was a notorious shooting captured on surveillance video in 1991 in which a Korean American liquor store owner in Los Angeles killed a fifteen-year-old African American customer for reportedly trying to steal a bottle of orange juice. In New York City, Black protesters led an eighteen-month-long boycott of Korean American stores in 1990 after an alleged assault by a Korean American shopkeeper on a Haitian American customer. The 1989 Spike Lee movie *Do the Right Thing* presents a fictional story of escalating tensions between African Americans, Italian Americans, Jews, Korean Americans, and Latinos in Brooklyn that erupt into a riot, resulting in the death of a Black man and the destruction of a local pizza shop. While such media portrayals were quite prominent then, they have largely faded away in recent years. Ethnographers of ESA have noted that white students in Australia, Canada, and the United States have imagined ESA students as coming from some vaguely undeveloped place, or, only recently, from the land of K-pop idols, if they even recognize South Korea at all.

In contrast, educational migration is a topic of a great deal of anguished self-reflection in South Korea. Some commentators look cynically at ESA as yet another site of class reproduction in a society where income inequality has risen sharply. Pointing to the array of consultants and brokers who steer elite families on the right path to managing their children's education, critics locate ESA as a dismaying site of status competition among the wealthy.

Educational migration is even part of South Korean popular culture—in dramas that fictionalize study abroad as a romantic and transformative time of freedom and leisure; in reality shows that feature young single returnees fresh from universities in the West looking for love back home; in variety shows in which returnees' multilingual abilities are ridiculed; and in prime-time shows featuring panels of male foreign university students in Seoul earnestly discussing current events.

Other commentators see ESA as squandering money that would be better spent domestically, pointing to the sizeable percentage of South Koreans who study abroad and the relatively scant number of foreign students in South Korea. In this framing, ESA is not understood as an export, a sign of the desirability of Korean goods, products, and people abroad, but is part of a global circuit of education migration in which South Korea's (and Asia's) best and brightest go the West, and third-rate students from China, Japan, and Vietnam come to South Korea.

From the perspective of the state, study abroad at the undergraduate and graduate level, particularly by men, is important for developing the nation, but the exodus of pre-university students is harmful to families and should be curtailed. The South Korean government's efforts to keep its children at home include support for the not terribly successful "English villages," which offer an immersive experience in reproductions of quaint British towns; programs that bring native speaker English teachers to local schools;[9] and policies designed to deter early study abroad by making reentry to state-sponsored primary and secondary schools challenging.[10] These state-sponsored initiatives are dwarfed by the private English language market, which has witnessed an explosion in the number of private English-medium kindergartens, campuses of foreign universities, and private English- medium high schools in South Korea in the past decade, all of which cater to the well-heeled. As English has become ever more entrenched as a necessary credential for advancement, with elite universities being encouraged to hire professors who can teach courses in English, interest in study abroad shows few signs of abating.

In this sense, ESA has come full circle. While leaving for Australia or the United States was, for a brief period, imagined as an escape from the intense schedule of after-school and weekend classes that middle- and upper-class children pursue in South Korea from early childhood through high school, going abroad is at this point just another extension of the domestic education market for many.[11] State-led efforts to dampen desires for study abroad do not seem to have worked; instead, the wealthy have once again figured out how to game the system, often by taking their children abroad as accompanying minors to the parents' own overseas postings. Although opinions about timing, ideal destinations, and the "right" way to go abroad may have changed over time, fueled in part by the ever-changing advice of an industry of consultants, what stands out to us is the persistence of the belief that it is good for South Koreans to leave for a spell to live, study, or work abroad.

CONCLUSION

In this chapter, we have shown how ESA is a rich site for examining the dynamics of globalization in South Korea. Both ESA and employment migration of young adults disillusioned with dead-end jobs are spurred by the promise of the West. However, there is also an increasing wariness of the moral corruption supposedly engendered by migration. Figures proliferate in the popular media of dissolute South Korean mothers with their children abroad and of escapee students who while away their time in a haze of drugs and partying. What are the costs and risks of leaving? What if your child is transformed, but not in the way you hoped? What if she can never fit back in?

The South Korean state has fueled these migrations through neoliberal moves that opened up the private education markets but also sought to stem them through efforts at equalization like providing less privileged students with access to foreign English teachers. ESA. in its early phases, was presented as a way for anyone with enough gumption and dedication to circumvent the power of the elite. Nowadays, public discourses about the inevitability of class reproduction cynically frame education migration as just one more vehicle through which the South Korean elite can ensure the brightest of futures for their own children.

NOTES

The preparation of this chapter was supported by the Core University Program for Korean Studies through the Ministry of Education of the Republic of Korea and the Korean Studies Promotion Service of the Academy of Korean Studies (AKS-2018-OLU-2250001) and the Canada Foundation for Innovation (#37510).

1. Lo et al. 2015.
2. Park 2009.
3. Bae and Park 2016.

4. Choi 2017.
5. Kang 2015.
6. Kim 2015.
7. An 2015; Shin 2015.
8. Park and Bae 2009; Song 2012.
9. Jeon 2012.
10. Kim 2015.
11. Kang and Abelmann 2011.

REFERENCES AND FURTHER READING

An, Sohyun. 2015. "'We Are More Racist': Navigating Race and Racism in (Korean) America." In *South Korea's Education Exodus: The Life and Times of Early Study Abroad*, edited by Adrienne Lo, Nancy Abelmann, Soo Ah Kwon, and Sumie Okazaki, 209–27. Seattle: Center for Korean Studies, University of Washington Press.

Bae, Sohee, and Joseph Sung-Yul Park. 2016. "Becoming Global Elites Through Transnational Language Learning?: The Case of Korean Early Study Abroad in Singapore." *L2 Journal* 8, no. 2: 92–109.

Choi, Lee Jin. 2017. "The Gendered Construction of 'Inauthentic' Female Bilinguals in South Korea: Authenticity, English and Gender." *Gender and Language* 11, no. 4 (December): 482–506.

Jeon, Mihyon. 2012. "Transnationalism, Globalization, and Language Management: Overseas Koreans as English Teachers in Rural Korea." *Journal of Sociolinguistics* 16, no. 2 (April): 238–54.

Kang, Jiyeon, and Nancy Abelmann. 2011. "The Domestication of South Korean Early Study Abroad (ESA) in the First Decade of the Millennium." *Journal of Korean Studies* 16, no. 1 (March): 89–118.

Kang, Yoonhee. 2015. "Going Global in Comfort: Korean Educational Exodus in Singapore." In *South Korea's Education Exodus: the Life and Times of Early Study Abroad,* edited by Adrienne Lo, Nancy Abelmann, Soo Ah Kwon, and Sumie Okazaki, 125–46. Seattle: Center for Korean Studies, University of Washington Press.

Kim, Jeehun. 2015. "The 'Other Half' Goes Abroad: The Perils of Public Schooling in Singapore." In *South Korea's Education Exodus: The Life and Times of Early Study Abroad,* edited by Adrienne Lo, Nancy Abelmann, Soo Ah Kwon, and Sumie Okazaki, 103–22. Seattle: Center for Korean Studies, University of Washington Press.

Korean Educational Statistics Service. 2018. "Statistics on Study Abroad Students." Accessed November 18, 2020. https://kess.kedi.re.kr/mobile/stats/school?menuCd=0101&cd=4218&survSeq=2018&itemCode=01&menuId=m_010105&uppCd1=010105&uppCd2=010105&flag=A.

Lo, Adrienne, Nancy Abelmann, Soo Ah Kwon, and Sumie Okazaki, eds. 2015. *South Korea's Education Exodus: The Life and Times of Early Study Abroad*. Seattle: Center for Korean Studies, University of Washington Press.

Park, Joseph Sung-Yul, and Sohee Bae. 2009. "Language Ideologies in Educational Migration: Korean *Jogi Yuhak* Families in Singapore." *Linguistics and Education* 20, no. 4 (December): 366–77.

Shin, Hyunjung. 2015. "Everyday Racism in Canadian Schools: Ideologies of Language and Culture among Korean Transnational Students in Toronto." *Journal of Multilingual and Multicultural Development* 36, no. 1: 67–79.

Song, Juyoung. 2012. "The Struggle over Class, Identity, and Language: A Case Study of South Korean Transnational Families." *Journal of Sociolinguistics* 16, no. 2 (April): 201–17.

ELEVEN

From "Wild East" to Global Pioneers

LIFE SCIENCE DEVELOPMENTS IN EAST ASIA

Margaret Sleeboom-Faulkner

JUST A FEW DECADES AGO, the notion that science was rooted in Western civilization remained virtually unquestioned. Although in the popular imagination East Asia was trying to emulate the West, it was thought unlikely that these latecomers would catch up, because it was taken for granted that the West defined the rules of good science. This chapter on regenerative medicine shows how the tables have been turned, illustrating how a "Wild East" of stem cell science has become a major player in determining this field's development. This area of research translates ideas from molecular biology and tissue engineering, therapeutic applications in regenerative medicine that aim to replace, engineer, and regenerate human cells, tissues, and organs.

To understand how changes in leadership of the field are taking place, we also need to adjust our perception of what exactly is regarded as scientific advancement. Rather than exclusively focusing on the work of what are regarded as the most advanced players in the field, it is necessary to broaden our vision to see how the rules for doing science are set. Building on over a decade of empirical research on international life science networks and collaborations across East Asia and beyond, I will argue that the dynamic of competition between nation-states is crucial in determining the growth of this field. The development of stem cell science in East Asia and the world does not just reflect the growing scientific capacity in East Asia; competitive political and regulatory moves are equally crucial in enabling scientific activity.

The West, and especially the United States, have shaped much of the world's economic infrastructure for biomedicine, including that of regenerative medicine and, in particular, the relation between academic institutions and industry. In the United States, the Bayh Dole Act (adopted in 1980), in conjunction with the 1986 Federal Technology Transfer Act, devolved the right to patent the fruits of federally funded research from the government to the institutions that had received these funds. This arrangement greatly encouraged the collaboration between universities and industry and was subsequently adopted in various forms in many other countries, including in East Asia and Europe.

At the time, research regulation for new medicinal products was based on the pharmaceutical model of Western evidence-based science and its notions of the double-blind research in clinical trials (RCT), control groups, risk, fairness, and ethics. The formalized ethics review of research is built on individualized notions of patient autonomy and ideas of ethical sourcing of research materials. These notions and ideas have had a major impact on the development of human embryonic stem cell research. Embryonic stem cell science, based on the technology that was used for cloning "Dolly the Sheep" in 1996, promised the start of an era of tailor-made cures for serious medical conditions. The idea was that the nucleus from healthy cells of patients would be transferred into egg cells (oocytes). The resultant embryos would then be used to regenerate numerous healthy cells to cure the patient. As this required the destruction of nonviable or redundant embryos, in 2001 US President George W. Bush announced a moratorium on federal state funding for this kind of research. Bush's decision reflects specific religious and other cultural views about the status of the embryo. Science would have to switch from using embryonic to less controversial adult (somatic) stem cells. However, the use of adult stem cells can also be seen as problematic. Critics maintain that their use cannot be justified without strict scientific evidence regarding the safety and efficacy of clinical trials that is subject to a formalized ethics review. Some so-called therapeutic applications, these critics argue, have in fact caused unintended growths, while their efficacy may not be due to the use of stem cells themselves but to specific growth factors contained in the cloned cells.

Because of these restrictions and debates in the United States, stem cell medical tourism emerged in what was referred to as the "Wild East." Patients from different parts of the world visited clinics that provided stem cell interventions and that were not approved of by the scientific community in the West. These practices in the East were contrasted with authoritative "Western" regenerative medicine, as defined, for example, by the International Society of Stem Cell Research (ISSCR). The regulations in the West would protect patients from what were regarded as quack practices, such as the fetal therapy provided by Huang Hongyun in China or the cloning practices of Woo-Suk Hwang and his team in South Korea.

This dichotomization between a fraudulent East and an authoritative West became untenable with the discovery of induced pluripotent stem cells (iPSc) in Japan in 2006 by Shinya Yamanaka, who, together with British scientist John Gurdon, was awarded the Nobel Prize in Physiology or Medicine in 2006. IPS cells are cells that have been "reprogrammed" back to an embryonic-like stage, after which they can be multiplied and administered to patients as an ethical alternative to human embryonic stem cells. Yamanaka was the first to use this new technology for reversing the history of somatic cells in mice, and he is a pioneer in its application to humans. Yamanaka's success led scientists worldwide to jump on the bandwagon of iPS research and to compete to create the first successful clinical applications, which caused Japanese politicians and scientists to worry that Japan might lose its leading edge in iPS science. In response, it was decided to give iPS research priority in Japan's national life science endeavors.

What is of particular interest to the argument here is how the regulation of regenerative medicine in Japan and other countries became a crucial factor in the global competition for scientific leadership. The race to develop clinical applications for iPS research was accompanied by diverging standards of acceptable scientific evidence and the conditions that have to be met to bring a medicinal product to market. Governments, industry, universities, hospitals, and clinics all had a stake in the hype around potential discoveries of a cure in the form of patents, knowledge, reputation, profit, and fame. Most tried to benefit from the financial injections into this area of research and the widespread hope and belief that an efficacious therapy for some disease would be discovered soon, regardless of whether or not that would happen through clinical studies, clinical experimentation, or even last-resort treatment. In this new global configuration of scientific competition, Asian scientific and industrial activities increasingly codetermine the rules.[1] Scientific and regulatory developments in South Korea, China, and Japan show how international competition and collaborations in conjunction with government policies and investments have changed the global power constellation in the field.

SOUTH KOREA

Until the beginning of this millennium, South Korea's promising work on regenerative medicine was regarded as simply copying Western methods and achievements. This image was a thorn in the side of Korean scientists—for instance, at the Center for Democracy in Science and Technology—who wanted the country to be an advanced model of transparent and responsible science. In 2004, Seoul National University star scientist Woo-Suk Hwang and his team amazed the world by announcing the world's first successful case of human somatic cell nuclear transfer with the prospect of curing patients with serious, intractable diseases, such as spinal cord injury or amyotrophic lateral sclerosis (ALS). In the course of 2005 and 2006, however, it transpired that Hwang's team had fabricated their data. Moreover, the eggs needed for this technique had been sourced from paid donors, some of whom worked at Hwang's own laboratory. Although politically active researchers and women had earlier publicly protested these ethical violations, an international scientific scandal was needed to attract attention to them.

The South Korean government tried to avoid a further tarnishing of the reputation of Korea's stem cell research by strengthening its regulations regarding adult stem cell research. However, these were still very permissive of research that violates scientific practices by Western standards. South Korea's Bio-Vision 2016 (2007–2016) innovation strategy announced support for national biotechnology by means of an expansion of research and development infrastructures, the globalization of bioindustries, and a regulatory and legal overhaul. Inspired by policies in the United States that enabled investigator-led projects and fast-track regulatory pathways, South Korea was the first to legislate the governance of stem cell research, which, as regulatory documents indicate, meant a push in the direction of a deregulation of South Korea's national biomedical industry. For instance, the 2010 Regulation on Review and Authorization of Biological Products introduced directions for autologous cartilage and skin cell therapy that authorized marketing already before the submission of clinical data confirming therapeutic efficacy. It also redefined the notion of "orphan drugs." Orphan drugs are developed to treat rare medical conditions with government assistance. As it is hard to find enough participants in clinical studies for orphan diseases, guidelines for the development of orphan drugs are usually less prohibitive. By allowing less stringent conditions—for instance, by the substitution of exploratory studies for confirmatory studies—it was made easier to develop new medicinal products. Another policy document named the Number of Subjects for Clinical Studies Clause allowed a decrease in the number of required study subjects in clinical trials. The clause also introduced a fast-track review process for studies on life-threatening diseases, medical products for intractable diseases and medical products that could be effective in dealing with bioterrorism.

With these new, more permissive regulations, South Korea allowed research on a large number of stem cell products, many of which were developed by the company Chia-Bio. Despite initial caution, South Korea's research repertoire in regenerative medicine was extended to human embryonic stem cell research and now also includes iPS and other research based on embryos. Some Chinese and Japanese stem cell scientists whom I interviewed in 2013 openly expressed their envy of what they termed South Korea's "progressive" regulatory environment, which had enabled marketing approval for many new medicinal products. However, international experts strongly criticized South Korea's regulatory permissiveness.[2] South Korean companies like RNL (Revolution of Natural Life) have been the butt of criticism for setting up what are deemed rogue stem cell clinics and research facilities through international collaborations encouraged by South Korea's Bio-vision 2016.

CHINA

After President Bush's moratorium on federal funding for human embryonic stem cell research, American scientists threatened to take refuge in China to continue their work free from "prohibitive" ethical regulation. Western scruples about using fertilized human cells were thought to be absent in the East. Some Chinese scientists went along with this, claiming that "in the Confucian tradition, human beings achieve personhood only when they're able to participate in society."[3] Nevertheless, in January 2004, the Chinese Ministry of Science and Technology (MoST) adopted the new Ethics Guidelines for Human Embryonic Stem Cell Research, which explicitly forbade "human reproductive cloning" and only allowed human embryonic stem cell research within a period of fourteen days after fertilization or nucleus transfer. Furthermore, any trade in human gametes, fertilized eggs, embryos, and fetal tissues was explicitly prohibited. With these new guidelines in place, various universities experimenting with embryonic stem applications, such as Sun Yat-sen University, further built up their research capacity. Soon China covered all main areas of stem cell research, both at universities and in hospitals. In the ninth Five-Year Plan (1997–2001), stem cell research was supported by the government, and in the eleventh and twelfth Five-Year Plans (2007–16), the so-called 863 Program included funding sections for stem cell and tissue engineering and clinical application. The National Stem Cell Advisory Committee (established in 2011) aimed to create a favorable environment for promoting high-level training in the field of regenerative medicine and strengthening international collaborations.

Unfortunately, government regulations had only a limited effect. China became infamous for its international stem cell tourism with the company Beike Biotechnology as one of the best-known and most controversial therapy providers. This dubious reputation outraged many scientists in China, who pointed out that the government was spending considerable funding and efforts on bona fide regenerative medicine through its regulation and national science programs. However, only elite centers concentrated in major cities were expected to follow international regulatory standards that involved large investments into laboratories, equipment, institutions, and procedures. Many other laboratories lacked the capacity to do so, while local governments that had invested in local regenerative medicine projects favored rapid clinical application. Finally, in 2015, new draft regulation on clinical research and applications that involve human stem cells were issued, which clearly had adopted and adapted international guidelines, such as those that are currently valid in the United States and Europe. However, there were uncertainties around its implementation, partly owing to China's complex science infrastructure and partly as a result of the substantial capacity required for adequate oversight.

Even before the 2010s, especially in the main conglomerates, biotech parks had emerged and started to thrive, thanks to clearer rules about how to proceed. Here scientists forged ahead with stem cell processing, the production of new assays and laboratory experiments to satisfy the demand for stem cells, tests and knowledge needed for commercial clinical stem cell therapies. This development contributed to the gradual diminution of the difference between clinical studies of elite laboratories and those of private companies with their own links to hospitals and universities. Working together with hospitals that were willing to apply new therapeutic products to patients, scientists had little to lose and potentially much to gain. This is where ethical and research oversight remains patchy, and it explains—partly—why stem cell scientist Dr. He Jiankui was able to experiment with germline intervention on embryos, as he announced in November 2018.

JAPAN

Japan, a country often regarded as Western in terms of its scientific development, struggled to profile itself as a frontrunner in the life sciences until the twenty-first century. In the middle of its economic slump in the 1990s, the Japanese government launched the Millennium Project, which was designed to encourage innovation in science and technology. This project stressed the importance of the life sciences. In September 2001, Japan decided to allow the creation of human embryonic stem cell lines for stem cell research. In 2004, the Japanese Cabinet Office's Council for Science and Technology Policy voted to allow the use of human embryonic stem cells from aborted fetuses in clinical research. However, owing to bureaucratic delays, sociocultural issues around the regulation of egg donation and embryo creation, and the fear of scandal, the field of human embryonic stem cell research fell far behind the corresponding and much less controversial field of mouse stem cell research.

National euphoria followed Kazutoshi Takahashi and Shinya Yamanaka's discovery of induced pluripotent stem cells in October 2006 and its application to human iPS in 2007. The government promptly announced radical policy changes, including the creation of special disciplinary areas (*sūpā-tokku*), the expansion of IPR facilities, support for collaboration with industry, and a new funding policy prioritizing iPS, which caused complaints about the reallocation of funding from other fields of research. In addition, worries were expressed about hurrying from research to clinical applications and overly relying on regenerative medicine.

Nevertheless, inspired by regulatory advances in South Korea, even more far-reaching radical regulatory changes were subsequently announced. In 2011, three ministries collaborated in launching the Highway to the Realization of Regenerative Medicine project, which yielded several laws that facilitated the further development of regenerative medicine research. An amendment to the national Pharmaceutical Affairs Act introduced in 2014 created a new category of medicines ("regenerative medicine products") and a review pathway designed to accelerate product approval. The newly established National Institute of Health allowed that merely *conditionally* approved regenerative medicine products could be used for "evaluative treatment." These policies were expected to accelerate the application and commercialization of regenerative medicine, and of the induced pluripotent stem cells that had been discovered by Takahashi and Yamanaka in particular. In sum, the developments in regenerative medicine have been a major step in redefining notions of risk, ethics, and healthcare provision in Japan that have pushed important regulatory changes.

THE GLOBAL DYNAMICS OF SCIENTIFIC COMPETITION

The role of East Asia in science has recently become much more visible owing to major achievements in the field of regenerative medicine. This has impelled governments to embark on significant regulatory changes with global consequences. Ironically, such changes started with South Korea's regulatory reforms inspired by earlier US efforts to accelerate product development. After the debacle of Woo-Suk Hwang's human somatic cell nuclear transfer, South Korea's life science strategy aimed to restore the country's scientific reputation in the new field of human embryonic stem cell research. However, the acceleration of its system for medicinal product approval and a flurry of international clinical collaborations with "rogue" stem cell clinics in other countries aroused the indignation *and* the envy of scientists abroad. China's stem cell science community, while emulating Western regulations in order to keep up with international expectations, initially struggled to implement such stringent regulations because of funding issues, institutional cultures, and local developments. However, China has gradually adapted these regulations to its own conditions and is becoming a major international player in the field. Japan followed a different pathway, fearing that it would fail to be the first to take the Japanese discovery of iPS to clinical applications. A radical regulatory overhaul shook the world of regenerative medicine when Japan decoupled its regenerative medicine model from the traditional model of clinical trials, by allowing products to reach the market before they had been proved safe.

The rest of the world's stem cell industry responded. After the initial criticism of Japan's deregulation, Western regulators took their own measures. In

Europe, the European Medicinal Agency (EMA) adopted Safe and Timely Access to Medicines for Patients (STAMP, EU, 2015) and Accelerated Access Review (AAR, 2015). In the United States, political groups like the Heartland Institute, which advocate what they called "Free To Choose Medicine" (FTCM), lobby to deregulate regenerative medicine.[4] The Japanese Foundation for Innovative Regenerative Medicine (FIRM), a corporate industry group, signed a memorandum of understanding with the Alliance for Regenerative Medicine (ARM), a US-based lobbying organization in March 2015. This agreement enabled Japan to advertise its new regulations and the advantages of collaborations with Japanese enterprises, which led to a flurry of collaborations to start clinical trials in Japan. Furthermore, in the United States, lobby groups submitted the REGROW Act, which aimed to open the market to regenerative medicine products on completion of a phase II study rather than the usually required full clinical trial. The act was justified by arguing that Europe and Japan had outpaced the United States in modernizing their policies to grant patient access to safe cell therapies.

The notion that Western science can define the parameters of "good science" has gone. Former assumptions that Eastern countries necessarily would have to emulate august Western practices of knowledge production have become outdated. The practice of global science today clearly shows how science now is not merely coproduced but also co-defined by Asian countries. This, however, does not mean that such practices occur in an inclusive or systematic manner. Regulatory agencies and societies for stem science collaborate in redefining the rules of science in ways that are contingent on international economic, political, and scientific developments. Not just scientific knowledge but also the authority to define the internationally valid rules and regulations that frame and condition scientific production themselves have become subject to competition in the world of global science.

NOTES

I would like to thank coauthors, colleagues, and collaborators Nattaka Chaisinthop, Choonkey Chekar, Haidan Chen, Jessica Chang, Adrian Ely, Alex Faulkner, Carolyn Heitmeyer, Seyoung Hwang, Kazuto Kato, Masae Kato, Koji Kawakami, Marina Marouda, Prasanna Patra, Achim Rosemann, Doug Sipp, Yeyang Su, Suli Sui, Azumi Tsuge, and Xinqing Zhang, and I apologize to those whose work I have not been able to refer to by name and title here.
    1. Sleeboom-Faulkner et al. 2016.

2. Wohn 2012.
3. Mann 2003.
4. Sipp and Sleeboom-Faulkner 2019.

REFERENCES AND FURTHER READING

Mann, Charles C. 2003. "The First Cloning Superpower." *Wired Magazine,* January 1, 2003.

Sipp, Doug, and Margaret Sleeboom-Faulkner. 2019. "Downgrading Regulation in Regenerative Medicine." *Science* 365, no. 6454 (August): 644–46.

Sleeboom-Faulkner, Margaret, Choon Chekar, Alex Faulkner, Carolyn Heitmeyer, Marina Marouda, Achim Rosemann, Nattaka Chaisinthop, et al. 2016. "Comparing National Home-Keeping and the Regulation of Translational Stem Cell Applications: An International Perspective." *Social Science & Medicine* 153 (March): 240–49.

Sleeboom-Faulkner, Margaret. 2019. "Regulatory Brokerage: Competitive Advantage and Regulation in the Field of Regenerative Medicine." *Social Studies of Science* 49, no. 3 (June): 355–80.

Wohn, D. Yvette. 2012. "Korea Okays Stem Cell Therapies despite Limited Peer-Reviewed Data." *Nature Medicine* 18, no. 3 (June): 329–30.

TWELVE

A Concise History of Worlding Chinese Medicine

Mei Zhan

WHAT IS "TRADITIONAL CHINESE MEDICINE"? This question is directed at me time and again at academic conferences and colloquia, as well as in lay settings ranging from holiday gatherings to taxi rides. Having spent more than two decades in Shanghai and the San Francisco Bay Area conducting research on the translocal movements and transformations of Chinese medicine, I usually answer, "Well, it is not really 'traditional,' or 'Chinese,' or, for that matter, exactly the kind of 'medicine' that we commonly assume it is. It is so much *more* than all that."

What we have come to know as "traditional," "Chinese," and "medicine" was, and continues to be, a set of knowledges, practices, and worldviews constituted through translocal encounters and entanglements with modernity, materialism, science, and biomedicine. They conjure up particular visions and understandings of what constitutes our everyday worlds and our places in them, which I call the "worlding" of traditional Chinese medicine.[1] In what follows, I will focus, first, on how traditional Chinese medicine became professionalized and standardized as "Traditional Chinese Medicine" (TCM) through complex interactions with biomedicine. Second, I will look at how TCM was propagated as a type of preventive medicine for the rural poor of the developing world and has now been reinvented as a holistic medicine for the aspiring cosmopolitan middle class. Finally, I will turn to recent efforts in promoting "classical medicine" that suggest new possibilities in unpacking TCM and rethinking the reaches and goals of medicine and healthcare more broadly.

To begin with, historians and anthropologists have long argued that the emergence of traditional Chinese medicine as a profession took place around the turn of the twentieth century amid struggles with Western biomedicine. This was a time when traditional Chinese medicine was seen as an ambiguous symbol both of an enduring Chinese culture and national consciousness and of China's backwardness and humiliation at the hands of Western and Japanese powers.

As Western biomedical and bioscientific institutions began to take hold in Chinese cities, local practitioners of Chinese medicine began organizing themselves to set up small academies and clinics. They reexamined the philosophical and medical concepts of Chinese medicine through the prism of Western medicine and bioscience, and they petitioned the Nationalist government of the Republic of China (1912–49) to recognize the legitimacy and legality of this medical practice. During these encounters and entanglements, traditional Chinese medicine was reinterpreted as a medical practice grounded in *jingyan*, commonly translated as "experience" in the empiricist sense. Traditional Chinese medicine was thus remolded into a lesser science befitting the modernist empiricist position that became "so entrenched in Chinese medical language, it is difficult to imagine that for a long time Chinese people lived comfortably without it."[2]

In the decades following the founding of the People's Republic of China in 1949, traditional Chinese medicine, by then established as an experiential medicine, was institutionalized as a uniquely Chinese medical and scientific discipline—"TCM." Biomedical professionals collaborated with TCM practitioners in creating TCM institutions, compiling the basic theories of TCM and conducting laboratory and clinical TCM research. In Shanghai, for example, a group of biomedical practitioners was apprenticed to traditional herbal healers and acupuncturists. Some went on to play instrumental roles in founding and operating state-run TCM hospitals and colleges. The No. 11 Hospital, a biomedical hospital in Shanghai, was reorganized and renamed Shuguang Hospital of Traditional Chinese Medicine in 1954. In 1956, the Shanghai College of Traditional Chinese Medicine was established to promote "two-fisted Chinese medicine," which embraced biomedical concepts and techniques alongside TCM.[3]

At the same time, biomedical and TCM practitioners collaborated in compiling standardized textbooks, and especially in crafting a body of "basic theory" of TCM. Taking to heart Chairman Mao's call to elevate experience to the level of theory as part of Marxist-Maoist materialism, textbooks defined TCM as the dialectical cumulation and transformation of life-and-death struggles between the working class and nature. Within this conceptual and institutional framework, "unscientific" and "superstitious" practices—itinerant doctors and divination, for instance—were excluded from TCM, which by then mainly consisted of herbal medicine, acupuncture, and *tuina* (a form of therapeutic massage). At the same time, the holistic concept of *yinyang* was redefined as a theory of dialectics, whereas *wuxing* (commonly translated as "five elements," "five phases," or "five agents") was understood to be a rudimentary and empirical form of materialism.

ACUPUNCTURE IN AND OUT OF THE "PROLETARIAT WORLD"

Standardized TCM became an integral part of China's socialist healthcare system. In particular, "a bunch of needles, a handful of herbs, and a pair of hands"—a reference to acupuncture, herbal medicine, and tuina respectively—were implemented as part of the low-tech, low-cost, and mobile healthcare and socialist preventive medicine, particularly for China's poor among the large rural population. In the 1960s and 1970s, as China jostled with the United States and the Soviet Union in global politics, TCM, and especially acupuncture, became instrumental in China's efforts to position itself as the champion of a racialized proletariat world. China implemented infrastructure projects in developing countries in Africa, Southeast Asia, and Latin America. Although Chinese-built railways and dams tended to draw local suspicions and protests, medical teams were by and large welcomed in these developing countries.

Low-cost and low-tech acupuncture distinguished China's medical teams from those of the Soviet Union or the United States. Chinese newspapers in the 1970s routinely reported the success and even the "miracles" of Chinese medical teams in Africa, and one such report even stated, "*We* Blacks stick together."[4] In Zanzibar, acupuncture was so highly regarded that people with a bad temper were often told to take it to the Chinese because "they even have a cure for that."[5] In Mauritania, Chinese instructors trained the first native acupuncturist who exclaimed "Chinese acupuncture is particularly useful in our country, where there is a lack of doctors and medicine."[6] Today, as the Chinese government continues to send teams—albeit smaller ones than before and with less fanfare—Chinese entrepreneurs take the opportunity to set up and expand acupuncture and herbal clinics in African countries.[7]

A NEW "PREVENTIVE MEDICINE"

In July 1971, a few months before Richard Nixon's historic trip to China that led to the normalization of China-US relations and a bilateral relationship, the *New York Times* journalist James Reston visited Beijing. During his trip, Reston came down with acute appendicitis and had to undergo emergency surgery. After surgery, he was offered acupuncture as an option for postsurgery pain relief. Acupuncture, by then, was sometimes used as an analgesic technique in combination with biomedical surgeries in both TCM and biomedical hospitals in China. Reston chose acupuncture treatment, and he wrote a front-page article titled "Now, About My Operation in Peking," in which he gave a vivid account of his encounter with acupuncture that generated an acupuncture frenzy among the *New York Times*' readership and the larger scientific, medical, and lay communities in the United States. It is noteworthy that Reston's encounter took place at the Anti-Imperialism Hospital—founded as the Peking Union Medical College Hospital in the 1910s. One of the first biomedical hospitals, it had been supported by the likes of the Rockefeller Foundation and it had played a pivotal role in marginalizing traditional Chinese medicine. When the Anti-Imperialism Hospital became the site where TCM was launched into the American media and public interest in the 1970s, history came full circle.

As US-China relations became normalized, and as China entered the post-Mao reform period at the end of the 1970s, American biomedical professionals and acupuncturists, the latter of whom had mainly learned their trade outside mainland China, flocked to Chinese cities. On their arrival, they were shocked to see that, contrary to their preconceptions of a closed and isolated Communist China, there was already a world of Chinese hospitals with students and doctors from developing countries studying TCM. Some acupuncturists were also surprised by the fact that many ordinary Chinese, especially well-educated urbanites, were suspicious of herbal medicine and acupuncture, which they considered "backward" or even "unscientific."

Barbara Bernie, the founding president of the American Foundation of Traditional Chinese Medicine in San Francisco, told me that during her first trip to China she started offering acupuncture treatment to the local Chinese people who visited her at her hotel in order to convince them of its efficacy and legitimacy.

In the United States, acupuncture and herbal medicine spearheaded the legalization and mainstreaming of complementary and alternative medicines. They were and continue to be used for conditions where conventional biomedical treatments are less effective or ineffective. These include cancers and other terminal illnesses that cannot be resolved by surgery, chemotherapy, radiation, or other established biomedical therapies. Those who suffer from chronic illnesses—insomnia, pain, depression, fatigue, and so forth— or from mind-body illnesses that are difficult to diagnose as "diseases" increasingly turn to acupuncture, herbal medicine, and other "complementary and alternative" treatments. Today in the United States, TCM does not serve as an inexpensive form of preventive medicine for the poor rural population but as an alternative or supplement to biomedicine catering to the well-off and cosmopolitan middle class. When I was conducting fieldwork in the San Francisco Bay Area in the 1990s, on hearing about my project, many hip, local friends told me "you should interview my acupuncturist!"

The steady rise of acupuncture and herbal medicine in the United States also shaped the reinvention of traditional Chinese medicine as a new kind of preventive medicine for the aspiring middle class in China. In the 1990s, as China strove to "get on track with the world"—that is, with the developed rather than the developing countries—traditional Chinese medicine in China too came to be reinvented as a holistic, preventive medicine perfect for the body and mind. Entrepreneurially-minded herbal doctors and acupuncturists in Chinese metropolises such as Shanghai and Beijing have quickly caught on to this new trend in the worlding of traditional Chinese medicine. In everyday clinical practice and pedagogy, they purposefully promote traditional Chinese medicine as part and parcel of the cosmopolitan lifestyle of the aspiring urban middle class. Rather than targeting the rural poor, they treat "subhealth" conditions afflicting the urbanites—that is, a state of being not "healthy" yet not diagnosably "ill." In practice, subhealth conditions include a wide range of experiences such as pain syndromes, insomnia, fatigue (which continues to be linked to premature and sudden death among young, urban, white-collar Chinese), and, increasingly, allergies and other respiratory and heart syndromes that are likely the consequences of urban pollution. Getting on track with the world, to a certain extent, also means getting on track with middle-class experiences, including suffering from subhealth, for which traditional Chinese medicine may provide temporary relief if not a permanent cure. In China, just as much as in the United States before, the reinvention of traditional Chinese medicine as a holistic, preventive medicine is therefore an essential part of the production of middle-class worlds and lifestyles.

ACTIVATING THE CLASSIC

Today, "getting on track with the world" is no longer a mere aspiration. As my interlocutors in China tell me, "We have already gotten on track with the world." What this means for healthcare and medicine is profoundly ambiguous. To begin with, China started a series of reforms in the mid-1990s that aimed at transforming healthcare from a social good provided by the state to a service provided by the market. These reforms have resulted in, among other problems, drastically lower healthcare efficiency and worsening relations between the medical establishment and patients and their families. Violence against medical professionals—ranging from harassment to murder—has become all too common at hospitals and clinics. At the same time, the scramble for the market has also led to increased frictions between biomedicine and TCM, as debates over the legitimacy, efficacy, and ethics of traditional healing practices intensify. These frictions are not restricted to the medical or healthcare domain. The legitimacy of traditional Chinese medicine is a common topic of debate on Chinese social media platforms such as Weibo and Weixin. Some commentators have playfully suggested that a person's opinion on Chinese medicine should be used as a criterion in *xiangqin* (arranged dating) to quickly weed out unsuitable potential spouses.

One possibly unexpected outcome of these debates and conflicts is the emergence of an experimental movement to "bring medicine back to life." Spearheading these experiments are firms that promote a new kind of "classical" (*gudian*) or "ancient" (*gu*) Chinese medicine. First appearing in cosmopolitan China in the early 2010s, these small startups were propelled by the rise of social media, which enabled them to tap into otherwise unprofitable niche markets. They were funded by venture capital, or by investors and co-owners with previous entrepreneurial experience or capital earned in China's transnational market economy. The number of new firms has increased significantly after the Chinese leadership called for "mass entrepreneurship and innovation" at the World Economic Forum (WEF) in 2014, and subsequently made the development of a knowledge-based economy a centerpiece of the thirteenth Five-Year Plan.[8] Further, the new classical medicine, although it remains very loosely defined, self-consciously and strategically distinguishes itself from the secularized and scientized TCM taught and practiced at state-run colleges and hospitals, even though almost all these firms actually have some kind of connection to TCM institutions.

Through a wide range of online and offline pedagogical, clinical, commercial, and outreach activities, proponents and participants of classical Chinese medicine purposefully embrace practices that were marginalized by or excluded from TCM for having religious, spiritual, or superstitious connotations, as well as ideas that were redefined through the scientistic framework of Marxist-Maoist materialism. Suspicious of rationalism and scientism even while deeply enmeshed in it, they argue that classical Chinese medicine is in fact much larger than "medicine." It must be taken seriously as an immanent "way" or "method" (*dao* as in Daoism) for thoughtfully inhabiting modern worlds and lives. By critically rereading classical texts and learning self-healing concepts and techniques, those who embrace classical medicine strive to take medicine, health, and life back into their own hands. In doing so, they aspire to learn to live and even thrive in a precarious modern world full of contradictions.

The emergence of classical medicine is therefore by no means a simple effort to resurrect the ancient or to revive the religious. Part of this movement includes tapping into new trends in traditional Chinese medicine worldwide. Interestingly, acupuncturists from the United States, Canada, France, Britain, Japan, and other parts of the developed world are now brought into exchanges with practitioners in China. In some cases, former international students trained at TCM colleges in China come back to teach their Chinese colleagues and former teachers their interpretations of classical ideas, as well as new techniques that cultivate the "postmodern" body and mind. Instead of subscribing to the Marxist-Maoist materialist narrative that the relationship between humans and nature is one of continuous struggle and conquest, advocates and practitioners of classical medicine collectively articulate hopes for better –even if elusive—coexistence in a world of disharmony.

In sum, whether taking the form of institutionalized TCM or loosely clustered "classical medicine," the worlding of traditional Chinese medicine takes place *through* and *as* constantly shifting translocal projects and processes. Despite efforts to pin it down—as culture, science, tradition, or philosophy—traditional Chinese medicine remains alive and open to creative interpretations, experiments, and aspirations.

NOTES

1. Zhan 2009.
2. Lei, 2015, 334.
3. Zhan 2009.
4. Hutchison 1975, 179 (italics added).
5. Hutchison 1975, 222.
6. "Quanxin quanyi wei Maolitaniya renmin fuwu" [Serve the people of Mauritania]. *Renmin ribao*, February 10, 1970, 5.
7. Hsu 2008.
8. Chinese State Council 2016.

REFERENCES AND FURTHER READING

Andrews, Bridie. 2014. *The Making of Modern Chinese Medicine, 1850–1960*. Vancouver: University of British Columbia Press.

Barnes, Linda. 2005. *Needles, Herbs, Gods, and Ghosts: China, Healing, and the West to 1848*. Cambridge, MA: Harvard University Press.

Chinese Ministry of Science and Technology. 2016. *Zhongguo gongmin kexue suzhi jizhun* [Basic standards for the scientific quality of Chinese citizens]. Accessed May 31, 2019. http://www.most.gov.cn/mostinfo/xinxifenlei/fgzc/gfxwj/gfxwj2016/201604/t20160421_125270.html.

Farquhar, Judith. 1994. *Knowing Practice: The Clinical Encounter of Chinese Medicine*. Boulder, CO: Westview Press.

Hsu, Elisabeth. 2008. "Chinese Medicine as Business: Chinese medicine in Tanzania." In *China Returns to Africa: A Rising Power and A Continent Embrace*, edited by Chris Alden, Daniel Large, and Richardo Soares de Oliveira, 221–36. New York: Columbia University Press.

Hutchison, Alan. 1975. *China's African Revolution*. London: Hutchinson.

Lei, Sean Hsiang-lin. 2015. *Neither Donkey nor Horse: Medicine in the Struggle over China's Modernity*. Chicago: University of Chicago Press.

Scheid, Volker. 2002. *Chinese Medicine in Contemporary China: Plurality and Synthesis*. Durham, NC: Duke University Press.

Taylor, Kimberly. 2005. *Chinese Medicine in Early Communist China, 1945–1963: A Medicine of Revolution*. New York: RoutledgeCurzon.

Zhan, Mei. 2009. *Other-Worldly: Making Chinese Medicine through Transnational Frames*. Durham, NC: Duke University Press.

PART FOUR

East Asian Mobilities and Diversities

Frank N. Pieke

EVEN MORE THAN THE FLOWS of goods, finance, information, or data, the mobility of people is at the core of globalization and transnationalism. East Asia has historically been an important source of international migrants. While Japanese, Taiwanese and Korean migrants are concentrated mainly in the New World, over 40 million overseas Chinese (Chinese migrants and their descendants) are found all over the world, with the largest number still living in Southeast Asia. Despite having numerically the largest ethnic Chinese population by far, many countries in Southeast Asia have restricted or even completely banned further Chinese immigration, and in some cases such decisions were already made decades ago. Singapore, however, is deliberately growing its population through highly selective immigration schemes, predominantly from China. Elsewhere in Southeast Asia, Chinese investments, trade, and infrastructure buildup are supported by Chinese workers, entrepreneurs, and professionals, although it is unclear how many of these people will actually remain there.

The long and multilayered history of the Chinese in Southeast Asia is beautifully captured by Kwee Hui Kian in chapter 13, "Of Married Daughters and Caged Chickens: The History and Significations of Being 'Chinese' in Southeast Asia." It is often suggested that the term "overseas Chinese" is wrong because it implies an unchanging identity and a persistent focus on China, ignoring the acculturation and integration of the descendants of Chinese migrants into local societies. While this criticism of the term "overseas Chinese" may be true, Kwee shows that many Chinese descendants in fact do produce new meanings of being Chinese for themselves, continuing to link their life with China in the contemporary world. Despite—or perhaps because of—continued experiences of discrimination or persecution like during the 1998 anti-Chinese riots in Indonesia, many overseas Chinese remain proudly Chinese, thinking of China's rise and global power as a guarantee of their safety amid the often volatile societies of Southeast Asia.

East Asian emigration before the Second World War consisted mainly of indentured laborers, farmers, and workers who aspired to a better life, but since the 1960s East Asian migration has diversified and has increasingly come to include the middle classes and elite. Students, professionals, and entrepreneurs—first from Taiwan, South Korea, and Japan and, since the 1980s, in ever larger numbers from China—found their way initially to North America and later also to other parts of the world. These flows of people and growing diasporas gradually tie East Asian societies ever more strongly to the United States, becoming a major geostrategic force shaping the relationships between the United States and China, South Korea, Taiwan, Hong Kong, and Japan.

In chapter 14, "The Korean Diaspora in the United States," John Lie discusses the earliest beginnings of Korean migration to the United States against the background of Japanese colonialism and the expansion of American power in Northeast Asia at the end of the nineteenth century. However, mass emigration from Korea to the United States only started after the US Immigration and Naturalization Act of 1965 lifted the ban on Asian immigrants. While highly educated immigrants and adoptees were prevalent initially, in the 1980s students and people with a lower income or educational status started to make up the majority of immigrants. In the twenty-first century, the United States is not only a guarantor of South Korean geopolitical security but also a model for South Korea. South Koreans educated in the United States and Korean Americans have become important factors in South Korean business, trade, science and technology, and cultural life.

In chapter 15, "The Japanese Diaspora in the Americas and the Ethnic Return Migration of Japanese Americans," Takeyuki Gaku Tsuda scrutinizes the long-term diasporic connections between the United States and East Asia on the basis of his research on the Japanese in America, many of whom are now already fourth- or even fifth-generation descendants of the original immigrants. Japanese Americans have returned to Japan as students, professionals, and tourists. Their experiences vary considerably, depending on generational distance from the homeland. The volume and significance of ethnic return and the level of homeland immersion does not naturally decline across the generations in a unilinear manner. The most recent generations of Japanese Americans are highly assimilated. Increasingly valorizing their ethnic heritage and homeland, many have become more rather than less engaged with Japan than their parents or grandparents.

Outside Southeast Asia and North America smaller but growing communities of Chinese (including many ethnic Chinese from Southeast Asia) exist across Europe. The number of Chinese working or even settling in Latin America and especially in Africa is increasing very rapidly, in part because of the growing economic and political footprint of China on these continents. In chapter 16, "Chinese Labor Migrants in Asia and Africa," Miriam Driessen and Biao Xiang report that at the end of 2016 the number of Chinese workers sent overseas as part of contractual projects and labor cooperation agreements amounted to nearly one million. With strong echoes of the characteristics of nineteenth-century Chinese indentured coolie workers, many of whom were born in rural China or in a city to rural migrant parents, Chinese labor migrants in Asia and Africa are driven to create stable and secure lives in China rather than a better life abroad. Moving to new places and changing jobs frequently are a common experience. The Chinese reforms have freed Chinese from the fetters of state socialism, and the relentless effort to achieve social upward mobility has become the norm. Yet sustaining a middle-class lifestyle often requires spatial mobility, especially for those who come from a poor or rural background. Owing to the security provided by land rights back in China, rural citizens can take on the risks of migration. In addition, the expansion of social welfare in China provides another safety net.

New East Asian flows of people also include migration to other countries in East Asia. Japan currently has several hundred thousand Chinese students and "interns" (de facto short-term labor migrants); Chinese of Korean descent have become a distinctive community in South Korea, as have North Korean refugees. There are also reportedly hundreds of thousands of North Koreans in China, whom the government refuses to recognize as refugees or migrants and who continue to run the risk of involuntary repatriation. South Koreans and Taiwanese are the largest foreign communities in China. As Chinese "compatriots," the latter have almost the same rights as full citizens of the People's Republic of China.

A distinctive flow of East Asian long-term migrants are women emigrating for marriage to a richer area or country in East Asia. These include Vietnamese and Burmese women in China, Korean Chinese in South Korea, and Chinese in Taiwan. In chapter 17, "Uncertain Choices of Chinese- Foreign Children's Citizenship in the People's Republic of China," Elena Barabantseva, Caroline Grillot, and Michaela Pelican examine three different familial contexts in

China—namely, Chinese-Vietnamese, Chinese-Cameroonian, and Chinese-Russian families. The gendered, socioeconomic, and racial dimensions affecting Chinese-foreign families are implicated in how decisions about their children's nationality are made: are they Chinese or foreign? The citizenship of Chinese-foreign children is increasingly relevant because of their growing numbers, the effects of the household registration system, nationality and immigration laws, and wider debates on identity and belonging in China.

While children of mixed descent problematize a reading of the nation based on blood ties rather than legal citizenship, minority groups do so even more, especially if their transnational ties force us to look beyond the nation and national categories in the conceptualization of migration, ethnicity, and diaspora. Louisa Schein and Chia Youyee Vang, the authors of chapter 18, "From Hmong Versus Miao to the Making of Transnational Hmong/Miao Solidarity," analyze how Hmong (Miao) from Laos dispersed across the globe after the Vietnam War fashioned connections to homelands in Asia, overcoming barriers and distances shaped by the countries of residence and those of Hmong (Miao) origin in East and Southeast Asia. Hmong (Miao) have created transnational communities of belonging through what they call the "identity exchanges" that are part of familial, cultural, economic, religious, medical, and touristic encounters between Hmong (Miao) in disparate locations, including the Miao ancestral homelands in central and southern China. Over the last several decades, Hmong (Miao) have moved toward being less marginalized within the nation-states that they belong to and they have developed transnational communities comprising many distinct elements.

Transnationalism and diaspora that connect multiple locations and nation-states are even more charged when a group is suspected of political subversion of the nation or nations that they inhabit. The case of the Uyghurs in or from Xinjiang in China throws these issues into stark relief. In chapter 19, "An East Asian Nation without a State: Xinjiang and China's Non-Chinese," Ildikó Bellér-Hann shows that, following 9/11, the government presented Uyghur protests in Xinjiang and attacks against Chinese targets as a matter of international terrorism and a threat to China's territorial integrity and internal stability. Uyghur terrorism escalated even further in 2015 and 2016. The Chinese government responded with massive surveillance and repression, while at the same time continuing to invest heavily in the development and modernization of Xinjiang in the context of China's Belt and Road Initiative. Under pressure from China, transnational political and commercial activities of Uyghur communities in Central Asia have been restricted.

Nevertheless, the Uyghur diaspora in Europe, the United States, the Middle East, and Turkey has managed to internationalize the Xinjiang problem, even though it has still received relatively little official support. This situation only started to change in 2019 when first the United States and, later, the European countries stepped up their criticism of China's Uyghur "reeducation" camps as part of their generally tougher and more confrontational approach to China in the context of the US-China trade war and Europe's "systematic rivalry" with China.

THIRTEEN

Of Married Daughters and Caged Chickens

THE HISTORY AND SIGNIFICATIONS OF BEING "CHINESE" IN SOUTHEAST ASIA

Kwee Hui Kian

"IT'S EASY FOR YOU TO DISAVOW BEING CHINESE, much more difficult for me," Mr. Huang said, as he pondered over our discussion.[1] Born in a small town in West Kalimantan, Indonesia during the 1940s, Mr. Huang was recounting his experiences growing up and living in Pontianak. It wasn't easy to get him to talk about himself. We became acquainted in 2008 when I first visited the temple he helped to manage in the provincial city. Over the years I went to the temple several times and tried to chat with him, but he would remain reticent. It was only in mid-2018, when we met for the fourth time and after the recommendation of a close friend, that he decided that it was all right to share his thoughts on his life.

"I am now in my seventies. If the authorities want to lock me up for what I have said, that would not be for too long a time." Mr. Huang has remained circumspect and prudent for a large part of his adult life. When there was a ban against the use of Chinese languages in public arenas under the New Order of President Suharto (1966–98), he discreetly worked on developing his Chinese writing and reading skills, which were acquired during his few years of education at a Chinese primary school. Even after Suharto had fallen from power and the fourth Indonesian president, Abdurrahman Wahid, abolished all the discriminatory legislation against the Chinese, Mr. Huang did not immediately embrace the new freedom of cultural expression.

In my lifetime I have encountered many anti-Chinese incidents in Pontianak. In 1958, the president issued an order prohibiting people without Indonesian citizenship from trading in small towns and villages, and the lives of many Chinese were badly affected. During the anti-Communist suppression in

1965 and after, there were mass arrests of Chinese people who were indiscriminately regarded as Communist sympathizers. In 1998, the provincial governor implicitly encouraged people to loot shops and warehouses owned by the Chinese during the economic crisis. And even as recently as 2008, a dispute between a Chinese and a non-Chinese over a minor car accident turned into a riot and the destruction of many Chinese residences in the street of Gang Tujuhbelas.

It was only during the early 2010s that Mr. Huang decided that the political situation was sufficiently benign to start attending talks and seminars organized by the Chinese embassy and the Confucius Institute in Pontianak.

> "Chinese Indonesians are our married daughters"—that's what the Chinese ambassador said! I remember these words clearly. Do you know what this means? China is saying that if our daughters are bullied by their in-laws, we will not hesitate to step in.

My facial expression must have changed at that point because Mr. Huang suddenly stopped and asked me how I regarded China.

"I think people my age and younger probably see themselves as Singaporeans before being a Chinese. China is where our ancestors came from, but it's another country altogether," I said, choosing my words carefully.

"It's easy for you to disavow being Chinese, much more difficult for me . . ."

. . .

Mr. Huang's words have stuck in my memory. In recent years, experts in the fields of Sinophone literature, Chinese overseas migration, and diaspora have proposed that terms like "overseas Chinese," "Chinese diaspora," and "Chinese migrants" should be expunged as references to people of Chinese ancestry who were not born in China itself. These terms suggest an implicit and wrong assumption of an "unchanging" and "static" identity, and they fail to acknowledge that the people they supposedly describe have become acculturated to the local society, having created and embraced creolized and hybrid identities. Another objection often raised is that these terms also imply a Chinacentric disposition toward these subjects and disregard their positionality of being more "at home" outside China. A further criticism is that "China" should not necessarily be equated with the government of the

People's Republic of China. Some Chinese outside China (e.g., displaced people from Tibet or Falungong practitioners) might in fact engage in politics directed against the actions of the authorities in Beijing.[2]

Academic interventions that are seeking to unpack and deconstruct ethnicity and other forms of identification are most useful. They are important reminders that the meanings embedded in the term "Chinese"—whether used as a noun or an adjective—are not a given but are constantly changing depending on geographical location, time period, and historical context. But to suggest disregarding or terminating the term *Chinese* seems to be throwing out the baby with the bathwater.

When conducting fieldwork and interviews in Indonesia, Malaysia, and Singapore, I often encounter individuals like Mr. Huang who identify themselves as Chinese and who do so with pride. Indeed, many people close to Mr. Huang's age who have also have had some experiences studying in Chinese schools, the majority of which were established with private funds rather than funds from the colonial governments, often refer to themselves in Mandarin Chinese as *zhongguoren*—that is, as people of the Chinese nation.[3]

Mr. Huang's reflections and experiences show that the term *Chinese* is loaded and difficult to dismiss merely as an imagined identity imposed by academic observers or political interests. While the latter may be true, many subjects also produce new imaginations and meanings of being Chinese for themselves. Especially among the descendants of migrants from South China in Indonesia and other parts of Southeast Asia, many continue to link their fate with China in the contemporary world. This chapter builds on my conversations with Mr. Huang to present the history of these migrants and their descendants in Southeast Asia. It also discusses the ways in which different meanings of being Chinese have come to be attached to these descendants, and the implications of the varying signification for these subjects from the turn of the twentieth century to the present.

·   ·   ·

"We Chinese (*tenglang, tangren*) have traditions and values different from the Indonesians (*yinniren*)," Mr. Huang asserted at one point when he was telling me how his closest friends and associates were all ethnic Chinese. He grew up in a predominantly Chinese neighborhood in a province where about 10 percent of the population is ethnic Chinese.

As much as Mr. Huang may regard being Chinese as a truism, the migrants from South China and their Southeast Asian-born descendants have not always identified as Chinese, with their destinies being forever linked to China. Since the twelfth century, Chinese migrants have ventured to Southeast Asia, mainly for the sake of trade. Many settled down, married, and had children, and their descendants eventually blended with the local population. In order that the migrant settlers would become their subjects, local kings sometimes required them to convert their religions. In other cases, the acceptance of their status of subjects was sufficient. This usually entailed submitting tribute, performing statutory labor, or joining the king's military expeditions. Over time, the settlers and their descendants became indistinguishable from the native population and were known as Siamese, Javanese, Malays, and as other local identities. People who opted for a sojourning status were required to pay higher taxes; they were also eventually expected to return to their homeland. Even as the number of migrants increased to several thousand annually in many parts of Southeast Asia during the eighteenth century, such systems of absorption persisted.[4]

European companies and state enterprises started entering the Southeast Asian commercial scene in the sixteenth century, and they established their trade enclaves in Malacca, Manila, Batavia (today's Jakarta), and other regions. The way they regarded their subjects differed from the way in which the local kings had done this, however. Perceiving themselves as superior, they did not allow their Asian subjects to acquire European identities. Instead, the subject population had to keep a supposedly original identity, which broadly distinguished between "natives" and "nonnative Orientals," the latter meaning the migrants and traders hailing from the Middle East, South Asia, or China.[5]

The Dutch went to the greatest extreme in preserving the Chinese identity of their subjects in the Indonesian archipelago. Considering the Chinese as the most industrious and taxable population, the Dutch administration designed a revenue system specifically for the commercial, social, and entertainment activities of these migrants and their descendants. These included gambling, alcohol, opium consumption, pig slaughter, and sales, as well as those economic activities that were dominated by the Chinese—rice and tobacco trading in Central and East Java, gold mining in western Borneo (today's Kalimantan), and sugar milling in Batavia. Most importantly, a poll tax was levied on all Chinese males. Many of these tax policies were later copied by other European colonial regimes in Southeast Asia.[6]

Since intermarriages with local women were common before the twentieth century, as the migrants were predominantly male, the offspring of Chinese fathers might in principle have opted to enter into the "native" group and thus avoid paying taxes. To preempt this potential loss of revenue, the Dutch regime classified subjects of mixed race as *peranakan* and subsumed them under the "Chinese" category, regardless of what these subjects' own opinion on the matter might have been. In the course of the nineteenth century, the "Chinese" and "natives" were further molded into separate legal identities governed by distinct sets of criminal and civil laws.[7]

As the Dutch and other European colonial regimes further developed the rhetoric of their civilizing influences over the "natives" at the turn of the twentieth century, the category of "Chinese" became a dual metaphor. "Hardworking Chinese" featured as a whip for the "lazy natives"; at the same time, the Chinese, rather than the European colonizers, were presented as the real villains of the exploitation and impoverishment of the natives. In these colonial fairy tales, it was of course the sage and benevolent European regime that emerged as the protector of the oppressed natives.[8]

These narratives, no matter how carefully crafted, did not end cross-ethnic collaboration between the natives and the Chinese. In Mr. Huang's home province in West Kalimantan, a sworn brotherhood was forged between the Chinese and other local peoples to stage a rebellion against the Dutch government in 1914. The root of the grievance was a newly appointed resident (colonial official). Eager to demonstrate his effective administration, he increased local tax revenues by more than 60 percent and also demanded that all adult men perform statutory labor.[9]

· · ·

The revolt ended in the rebels' favor, with the dismissal of the resident and the abolition of compulsory labour. However, several developments had already been set in motion since the 1840s that would have long-term implications for ethnic relations in Southeast Asia and other parts of the world.

Firstly, the extent of emigration from South China increased to an unprecedented level during the global "age of migration"—from the 1840s to 1940s. From a net emigration of about three million during the early nineteenth century, the total number of departures stood at nineteen million during the late nineteenth and early twentieth centuries, with more than 85 percent leaving for Southeast Asian destinations.[10]

Furthermore, after the defeat during the First Opium War (1839–42), China no longer had the military strength to protect its existing wealth; nor did it have the technological capabilities to compete in the global political economy. The Qing authorities knew they needed to play catch-up fast, lest they lose even more sovereign rights to their Western European rivals. Gradually, they also turned their attention to the migrants from South China residing overseas. The Qing government had disdainfully regarded these people as "abandoned subjects" who had left the Middle Kingdom at their own behest. By the 1860s, it came to realize that these migrants, especially those who have lived for generations under European rule in Southeast Asia, might actually have the knowledge and capital that would help the ailing regime.

During the last decades of the nineteenth century, imperial agents were dispatched overseas to woo the migrants' support and possible investment in modern infrastructure and industries. In the Qing discourse, the migrants were now regarded as "patriotic Chinese." From 1909 on, Chinese nationality was offered to anyone "who had Chinese blood." Promises were made on this condition: Help China grow strong, and she will protect you in the international arena. This was particularly attractive to migrants facing intense discrimination in North America and other white settler colonies.

The migrant communities were urged to form commercial organizations and schools—the former to establish institutionalized economic links with the home regimes and the latter to cultivate new generations of patriotic Chinese. Limited as the Qing government's budget might have been, occasional displays of concern for the migrants were deemed necessary, and imperial naval steamships were dispatched to this clientele overseas to show that China was ready to protect their interests should trouble arise. The Qing successor regime, the Republic of China (1912–49), readily adopted similar narratives and measures, offering positions in military training facilities and universities in Guangzhou, Xiamen and other coastal cities for returning overseas Chinese youths.[11]

In other words, if the European colonizers were interested in the "Chinese" as useful economic animals and revenue providers, the Chinese authorities were essentially interested in similar things. The only difference is that the latter offered a modicum of recognition for the targeted audience—that is, as nationals with equal stake in a common future.

Indoctrination and inculcation of a China-oriented ideology at Chinese schools overseas also began to pay off. Although the Chinese state only gained the attention and investments of a limited elite group of merchants at the turn of the twentieth century, support grew rapidly and became overwhelming during the 1930s. With the Japanese aggression in 1937, thousands of idealistic youths from Southeast Asia departed for China to join the resistance efforts. Many more felt the connection of their fates with the fatherland when the Japanese troops invaded Southeast Asia, often singling out Chinese migrants and their descendants in punitive arrests and executions. Little wonder, then, that when China became one of the victors of the Second World War, Chinese people living overseas in Bangkok, Manila, and many other cities in Southeast Asia flew the Chinese flag, enthusiastically expressing a sense of nationalist pride.[12]

An abstract national signifier has thus become real. Ethnic identity, once fluid, has also been gradually solidified. Looking back, however, we can say that the timing could not have been more inopportune. It was also at this point in history that Southeast Asian nationalist efforts came to fruition. The Japanese invasion had fatally undermined the myth of European superiority. After the war, the anticolonial struggle in many countries turned militant when negotiations for independence failed. Nationalism in Southeast Asia often rested on the identity of the dominant group in the country or— and often even more damagingly—turned against a group considered to be from foreign stock: the Chinese. Even the loyalty of those ethnic Chinese who had taken up local citizenship became suspect.

To cap it all, the Cold War between the Soviet Union and the United States and their allies broke out after the Second World War. With China joining the Soviet camp when the Chinese Communist Party won the Chinese Civil War in 1949, the future became even more foreboding for the Southeast Asian Chinese. Already in a precarious political position, they also found themselves labeled a "fifth column"—potential stooges of Red China's ambition to export its revolution to other Asian countries and beyond.

. . .

It was during this momentous period in history that Mr. Huang came of age. Like most of his peers, he went to a Chinese school and started working after completing his primary education. Disaster struck in 1967, when he was arrested and imprisoned for several years because he was photographed accepting a trophy from the Baperki organization. This pro-Sukarno, left-leaning organization was among those persecuted by the New Order military regime that came into power after the attempted coup allegedly planned by the Indonesian Communist Party in September 1965.

Mr. Huang was neither a member of the organization nor did he participate in any of the learning cells, singing troupes, arts associations, farmers' groups, or workers' unions established by the Communist Party. An enthusiastic soccer player, he joined the team in his kampong and was made captain. His team took part in and won many competitions, including one that was organized by the Baperki. It was this moment that was caught on camera and used as proof of his alleged membership in Baperki, while in actual fact he was merely representing the team to accept the trophy.

This experience left an indelible imprint on his life. Through the decades, he was always on guard. I am struck by how he was able to focus on our conversation while constantly remaining watchful and aware of his surroundings, readily attending to people coming to the temple who require his advice and services. Moreover, he had learned to keep his opinions to himself.

"For a long time and even today I do not openly share my views and perspectives. Only with a few intimate friends, and only behind closed doors."

. . .

Across Southeast Asia, the political readjustments from the 1950s to 1970s caused major upheavals in many individual lives, especially among ethnic Chinese and even more so for those with Communist connections. In Singapore, the authorities arrested and imprisoned thousands of Chinese school students and workers involved in leftist demonstrations, sending their leaders into exile. Meanwhile, their counterpart in neighboring Malaysia successfully cut off food and other supplies to the Communist guerrilla fighters with the forced relocation of farmers in the hills to so-called "new villages." Most of the displaced people were ethnic Chinese. In the aftermath of the May 1969 race riots, pro-Malay constitutional regulations were widely implemented, relegating the ethnic Chinese and Indian Malaysians to the status of second-class citizens in Malaysia.

Martial law was also imposed at various times in the Philippines and Thailand in the name of combating Communist influences. To display to their American patrons that they were in control, the Thai military regime resorted to excessive violence during the July 1974 riots in Bangkok's Chinatown, which ended with dozens dead and over a hundred wounded. Even in socialist Vietnam, the ethnic Chinese were the first to bear the brunt when Vietnam signed a treaty of friendship with the Soviet Union and officially took their side against China in the late 1970s. Over a hundred thousand fled overland to Guangxi province in China and even more left by sea.

Indonesia saw the worst. In 1965 and 1966, the military regime killed more than five hundred thousand people with allegedly Communist connections. West Kalimantan escaped this ordeal only to face the expulsion of over one hundred thousand ethnic Chinese from the interior parts of the province between 1967 and 1972. During this period, the authorities realized that the Communists in both West Kalimantan and in Sarawak, the neighboring Malaysian state, were still active in the jungle, and they resorted to the extreme measure of uprooting all ethnic Chinese inhabitants living inland to cut off supplies to the guerrillas.

Unlike other postcolonial Southeast Asian countries, where education in Chinese languages was still allowed on the condition that the contents of the instruction be modified to suit the new national environment, the Suharto New Order regime instigated the public "erasure" of things Chinese. In addition to shutting down all Chinese-language schools and media, the regime also discouraged the use of the Chinese language and Chinese-sounding names as such, and it prohibited the open celebration of Chinese New Year and other festivals, as well as the import of materials bearing the Chinese script.[13]

During these troubling years, the Chinese authorities avoided intervening. After the end of the Chinese Civil War in 1949, the Nationalists on Taiwan and the Communists on the mainland continued to claim the allegiance of the overseas Chinese. This time, however, they distinguished between those who were Chinese nationals and those who were not—a process made somewhat easier now, since the ethnic Chinese in Southeast Asia had already been encouraged to take up local citizenship during the 1950s. However, the overseas Chinese policies of Nationalist and Communist China had little impact during the 1960s and 1970s, since Taiwan's resources were limited, on the one hand, and the mainland became mired in the domestic woes of the Great Leap Forward and the Cultural Revolution, on the other.

After Deng Xiaoping took over the Communist Party leadership in the late 1970s, China readily rekindled its connections with the Chinese overseas. Embarking on what it called "socialist modernization," the People's Republic invited them to partake in the project through investments, donations, or remittances. The lines between Chinese nationals (*huaqiao*) and ethnic Chinese (*huaren*) with no Chinese citizenship abroad were deliberately blurred, reminiscent of the turn-of-the-century Qing tactics. All Chinese people overseas—the majority of whom were in Southeast Asia—were called on for assistance based on their supposedly common descent, blood, and culture.

The Chinese state's efforts paid off. Between 1979 and 2000, the overseas Chinese contributed about 65 percent of foreign direct investment in China. China enjoyed a double-digit growth from 1978 to 2005, and it officially became the world's second largest economy in 2006.[14] From the late 1990s on, the newborn economic giant began to spread its wings abroad, and Southeast Asian countries, especially those to the immediate south of China in the greater Mekong subregion, were among the earliest to experience China's outbound investments. These ranged from small-scale retail trade and agricultural ventures to telecommunications, factories, and real estate, as well as to hydropower plants and high-speed rail construction, with the latter often being dominated by state-owned companies. In recent years, China's economic presence in Southeast Asia was taken up a notch when China launched its increasingly ambitious and comprehensive "Belt and Road Initiative."[15]

Alongside these "go global" economic endeavors, is the extension of China's soft power to boost its international image. In Asia alone, the Chinese state has established more than a hundred Confucius Institutes to date to facilitate Chinese cultural exchanges and to foster the learning of the Chinese language. In addition to projecting a positive image of China through the CCTV and Phoenix television networks, the Chinese bureaucracy and embassy have also provided informal advice in news stories related to China to friendly press and news agencies in Southeast Asia. The Chinese state offers assistance to private Chinese-language learning facilities and schools through the Overseas Chinese Affairs Bureau. This includes the dispatch of volunteer teachers, giving funds for renovating the premises, and also awarding scholarships and higher studies opportunities in China.

What the emergence of a strong and prosperous China might mean for Southeast Asians of Chinese descent is a subject of great sociopolitical interest, given their unpropitious fate during the latter half of the twentieth century. Recent events have signaled optimism in the domestic assessment and future prospects of ethnic Chinese in many countries. The government of Mahathir Mohamad, who was again elected as Malaysian prime minister in May 2018, is looking to revise the decades-long pro-Malay policies in favor of an ethnically blind award system for government contracts and scholarships, as well as for enrollment in state universities. In Thailand, since the late 2000s, the contestation between the Yellow Shirts and Red Shirts has seen the active participation of ethnic Chinese Thais on both sides. These protagonists not only profess deep Thai patriotism but they also openly assert their Chinese ancestry, neutralizing the image of apathetic and politically passive (read: disloyal) Thai Chinese.[16]

Many governments seem to realize that the retention of Chineseness—in whatever way the local Chinese define it—is not antithetical to their becoming loyal Southeast Asian citizens. However, there is a persisting precariousness in the position of the Chinese in Indonesia. Despite his effectiveness in fighting floods, reducing traffic jams, and combating bureaucratic corruption as the governor in the national capital, Basuki Tjahaja Purnama—known popularly as Ahok after his Chinese name—not only lost his bid for a second term in the 2017 Jakarta gubernatorial election but was also imprisoned for two years for allegedly insulting the Islamic religion. And although the current president of Indonesia, Joko Widodo, enjoyed a popularity margin of more than 60 percent after three years of presidency, claims that he is of Chinese descent, however false, are still made by his political rivals and even seemed to have a somewhat adverse effect on his popularity rating.

It is no wonder that Mr. Huang remains apprehensive about the future.

. . .

After prison time, Mr. Huang kept his head low, running a vegetable stall at a local market for a living. He improved his Chinese reading and writing skills and he now writes beautiful calligraphy, which he put to use in the temple where he is helping out. When his son fell in love with a girl of Javanese parentage, Mr. Huang went out of his way to end their relationship. Accompanied by his son, he visited the girl's family and announced that he would never agree to their relationship. He feels sorry about the whole situation. As a kind of compensation fee, he bought the girl's family a shophouse. "You may call me old-fashioned. But we are Chinese, our customs and values will never be the same as theirs."

Mr. Huang diligently keeps himself updated about the Indonesian sociopolitical situation. He cited Ahok's political debacle and sees little reason for optimism about the prospects of the ethnic Chinese in Indonesia.

Many government people are just anti-Chinese. Even though we are WNI (Indonesian citizens), Indonesian officials always treat us—these "pork-oiled faces"—as outsiders. We have to be in the know, otherwise we might get killed without being aware of the danger.

Mr. Huang's opinions might perhaps seem extreme, but they are not uncommon among Chinese Indonesians of his generation who have experienced unwarranted persecution. Many younger people, however, see themselves as both "Chinese" and "Indonesian." Acui, a Pontianak Chinese in his forties, felt inspired rather than disheartened by Ahok's experiences. After the downfall of Suharto, he became a political activist to pursue equal rights for Chinese Indonesians. Acui expresses much disdain for the "older generation," who are happy to maintain the status quo and take a back seat in Indonesian politics and the public sphere.[17] "Why," he asks, "should it be the case that non-Chinese Indonesians may enjoy full freedom of cultural and political expression but not us?" Since 2004, he has repeatedly run for the provincial and national legislative council elections. For him "Chinese" is a code word for resistance.

Jacobus, on the other hand, sees "Chinese" as a window on global opportunities. Born of mixed Dayak and Chinese parentage, he is married to a Chinese Indonesian. When I asked what languages their children speak, he told me Indonesian and English.[18]

"If they are interested in learning another language, I would rather they learn Chinese than Dayak."

"Why?"

"China is an economic powerhouse. If they learn Chinese, they will have access to wider horizons and bigger opportunities."

. . .

"But China did not do anything for the Chinese Indonesians—the government did not raise a word of protest when the anti-Chinese riots occurred in 1998," I pointed out, after mulling over what Mr. Huang had said about the ambassador's words—namely, that "Chinese Indonesians are our married daughters." His interpretation seemed too optimistic and his expectations of China's assistance too sanguine. I can't help but recall a traditional Chinese saying: "A married daughter is equivalent to discarded water" (*jiachuqu de nü'er shi pochuqu de shui*). She is of no concern to her parents anymore.

Leaving thousands of shops destroyed, over a thousand people dead, and more than 168 women raped, the May 1998 riots in Jakarta were the worst anti-Chinese violence in recent decades. However, much as the People's Republic of China has been eager to attract the transnational investments and donations of ethnic Chinese abroad on the basis of blood and cultural ties, it failed to condemn the Indonesian government, stating that it would not interfere in a "domestic affair."

"Yes, you may be right that China did not react during the 1998 crisis. But her economic rise is very important for us. At least these Yinniren have been more polite in the way they treat us. If China had remained weak and poor, they would not think twice about putting us down."

"If China is not strong today, we are merely chickens in the cage—waiting to be slaughtered."

NOTES

1. Interviews, June 29, 2018, and November 1, 2018. The name has been changed for privacy reasons.
2. Shih 2013; Ang 2001.
3. The conversations with Mr. Huang were conducted in a mixture of Mandarin and Teochiu Chinese and Indonesian.
4. Reid (1998) 2001.
5. Skinner (1996) 2001.
6. Kwee 2013.
7. Hoadley 1988.
8. Kwee 2000.
9. The 1981.
10. McKeown 2004.
11. Kwee 2000.
12. Wongsurawat 2016; Chu 2010, 281–332.
13. Heryanto 1998.
14. Barabantseva 2011, 108–37.
15. Nyiri and Tan 2017.
16. Tejapira 2009.
17. Interview, November 19, 2018.
18. Interviews, May 20, 2018 and August 18, 2018. The name has been changed for privacy reasons. The Dayaks are one of the three main ethnic groups in West Kalimantan.

REFERENCES AND FURTHER READING

Ang, Ien. 2001. *On Not Speaking Chinese*. London: Routledge.
Barabantseva, Elena. 2011. *Overseas Chinese, Ethnic Minorities and Nationalism*. London: Routledge.
Chu, Richard. 2010. *Chinese and Chinese Mestizos of Manila*. Leiden: Brill.

Heryanto, Ariel. 1988. "Ethnic Identities and Erasure: Chinese Indonesians in Public Culture." In *Southeast Asian Identities*, edited by Joel S. Kahn, 95–114. Singapore: Institute of Southeast Asian Studies.

Hoadley, Mason C. 1988. "Javanese, Peranakan, and Chinese Elites in Cirebon: Changing Ethnic Boundaries." *Journal of Asian Studies* 47, no. 3 (August): 503–17.

Kwee Hui Kian. 2000. "Enunciating 'Chineseness' in Late-Nineteenth and Early-Twentieth Century Singapore." Master's thesis, National University of Singapore.

——2013. "Chinese Economic Dominance in Southeast Asia: A *Longue Durée* Perspective." *Comparative Studies in Society and History* 55, no. 1 (January): 5–34.

McKeown, Adam. 2004. "Global Migration, 1846–1940." *Journal of World History* 15, no. 2 (June): 155–89.

Nyiri, Pal, and Danielle Tan. 2017. *Chinese Encounters in Southeast Asia*. London: Routledge.

Reid, Anthony. (1996) 2001. "Flows and Seepages in the Long-Term Chinese Interaction with Southeast Asia." In *Sojourners and Settlers: Histories of Southeast Asia and the Chinese*. edited by Anthony Reid and Kristine Alilunas-Rodgers, 15–50. Honolulu: University of Hawai'i Press.

Shih, Shu-mei. 2013. *Sinophone Studies*. New York: Columbia University Press.

Skinner, G. W. (1996) 2001. "Creolized Chinese Societies in Southeast Asia." In *Sojourners and Settlers: Histories of Southeast Asia and the Chinese*, edited by Anthony Reid and Kristine Alilunas-Rodgers, 51–93. Honolulu: University of Hawai'i Press.

Tejapira, Kasian. 2009. "The Misbehaving Jeks: The Evolving Regime of Thainess and Sino-Thai Challenges." *Asian Ethnicity* 10, no. 3 (November): 263–83.

The, Siauw Giap. 1981. "Rural Unrest in West Kalimantan: The Chinese Uprising in 1914." In *Leyden Studies in Sinology*, edited by W. L. Idema, 138–52. Leiden: Brill.

Wongsurawat, Wasana. 2016. "Beyond Jews of Orient: A New Interpretation of the Problematic Relationship between the Thai State and Its Ethnic Chinese Community." *Positions* 24, no. 2 (May): 555–82.

FOURTEEN

The Korean Diaspora in the United States

John Lie

WHEN DID KOREANS EMIGRATE TO THE UNITED STATES? Before we can answer that question, we need to first ask, when did Koreans become Koreans? Most contemporary Koreans, North and South and diasporic, have a ready answer: Koreans became Koreans with the birth of Dangun, the off-spring of Hwanung, the son of the "Lord of Heaven," Hwanin, and a bear that became a human female by dint of eating garlic and mugwort in the dark for a hundred days. The interspecies interaction is said to have spawned the first Korean in or about 2,333 BCE. The Dangun myth lies at the root of the oft-repeated claim of "five thousand years of Korean history" (never mind that the numbers add up to only 4,353 as of 2020). As Jeong Young-Hun of the Academy of Korean Studies in South Korea says, "Dangun is a basis for Koreans to feel the necessity for pursuing harmony and unification. . . . Dangun is a basis for seeing unification as something possible."[1] This magical, mythical thinking would unite all Koreans, North, South, and diasporic, past and present. Stories of origins, conveniently shrouded in the fog of the past, are not just stories but also tales that divide insiders from outsiders.

The fantastic genealogy from Dangun to contemporary Koreans faces the recalcitrant reality of intervening and inconvenient facts. There was not, for example, a consensus on what to call Dangun's descendants. The nominal absence runs right up to the present: North Korea in Korean is called Joseon; South Korea in Korean is called Han'guk (the country of Han). Joseon is a name of a dynasty; Han harks back to a Sinic toponym that was in principle applicable to three countries named Han in the Korean peninsula. To be sure, it would be difficult to deny the distinctiveness of the Korean polity during the five-century-long Joseon Dynasty (1392–1897). There was something of a proto-Korean sentiment among the Joseon elite, but there was nothing close to popular national identification for people living in the Korean peninsula as Korean people. Nominal confusion, national disintegration, and status division forestalled a sense of widespread Korean identification until the twentieth century.[2]

THE EMERGENCE OF KOREAN NATIONALISM

When and where did Korean popular nationalism emerge? In the late nineteenth century: Western- and Japanese-educated elites in the Korean diaspora invented the modern idea of Korean nationhood and peoplehood.[3] Given the pervasive Western belief in the concept of the nation-state (one nation, one people) and the apparent success of the idea in neighboring Japan, it should be not surprising that some ethnic Korean intellectuals, on their path from a Sinocentric to a Eurocentric (and Japanocentric) worldview, would embrace popular nationalism. Two of the first ethnic Koreans to be naturalized US citizens, Philip Jaisohn (Soh Jaipil) and Sin Chaeho, were extremely influential in planting the idea of modern nationhood in educated fellow Koreans. Although Jaisohn's nationalism did not preclude him from marrying an American woman or settling in the United States, he was not only the first naturalized US citizen of Korean origin; he was also the first ethnic Korean to write a work of fiction in English; loosely based on his life, it is called *Hansu's Journey*.[4] Ironically, US journalistic accounts often referred to him as Japanese (this was technically correct, as Korea was part of Japan at the time).[5] His daughter, in turn, was not only of mixed ancestry but also eloped with a white American; therefore, the first US-born Korean American was not only reported to be of Japanese ancestry but has also been lost to history.

During Japanese colonial rule (1910–45), diasporic Koreans waged much of their anticolonial, independent struggles outside the Korean peninsula. After the Second World War and the end of Japanese rule, South Korea was led by Syngman Rhee, who had spent three decades in the United States, and North Korea was ruled by Kim Il-sung, who had engaged in guerilla struggles against the Japanese in Manchuria. Again, Korean nationalism was born and nurtured by Koreans living outside the Korean peninsula. These diasporic struggles, however, would be elided in the nationalist historiography in both North and South Korea and replaced by the bizarre tale of bestiality called the Dangun myth discussed above or by an account of Kim's semisacred birth in the same place as Dangun.

If it is unavoidable that countercolonial struggles had to be waged beyond the Korean peninsula, ruled as it was by the Japanese, why did ethnic Koreans, such as Jaisohn, Sin, or Rhee, seek their education and even livelihood specifically in the United States? After the decline and collapse of the Qing Dynasty, which ended the long Korean subservience to a series of Chinese dynasties and classical Chinese culture in the late nineteenth century, there were two potential lodestars for ambitious Koreans. Japan was to dominate Korean life in the first half of the twentieth century, and many ethnic Koreans ended up in the Japanese archipelago, numbering well over two million by the early 1940s.[6] Yet Japan, as the colonial ruler in Korea, repelled as much as it attracted. Another power that was a major presence in the Korean peninsula by the late nineteenth century, the United States, had no such baggage. The protagonist in Younghill Kang's autobiographical novel *The Grass Roof*, which was published in 1931, describes his teacher as follows: "What glamour he cast over the great colleges in America. . . . He made me see that the road of a scholar's future prominence lay toward America."[7] Such stories of America as the land of promise and plenty would reverberate in the Korean peninsula.

The self-proclaimed idealism and innocence of the United States belie its expansionist and imperialist reality. In Northeast Asia, the United States made its mark early, concluding in succession the 1844 Treaty of Wanghia, the 1854 Convention of Kanagawa, and the 1882 Treaty (a.k.a. Shufeldt Treaty) with China, Japan, and Korea, respectively, and opening these countries to US trade and missionary work. US missionaries and businesspeople roamed the Korean countryside; the cross, the flag, and the dollar worked in intimately intertwined fashion. It is therefore not surprising that the first Koreans to venture to the United States, being the recipients of these blessings of Western modernity, were themselves educated and often Christian. The first organized Korean emigration to the United States—a unified venture of Christian missionaries and sugar and pineapple plantation owners—occurred between 1903 and 1905. It ensconced about seven thousand Koreans in the then US territory of Hawaii. Educated and Christian though they may have been, they found themselves toiling in sugar and pineapple plantations as low-waged field hands.

GROWTH AFTER THE SECOND WORLD WAR

The Korean population in the United States did not exceed two thousand until the end of the Second World War. Why weren't there more Koreans like Rhee who would fight for Korean independence in the land of the free and the home of the brave?

Chain migration is an oft-deployed concept in migration studies: Initial settlers spread the word and bring their relations and friends to the new land of promise and plenty. In the case of ethnic Koreans in the first half of the twentieth century, however, the United States was not only distant; there was also a ready alternative—namely, the relatively affluent and nearby Japan. But there is more: the United States remained inhospitable and largely closed to Japanese subjects, as Koreans were then considered to be, owing to the 1907 Gentlemen's Agreement, which effectively ended Japanese emigration to the United States. Furthermore, the 1924 Immigration Act, including the ethnoracial Asian Exclusion Act, turned the spigot of the movement of Asians to the United States to a trickle.[8] Those who dwelled in the United States also suffered. Mary Paik Lee arrived in Hawaii in 1905 with her Christian minister father who started work on a sugar plantation. She faced considerable prejudice and discrimination: "Orientals were told at the door that they were not welcome" at barber shops, theaters, and churches, and by the end of her life she attended a black church, "because it is there [that] I feel most comfortable."[9]

MASSIVE GROWTH

When did ethnic Koreans come to the United States in large numbers? Shaped by the US Civil Rights Movement and antiracist sentiments and activities, the 1965 Hart-Cellar Act lifted the systematic disadvantage that Asians faced in order to enter the United States. By 1970, the number of ethnic Koreans had reached nearly seventy thousand, and the growth thereafter was explosive: 350,000 by 1980 and 800,000 by 1990. The 2010 US Census counted roughly 1.7 million Korean Americans; by 2020, some estimates exceeded 2.5 million.

Needless to say, the 1965 opening of the metaphorical gate to the United States was neither total nor unfettered. Entry depended in part on chain migration in the form of family unification. Family in the United States included not only the small population of prior immigrants but also more recent arrivals, most importantly those associated with the US military, especially South Korean wives of American GIs. Yet Koreans often scorned them, sometimes because of Korean racist prejudice against intermarriage and people of mixed-race ancestry. For example, the South Korean mother of Hines

Ward, a celebrated American football player, recalls that, when she and her son visited South Korea, "even Korean people who looked educated spat when we walked by," presumably because of Ward's African American ancestry.[10] Korean adoptees—in total one hundred thousand in the post-Second World War period –constituted another significant slice of Korean emigration to the United States in the 1950s and 1960s. Like Hines Ward, adoptees also faced considerable discrimination when returning to South Korea.[11]

By the 1970s, highly educated and skilled South Koreans became more numerous: medical doctors, professors, and businesspeople. One of the more striking statistics of the movement of South Koreans to the United States is that half the medical school graduates of Seoul National University—for long one of only two medical schools in South Korea and one of the most prestigious universities in South Korea— between 1952 and 1985 was in the United States by the late 1980s.[12]

It is not surprising that the United States, which, like many societies, faces a chronic shortage of physicians, especially those who are willing to work in the countryside, welcomes qualified medical doctors. But why were South Korean physicians apparently so eager to abandon lives of relative privilege and prestige in South Korea? The key word is *relative*; in the 1870s and 1980s, South Korea to most South Koreans was not only materially impoverished but also politically unpalatable and extremely insecure.[13] The destructive Korean War (1950–53) was indelibly etched onto many Koreans' memories. As the war did not end with an official armistice between North and South, the pervasive sense of insecurity was never erased in subsequent decades: the specter of another and perhaps even more destructive war always remained.

Politically, Rhee was widely seen as not only corrupt but also authoritarian. He was replaced by military strongman Park Chung-hee after the 1960 student revolution, which was itself followed by the 1961 military coup. As for the state of the economy at that time, suffice it to say that per capita South Korea's GDP was lower than that of some Sub-Saharan Africa countries. When ethnic Koreans in Japan sought to return to the Korean peninsula in the late 1950s and early 1960s, most believed that North rather than South Korea was the more progressive and prosperous place to go to. This was not a delusion born of a misguided political ideology: the CIA itself estimated that the South Korean economy started to supersede that of North Korea beginning only in the early 1970s.

In contrast to the sorry state of South Korea, the United States was nothing short of a promised land. Not only had it triumphed in the Second World

War, defeating the colonial power Japan in the process, but it was also widely believed to have saved South Korea from defeat and ruin in the Korean War. American Gis, who still remained a visible presence in Seoul and throughout South Korea, seemed physically strong and materially well-off, dispensing the blessings of US material culture, such as Coke or Hershey's, on South Korean children. When South Koreans could only dream of a morsel of meat, Americans were believed to be downing one huge steak after another.

The extent of many South Korean elites' lack of faith in the future of South Korea and the corresponding trust they placed in the United States can be gleaned from the surprising absence of Korean-language retention among their offspring. Assimilation was the goal.[14] South Korean immigrants to the United States between the 1950s and 1970s and beyond were eager to enter and be part of the imperial core.

THE AMERICAN DREAM AND ITS DISCONTENTS

Did the Korean diaspora in the United States live up to the immigrants' hopes from the American Dream? Both Korean Americans and Americans in general often touted the spectacular achievements of Korean Americans, and this good news traveled back to the homeland. Yet there are also reasons to be skeptical of the triumphalist account of the Korean diaspora in the United States. In spite of their presumed economic and educational achievements, Korean Americans don't do much better than the American average in terms of either per capita income or years of schooling. Just as Mary Paik Lee's minister father became a plantation worker in Hawaii, many first-generation Korean immigrants, though often highly educated, found themselves operating a small grocery store or laundry shop. Not surprisingly, there is also a generational rift between parents with inadequate English and their assimilated, native-English-speaking children. As the protagonist of Chang-Rae Lee's novel, *Native Speaker*, puts it: "What belief did I ever hold in my father, whose daily life I so often ridiculed and looked upon with such abject shame?"[15] Furthermore, there are subjective accounts that suggest that the immigrants often faced lives of hardship, whether from ethnoracial discrimination or the general difficulties of life in the United States. The 1992 Los Angeles riots, during which Korean American shopkeepers were often condemned as racist and exploitative, cast serious doubt on the triumphalist narrative. It is not surprising, then, that a sizable number of Korean

Americans began to seek opportunities in the South Korea that their parents had left behind. Steven Yeun, one of the first Korean American actors to received widespread recognition in the United States, observes: "It's been like, 'Here's what an Asian person looks like to a majority white audience.'... But if you go to [South] Korea, the characters are just humans because they're not thinking about it like that."

In 2020 it continues to be difficult to name an entrepreneur of note, a singer of general renown, or a cultural figure of widespread repute among Korean Americans. To be sure, it is not that there aren't successful Korean Americans. The contrast with the Korean diaspora in Japan is especially stark, despite the discrimination, hardship, and struggle they have had to face. Yet Son Masayoshi remains perhaps the best-known entrepreneur in contemporary Japan, while there are numerous ethnic Korean popular singers and Kang Sangjung is probably the representative intellectual in Japan. My point is not to tout the superiority of Korean-Japanese achievements, but rather to question the widespread belief in the successes of Korean Americans. The United States is far from the land of ethnoracial equality. Korean Americans, along with other Asian Americans, face a glass, or the so-called bamboo, ceiling that blocks their upward mobility; they often even feel that they remain aliens and foreigners.

Why, then, do South Koreans continue to come to the United States? Since the 1980s, the corporate or professional elites no longer come in large numbers. Rather, people with lower income and educational attainment are an increasing proportion of new immigrants, together with Korean students seeking high school, college, or postgraduate education in the United States (as is discussed in more detail in chapter 10 by Adrienne Lo and Leejin Choi of this book).[16] As the oft-repeated mantra among South Korean youths about "Hell Joseon" puts it, South Korea, despite its newfound wealth and democratic politics, is a country replete with problems—from the undue pressures to succeed in school examinations to the dearth of well-paying jobs with suitable working conditions. The United States remains an escape valve of sorts, whether for those who would opt out of the educational rat race or find greener pastures to avoid environmental pollution or gender discrimination.

Korean Americans can be found in all fifty states, but they are concentrated above all in Los Angeles, New York, and other large cities. The estimated population in 2020 runs as high as 2.5 million, though the 2010 census registered roughly 1.8 million. The first generation, which was born in South Korea, still holds numerical majority, and the occupations most associated with them are dry cleaners and greengrocers, though there is great occupational diversity. Given the preponderance of first-generation Korean Americans, they tend to retain Korean language fluency and other cultural attributes, perhaps most obviously in their attachment to Korean food. Another notable feature is the extremely high percentage of Christians (as high as 80 percent).

KOREAN AMERICANS, KOREAN DIASPORA, AND SOUTH KOREA

Is the movement to the United States a one-way street? Have Korean Americans had an impact on South Korea? A transnational movement of people, commodities, and ideas exists not only between South Korea and the United States but also around the world. Moreover, diasporic Koreans do not simply stay in one place or move along simple, unidirectional routes. Tens of thousands of South Koreans who emigrated to Brazil or Argentina subsequently moved on and ended up elsewhere, including in the United States. Those who went to the United States, in turn, have often returned to South Korea.

One decisive transformation of South Korea in the past three decades is its greater orientation toward the United States. Although the United States has been the most important foreign power for South Korea since its founding, the impact of Japanese influence was profound well into the 1980s. Indeed, it is difficult to understand the nature and direction of South Korean industrialization in the 1960s and 1970s without appreciating the pervasive role of ethnic Koreans in Japan. Since the beginning of the twenty-first century, however, Japanese influence has been in steady decline, replaced not only by South Koreans educated in the United States but also by Korean Americans. This is true not only in matters of business and trade or science and engineering but also in terms of cultural life. From movies and television shows, to popular music and fine cuisine, the impact of Korean Americans is profound. Indeed, we cannot appreciate the rise of K-pop, for example, without taking into account the significant role of Korean Americans in particular and that of the United States in general (for more on this, see Jung-Sun Park's chapter 7 in this volume).[17]

The Korean diaspora in the United States is part of the worldwide Korean diaspora. However, because the United States is not only a guarantor of South Korean geopolitical security but also a model for most things, Korean Americans remain US-centric and relatively unaware of other diasporic populations. South Korea's recent turn to China may augur a distinct trajectory for the Korean diaspora in the United States—just as much as Koreans once turned away from China to Japan and then to the United States—but that possibility remains mere conjecture at this point.

NOTES

1. Josh Smith and Jeongmin Kim, "North Korea's Box of Bones: A Mythical King and the Dream of Korean Unification," Reuters, October 20, 2018, https://www.reuters.com/article/us-northkorea-southkorea-unification-myt/north-koreas-box-of-bones-a-mythical-king-and-the-dream-of-korean-unification-idUSKCN1MV022.

2. See Lie, forthcoming.

3. Lie 2017.

4. Jaisohn 1922.

5. See, e.g., *Washington Post*, February 3, 1915, 3. See also Mark E. Dixon, "Making a Difference from a Distance," *Mainline Today*, August 25, 2014, http://www.mainlinetoday.com/Main-Line-Today/September-2014/Making-a-Difference-From-a-Distance/.

6. See Lie 2008.

7. Kang 1931, 182.

8. See Abelmann and Lie 1995, 49–84.

9. Lee 1990, 105, 130.

10. "Hines Ward's Mother Recalls Hard Road to Success," *Chosun Ilbo*, February 8, 2006, http://english.chosun.com/site/data/html_dir/2006/02/08/2006020861017.html.

11. On the adoptees, see Kim 2010. On South Koreans and race, see Kim 2008.

12. Shin and Chang 1988.

13. See Lie 1998.

14. Abelmann and Lie, 1995, 49–84, 148–83.

15. Lee 1995, 53.

16. See Lo and Choi, chapter 10 of this volume.

17. See Park, chapter 7 of this volume; Lie 2015.

REFERENCES AND FURTHER READING

Abelmann, Nancy, and John Lie. 1995. *Blue Dreams*. Cambridge, MA: Harvard University Press.

Jaisohn, Philip. 1922. *Hansu's Journey*. Philadelphia: Philip Jaisohn.

Kang, Younghill Kang. 1931. *The Grass Roof.* New York: Scribner.

Kim, Nadia Y. 2008. *Imperial Citizens*. Stanford, CA: Stanford University Press.

Kim, Elena J. Kim. 2010. *Adopted Territory*. Durham, NC: Duke University Press.

Lee, Mary Paik. 1990. *Quiet Odyssey*. Seattle: University of Washington Press.

Lee, Chang-Rae. 1995. *Native Speaker*. New York: Riverhead Books.

Lie, John. 1998. *Han Unbound*. Stanford, CA: Stanford University Press.

————. 2008. *Zainichi (Koreans in Japan)*. Berkeley: University of California Press.

————. 2015. *K-pop*. Berkeley: University of California Press.

————. 2017. "Korean Diaspora and Diasporic Nationalism." In *The Routledge Handbook of Korean Culture and Society*, edited by Youna Kim, 245–54. Abingdon: Routledge.

————. Forthcoming. Introduction to *A Critical Companion to South Korean Culture and Society*, edited by Theodore Jun Yoo. Berkeley: Institute of East Asian Studies, University of California, Berkeley.

Shin, Eui Hang, and Kyung-Sup Chang. 1988. "Peripherization of Immigrant Professionals: Korean Physicians in the United States." *International Migration Review* 22, no. 4 (December): 609–26.

FIFTEEN

The Japanese Diaspora in the Americas and the Ethnic Return Migration of Japanese Americans

Takeyuki Gaku Tsuda

THE JAPANESE DIASPORA CONSISTS OF various communities of Japanese descendants (known as *Nikkei* or *Nikkeijin*), which are scattered primarily throughout the Americas. Substantial Japanese emigration from Japan to the Americas started in the 1880s, initially to North America (mainly the United States but also Canada) and lasted for several decades. Immigration to Latin America began in the early 1900s (predominantly to Brazil, but also to other South and Central American countries) and continued into the 1960s. Many of these immigrants were from Japan's rural areas, which were suffering from overpopulation and economic difficulties, and they went to the Americas to fill labor shortages as agricultural workers.

Beginning in the late 1960s, Japanese again began emigrating from a now economically prosperous Japan as businessmen, professionals, and students. They initially went to the United States and Europe, but more recently have also started migrating to other countries around the world. However, the post-1960s emigration of highly skilled Japanese has been relatively limited compared to emigration from other East Asian countries, and a majority of them reside abroad only temporarily. Currently, the two largest communities in the Japanese diaspora consist of Japanese Brazilians and Japanese Americans, although there are much smaller Nikkei communities in Canada, China, Peru, and Argentina, among other countries.

In recent decades, there has been a significant amount of return migration of Nikkeijin in the Japanese diaspora to the ancestral homeland of Japan. This ethnic return migration primarily consists of Japanese Brazilians (as well as much smaller numbers of Nikkei from other South American countries). They started to migrate to Japan in the late 1980s, mainly as unskilled factory workers in response to an economic crisis in Brazil and a severe labor shortage in a booming Japanese economy. However, despite being initially welcomed by the Japanese government as coethnic descendants, the Japanese Brazilians have been ethnically excluded in Japan and treated as foreigners because of their Brazilian cultural differences. As a result, they have become a socioeconomically marginalized and alienated ethnic minority in their ancestral homeland.[1]

In addition, there is also a much smaller number of ethnically Japanese American return migrants to Japan. They do not have strong economic incentives to migrate to Japan, and they return mainly as students, business personnel, highly skilled professionals, or tourists. Among the fifty-five Japanese Americans in my research sample, only twenty-two had visited Japan at some point in their lives. Most of them had been brief sojourners in the country, and only about one-fifth of them had lived there for more than a few months.

JAPANESE AMERICANS AND ETHNIC RETURN MIGRATION

Japanese Americans are one of the oldest Asian American groups in the United States. Although most Asian Americans are primarily the product of the mass Asian immigration to the United States after 1965, much of Japanese immigration occurred between the 1880s and 1924, when the United States prohibited further Asian immigration until after the Second World War. As a result, the "Japanese diaspora" is now becoming older and mainly consists of Japanese descent Nikkeijin of the second, third, and fourth generations. The population of elderly second-generation Japanese Americans, who were interned in concentration camps during the Second World War, has dwindled. After the war, their descendants and the modest number of more recent immigrants from Japan did not experience as much racial discrimination and have grown up in a bilingual and bicultural environment in an era of multiculturalism and greater ethnic tolerance.

This chapter will examine differences in the ethnic return migration experiences of Japanese Americans in Japan from the second to the fourth generations. Generational differences are especially important for diasporic return migrants, such as Japanese Americans, who have been living outside their ethnic homeland for well over a century. As a result, there is considerable internal generational diversity within this ethnic group, whose members range from bicultural second-generation Japanese Americans to those of the fourth generation, who have become completely assimilated to American culture.

In the case of the Japanese Americans, I found that the degree of ethnic return and the level of homeland immersion do not naturally decline across the generations in a unilinear manner because of increasing cultural assimilation and social incorporation into mainstream American society. Instead of following such a predictable pattern, the level of homeland engagement and its impact on the ethnic identity of different generations of Japanese Americans is much more complicated and contingent, and it also depends on their specific historical and contemporary ethnic experiences.

PREWAR SECOND GENERATION: RELATIVE DISENGAGEMENT

Japanese Americans of the prewar second generation (called *nisei*) are descendants of Japanese who immigrated to the United States before the Second World War. Although they are only one generation removed from Japan, they are relatively disengaged from their ethnic homeland. Since the prewar nisei grew up during the 1930s and 1940s, they experienced considerable discrimination because of American hostility toward Japan and Japanese Americans; many were interned in concentration camps during the war. As a result, many of them eventually distanced themselves from their Japanese heritage, assimilated to American society, and emphasized their national identity and loyalty as Americans.[2]

The elderly second generation nisei I interviewed continue to be influenced by these formative youth experiences; as a result, they have not developed transnational ties to Japan or a stronger affiliation with their ethnic heritage later in their lives. Although most of them have actually visited Japan, they went as tourists. Their short trips neither had much impact on their ethnic consciousness nor increased their connection to their ancestral heritage. "It was just like being a tourist in a foreign country," Jim Sakura explained. "I just went to see another country, how other people live. I didn't feel like I was connecting to my roots or anything. No, nothing of that sort."

In general, the prewar nisei enjoyed their vacations in Japan, had a wonderful time touring different parts of the country, and were treated well by the Japanese with whom they interacted. However, because these trips to Japan were brief, one-time visits, and their experiences in the country were rather superficial, they did not develop a greater transnational identification with Japan. Instead, they experienced their ethnic homeland as essentially a foreign country.

"It was great to reconnect with my relatives and see photos of my grandparents. I felt like I went back to my roots," Mike Oshima recalled. "But it didn't make me feel more Japanese or anything. I'm really a clueless foreigner in Japan. It actually reinforced in my mind that I'm an American of Japanese descent."

THE POSTWAR SECOND GENERATION: AT HOME
IN THE ETHNIC HOMELAND

The descendants of Japanese immigrants who arrived in the United States after the 1960s, or *shin-nisei* (the "new" second generation) as they are known, are generally still young. Like the prewar nisei, they are second-generation immigrants; but they are nevertheless members of a completely different generation. They came of age primarily after the 1980s and 1990s, and they grew up in a much more ethnically diverse, pro-Japanese, and globalized environment. As a result, they have retained their Japanese cultural heritage to a much greater extent than the prewar nisei, and their ethnicity and identities are bicultural and transnational.

Compared to their prewar, second-generation predecessors, the postwar shin-nisei have much more sustained and significant transnational engagements with their ethnic homeland of Japan. Their transnationalism has been inherited from their immigrant parents, who have taken them to Japan on numerous occasions. However, they have also sustained their transnational lives on their own and some have lived in the country as ethnic return migrants for extended periods for personal, educational, or professional reasons. In addition, because they are fully bilingual and bicultural, their level of interaction and engagement with the Japanese in Japan runs deeper than the older Japanese Americans.

In general, these shin-nisei have quite positive experiences in their ethnic homeland. They report that their cultural adaptation to Japan is quite smooth, and they feel comfortable living there. For the shin-nisei, Japan was never truly a foreign country, and they are able to sufficiently speak and "act Japanese" to the point where they have little trouble being socially accepted. As a result, they feel very much "at home" in their ethnic homeland. My interviewees also generally felt that Americans are well-regarded in Japan.[3]

Most of the shin-nisei strengthened their identification with Japan as a result of living in the country. Although some of them felt more American in Japan because of the cultural differences they encountered, they also developed a transnational ethnic consciousness based on a dual affiliation with both America and Japan to some extent. For instance, Yuki Noguchi spoke about his experiences as follows:

> In Japan, I definitely feel my Americanness more because I notice more differences than similarities [with the Japanese], even though I can do a decent job of getting by. But I also have a Japanese side I can activate, and a lot of times, I do, for courtesy's sake. I don't need to advertise that I'm from the US.

THIRD-GENERATION SANSEI: TOURISTIC ENCOUNTERS WITH THE ETHNIC HOMELAND

Third generation Japanese Americans (called *sansei*) are perhaps the largest group of Japanese Americans today; they are usually middle-aged. As descendants of the prewar, second generation nisei, they have followed the assimilative path of their parents and were raised in Americanized families in white, middle-class suburbs. As a result, the third-generation sansei have become well integrated in mainstream American society and have experienced further upward socioeconomic mobility, cultural Americanization, and intermarriage, usually with white Americans. Those that I interviewed characterized themselves as detached from their Japanese cultural heritage and their ethnic homeland of Japan.

Compared to other generations of Japanese Americans, over half of my sansei interviewees had never even visited the country. Among those who had never visited, close to half did not even have any interest in doing so in the future. For instance, John Sakata said:

> I was born and raised here. The only connection [to Japan] I have is that I'm of Japanese ancestry, and that's it. For me, to go to Japan and see the temples and shrines and other things doesn't interest me. There are too many places in the US I still haven't seen.

Those sansei I interviewed who had been to Japan generally traveled to Japan as tourists. My interviewees spoke highly, if not ravingly, about their trips and vacations to Japan, recalling nostalgic images of cherry blossoms and festivals, shrines and gardens, art and pottery, beautiful and idyllic scenery, bullet trains, good restaurants and food, and a generally clean, orderly, and safe society. However, because of their relatively short sojourns as tourists, most sansei have a rather superficial encounter with Japan and their

FIGURE 15.1. Obon Festival in San Diego to commemorate the ancestors (2006). Source: Takeyuki Tsuda.

interaction with Japanese is limited to service workers in restaurants, hotels, and department stores, where they are in the privileged position of customers and are treated in a courteous manner. Although the sansei usually do not speak Japanese (despite looking Japanese), they generally reported that the Japanese did not react negatively as a result.

Despite the positive experiences the sansei have in their ethnic homeland, it is not surprising that such short vacations as foreign tourists did not make them feel more connected to their ethnic roots and heritage. "I didn't go [to Japan] because I wanted to explore my roots," one sansei noted. "It was a nice country, but a completely foreign country as far as I'm concerned."

FOURTH-GENERATION YONSEI: RECOVERING ANCESTRAL HERITAGE THROUGH RETURN MIGRATION

In recent years, fourth generation Japanese American youth (called *yonsei*) have attempted to recover their ethnic heritage and reconnect with their ancestral homeland. This ethnic revival is a response to their continued

FIGURE 15.2. Taiko performance at the Obon Festival, San Diego (2006). Source: Takeyuki Tsuda.

racialization as "Japanese," which has caused them to become concerned about their overassimilation to American society in an era of multiculturalism, where cultural heritage and homeland have come to be positively valued. As a result, a significant number of yonsei are studying Japanese, majoring in Asian studies, living in Japan as college exchange students, or participating in Japanese *taiko* drum ensembles in local ethnic communities.

Almost all the yonsei in my research sample had lived in Japan as college students on foreign exchange or study abroad programs, generally for one semester or a year, or planned to do so soon. One-third had been to Japan multiple times. In addition, the yonsei I interviewed reported quite positive and fun experiences in their country of ethnic ancestry. Those who lived in Japan as study abroad students mainly associated with Japanese students who were educated and cosmopolitan, often spoke (or wanted to practice) English, and were quite eager to meet and talk to American students.

My yonsei interviewees also reported that the Japanese they encountered outside their host universities were also quite courteous and polite, even toward foreigners who did not speak Japanese all that well. Although the Japanese were sometimes initially confused or surprised when meeting Japanese-looking people who could not speak the language, and may have even initially seen them as disabled, strange, or uneducated,[4] the treatment was reported to be quite nice and courteous once it became apparent that they were Americans.[5]

Because of their overall positive experiences in Japan, a good number of yonsei I interviewed reported an increased identification with their ethnic homeland and a greater connection to their ancestral roots. Although about half of my interviewees mentioned that they felt quite American in Japan, this was simply a recognition of their cultural differences with the Japanese.[6] "I feel somewhat of a stronger affinity with Japan now," Sandy noted. "It's because I know more about Japanese culture and how it works. Now, I want to learn more, so that Japan becomes more natural for me, so when I go back, I can fit in more."

CONCLUSION

As ethnic return migrants from a highly developed country at the top of the global hierarchy, Japanese Americans undoubtedly experience a much more positive ethnic homecoming than their counterparts from developing countries, such as the Japanese Brazilians. Despite their status as cultural foreigners in their ethnic homeland, they return as privileged, professional migrants, students, or well-treated tourists who are generally part of the global elite and who interact with more well-educated, cosmopolitan Japanese. In addition, Japanese Americans benefit from the global stature of the United States and are respected in Japan as Americans.

Although Japanese Americans generally have positive experiences in Japan overall, their diasporic returns do vary considerably by immigrant generation. This chapter has cautioned against the facile assumption that ethnic returns and their importance for ethnic heritage and identity naturally attenuate and weaken over the generations, as ethnic minorities are progressively assimilated and socially integrated into mainstream host societies. Although the third-generation sansei are less likely to visit Japan than the prewar, second-generation nisei, the level of engagement and immersion of the nisei is not necessarily greater than that of the sansei. In addition, the most recent and younger generations of Japanese Americans have become more transnationally engaged with Japan than their earlier generational predecessors. Although the fourth generation yonsei are the most assimilated and Americanized of all Japanese Americans, they are also among the most transnationally engaged in their ethnic return migration. They are concerned about their overassimilation to mainstream American society in a multicultural and globalized world that increasingly valorizes ethnic heritage and homeland.

Therefore, for immigrant-origin minorities like the Japanese Americans, who are many generations old and are characterized by considerable internal diversity, it may be difficult to generalize about their ethnic return migration experiences. Instead of assuming that ethnic minorities are less likely to return migrate and engage with the homeland with each successive generation, we must examine how the various generations negotiate their ethnic positionality in response to multiple historical, cultural, and racial factors.

NOTES

This chapter is based on one-and-a-half years of fieldwork and participant observation with Japanese Americans in San Diego and Phoenix between 2006 and 2009. For an extensive discussion of the methodology for this project, see Tsuda 2016, introduction. The ethnographic materials used in this article are excerpted from Tsuda 2016, chapters 1, 2, 3, and 5.

1. Tsuda 2003.
2. See Tsuda 2016, 45–80.
3. See also Yamashiro 2011, 1512–13.
4. Tsuda 2003, 156–94; Yamashiro 2011, 1511.
5. See also Asakawa 2004, 111.
6. See also Yamashiro 2011, 1512–13.

REFERENCES AND FURTHER READING

Adachi, Nobuko, ed. 2006. *Japanese Diasporas: Unsung Pasts, Conflicting Presents, and Uncertain Futures.* London: Routledge.

Asakawa, Gil. 2004. *Being Japanese American: A JA Sourcebook for Nikkei, Happa . . . & Their Friends.* Berkeley, CA: Stone Bridge Press.

Fugita, Stephen, and David O'Brien. 1991. *Japanese American Ethnicity: The Persistence of Community.* Seattle: University of Washington Press.

Hirabayashi, Lane Ryo, Akemi Kikumura-Yano, and James A. Hirabayashi. 2002. *New Worlds, New Lives: Globalization and People of Japanese Descent in the Americas and from Latin American in Japan.* Stanford, CA: Stanford University Press.

Takamori, Ayako. 2010. "Rethinking Japanese American 'Heritage' in the Homeland." *Critical Asian Studies* 42, no. 2 (May): 217–38.

Tsuda, Takeyuki. 2003. *Strangers in the Ethnic Homeland: Japanese Brazilian Return Migration in Transnational Perspective.* New York: Columbia University Press.

———. 2016. *Japanese American Ethnicity: In Search of Heritage and Homeland across Generations.* New York: New York University Press.

Yamashiro, Jane. 2011 "Racialized National Identity Construction in the Ancestral Homeland: Japanese American Migrants in Japan." *Ethnic and Racial Studies* 34, no. 9 (September): 1502–21.

———. 2017. *Redefining Japaneseness: Japanese Americans in the Ancestral Homeland.* Stanford, CA: Stanford University Press.

SIXTEEN

Chinese Labor Migrants in Asia and Africa

Miriam Driessen and Biao Xiang

CHINESE WORKERS HAVE LONG ENJOYED a reputation of being hardworking. The Chinese coolies who were contracted to build America's first transcontinental railway in the nineteenth century are engraved in the public imagination as the epitome of industrious workers, and so are the Chinese workers in the gold mines of colonial South Africa. "If you see a man working in the desert, it must be a Chinese," grinned an Ethiopian driver of a Chinese company with a mixture of admiration and scorn. "It's just too hot for Ethiopians to work there." Persistent rumors about Chinese convicts being sent to work on construction sites in Africa hark back to the image of coolies in America, reflecting the widespread disbelief among Africans in the willingness of Chinese laborers to toil under the toughest of circumstances. "You should see them busy with hammers, splitting rocks in the desert at the border with South Sudan. They must be prisoners," whispered an Ethiopian engineer. "Who else is willing to do this work?"

African bewilderment at the sight of Chinese workers bustling around on construction sites is not unfounded. Chinese laborers work hard, and hope to work even harder. In Japan, South Korea, and Singapore a common complaint by Chinese workers was that there is too little overtime. For them, working additional hours is critical for accumulating savings. Yet why are still so many Chinese willing to move abroad to take up work, often under very challenging circumstances, despite their country's unprecedented economic development and growing affluence in recent decades?

At the end of 2016, the number of Chinese workers dispatched overseas as part of contractual projects and labor cooperation agreements amounted to nearly one million. Ninety percent of them work in Asia and Africa, with Japan, Singapore, and Macau being the top destinations.[1] From the migrants' perspective, wage work in developed countries such as Japan and South Korea and in emerging economies in Africa like Ethiopia provides advantages over employment in China. Living expenses in Chinese cities are soaring, leaving rural-urban migrants with little money at the end of the month. By moving overseas, migrants are able to earn "dry money"—money that can be saved and invested. But "dry money" demands hard work.

Typically born in rural China or in the cities to rural parents, Chinese labor migrants in Asia and Africa come from similar socioeconomic backgrounds. Migrant men and women are driven to create stable and secure lives for themselves and their families in China rather than a better life abroad. They are deeply worried that they may be left behind in the fierce competition for wealth in China, and they hope to live a life free from struggles— financial, social, or otherwise. Yet without the willingness to migrate and work hard, they cannot attain their dreams of living a worry-free, middle-class life at home. They work hard, chiseling away in the punishing sun in Africa and toiling at midnight hours in factories in Japan and Singapore to avoid having to work hard in the future.

HYPERMOBILITY

Being hypermobile—moving to new places and changing jobs frequently—is a common life trajectory of Chinese workers and, in their eyes, the best way to earn and save money. Take Liu as an example. Born in 1983 in Northeast China, Liu first moved to the town close to her home village at the age of sixteen to work as a room cleaner and kitchen assistant in a hotel. After that she worked in a plastic manufacturing workshop, a restaurant, a textile factory, a brewery, and another restaurant, moving from one city to another. She changed jobs for various reasons: poor pay, tough working conditions, harassment by a manager, conflicts with roommates, following good friends, or simply boredom.

In 2006, Liu went to Japan as an "industrial trainee"—a Japanese euphemism for an unskilled, temporary foreign laborer. The work in a small garment factory was tough and physically taxing. She lost "a layer of the body," as she put it, when she came back three years later. But the salary was good. She brought home nearly CNY 300,000 (US$45,000). Five months after her return, she married Wan, who was a taxi driver at the time. Their first two years of marriage were the happiest in their lives. Liu took, in her words, "a good rest," and returned to her natal village to look after their newly born daughter.

In 2010, Liu and Wan bought an apartment in the city. But living costs there were much higher, and savings were running out. Liu opened a laundry shop in the neighborhood, and then converted it into a convenience store. Neither enterprise was successful. In 2012, Liu went to South Korea on a tourist visa and worked in a restaurant; this job was arranged by a middleman of Korean ethnicity for a brokerage fee of US$12,000. Yet fate struck unexpectedly when she was apprehended and deported six months later.

Immediately after Liu's return, Wan went to Japan to work for a construction company. After Wan returned in 2015 with savings of around US$25,000, he "took a rest" and worked as a freelance technician. Liu had joined a large retailer company as a shop assistant. Her pay was moderate, but she had her social security covered, including pension, medical care, and insurance against work-related injuries. It was the first time that Liu signed a formal employment contract in China.

Paradoxically, in a moment of relative stability, anxiety creeped in again. "Money came in slowly but went out fast." In 2015, Wan and Liu and three relatives joined a pyramid sales scheme. "Many people became millionaires in less than a year!" Liu quit her job, rented a shop in a prime location, and recruited new members as quickly as possible. Nine months later, the founders of the scheme were arrested for deception and the pyramid collapsed. The family lost more than US$10,000. Wan regretted not joining the scheme earlier. Liu became a Buddhist, spending much time visiting different shrines. In the meantime, Wan was working multiple odd jobs. Going overseas to work, which they had ruled out after Wan returned from Japan, seemed a realistic option again.

Liu and Wan's life trajectories are common among unskilled Chinese workers, who alternate ventures in China with wage work overseas. They rarely sit still. In moments of relative stability or boredom, they become restless and move on to another job. "Taking a rest" is merely to gather pace and start a new challenge. The lives of Liu and Wan and many other migrants in China and abroad are characterized by frenzied activity.

Most of the wage jobs migrants take on are manual and low-skilled. In 2015, 49 percent of the Chinese workers overseas were in construction, 16 percent in manufacturing, followed by 5.7 percent in agriculture.[2] Managerial oppression is rampant. Migrant workers often reside in dormitories attached to factories or camps on construction sites with severely restricted freedom of movement. Few migrants could endure more than three years in one go. Migrants, whom Biao met in Japan and Miriam met in Ethiopia, said that the first thing they would do after returning to China was to spend some time "sleeping and eating properly." For this reason, married couples like Wan and Liu take turns moving overseas. Wan went to Japan because Liu insisted that it was his turn to migrate.

This form of rotation, however, was less common in the case of Chinese migrants in Ethiopia, where migrant men asserted that Africa is not a place for women—*Chinese* women, that is. Most of their spouses, if they were married, took care of the children and grandparents, or, more commonly, worked closer to home. Women who chose to stay at home initially often became restless and took up work again. Like their husbands, they remained on the move.

DRY MONEY

Employment overseas does not necessarily provide more income. Most crucially, work abroad allows migrants to *save* money. "You can't save much when you are working in China. You have friends and you go out in the evenings," one taxi driver told Biao, relaying his plans to go to South Korea. "When you are abroad, all the money that you earn is dry money." "Dry money" goes straight into the savings account. Chinese migrants in Ethiopia also mentioned the ability to save money as the main reason for taking up employment there, bemoaning high living expenses in China, including soaring house prices and high costs of social life, leaving little money to save.

Savings are crucial because migrants use the fruits of wage labor as an investment. One migrant paid US$3,300 to go to Singapore without checking how much exactly the wage would be. He was so taken by the middleman, who told him "[by going to Singapore] you may well catch the first barrel of gold in your life," that he signed the contract on the spot. The "first barrel of gold"—evoking the image of the nineteenth-century California gold rush—has been a popular metaphor in China since the early 2000s. It stands for start-up capital. Since migration is seen as an investment for future returns, it is thought to be crucial that one leaves at the first opportunity. China is developing so rapidly and you are not getting any younger; you may lag behind forever if you are late. Anxious to earn "quick money," migrants pay high fees to intermediaries—ranging from US$3,000 to 9,000—not only to acquire a job overseas but also to get it quickly.

The importance migrants attach to saving and investing is reflected in their views of the spending habits of members of the host countries. "In Ethiopia, rich people work hard, but poor people who get one birr per day by begging in the street only think about how they will spend that one birr, not about how they will earn two birr the next day," explained Wang, a self-made migrant entrepreneur who came to Ethiopia in 2007 as an employee of tele-communications equipment giant ZTE. In contrast to most of his expatriate colleagues at the time, he did not intend to return to China—at least not in the short term. Before he moved "from Jiangsu to Ethiopia," as he put it, he had worked in various factories. He was reluctant to return, because he earned much more overseas.

During his time at ZTE he had become fluent in Amharic, mostly through chatting with Ethiopian security personnel. After his contract ended, he decided to stay, and he converted to orthodox Christianity—the dominant religion in Ethiopia. He started an Ethiopian restaurant and a computer store in the town of Dilla in southern Ethiopia. At the age of twenty-five, he had, by local standards, become a successful entrepreneur. However, his time was running out when Miriam first met him in Addis Ababa in 2011. Wang's visa was two months overdue and he was anxiously trying to find ways to renew it.

Although Wang admits having gained respect for Ethiopians, he also considered them spendthrifts. "Ethiopians are lazy. At first, they work hard. But after they get their salary, they start to get lazy." In Wang's eyes, Ethiopians lack the drive to improve their lives by saving and investing—*the* ideal among Chinese workers. Some migrants attributed laziness to Ethiopians' belief in God. Religion, they held, produced complacency. Chinese migrants like Wang were quick to point out that discipline and diligence were what set Chinese workers apart from Africans. "The Chinese are not here to enjoy themselves. They are here to work hard," Wang asserted, reiterating a mantra among Chinese migrants who, whether in Japan or Ethiopia, sought to maximize returns.

The uncertainty migrants embraced in the process was contained uncertainty. Labor migration is a relatively secure and predictable form of wage work, and one that guarantees returns. Chinese companies in Ethiopia, for instance, offer all-in packages and clearly set trajectories. In the period abroad, the employer is the provider of housing, transport, food, and limited health care, commanding full control over expatriate staff. The threshold for migration to Africa is low; much lower than that for migration to developed countries such as Japan, South Korea, or Singapore. Migrants moving to these Asian countries often go through migrant brokers who demand high fees. By contrast, the increasing number of Chinese men who move to Africa to work as laborers contracted by Chinese construction, mining, and agriculture enterprises are either recruited directly online or on a university campus, or they enter the company via kin or acquaintances. Chinese laborers in Ethiopia typically work for Chinese companies, whereas Chinese migrants in Asia often work for local Asian firms.

Migrants invest the savings from wage labor in housing or commercial ventures in order to have its value multiplied. Apart from buying housing in cities in China, returnees also purchase commercial real estate or cars that they rent out as taxis. Becoming a rentier-style property owner is a widely shared dream among migrants. The majority of migrants work in large cities where wages are higher but properties are prohibitively expensive, forcing them to buy apartments in small towns close to home villages instead.

Chinese migration is no longer about American or Japanese dreams. Rather than fantasizing about greener pastures elsewhere, migrants pursue *Chinese dreams*. They hope that intensive labor abroad will lift them onto the train of rapid wealth accumulation in China and relieve them from the struggles they go through in the present.

FAMILIAL ENTREPRENEURIALISM

"Why do the Chinese work so hard?" This was the question Stevan Harrell (1985) asked in his attempt to trace the origin of Chinese diligence. The Chinese penchant for hard work, according to Harrell, lies not so much in the socialization of the value of hard work or the desire for its financial rewards as in an ethic of entrepreneurship—"the investment of one's resources (land, labor, and/or capital) in a long-term quest to improve the material well-being and security of some group to which one belongs and with which one identifies" (216). Entrepreneurship in this context is geared not only toward material gain, but also, and arguably more importantly, toward the generation of stability and security, the founding of hedges against adversity and loss. The principal beneficiary of entrepreneurial strategies, Harrell argues, is the family.

Migration and the search for security-generating opportunities inside and outside China speak to this entrepreneurial ethos. Yet, irrespective of where they go, migrants retain close bonds with their families. Migration is temporary, at least initially, and remittances flow back home.[3]

Chen Lin, a draftsman from Guizhou who had worked on road-building projects in the Central African Republic and Ethiopia, spent the salary of his first year abroad on the down payment of an apartment for his sister and brother-in-law near their home village. "Technically, my sister is not part of our family anymore, but since our father is no longer among us, I have to help her." When Miriam met Chen in Ethiopia, he was spending a good part of his salary on a second project: building a house for himself, his mother, and his family-to-be. His mother oversees the daily construction work and his sister manages the finances, while Chen Lin works in Ethiopia. This is an example of collective care and support within the family that migrant work and remittances enable.

Chen Lin cites "reality" as the main reason why he decided to relocate to Africa for work after graduating from college. Linked to societal pressure and uncertainty, "reality" in contemporary China is taken to bereave youths of the power to make the major decisions in life. "Only when you have a certain economic base, you are able to pursue your dreams," Chen explains. "This is the reality in present-day China." Questioning or challenging reality will eventually work against you. Chen had preferred to stay in China, close to his mother and sister, yet the burden of responsibility for the family's wellbeing weighed heavily on him. Moving to Africa for a job earned him more money—and "*dry* money" at that.

Many migrants frame moving away as a "way out." Apart from meaning an escape from a condition of insecurity, a "way out" is also taken to be a break away from a state of immobility or being stuck; financially, socially, or otherwise. But if the entrepreneurial ethos is intrinsic to Chinese culture, what precisely accounts for the seeming *increase* of entrepreneurialism in recent years? Why do migrants continue to work hard, or work even harder, despite the fact that their lives in China have significantly improved?

PROSPERITY AND RISKS

Chinese migrant workers do not work exceedingly hard and move constantly because their survival is at stake but because they are eager to move up economically and are ready to take risks. In China, entrepreneurialism among rural citizens has long been enabled by land ownership structures, in which rural land rights are tied to rural *hukou* (household registration) status. For a long time, land was a common-pool resource of village communities, and access to land depended on village membership. Virtually all rural residents had access to land that was nontradable and provided a subsistence base. Owing to the security provided by land rights, rural citizens could take on the risks of migration. In the event of misfortune or hardship, they were, and to a certain extent still are, able to resort to the land "to take a rest."[4] Only recently have many agricultural hukou holders lost their connection with the land, even though they still hold certain entitlements to use the allocated agricultural and residential land.

The children of the first generation of rural-urban migrants who have reached adulthood hardly have any experience of living on the land. Why can these migrants still afford to take the risks of quitting protected jobs and investing in speculative businesses again and again, instead of concentrating on improving the conditions of their wage jobs? The answer lies partly in the expansion of social welfare in China since the late 1990s and especially since the early 2000s. The state has created a safety net, albeit a very preliminary one, that in a way enables citizens to alternate between wage work and unpredictable business ventures.[5]

Welfare provision, however, continues to be far from perfect, driving Chinese people to work hard in order to secure an economic foundation for themselves and their families. Development typically spawns migration, as more resources for migration become available and successful migrant stories trigger the imagination of would-be migrants. This has certainly been the case in both rural and urban China.

Following three decades of unprecedented economic growth, socially upward mobility has become the norm in Chinese society. The country's market reforms, beginning in the late 1970s, were aimed at setting individuals free and encouraging them to grab life with both hands. In a context in which self-actualization has become the norm, those who fail to meet this norm risk being seen as having failed. Consequently, it has become an expectation, if not a duty, for young, able-bodied citizens, especially men, who traditionally carry the responsibility of securing the well-being of the family, to improve their lives and those of family members.

In short, Chinese industriousness can be explained by the entrepreneurial ethos that has been enabled by land ownership structures combined with increased state welfare provision, boosted by migrant remittances, inspired by success stories of migrants and returnees, and necessitated by high expectations of upward mobility and progress. In the face of increasing competition for resources, sustaining a middle-class lifestyle requires spatial mobility, especially for those who come from a poor rural background. This explains why, in the face of increased prosperity, Chinese workers continue to be disciplined and diligent workers, braving the natural forces of the wind, sun, and rain in even the remotest corners of the world.

NOTES

1. Ministry of Commerce 2017.
2. CHICA 2016, 10.
3. Chu 2010; Murphy 2002.
4. Lee 2007; Solinger 1999.
5. At the end of 2015, 858 million Chinese were covered by the basic pension insurance scheme (State Council 2016, part 2, 3), and 66 million were covered by the minimum livelihood assistance. Neither schemes existed before 1997. By the end of 2015, more than 95 percent of Chinese citizens were covered by medical insurance (State Council 2016, part 2, 3).

REFERENCES AND FURTHER READING

CHICA (China International Contractors Association). 2016. *Guoji Laowu Hezuo Niandu Baogao 2015* [Annual report on China's international labor collaboration 2015]. Beijing: CHICA. 2016.

Chu, Julie Y. 2010. *Cosmologies of Credit: Transnational Mobility and the Politics of Destination in China*. Durham, NC: Duke University Press.

Harrell, Stevan. 1985. "Why Do the Chinese Work So Hard? Reflections on an Entrepreneurial Ethic." *Modern China* 11, no. 2 (April): 203–26.

Lee, Ching Kwan. 2007. *Against the Law: Labor Protests in China's Rustbelt and Sunbelt*. Berkeley: University of California Press.

———. 2017. *The Specter of Global China: Politics, Labor, and Foreign Investment in Africa*. Chicago: University of Chicago Press.

Ministry of Commerce. 2017. "2016 Nian duiwai laowu shuchu hezuo jianmin tongji" [Brief Statistics on China's Foreign Labour Service Cooperation 2016]. Accessed July 25, 2019. http://hzs.mofcom.gov.cn/article/date/201701/20170102504425.shtml.

Murphy, Rachel. 2002. *How Migrant Labor is Changing Rural China*. Cambridge: Cambridge University Press.

Ong, Aihwa, and Li Zhang. 2008. Introduction to *Privatizing China: Socialism from Afar*, 1–19. Edited by Li Zhang and Aihwa Ong. Ithaca, NY: Cornell University Press.

Solinger, Dorothy. 1999. *Contesting Citizenship in Urban China: Peasant Migrants, the State, and the Logic of the Market.* Berkeley: University of California Press.

State Council (People's Republic of China). 2016. *Government Work Report.* The Fourth Meeting of the 12th National People's Congress. March 5, 2016. http://www.gov.cn/guowuyuan/2016-03/17/content_5054901.htm.

Wang, Gungwu. 2000. *The Chinese Overseas: From Earthbound China to the Quest for Autonomy.* Cambridge, MA: Harvard University Press.

———

SEVENTEEN

Uncertain Choices of Chinese-Foreign Children's Citizenship in the People's Republic of China

Elena Barabantseva, Caroline Grillot, and Michaela Pelican

THE CITIZENSHIP OF CHINESE-FOREIGN CHILDREN being brought up in China is an area of increased political relevance because of their growing numbers, the effects of the household registration system, nationality and immigration laws, and wider debates on Chinese identity and belonging. International business, trade, and education mobility have become important channels for personal contacts, cross-border intimate relations, and the formation of Chinese-foreign families, including children. These transformations take place at the intersection of population and family spheres of governance and have triggered changes in the politics of Chinese citizenship.

The regulatory mechanism of the People's Republic of China (PRC) for international marriages has evolved since 1986, when the concepts of "Chinese-foreign marriage" and "cross-border marriage" were introduced.[1] Yet the PRC's official statistics only include marriages registered in the territory of China, and they exclude unregistered informal marriages and Chinese-foreign marriages registered outside of China, thus making estimations of the number of Chinese-foreign marriages difficult.

While Chinese-foreign marriages have attracted considerable research interest, the focus so far has been either on the couple or on the migrant spouse. Researchers have noted challenges to the foreign spouses' legal and social status;[2] the importance of a racialized sexual stratification in finding a spouse;[3] the frequent interlinkage of intimate and business relations; changing intergenerational attitudes;[4] and shifts in public perceptions of Chinese-foreign marriages.[5] The children of Chinese-foreign couples, however, have been given much less attention. Unlike their foreign parents, who do not have a route to full citizenship in China and who can, at best, hope for the status of long-term residents, children born to Chinese-foreign couples are automatically entitled to Chinese citizenship in accordance with the 1980 nationality law.[6] Under the strict, single citizenship regime of the Chinese government, adopting Chinese citizenship means forfeiting the right to the foreign parent's citizenship by the age of eighteen.

Which citizenship to pass on to the child is not an easy and straightforward decision for parents in an environment of unknown possibilities and an uncertain future. In our analysis of this complex decision-making process, we focus on three examples of Chinese-foreign families that have attracted considerable attention in Chinese public and media debates. Our analysis is based on our own research and repeated interactions and interviews with these families. Elena did research on Chinese-Russian marriages and families; Michaela focused on Chinese-Cameroonian ones; and Caroline and Elena both worked on Chinese-Vietnamese couples and families. Our aim was not to draw comparisons across starkly different socioeconomic and political-cultural contexts but to juxtapose what is at stake in these three contexts. We argue that decisions are shaped by gendered, racial, and socioeconomic boundaries in China, which highlight the moral, legal, and sociocultural dimensions of Chinese citizenship.

MARRIAGE MIGRATION, MIXED CHILDREN, AND CITIZENSHIP IN CHINA

Citizenship in China entails at least three facets that frame an individual's legal rights and entitlements: nationality, ethnicity (officially *minzu* or "nationality"), and household registration. In addition to recognition as a Chinese national and a member of one of the fifty-six nationalities that constitute the Chinese nation, a citizen's household registration serves as a basis for economic and social status and access to healthcare, schooling, and pensions.

China faces a looming demographic crisis. Pointing to the decreasing number of marriages since 2003, a rising divorce rate, and an already very low fertility rate that continues to fall despite the abolition of the one-child policy in 2016, a *People's Daily* editorial in August 2018 identified having children as a matter of national concern.[7] Control of population quantity and population quality has been at the core of China's family planning policies since the late 1970s.[8] This now also comprises an officially recognized demographic need for more children, including, although in a tiny proportion, children of Chinese-foreign parentage. We refer to our three cases as historical, unexpected, and favored to highlight the dominant media and public attitudes toward these types of marriages, on the one hand, and to trace how different discursive trajectories relate to parental decisions regarding the citizenship of children of Chinese-foreign parents, on the other.

THE HISTORICAL: CHINESE-VIETNAMESE MARRIAGES

Chinese-Vietnamese marriages have long been part of the social landscape, despite constant political ups and downs, including military conflicts between the two countries and the consequent strengthening of border monitoring and restrictions on migration. The current discourse on illegal migration and criminality that has informed public perceptions of marriages between Chinese men and Vietnamese women ignores these historical roots. It also conveniently neglects the commodification of marriage arrangements, including coerced marriage as well as customary marriages among highland ethnic groups that live on both sides of the border. Nowadays, such marriages have in fact increased, owing to more frequent population movement and commercial exchanges across the border.

Accurate official data on the number of Chinese-Vietnamese marriages remains difficult to obtain. This reflects the complex administrative procedures involved in registering an international marriage and the lack of accurate information on these procedures available to the mostly rural population. As a result, many Chinese-Vietnamese families do not enjoy a fully legal status.

Rural Chinese bachelors prefer Vietnamese women as wives because of their reputation for being family-oriented, undemanding, humble, hardworking, and accepting of patriarchal norms.[9] These traits are increasingly difficult to find among young Chinese women, many of whom look for opportunities to move out of their rural homes in search of a better life in the city. Vietnamese women are perceived to be content with the role of providing heirs for the family, taking care of domestic chores, and remaining invisible in Chinese society.

THE FAVORED: CHINESE-RUSSIAN MARRIAGES

Chinese-Russian marriages started attracting media attention in the late 1990s and early 2000s and have received overwhelmingly positive coverage in Chinese official and popular publications. Mobility has been an important factor in enabling these encounters. In the late 1990s and early 2000s, the majority of couples and families were formed as a result of Chinese (mainly men) who moved to Russia for education or business. In the 2000s, similar opportunities became available for Russians (both men and women) to move to China.

The majority of Russian women who took part in the research project for this article had a college degree. Originally, the majority did not have any plans to marry Chinese men or to stay in China for other reasons. Their marriage to their Chinese husbands was registered and legalized either in China or Russia. Even though some of these women have a student or business visa, most of them aspire to get a family reunion visa (Q1) in China, which allows them, after five years of marriage, to apply for the ten-year residence card that will grant them the right to work.

THE UNEXPECTED: CHINESE-CAMEROONIAN MARRIAGES

China's economic growth and engagement in Africa have laid the groundwork for the increasing presence of African men and women in China. Many are from middle-class backgrounds and were attracted to China by funded education or business opportunities. The growing visibility of Chinese-African families within trading communities in cities like Guangzhou has become an unexpected and a frowned-on phenomenon in a society that favors the idea of racial purity and holds strong prejudices, particularly against people of African descent.[10]

Different from Chinese-Russian and Chinese-Vietnamese families, the vast majority of Chinese-African couples and families are made up of a Chinese woman and an African man who met in a business-related context in China. Often, romance goes hand-in-hand with business partnerships as the new couples join forces to realize their economic and family ambitions. Many of the Chinese women are rural migrants who seek a life in the city; for them, marriage to an educated or well-to-do foreigner is an opportunity of upward social mobility. Many of the African husbands are in a vulnerable legal and economic situation in China, as they are often only granted a short-term visa (valid for three to six months), which they have to renew on a regular basis. With increasingly stricter visa regulations, maintaining a legal status has become more difficult; this, in turn, has forced many Africans to overstay their visa or to return to their countries of origin.[11] While a business partnership or marriage to a Chinese woman may help the African husband mitigate his economic and legal insecurity, it ultimately cannot guarantee him a long-term stay or citizenship in China. Unlike Russian women, African men prefer a business or student visa to a family reunion visa, as they are focused on doing business and generating a stable income to support themselves and their families. This is also a strategy to counter the structural dependency and the experience of disempowerment that several of our interlocutors noted regarding spousal relations in China, which differ considerably from those in Cameroon. Moreover, many Chinese-African couples are not legally married, which rules out the possibility of a spousal visa.

Marriages between Chinese women and foreign men are generally viewed in a critical manner by the Chinese media and public, especially because foreign husbands are increasingly seen as competitors in the demographically skewed marriage market. However, anxieties about Chinese women dating foreign men already surfaced in the 1980s in the context of the Nanjing student uprisings against African students, and they have recently become the topic of a national security campaign.[12]

CONTESTATIONS OVER A CHINESE-FOREIGN CHILD'S CITIZENSHIP

In Chinese-Vietnamese Families

The similarities between Vietnamese and Chinese cultural backgrounds constitute the ground for shared family standards and values: exogamy and patrilocal residence rules; the importance of family ancestral lines; a patriarchal ideology and a marginal position of women within the family, and so forth. In a manner that is similar to what they're used to regarding the marriages in their natal societies, Vietnamese mothers do not discuss the surnames of their children or challenge their belonging to his father's family line.

In the Chinese-Vietnamese families, it is taken for granted that the child should be registered as a descendant of its father. When parents are not officially married—which is the case with many of the couples we investigated—the Chinese father must pay a fine in order to register his child's birth in violation of the state's family planning. If the father has exceeded the number of children that he would be allowed (for instance, when he already has other children from a previous marriage), it might be even more difficult to either comply with or circumvent family planning. Corruption or using personal connections sometimes helps, even though the price might be high. In other cases, relatives may also provide a solution—for example, by registering the child as the father's brother's (the uncle's).

Such arrangements are common among Chinese-Vietnamese couples who live relatively far from the border. However, when they live in the borderlands other solutions are possible. If the child is a girl, or if the father does not want to be identified as a lawbreaker, the couple may decide to register their offspring in Vietnam. Although household registration systems exist in both countries, Vietnam recognizes children born out of wedlock and allows single mothers to register their children on their own household registration without paying a fine. However, by doing so, the father must accept that his child would never be eligible for education, health care, or inheritance in China. This also means that since no official affiliation is recognized in China, his wife may vanish with the couple's child in case of a conflict or separation. This is why, given the value attributed to a male heir in China, couples only resort to a child's registration in Vietnam when all other possibilities have been ruled out.

In Chinese-Russian Families

The popularity of Chinese-Russian families in Chinese discourses can be explained by the high esteem they have for their Eurasian offspring, an esteem informed by a deep-seated, racially hierarchical view of the world.[13] As one of the research participants observed, "Eurasian children are cleverer, and, according to the Chinese, are very beautiful."[14] Chinese advertising agencies capitalize on this, and they frequently circulate adverts in WeChat groups in search of Eurasian baby models, offering them a pay rate equivalent to an adult model of up to CNY 400 per hour. Despite the fascination with Eurasian children because of their lighter complexion, the children are actively absorbed into the Chinese civilizational sphere through dominant family norms and citizenship practices. The multiple claims made on the children by the Chinese father, his family, and the state are a cause of concern for the mother's parental rights. For many of these women, securing their maternal rights and ensuring that the child has Russian citizenship is a priority.

Throughout the 2000s, a series of prominent cases involving Chinese husbands who hid children from their mothers in the Chinese countryside shook the Russian population in China. Many women became aware of the risks of registering their children as Chinese rather than as Russian citizens. Some women who took part in this research blamed the effects of family planning policies in China and traditional marriage values that treat the wife and her children as the property of the husband's family. The risk that their children may automatically assume Chinese nationality through their fathers generates for the women a fear that at some point they might be separated from their children. Some women, therefore, prefer to give birth in Russia, where they then register their children as Russian citizens to ensure their maternal rights. The citizen status of a Chinese-Russian child is a complex phenomenon wherein competing citizenship practices manifest themselves and struggles over identity and parental rights play out.

In Chinese-Cameroonian Families

In many Chinese-Cameroonian families, the African husband's role in decisions regarding the citizenship and upbringing of his children is limited because of his often insecure economic and residence status. In general, administrative procedures are taken care of by the Chinese wife, sometimes with her parents. They know the language and the system, and they have the social network to facilitate administrative procedures.

Neither Cameroon nor China allows dual nationality. Faced with the need to choose between one country or the other, the families that took part in this research opted for their children to have Chinese citizenship. This choice is largely based on pragmatic considerations. First, as long as the couple is based in China, Chinese citizenship will entitle the child to stay in China without having to undergo the costly and risky procedure of regularly renewing a visa. Second, Chinese citizenship will provide access to social services. This depends on the child's inclusion in the mother's household registration, which is often in a rural area different from the place in which the couple currently lives. A third and major reason is that Cameroonian citizenship can still be acquired at a later stage. In Cameroon, there is a whole industry of producing birth certificates, passports, marriage certificates and so on, either legally or illegally. Cameroonian fathers are more concerned about securing their children's legal status in China, which, in their experience, is very difficult to obtain with a Cameroonian passport.

For children of African-Chinese descent, social recognition poses a problem. When Lou Jing, daughter of a Chinese mother and African American father, participated in the Shanghai Dragon Television's talent show, public opinion was divided on whether she was, in fact, Chinese.[15] Lou Jing's experience of racialization and alienation is shared by other children of Chinese-African descent, and it is a constant worry for many parents.

CONCLUSION

Our research shows that, in general, Chinese-foreign children are valued more than their foreign parents. Like almost all other foreign residents in China, foreign parents remain temporary or incomplete members of society, and their role is largely restricted to the reproductive sphere. This is particularly the case for foreign wives who serve as mothers of future Chinese citizens, while foreign fathers are seen as competitors over Chinese women and as being of limited importance in the upbringing of their children. Importantly, in order to be entitled to long-term residency in China, foreign parents are expected to demonstrate their economic worth to Chinese society, as well as their loyalty—and utility—to the Chinese family.

These common conditions manifest themselves differently across our three cases. Parents' negotiations and specific citizenship arrangements are informed by their visions of family norms and their perceptions of what will ensure a better future for their children. The fact that similar cultural values are held by parents in Chinese-Vietnamese households and the relatively low social status of the Vietnamese wives facilitate the acquisition of Chinese citizenship for their children. In Chinese-Russian families, contrasting family norms and values and the relatively high status of the Russian wives constitute a common cause of family tensions. The marginal socioeconomic position of rural migrant Chinese mothers and the societal prejudice toward Cameroonian fathers prompt Cameroonian-Chinese couples to look for pragmatic solutions to choosing their children's citizenship that will guarantee them legal status, or at least continued residence, in China.

Against the backdrop of the growing internal diversity of Chinese society, the current immigration regime is rather restrictive; moreover, it is not showing signs of changing any time soon. The spirit of Chinese market reform emphasizes labor and the economic value of human capital that benefits China's economic transformation. Current immigration laws and regulations favor highly skilled Chinese returnees, and thus continue the centuries-long tradition of privileging blood ties and lineage as the foundational principle of national belonging. While foreign spouses will continue to face legal and social obstacles to integration into the Chinese populace, children of Chinese-foreign backgrounds are more valued as Chinese nationals but are likely to continue to have to confront social stigmatization in the years to come.

NOTES

1. Wang 2014. In this chapter, we prefer the term *Chinese-foreign marriage/families* over the alternative terminologies of *international, cross-border, interracial,* or *mixed marriage/families.* The term *Chinese-foreign marriage/family* best captures the commonalities shared by the three cases under study here.

2. Barabantseva and Grillot 2018; Farrer 2008.

3. Lan 2017.

4. Nehring and Wang 2016.

5. Wang 2014.

6. Nationality Law of the People's Republic of China, effective as of September 10 1980, http://www.npc.gov.cn/englishnpc/Law/2007–12/13/content_1384056 .htm, last accessed 13 June 2019.

7. Zhang, Yiqi "Sheng wa shi jia shi ye shi guo shi" [Having babies is a family matter, as well as a national matter], *Renmin Wang,* August 6, 2018, http://politics .people.com.cn/n1/2018/0806/c1001–30210179.html. In August 2018, a series of publications on the possible ways of encouraging Chinese citizens to have more children hit Chinese official media outlets. The proposal to establish the reproduction fund that would financially penalize couples for not having a second child has been met with particularly harsh reactions from Chinese netizens, see Feng 2018.

8. Greenhalgh 2010.

9. Grillot 2010.

10. Dikötter 2015; Lan 2017.

11. Lan 2017.

12. Barabantseva and Grillot 2019

13. Dikötter 2015.

14. Interview May 31, 2017.

15. Leung 2015.

Barabantseva, Elena, and Caroline Grillot. 2018. "Le Statut de 'Visiteuses de Famille': Mythes et Réalités sur les Epouses Russes et Vietnamiennes en Chine" [The status of ' family visitors': Myths and realities of Russian and Vietnamese wives in China]. *Cahiers de Genre* 64: 105–27.

———. 2019. "Representations and Regulations of Marriage Migration from Russian and Vietnam in the People's Republic of China." *Journal of Asian Studies* 78, no. 2 (May): 285–308.

Dikötter, Frank. 2015. *The Discourse of Race in Modern China*. Rev. ed. London: Hurst.

Grillot, Caroline. 2010. *Volées, Envolées, Convolées … Vendues, en Fuite ou Resocialisées: Les "Fiancées" Vietnamiennes en Chine* [Stolen, vanished, wedded … Sold, runaway, or resocialized: The Vietnamese "brides" in China]. Paris: Connaissances & Savoirs.

Farrer, James. 2008. "From 'Passports' to 'Joint Ventures': Intermarriage between Chinese Nationals and Western Expatriates Residing in Shanghai." *Asian Studies Review* 32, no. 1: 7–29.

Feng, Jiayun. 2018. "Subsidies for Having Kids? The Chinese Internet is Not Impressed." SupChina. August 16. https://supchina.com/2018/08/16/subsidies-for-having-kids-the-chinese-internet-is-not-impressed/.

Greenhalgh, Susan. 2010. *Cultivating Global Citizens: Population in the Rise of China*. Cambridge, MA: Harvard University Press.

Lan, Shanshan. 2017. *Mapping the New African Diaspora in China: Race and the Cultural Politics of Belonging*. New York: Routledge.

Leung, Wing Fai. 2015. "Who Could be an Oriental Angel? Lou Jing, Mixed Heritage and the Discourses of Chinese Ethnicity." *Asian Ethnicity* 16, no. 3 (June): 294–313.

Nehring, Daniel, and Xiying Wang. 2016. "Making Transnational Intimacies: Intergenerational Relationships in Chinese-Western Families in Beijing." *Journal of Chinese Sociology* 3, no. 1 (June): 1–24.

Wang, Pan. 2014. *Love and Marriage in Globalizing China*. London: Routledge.

EIGHTEEN

From Hmong Versus Miao to the Making of Transnational Hmong/Miao Solidarity

Louisa Schein and Chia Youyee Vang

HOW DOES A DIASPORIC GROUP build a transnational network that is shaped by the nation-states in which they live and in turn impacts who they imagine themselves to be? This chapter offers dual perspectives from a Hmong American scholar with Lao origins and a white American researcher; both have documented and played roles in the formation of a global identity for Miao and Hmong based in Asia and in the countries of refugee resettlement. We chronicle myriad ways that Hmong dispersed from Laos after the Vietnam War fashioned connections to homelands in Asia, asking how specific practices produced and overcame sociocultural distances engendered by national locations.

The strands that have come to link Hmong in Asia to those in diasporic locations in the Americas, Europe, Australia, and New Zealand are braided together into complex interchanges. They include familial, academic, cultural, economic, marital, religious, medical, media, and touristic engagements that bring diasporic and Asian players together—often in profoundly asymmetrical ways. Nonetheless, the drive to form transnational solidarity has been a strong and consistent impetus. Since the 1980s, we argue, perceptions of transnational identity and of homelands have shifted considerably, giving unexpected insights into how a globalizing Asia is being lived.

DIASPORIC FORMATION

The group that is officially called Miao in China numbers 9.4 million. Because of long separations, owing to centuries of migration across Chinese territory, members of this group go by several different ethnonyms and speak mutually unintelligible dialects. Only a couple of subgroups of "Miao" have migrated since the mid-1800s to Vietnam, Laos, Thailand, and Burma. These latter groups, who are also internally diverse, all call themselves "Hmong" and recognize each other by both language and a kin ethic: Wherever they go, those of the same surname regard each other as "brothers" and "sisters" and offer support and hospitality regardless of whether they have ever met.

Hmong arriving in Southeast Asia lived alongside other ethnic minorities in highland areas. Isolation from lowland societies did not, however, make them immune to the larger political and military transformations of the nineteenth and twentieth centuries. French colonialism and US imperial projects during the twentieth century ensnared them in global political and military struggles. Some aligned themselves with nationalists fighting for independence; others collaborated with imperial powers. Contentiousness expanded as French colonial rule in Indochina ended in 1954 and US Cold War urgency increased. Although Lao neutrality was declared in 1954, the people of Laos eventually were pulled into a war centered in Vietnam.

While the Hmong were spread across Vietnam, Laos, and Thailand before the American War, those who migrated to the United States are from Laos, where they took part in US covert operations from 1961–75.[1] Initially a few hundred, the Hmong clandestine army numbered over 40,000 by the late 1960s. This clandestine army, which was supported by the US Central Intelligence Agency (CIA). sustained severe losses. Following US disengagement from Southeast Asia, those who had aligned themselves with the Americans faced retribution. Two weeks after the fall of Saigon on April 30, 1975, roughly 2,500 Hmong military officials and their families were airlifted by the CIA to Thailand. Thousands more sought a way out of Laos on their own. Those who crossed the Mekong River seeking asylum in Thailand transited in United Nations refugee camps, prior to resettlement in third countries. Since 1975, the vast majority have resettled in North America (about 145,000 in the United States and 2,000 in Canada), Europe (15,000 in France and 150 in Germany), and Oceania (2,000 in Australia and New Zealand). One of the authors of this article (Vang) and her family were among those who rebuilt their lives in the United States. France also sent about one thousand Hmong to French Guiana. Argentina accepted 266 families, of which twenty-five were Hmong.[2]

Especially because departure from Asia was abrupt and involuntary, Hmong arriving in foreign countries harbored acute longings for homelands left behind. Hmong stories, legends, and cultural practices had long referenced *Suav Teb* (China, or the land of the Han) as both place of origin and mythical site to which souls of the deceased should return. Hmong called funeral incantations and shaman trance speech *lug/lus suav* ("Chinese speech"), for their phonetic resemblance to Chinese. Refugees' memory and grief for lost lands and lifeways extended to "homelands" that encompassed the Lao land they had inhabited, the Chinese regions from which their ancestors came, and the refugee camps in Thailand where they had last sojourned. As they resettled into urban and industrialized lives in the West, an imaginary of these homelands became stabilized as a rural and underdeveloped zone where culture remained suspended in time, traditions preserved. In the late 1970s, no one was sure they would ever see these lands again, which intensified nostalgic feelings.

In 1982, Schein visited China as a junior researcher on the Hmong. The country was in the early process of opening to foreigners after being closed for three decades during Maoism. That year, Schein was not permitted to visit the Miao countryside, but was introduced to Miao "teachers" in Beijing. To her shock, she found that the Hmong language she knew was not recognizable to the Miao she met from various parts of China, nor were customs and clothing styles similar. Miao intellectuals and cultural workers she encountered were anything but peasants; they had been through a socialist revolution and had obtained a higher education. These elite identities were unknown, perhaps unfathomable, to Hmong in the diaspora, whose image was of highland farmers remote from—even antagonistic toward—Han Chinese centers.[3]

Schein returned to the United States with audiotapes and photos to share with Hmong friends. Rather than regarding them with curiosity, however, Hmong Americans confronted the material with profound disillusionment, suspicious that Schein, as a clueless white American, had been introduced to *other* ethnic minorities, not their ancestors' people. In that moment, Hmong émigrés' language and cultural gaps with what Schein had gathered were too vast to allow for identification. But in the end such gaps proved bridgeable. Four decades on, dense webs of interaction have been spun between China, Southeast Asia, and Western countries. In what follows, we explore the many—not uncomplicated—ways by which diasporic Hmong reconnected with coethnics in Asia through what Schein elsewhere has called "identity exchanges" and through continuously revising homeland expectations.[4] In the process, the Hmong/Miao *subnational* status as minorities in every country they inhabited came to be supplemented by a *supranational* connectivity

YOUR MOUNTAIN LIES DOWN WITH YOU

Mai Der Vang

Mourn the poppies, the mangosteen and dragonfruit.

But you come as a refugee, an exile, a body seeking mountains
Meaning the same in translation.

Here they are.

Place your palms on the grasslands. Feel the foothills rise
with gray pine and blue oak.

Here, rest not by the lotus of your old country but with
carpenterias and fiddlenecks of spring.

These woodlands may be unfamiliar, their sequoias thicker
than bamboo, and the rains unable to assemble monsoons.

Still, look out to the distance from where you lie.

You will see Mount Whitney is as beautiful as Phou Bia.

The moon is sharp enough to cut your ear as the one from your village.

And notice how these budding magnolias gesture
like the petals on a *dok champa*.

Is that the jungle flower you plucked when you fled, the one you
cradled
all the way to the ghettos of Saint Paul where you first settled?

You cried every time you saw its picture.

Grandfather, you are not buried in the green mountains of Laos
but here in the Tollhouse hills, earth and heaven to oak gods.

Your highlands have come home,
and now you finally sleep.

that superseded borders and citizenship, even as it created unequal power relations.

THE BLOSSOMING OF TRANSNATIONALITIES

As Hmong immigrants began to gather resources and qualify for passports, the late twentieth century saw burgeoning travel to Asia, first to refugee camps in Thailand, then to reunifications with family in Laos. In this era of intense flows, return visits were complemented by new refugee departures from Southeast Asia that continued into the 1990s. Since only Hmong *from Laos* were granted refugee status as a result of their relationship with the United States during the Vietnam War, the globalizing process has been almost entirely in the hands of those of one national origin. The Lao-Hmong have largely shaped perceptions, interactions, agendas, and actual exchanges.

Such exchanges soon became highly material. Most Lao-Hmong refugees in Thailand and some Hmong in Laos itself increasingly anticipated, even depended on, remittances from their overseas relatives. In ensuing decades, these financial transfers became intrinsic to the Lao economy. Business relations quickly followed. Hmong American women discovered a market for their colorful textile handicrafts and began importing small pieces sewn by women in camps and villages. As Hmong living in Western countries became savvy about the marketability of certain commodities, such as small purses or cushions, they began to contract with women in Thailand to produce merchandise in bulk. Some who settled in Amish country in Pennsylvania gleaned the high returns to be garnered on Amish quilts and outsourced the designs to Southeast Asia for needlework and assembly. The commodification of handicraft also impacted gender roles; some Hmong men in the refugee camps taught themselves the time-honored women's sewing skills in their quest for sources of income. In the 1990s, entrepreneurial Hmong American men pursued business ventures in Laos, including hotels and real estate. Since foreigners could not own businesses, they either used the name of a close Hmong Lao relative or, occasionally, married a local woman and established the enterprise in her name. One midwestern Hmong couple renounced their American citizenship and moved back to Laos to build a hotel.

Types and goals of return visits proliferated gradually. A mushrooming economic and cultural niche was video making. As portable camcorders proliferated, documentation of homeland trips became popular. Especially prized were videos shot in Vietnam and China, where most Hmong from Laos had never traveled. Voyagers morphed into directors as they began to edit their tourist footage, add narration, and circulate packaged products, sometimes for profit. Indeed, commercialized videos may have expanded the geographic scope of homeland imaginaries as videographers marketed their works as showcasing "where we came from." Not only did visual imagery and, later, analog and digital communications technologies make Hmong (Thailand and Laos), "Meo" (Vietnam), and "Miao" (China) more familiar but they also promoted the envisioning of a unitary worldwide community. When Schein visited the far north of Vietnam in the 2000s, she found local Hmong chatting with Hmong in the United States via social media at internet cafes.

The initial diasporic demand for "homeland videos" (Schein 2004b) spawned a burgeoning enterprise that involved a range of players. Hmong Americans established production companies, purchased editing equipment, and began putting out videos for mass circulation via ethnic shops and festivals. Quickly, the creatively inclined realized that the market would also welcome narrative videos. Within a few years, the variety of products included not only homeland documentaries but also melodramas, martial arts stories, ghost stories, remakes of old legends, music videos, comedies, war stories, and histories. In Hmong language, for consumption by Hmong audiences, this exploding field also included dubbed films from the mainstream Hong Kong, Thai, and other movie industries. Cassette tapes and eventually CDs were also produced to circulate older and newer forms of Hmong music. A transnational business model developed in which overseas Hmong created scripts, gathered equipment, then traveled to Asia to access scenic settings, acting labor, crew, and inexpensive postproduction. Shooting in Asia was also valued for its pedagogical function in tutoring second-generation youth in the lifeways, language, and heritages of their Asia-based forbears.

Perhaps the most popular among the dramatic genres were romances, often in the tragic vein. A highly gendered norm developed around the spectacularizing of the longed-for "homeland woman," young and traditionally adorned.[5] Iconic, she epitomized the lost past, thus becoming an object of male desire. Romantic tearjerkers staged time-honored stories of young love (often star-crossed), newer scenarios set in war or refugee eras, and contemporary trans-Pacific sagas replete with all the structural tensions that were emerging with transnationality. A diasporic "courtship" genre became wildly popular. In variant stories, Hmong American men would go to Asia to seek brides, girlfriends, or trysts; highly fraught scenarios would ensue as young women were cruised, pressured. or taken advantage of by these relatively well-off visitors endowed with First World residency.

As Schein has argued elsewhere, much of the popularity of the diasporic courtship genre was its function of voicing social critique.[6] For indeed, in the 1990s, and up to the present, a chief regret among diasporic and homeland Hmong alike is that gendered and sexual exploitation has divided the community and severely taxed potential solidarities across the Pacific. While transnational marriages *could* fulfill multiple needs—of forming kin alliances, channeling remittances, and allowing Asia-based spouses to emigrate—the lived reality has been much more multifaceted and ambivalent. Numerous promises of marriage have been broken, sometimes because men were already married in the West. Betrothed fiancées have been suspended in waiting for their grooms for years, occasionally resulting in their suicides.[7]

VOYAGES, EXCHANGES, ASYMMETRIES

Gendered returns are much of what makes the transnational connections between Asia and the West so starkly asymmetrical. Layered onto the existing structure of First World as mobile and wealthier versus developing world as earthbound and often mired in poverty is the preponderance of diasporic *men* traveling to Asian villages (though women also travel), where they achieve prestige and recognition for their newfound cosmopolitan status and their wielding of potent currencies—American, French, Australian, and so on. Men's returns take a related form in health quests, documented by Mai See Thao, in which aging, chronically ill men seek to restore youthful wellness and masculinity by tapping into homeland purity and vitality.[8]

Healing returns are multipurpose and extend way beyond remasculinization. In an era in which "integrative" medicine has been on the rise, Hmong can be considered pioneers for considering alternatives and regularly electing more naturopathic options, especially those accessed in Asia. What in other contexts has been called "medical tourism" appears here more like homeland health-seeking. Patients with acute, terminal, and chronic illnesses—wary of the expense, invasiveness, and toxic side-effects of Western biomedicine and favoring less aggressive measures, including herbal treatment, skilled massage, and spiritual solutions such as shamanism—have journeyed to Southeast Asia, even to China, to seek the most suitable care. Demand has been high enough that clinics have been established in Hmong and other minority areas to treat international patients. Homeland affect is intrinsic to these quests. Patients say that the environment, fresh air, food, and water, as well as the soothing scenes of mountains and the slower pace of life, are much of what supports their healing. In a sense, as Thao interprets it, they seek to remedy the pain of displacement through a "place-specific cure."[9] Moreover, returnee travelers connect with their kin groups even when they cannot visit their own close relatives, accessing a clan hospitality system Lee calls hegemonic, which elicits feelings of solidarity following painful war separations.[10]

Meanwhile, the desirability of alternative treatment modalities has provided a business niche for Hmong entrepreneurs who import herbs and other natural remedies that are only available or affordable in Asia. Hmong stores and festival booths overflow with such commodities. One businessman based in Minneapolis-Saint Paul cured by a Miao healer in the forests of the China-Vietnam border subsequently contracted to harvest the specialized herbs from that biodiverse region, processing them into capsules and powders in a small factory he established in Wisconsin.

Christian community-building and proselytizing have been strong forces in forging bonds across the diaspora. Catholic and Protestant missionaries converted perhaps 5 percent of Hmong in Laos during the 1950s and 1960s. In the United States they organized churches to nurture their far-flung communities.[11] The Christian Missionary Alliance (CMA) and Catholic churches were particularly proactive about reaching out to Hmong remaining in Southeast Asia, traveling to Thailand, Laos, Vietnam, and China. Proselytizing has also worked through the media with large numbers of conversions resulting from radio broadcasts across Southeast Asia in Hmong language. At street markets in mountain towns, crudely copied evangelizing VCDs and DVDs could be purchased literally from "under the table." Hmong American missionaries provide Hmong language Bibles and song books to new converts. While missionaries work in small numbers, the US-based CMA has held several large "Yexusfest" international gatherings in Chiangmai, Thailand.[12]

Second and 1.5 generation Hmong interact differently with coethnics in Asia. Joining short-term educational tours and longer study-abroad programs, they favor Thailand and China as destinations. Since 2003, college study tours have offered visits to and even fieldwork in Hmong villages in China, Laos, or Thailand. K-12 (kindergarten through twelfth grade), Hmong-focused charter schools in Saint Paul, Minnesota have taken middle school students to Laos and Thailand. In 2009, Vang began designing short-term programs to Cambodia, Laos, Thailand, and Vietnam that included cultural exchanges with local Hmong professionals and service projects in village schools. In their postprogram published testimonials, participants of Hmong ethnicity expressed curiosity and awe. Two undergraduate students discussed the impact that travel had on them:

> My experience collaborating with the local village school was truly a wonderful learning experience. After hearing my parents speak so much about their homeland, I never thought I would have the opportunity to actually visit Laos, to breathe the same air my parents had, to walk on the same ground they had, and to live in a village like they had (Bruce Lee, 2013).

> When I returned home from this trip, my parents asked if my group had stopped at a rest area that was on a mountain in the Xieng Khouang Province. I said we had and showed this photo to them . . . My father's eyes watered a bit and he said to me, "Right past those two large mountains is where I grew up" (Ahong Xiong, 2013).My expectations prior to the 2017–2018 program was to gain a deeper understanding about the experiences of Hmong Christians living in Vietnam and Laos. . . . Three things . . . I have taken away . . . (1) the meaning of sacrifice (2) my "Hmong" privileges and (3) a deeper appreciation of my Hmong American identity (Navee Lor, 2018).

In the 2000s, the Minnesota Center for Hmong Studies fostered intellectual exchanges through the International Conference on Hmong Studies, which convened seven times between 2006 and 2018. The purpose was "to provide opportunities for emerging and established Hmong and non-Hmong scholars to share their research on Hmong related topics, to inspire and motivate students to engage in scholarly research, and to recognize distinguished scholars for their work in the field of Hmong Studies." Sessions with scholars and presenters from China were in high demand. and increased contact gradually reduced Hmong American resistance to recognizing "Miao," despite their differences. Beginning with the sixth conference (2016), Center staff added the word "Miao" where it had previously included only Hmong (i.e., "Hmong/*Miao* related topics" or "the field of Hmong/*Miao* Studies").

After several decades of educational visits to Asia by scholars, tourists, and students, the flow is reversing. Chinese Miao social scientist Zhang Xiao visited the United States as a Fulbright scholar and devoted much of her time to living with and collecting data about the lives of Hmong Americans. A surgeon from Beijing pursuing a medical anthropology PhD worked with Hmong in a Fresno hospital. Two minority PhD students from Beijing, one of whom had done participant-observation on Hmong farms in the California Central Valley, pursued long-term fieldwork in Hmong communities in the American Midwest. From the perspective of these junior scholars, the question of how Hmong have adapted to life in the West is of great intellectual import.

CONCLUSION

Kou Yang, one of the earliest Hmong Americans to organize educational trips to discover heritage among ethnic counterparts in China, described the potent feeling for Hmong participants of having a cultural ceremony performed as a send-off from a village in China: "It was like a dream, seeing one's own ancestors for just a brief time."[13] We suggest that this dreamlike perception on the part of diasporic Hmong looking "back" on the homeland has a dual function. On the one hand, it is a powerful force propelling far-flung Hmong actors to initiate and sustain connections with Asian countries. On the other hand, it masks some of the more asymmetrical qualities of these connections, because it provides a rationale for regarding those Hmong and Miao left spatially behind as also left behind in time, as exemplars of the past to be consumed culturally and socially. Hmong and Miao in Asia have been repeatedly frustrated by this ascribed status, especially when they see their goals for transnational connections so differently. They often seek concrete exchanges, collaborations, and durable material and marital links.

Indeed, what migrants actually encounter on their return visits is far from the static, timeless culture dreamed about as the quintessential panacea for acute loss and dislocation in the West. With socialist revolutions in China, Laos, and Vietnam, and the subsequent impact of modernization, globalization, and urbanization, Hmong and Miao cultures, subsistence, and social lives in Asia have dramatically transformed. In the same decades, diaspora has wrought drastic upheavals. Because culture on both sides of the Pacific remains inevitably in flux, we have highlighted the material contours and what we call the "identity exchanges" that have been the backbone and the sinews of connectedness. In these decades, Hmong and Miao have moved toward being less fractured as marginal minorities within their respective nation-states; they have formed a supranational body that comprises a complex organism with many distinct elements. Border-crossing—in person and

through communications technologies and palpable imaginings—has been
the lifeblood and the "circulatory system" that sustain this body as a whole.

DISCOVERING WHAT IT MEANS TO BE HMONG AMERICAN

Vlai Ly

My grandmother never talks about herself when I ask about her life
back in Laos. Instead, her stories always revolve so deeply around the
people she loved. Sitting . . . in Fresno, she tells me of the time my
father was almost left behind in Laos during the evacuation.

"We all got in the car but there wasn't any room for your dad. He was
just a little younger than you, just standing up there on the road while
we were all about to leave.

Your grandfather called his name one time, called two times, but
he didn't hear. He called a third time, then finally your father came
down very quickly, right when a soldier's truck came. He was able to
get in that truck with them. . . . There were so many loved ones who
didn't make it out of Laos. . . .

. . . "No one gets left behind"—these were her sentiments toward
everyone around her as the war waged on. . . .

In listening to the elder's stories, I begin to slowly understand the
seed that existed inside all of their hearts, a seed that we've inherited
as a new generation of Hmong Americans. This seed . . . is the idea
that our lives are not our own— that we create community and community creates us.

As gunfire exploded around them and airplanes ripped through
the sky, Hmong people drew their strength from that sense of community. When they had to flee from their villages, it was other Hmong
people that provided them a new home to travel with.

You can see this within the United States today. From California
to Massachusetts, we congregated together because other Hmong
people provided that familiarity and comfort as we built new lives in
a new land. Home is often thought of as a place or a location, but to
Hmong people, home is the people themselves.

It's taken me twenty-six years to truly understand that idea for
myself. . . .

While the Hmong values of family and community were present at home, the Western values of individualism and competition
consumed my life. This divide was especially jarring growing up in

Massachusetts, where the Hmong community was much smaller than the dense communities found in Minnesota and California. . . .

It wasn't until college that I started pulling together the various threads of my life in an attempt to understand the enigma of the Hmong American identity. I went to the University of Massachusetts Amherst, where I spent the majority of my college career fumbling around with what to do with myself. . . . At that age, for a lot of Hmong Americans, the possibilities of what we could do with ourselves seemed extremely limited.

Right before entering my last year of college, I inherited my uncle's DSLR camera and became engulfed in photography. . . . I created photography projects focused around the Hmong. . . .

To further my understanding of Hmong identity, I decided to move to Sacramento, California. . . .

My work there connected me with Noah Vang. . . . He invited me to be a part of the Hmong American delegation going to Guizhou, China to experience the Miao New Year's and reconnect with that part of our Hmong history.

China introduced me to the idea of a global community, one not separated by borders and differing ideologies. The trip culminated in a conference between many of the Hmong, Miao, and Chinese leaders from around the world. Here, they spoke about wanting to build global bridges between the various international communities in order to move forward together. Despite the conflict-filled history between China and Hmong people, I felt a genuine intention to move forward into the future together.

The trip to China only lasted for a week, and while it was a beautiful spectacle to experience, it was the simplicity and slow-paced trip in Laos that had the most profound impact on me.

My initial Western perspective was to view the chaotic traffic and dusty roads of Luang Prabang as "undeveloped," but my heart was transfixed by the strangely beautiful thread that tied the community together.

I fell in love with the communal atmosphere there. People's lives weren't defined by what kind of work they did. Instead, work was just a simple means to get by while they put their energy into the people they loved and the community around them. Status and salary wasn't [*sic*] a factor in determining a person's self-worth. For the first time in my life, I was free from that deep sense of consumerism and materialism that plagued my life back in America.

The elders always tell me that they miss living in Laos, and I finally understood why.

Despite the long hours walking back and forth between the farmland and their house, they still yearn for that simplicity of life. It was a life devoted to spiritual and mental well-being for everyone around them, a life that was true to their values.

When I landed back into San Francisco, I was immediately faced with the stark cost that came with the comfort and luxury of America. Homeless people panhandling for money during Christmas week as hundreds of people walked by paying them no attention. An incoherent man being punched and thrown into the ground by security guards as everyone watched and recorded. The brief joy of being back home was taken over by this dense atmosphere of a spiritually and mentally sick country, lost to the values of community beyond their immediate circle.

I had spent my life stuck in limbo between the crossroads of my Hmong and American worlds, but in the clarity of that morning I finally felt as though I had . . . discovered what it meant to be Hmong American.

During my trip to Laos and China, . . . I realized that my life was not my own, that I create community and community created me.

My life is a continuation of my grandmother's story, of my parent's story—of the Hmong story that unites us all as a people. To know these stories is to know of the seed of community that exists inside all of our hearts. To be Hmong American means to use the tools provided through this country to uplift and empower the people around you so they can see the value in their own life's story. . . .

Originally published in Txhawb Hmong California Directory.

NOTES

1. Vang 2019.
2. Vang 2018.
3. She went on to produce a study of the Miao in China, partly in order to bring these stories to Westerners' awareness. See Schein 2000.
4. Schein 2004a.
5. Schein 2004b.
6. Schein 2004b.
7. Thoj 2002.
8. Thao 2018.
9. Thao 2018.

10. Lee 2018.
11. Vang 2010.
12. Ngo 2016.
13. Yang 2005:14

REFERENCES AND FURTHER READING

Center for Hmong Studies. "International Conference on Hmong Studies." https:// hmongcenter.csp.edu/

Lee, Sangmi. 2018. "Diasporic Kinship Hegemonies and Transnational Continuities in the Hmong Diaspora." *Identities* 27, no. 2 (March): 229–47.

Ly, Vlai. 2019. "Discovering What It Means to Be Hmong American." *Txhawb Hmong California Directory*. 11th ed. Annual Publication: 37-44.

Ngo, Tam T. T. 2016. *The New Way: Protestantism and the Hmong in Vietnam*. Seattle: University of Washington Press.

Schein, Louisa. 2000. *Minority Rules: The Miao and the Feminine in China's Cultural Politics*. Durham, NC: Duke University Press.

———. 2004a. "Hmong/Miao Transnationality: Identity Beyond Culture." In *Hmong/Miao in Asia*, edited by Nicholas Tapp, Jean Michaud, Christian Culas, and Gary Yia Lee, 273–90. Chiang Mai: Silkworm Books.

———. 2004b. "Homeland Beauty: Transnational Longing and Hmong American Video." *Journal of Asian Studies* 63, no. 2 (May): 433–63.

Thao, Mai See. 2018. "Bittersweet Migrations: Type II Diabetes and Healing in the Hmong Diaspora." PhD diss., University of Minnesota. ProQuest (AAT 10838352).

Thoj, Va-Megn, dir. 2002. *Death in Thailand*. Saint Paul, MN: C. H. A. T. Television Productions, Frogtown Media Productions. Videocassette (VHS).

Vang, Chia Youyee. 2010. *Hmong America: Reconstructing Community in Diaspora*. Champaign: University of Illinois Press.

———. 2018. "Thinking Refugee: The Politics of Hmong Place-Making in Argentina and French Guiana." *Amerasia Journal* 44, no. 2 (August): 1–21.

———. 2019. *Fly Until You Die: An Oral History of Hmong Pilots in the Vietnam War*. Oxford: Oxford University Press.

Yang, Kou. 2005. "Research Notes from the Field: Tracing the Path of the Ancestors—A Visit to the Hmong in China." *Hmong Studies Journal* 6, no. 1: 1–38.

Yang, Zhiqiang. 2009. "From Miao to Miaozu: Alterity in the Formation of Modern Ethnic Groups." *Hmong Studies Journal* 10, no. 1: 1–28.

NINETEEN

An East Asian Nation without a State

XINJIANG AND CHINA'S NON-CHINESE

Ildikó Bellér-Hann

DESPITE ITS FREQUENTLY ASSUMED HOMOGENEITY, socialist China, like its imperial and republican predecessors, is internally highly diverse. The fifty-five ethnic minorities officially recognized by the People's Republic of China make up less than 9 percent of the total population of the country; nevertheless, their role in upholding China's territorial unity and overall stability is crucial, owing to their position along international borders as well as the sheer vastness of the areas they occupy. It is no accident that four out of the country's five autonomous regions were established in these geopolitically important borderlands in the early 1950s. Of these, the Xinjiang Uyghur Autonomous Region (XUAR), situated in China's far northwest, makes up about one-sixth of the total area of China, shares international borders with eight countries, and is rich in natural resources. Today, the XUAR's total population of approximately 21 million people counts thirteen recognized ethnic groups. The Uyghurs represent approximately 45 percent, the ethnic Han Chinese 40 percent, while the remaining 5 percent is made up by the Kazakh, Hui, Kyrgyz, Mongols, and other smaller groups.

THE MAKING OF THE UYGHURS

The ethnogenesis of the modern Uyghurs has been a centuries' long, complex process with roots outside the territory of modern Xinjiang.[1] The designation "Uyghur" first appears in historical sources as the name of a Turkic-speaking nomadic tribal confederation with their headquarters in the Orkhon Valley in modern-day Mongolia; their nomadic empire north of Tang China was founded in the mid-eighth century. A century later, they were ousted by another nomadic confederation, and they migrated from their traditional territories toward the south and southwest. Those arriving in what is now known as Xinjiang intermarried with the local Indo-European sedentary population and gradually switched from a pastoral economy to farming.[2] While holding on to their native shamanic traditions, these old Uyghur communities encountered various religions emanating from western Asia and beyond, including Manichaeism, Buddhism, and Nestorian Christianity. With these came new scripts, which introduced a great deal of diversity into old Uyghur literate practices.[3] Despite this initial diversity in religious and literate traditions, linguistically the region soon became more homogenous: gradual Turkification was accompanied by the spread of Islam from the west, bringing with it the Arabic script, a process that started in the tenth century and was completed by the sixteenth century. After the Mongol period, the term "Uyghur" disappears from the sources. The Turkic-speaking Muslims of the region were referred to according to their place of origin, such as "the people from Kashgar," "the people from Kucha," and so on. By the late seventeenth and early eighteenth centuries, the small, fragmented oasis kingdoms under Muslim rulers were subordinated to Zunghar (western Mongol) domination. With the Qing conquest in the middle of the eighteenth century, Xinjiang and its Muslims became incorporated into the Manchu Empire.[4] Throughout the nineteenth and the first half of the twentieth centuries, Xinjiang was part of imperial and later republican China with several short-lived—but nonetheless important—attempts at independence. Today, socialist China claims the full territorial legacy of its imperial and republican predecessors and has a huge stake in holding on to Xinjiang on account of its size, strategic position. and resource wealth.

The XUAR was founded in 1955. Minority rights, though inscribed in the constitution, were only realized intermittently under Chairman Mao. Nevertheless, the Uyghurs profited from affirmative action policies for minorities, which were revived with Deng Xiaoping's reforms in the early 1980s. From the early 1990s, however, the authorities increasingly interpreted Uyghur assertions of cultural identity in terms of separatist aspirations that they were quick to repress. The emergence of new nation-states in Central Asia in the wake of the collapse of the Soviet Union, with several having Turkic-speaking Muslims as the titular population, exacerbated Beijing's fears. Throughout the 1990s. the Xinjiang problem was treated by Beijing as China's domestic affair. Following 9/11, the rhetoric changed and Uyghur protests in Xinjiang and attacks against Chinese targets were presented as a matter of international terrorism.[5] By the second decade of the twenty-first century. Uyghurs have little room left to maneuver. All aspects of their cultural and religious identity have come under attack. A small number of Uyghurs have reacted with increasingly frequent violent acts of protest. These "incidents" are countered by the government with massively enhanced security measures, surveillance, repression. and intimidation, on the one hand, but also by large-scale investment and development. on the other.

The promotion of wealth and economic prosperity is motivated not only by the desire to bring stability to this restive region but also, in the context of China's transnational Eurasian project, the Belt and Road Initiative (BRI, also referred to as the Silk Road Economic Belt), to promote Xinjiang as an international commercial hub. The legacy of Xinjiang's oasis cities along the historical Silk Road as major commercial and cultural centers are exploited by Chinese policy makers in their efforts to stabilize the region by means of top-down modernization policies. The XUAR's inclusion in this globalizing project stands in sharp contrast to its earlier isolation in the 1960s and 1970s. It resumes presocialist patterns of transregional connectivity that led Owen Lattimore to characterize Xinjiang in 1950 as the "pivot of Asia."[6]

The pivotal position of the Uyghurs at the intersection of East and Central Asia goes beyond the transnational economic role that Beijing assigns to Xinjiang. It is reinforced through multiple historical and cultural connections that tie the Uyghurs to various nation-states and diaspora populations outside China. As a member of the Turkic language family, Uyghur is related to a number of languages spoken by populations across Central Asia and beyond. Linguistic proximity connects the Uyghurs to the languages of four independent states in Central Asia—namely, Uzbekistan, Kazakhstan, Kyrgyzstan, and Turkmenistan—and beyond that to the states of Azerbaijan and Turkey, as well as many smaller ethnolinguistic communities in Mongolia, the Russian Federation, Iran, Afghanistan, and elsewhere in Central Asia, the Caucasus, the Middle East, the Balkans and Western Europe.

Other Turkic-speaking Muslim groups among Xinjiang's minorities, such as the Kazakhs, share numerous commonalities with Kazakhstani Kazakhs and diaspora Kazakhs living in Mongolia, Afghanistan, and Uzbekistan. Shared linguistic and cultural traits formed the basis of the positive response of some of Xinjiang's Kazakhs to the Kazakh government's repatriation program, which was launched in order to increase the number of ethnic Kazakhs who found themselves in the minority in Kazakhstan following that country's independence in 1991.[7] By contrast, the Uyghurs have no country outside

China to which they can go, despite the cultural and linguistic commonalities between Xinjiang (also known as Chinese or Eastern Turkestan) and the rest of Central Asia (sometimes referred to as Russian or Western Turkestan).[8]

Sunni Islam creates another common denominator between the Uyghurs and several other minorities (both Turkic and non-Turkic speaking) of Xinjiang, and more generally in Central Asia and the Middle East. Muslims in China are situated on the eastern edge of the Islamic world. The role of Islam in Uyghur self-identification and in relations across ethnic, regional, and national boundaries is fraught with complexity. In the early twentieth century, Muslim cultural reformism (Jadidism) spread via Muslim (especially Tatar) educators from the Russian and Ottoman Empires to Xinjiang, where it inspired cautious but significant changes in the traditional education system. These reformist ideas reached Xinjiang through progressive Uyghur traders who combined the pilgrimage to Mecca with commercial enterprise and cultural experience. Recently David Brophy has located the origin of modern Uyghur ethnonationalism in the convergence of Muslim reformist ideas with diaspora activities after the Russian October Revolution in 1917, which coincided with reemergence of the term "Uyghur".[9]

POLITICIZING UYGHUR IDENTITY

Today, in its unequal tug-of-war with the Uyghurs, Beijing exaggerates the role of Islam in Uyghur ethnic identity because it fears that religion can become a rallying point for Uyghur political discontent. The conflict that reemerged in the early 1990s in the more open atmosphere created by the early phase of the reform period has escalated gradually over the last three decades. Initially, the Uyghurs were emboldened by the more permissive policies. Some started to aspire to more meaningful political participation, as promised in the law on regional autonomy.

Shaken by the Tiananmen protests in 1989 and fearing that the emergence of the newly independent nation-states in neighboring Central Asia would serve as a model for the Uyghurs, Beijing dialed up the repression. The "strike hard" campaigns throughout the 1990s were not only directed against ordinary criminals but also against Uyghur separatists. Beijing presented this as joining the US War on Terror in the wake of 9/11 and received international support and sympathy. However, the number of violent incidents perpetrated by Uyghurs increased and started to be exported to other parts of China beyond Xinjiang's borders.[10] Parallel to this, Beijing also stepped up investment into Xinjiang, hoping that economic development would reduce ethnic unrest. The Great Western Development Drive launched in 2000 has indeed brought a great deal of investment into Xinjiang, but the authorities' hopes for an improved political atmosphere have not borne fruit.[11] The Uyghurs continue to view China's development program with a great deal of suspicion, seeing it as just another vehicle for stepping up Han immigration into the region.

Interethnic conflict between Han and Uyghurs during the protests in Urumqi in July 2009 soon turned into a full-scale riot that eventually took 197 lives and injured 1,721 people. Following the events in July, Beijing's campaign against the "three evil forces" (terrorism, ethnic separatism, and religious extremism) led to further animosity between the Han and Uyghur populations. Security measures, such as the permanent presence of troops in cities, checkpoints, and widespread high-tech surveillance, amounted to an undeclared state of emergency.

Between 2014 and 2016, the situation further deteriorated. Numerous attacks occurred in Xinjiang itself and in 2014 thirty-one people died when a bomb went off at Kunming railway station. Moreover, the Uyghur problem spread to other countries, making it much more visible and thereby damaging for the Chinese authorities. In response, hardliner Chen Quanguo was appointed as party secretary to Xinjiang in August 2016. Chen had earlier successfully brought the situation in Tibet under control by massively stepping up systematic policing, surveillance, and suppression. Under his rule in Xinjiang security measures have been increased and large sections of the population, reliably estimated to amount to more than one million people or 10 percent of the total Uyghur population, have been detained, arrested, or taken to the political reeducation camps that have sprung up all over Xinjiang. In the camps, inmates are educated to rid themselves of their Uyghur culture and religion and to become good Chinese citizens. The inmates include both members of the elite and villagers, and surveillance continues after release from the camp, making the Uyghurs in effect not only prisoners but also "strangers in their own land."[12]

Beijing's relentless tendency to respond to Uyghur resistance by further tightening the screw may turn Uyghur terrorism into a self-fulfilling prophesy. Uyghur fighters have been present in Afghanistan and Syria, of whom twenty-two that were captured in Afghanistan ended up in Guantanamo, later to be sent on to Palau and Albania. While the number of terrorist incidents has grown in recent years, most experts interpret these acts of violence as spontaneous expressions of individual frustration with religious and cultural repression rather than as premeditated terror attacks by an organized movement.

The politicization of Islam can be seen as a recent phenomenon largely provoked by harsh religious and cultural policies, which criminalize expressions of religious affiliation and brand all group members as potential terrorists. At the same time, Uyghur ethnonationalism, with its roots in the republican period and socialist ethnic policies, has rendered Islam an important constituent of Uyghur ethnic identity. Some young urban women have adopted foreign versions of Islamic dress codes.[13] Yet this external demonstration of faith and belonging does not, for most Uyghurs, translate into a primary identification with the transnational Islamic faith community (*umma*). That Uyghurs lack traditions of transnational "pan" identities which may partly be explained by the socialist minority policies that subordinated religious difference to ethnic identity. China's Muslims are fragmented along ethnic lines and have been isolated from Muslim communities abroad for decades. Moreover, Uyghur interpretations of what it means to be a Muslim vary considerably according to social class, gender, generation, education, and profession. Government policies themselves reveal ambivalence and inconsistencies concerning Muslims. While Uyghur Muslims are targeted with repressive policies both inside and outside their home region, the Chinese Muslims (the Hui, China's most populous Muslim ethnic group, who live in communities scattered throughout the country) enjoy a great deal of cultural and religious freedom, especially outside Xinjiang. Although the disciplinary and punitive measures employed against the Uyghurs have recently been extended to other Turkic-speaking Muslim groups in Xinjiang, notably the Kazakh, the Chinese Muslims have until recently largely been exempted.

THE UYGHUR DIASPORA

The Uyghurs' structural position within the People's Republic of China today is comparable to that of the Tibetans. Both are perceived by Beijing as the main threats to China's territorial unity and internal stability. The two groups' responses, however, both at home and in the diaspora, are very different. Uyghur violence takes aim not only at representatives of the Chinese state but also at civilians, both Han and Uyghur. This contrasts with Tibetan nonviolent forms of resistance and self-immolation. Moreover, compared to the Tibetans, the Uyghur diaspora lacks the high-profile charismatic leadership provided by the Dalai Lama and is much more fragmented.

Uyghur diaspora communities in neighboring Central Asia have developed since the nineteenth century. Their estimated number is three hundred thousand, with over 210,000 residing in Kazakhstan, 46,000 in Kyrgyzstan and 23,000 in Uzbekistan. In the Uyghur community in Kazakhstan in the 1990s, rival associations emerged with very different visions of their nation's future. As Beijing's hold over the Central Asian Republics became stronger, these associations gradually disappeared, went underground, or persisted in a depoliticized fashion.

China's setting up of the Shanghai Cooperation Organization with the Central Asian states in 1996 opened the border between the new republics and China and initially created new trading opportunities for China's Uyghurs. However, Uyghur shuttle traders were soon marginalized. One reason for that was state control over transnational business on both sides of the border, which favored the dominant groups in their respective countries; however, the Uyghurs' bad press as extremists, separatists, and terrorists also played a part.

While Uyghurs have languished, Chinese Muslims (known as Hui) have profited greatly from the transnational trade opportunities between China and Central Asia (although the most significant Chinese Muslim diaspora communities in Central Asia hail from Shaanxi or Gansu rather than Xinjiang). Smaller Muslim groups, such as the Tajik, the Uzbek, or the Kyrgyz. have been unable to profit significantly from transnational trade opportunities. The Kazakhs have fared better. Their transborder connections have received a boost from independent Kazakhstan's repatriation initiative to which numerous Kazakh families from China have responded positively.[14]

Large communities of Uyghur emigrants and refugees are found in Germany, France, and the United States. Since the 1950s, Turkey has become home to sizeable Uyghur and Kazakh diaspora groups that fled China in several waves in the wake of the Communist takeover of Xinjiang in 1949. While the Kemalists showed little interest in pan-Turkism, discursive support of the Uyghur cause has become stronger following the AK (Justice and Development) Party's ascendancy to power, which has based its proactive foreign policy on the principle of "civilizational geopolitics." While Turkey in recent years has repeatedly criticized Beijing's increasing heavy-handedness against the Uyghur Muslims in Xinjiang, it also stresses its ambition to cooperate with China, thus performing a careful balancing act.

The significance of the Uyghur diaspora in internationalizing the Xinjiang problem is increasing, especially since political activism inside the XUAR itself and the rest of China has become effectively impossible. The diaspora is increasingly using the internet. Online diaspora narratives challenge Chinese government website accounts of Xinjiang history.[15] Both sides tend to come up with wild exaggerations concerning the Uyghur and Han presence in Xinjiang, the nature of Uyghur indigeneity on Xinjiang soil, and Xinjiang's incorporation into the Chinese polity. Diaspora websites raise other contentious issues, such as China's bilingual education policy, which promotes the national language at the expense of the Uyghur mother tongue, as well as repressive religious policies. They frame Uyghur cultural traditions (e.g., music) as embedded in their Central Asian context. For its part, the government does not directly challenge the Uyghurs' Turkic or Central Asian heritage but rather adapts this narrative to promote a folklorized and commodified version of Uyghur identity for tourism by drawing attention to Uyghur festivals, food, dance, and music.

Historically, the Uyghurs embraced a moderate version of Islam and showed little, if any, inclination to join transnational political movements such as pan-Islamism or pan-Turkism. However, there is some evidence that the emerging urban Uyghur middle classes are responding to political pressure from Beijing and to processes of globalization with new consumption patterns (including Muslim attire) that reflect a closer alignment with Central Asian nation-states, Turkey, international Islam, or the West.[16]

UYGHUR-HAN TENSIONS AND THE FUTURE OF XINJIANG

Owing to the unequal power dynamics that have arisen ever since the incorporation of Xinjiang into the Chinese polity, the relationship between the region's Uyghur and Han populations has been fraught with tension. Throughout the socialist period and especially at times of political excesses, Uyghurs have tended to conflate the Chinese state and the majority Han population. Historical experiences, which culminated in violent conflict in 2009, and differences in religion, language, and social practices have all contributed to the perpetuation of mutual suspicion and avoidance of intermarriage between the two groups.

Both Uyghurs and Hans distinguish between those Han groups that have lived in Xinjiang for generations and have developed a certain cultural sensitivity toward the Uyghurs, and the newcomers, who have no such knowledge and are more likely to disregard rules of peaceful coexistence. Nevertheless, members of the two ethnic groups tend to live in relative segregation. The cultural differences between them have further been accentuated by the different policies targeting them.[17] Recent policies have sharpened interethnic conflict even more. More Han migrant workers and entrepreneurs have come to Xinjiang, marginalizing the Uyghurs in the labor market and the economy as a whole. State-sanctioned land grabs and investment in surveillance and communications technology and security confirm for the Uyghurs that the government is a government of and for the Chinese. This message is rubbed in even more by the "United as One Family" program that requires Han citizens regularly to visit Uyghurs in their homes in order to monitor their behavior and teach them Han cultural values. Existing fault lines in Xinjiang society are thus deepened by the state's simultaneous unleashing of the forces of Chinese capitalism represented by investors from eastern China and the implementation of extremely repressive measures. This approach may offer attractive short-term solutions, but it does not bode well for China's stability and unity in the long run.

NOTES

1. On the ethnogenesis of the Uyghurs, see Gladney 1990.
2. On the history of the nomadic "Old Uyghurs," see Golden 1992.
3. On the rich literate traditions of the pre-Islamic Turkic population of the Tarim Basin, see Róna-Tas 1991.
4. On the Qing conquest of Xinjiang, see Perdue 2005.
5. James A. Millward 2009.
6. Lattimore 1950.
7. As of 2015, approximately one million diaspora Kazakhs repatriated to the Kazakhstani homeland from neighboring countries. Of these, Kazakh immigrants from China make up more than 14 percent. See Cerny 2010.
8. Bellér-Hann et al. 2007.
9. Brophy 2016.
10. For a longitudinal study of Uyghur-Han relations. see Smith Finley 2013.
11. Millward 2007.
12. Mercator Institute of Chinese Studies (MERICS) 2019. See also Bovingdon 2010.

13. Leibold and Grose 2016.
14. Laruelle and Peyrouse 2009.
15. Culpepper 2012.
16. Erkin 2009.
17. On the Han living in Xinjiang, see Cliff 2016.

REFERENCES AND FURTHER READING

Bellér-Hann, Ildikó, Cristina Cesàro, Rachel Harris, and Joanne Smith Finley, eds. 2007. *Situating the Uyghurs between China and Central Asia*. Aldershot: Ashgate.

Bovingdon, Gardner. 2010. *The Uyghurs: Strangers in Their Own Land*. New York: Columbia University Press.

Brophy, David. 2016. *Uyghur Nation. Reform and Revolution on the Russia-China Frontier*. Cambridge, MA: Harvard University Press.

Cerny, Astrid. 2010. "Going Where the Grass is Greener: China Kazaks and the *Oralman* Immigration Policy in Kazakhstan." *Pastoralism* 1, no. 2 (January): 218–47.

Cliff, Tom. 2016. *Oil and Water. Being Han in Xinjiang*. Chicago: University of Chicago Press.

Culpepper, Rucker. 2012. "Nationalist Competition on the Internet: Uyghur Diaspora versus the Chinese State Media." *Asian Ethnicity* 13, no. 2 (February): 187–203.

Erkin, Adila. 2009. "Locally Modern, Globally Uyghur: Geography, Identity and Consumer Culture in Contemporary Xinjiang." *Central Asian Survey* 28, no. 4: 417–28.

Gladney, Dru. 1990. "The Ethnogenesis of the Uighur." *Central Asian Survey* 9, no. 1: 1–28.

Golden, Peter B. 1992. *An Introduction to the History of the Turkic Peoples- Ethnogenesis and State-Formation in Medieval and Early Modern Eurasia and the Middle East*. Wiesbaden: Otto Harrassowitz.

Laruelle, Marlène, and Sébastien Peyrouse. 2009. "Cross-border Minorities as Cultural and Economic Mediators between China and Central Asia." *China and Eurasia Forum Quarterly* 7, no. 1 (February): 93- 119.

Lattimore, Owen. 1950. *Pivot of Asia: Sinkiang and the Inner Asian Frontiers of China and Russia*. Boston: Little Brown.

Leibold, James, and Timothy Grose. 2016. "Veiling in Xinjiang: The Struggle to Define Uyghur Female Adornment." *China Journal* 76 (July): 1–25.

Mercator Institute of Chinese Studies. 2019. *Remaking a People: China's Coercive Policies in Xinjiang and What Europe Should Do about Them*. Berlin: MERICS.

Millward, James A. 2007. *Eurasian Crossroads. A History of Xinjiang*. New York: Columbia University Press.

———. 2009. "Introduction: Does the 2009 Urumchi Violence Mark a Turning Point?" *Central Asian Survey* 28, no. 4 (December): 347–60.

Perdue, Peter. 2005. *China Marches West: The Qing Conquest of Central Eurasia.* Cambridge, MA: Harvard University Press.

Róna-Tas, András. 1991. *An Introduction to Turkology.* Szeged: Universitas Szegediensis de Attila József Nominata.

Smith Finley, Joanne N. 2013. *The Art of Symbolic Resistance: Uyghur Identities and Uyghur-Han Relations in Contemporary Xinjiang.* Leiden: Brill.

PART FIVE

The Rise of China and East Asia as the New Center of the World

Frank N. Pieke

IT HAS BEEN SEVENTY YEARS since Mao Zedong proclaimed the founding of the People's Republic of China in Beijing. Since then, the country has undergone a tremendous transformation from a third-world country weakened by forty years of imperial collapse, warlordism, revolution, the Pacific War, and civil war to the second-largest economy in the world and a budding superpower.

In the 1970s and 1980s, Japan's rise was a cause for much concern about the decline of the West, almost as much, in fact, as China's rise is today. However, there is an essential difference. Japan had been devastated and defeated by the United States in the Pacific War. With its pacification and disarmament, any Japanese ambitions of becoming a global hegemon, imperial master, or superpower had been buried. Japan could only become—and also succeeded in being—a formidable economic power, but a power nonetheless that played within the confines of the rules of the existing Western-dominated world order and US and Soviet global supremacy.

China, however, is not content forever to play second fiddle. China's rise is engineered as part of a deliberate effort by the Chinese Communist Party to make China a great country and a great power that by mid-century will be able, if needed, to take US hegemony head-on. Not being dependent on the United States like Japan always continued to be, China only sticks to the rules insofar as this fits its own strategy. In other words, China's acceptance of the existing order is conditional. If required, it has the will, wherewithal, and increasingly also the military capacity to set its own rules, create its own institutions, and steer its own course. It does so in cooperation with other powers if it can, but it increasingly does not hesitate to go against its peers if it has to.

It is China's capacity and determination to become a great power that evokes such strong reactions among the established powers. In its China strategy paper of March 2019, the European Commission for the first time openly labeled China a "systemic rival" (European Commission, 2019); earlier in its 2018 Defense Strategy, the US administration had lumped China together with Russia as competitors of the United States who "want to shape a world consistent with their authoritarian model" (Department of Defense, 2018).

In the previous four sections, we already have given ample room to China's impact on the chief dimensions of globalization: goods, money, culture, science and technology, and people. In this final section of the book we will look at China's rise within our global square from a different point of view, homing in on the political and geostrategic aspects. In the first three chapters, we emphasize that the Chinese state's strategy of global expansion cannot simply enlist the bottom-up globalization of Chinese enterprises, migrants, institutions, and culture, but neither are the two completely separate. Bottom-up globalization provides both the tools for and sets the limits of state-led strategies and plans; conversely, China's global actors increasingly have to accommodate the plans of the party and the state, both in China itself and abroad.

Ruben Gonzalez-Vicente's chapter 20, "Global China's Business Frontier: Chinese Enterprises and the Reach of the State," interrogates the expansion of Chinese enterprises abroad. Chinese investments are often seen as the spearheads of a strategy carefully designed to "rejuvenate the Chinese nation," weaving an ever-growing network of economic activity that emanates from Beijing and seeking to capture resources and opportunities throughout the world. This picture fails to grasp the developmental challenges that China faces today and the decentralized and profit-oriented nature of China's international political economy. The chapter looks at the internationalization and localization abroad of Chinese enterprises as a logical aspect of the interwoven processes of capitalist accumulation and state-led global expansion, and their implications for the developmental impacts of Chinese foreign direct investment.

In chapter 21, "Common Destiny in Cyberspace: China's Cyber Diplomacy." Rogier Creemers argues that China's cyber power strategy lies at the heart of several intersecting policy agendas. The sharpening of geopolitical tensions with the United States as a consequence of China's growing global footprint has increased a sense of urgency with respect to Chinese dependence on foreign technologies, its vulnerability to external, cyber-enabled intrusions, and its lack of influence in global cyber governance processes. Creemers demonstrates that China not only seeks to redefine its place in this global order but increasingly wishes to reshape fundamental elements of the order itself. However, these ambitions remain defensive, focused on creating a safe and dependable international environment for the Party's domestic project. Chinese policy statements consistently state that China has no aggressive agenda in cyberspace. Instead, China argues for the recognition of the concept of "cyber sovereignty," which entails that cyberspace is bordered in the same way as geographical space. In other words, China asserts that it is entitled to manage its cyber territory, regulate online content and online processes as it sees fit, without interference from external actors.

In chapter 22, "Chinese Correspondents around the World," Pál Nyíri sketches the dynamics of the global expansion of China's news media. Describing the diversity of Chinese correspondents' positions and experiences, the chapter concludes that their limited embedding in foreign societies, the conservative nature of their media organizations at home, their financial constraints, and their personal priorities have all restricted the impact of PRC-based media outside China. However, Chinese media *have* become increasingly global owing to other factors—namely, the rise of social media platforms and the increasing collaboration between local, Chinese-origin freelancers and established media organizations. These collaborations blur the boundaries between China-based media and Chinese media overseas. While the worldwide expansion of PRC-based online platforms and PRC-generated content in foreign media is indeed likely to have a greater impact on influencing global public opinion of China, the rise of Chinese "influencers" abroad are in turn shaping Chinese views of the world.

In the two final chapters of this book we will focus on the international political economy and international relations dimensions of China's rise. Although globalization has set many of the patterns for China's role as a great power, its further rise will increasingly be determined by how China behaves and is perceived as a geostrategic player. Developments since the coronavirus crisis show that it is increasingly likely that US efforts to prohibit or even roll back Chinese globalization will continue, with American talk about "decoupling" and "conflict" quite possibly only being the beginning.

Richard McGregor and Hervé Lemahieu, in chapter 23, "Decoupling the US Economy," discuss the Trump administration's goal to roll back decades of globalization by actively seeking to disentangle the American economy from China's. China has in fact been doing something similar for years, but without telling everybody about it. As MacGregor and Lemahieu argue, however, both countries should be careful what they wish for, since they would suffer most from the decoupling of their economies. Moreover, a decoupled and deglobalized world will likely end up being divided into two camps, each of which may feel that it has less and less to lose and more to gain from competition, rivalry, and even outright conflict.

In chapter 24, "State-Led Globalization, or How Hard Is China's Soft Power?," Ingrid d'Hooghe and I are looking closely at an aspect of China's state-driven globalization that has aroused a great deal of suspicion—namely, gaining influence abroad by building up soft power. China has developed public diplomacy strategies promoting Chinese culture, values, and policies, as well as a positive domestic model. In the article, we specifically look at the following: the use of Chinese and foreign media and social media; the Confucius Institutes; work among the overseas Chinese populations that are both targets and actors of China's public diplomacy; and finally, the Belt and Road Initiative that is both a foreign policy strategy and a soft power tool. We conclude that there is much that is a threat to other countries in China's soft power strategy, which increasingly includes sharp power approaches of interference in the domestic political processes of other countries.

In the past as much as in the present, foreign observers often straddle the extremes when they look at China. Economically, the country impresses with its growth and sheer global footprint. These observers admire the successes of forty years of reforms and harbor at least some hope that China will finally become more like "us." Politically, however, it frightens. The list of reasons for this is long: the party's and the state's growing control over society and the buildup of a social credit rating system based on big data; the pursuit of global supremacy; the self-confident military buildup; the rapid technological development in fields like artificial intelligence; the suppression in Tibet and Xinjiang; the uncompromising albeit restrained attitude toward the demonstrations in Hong Kong in 2019; and Beijing's increasingly nationalist demeanor in territorial disputes in the South China Sea and elsewhere.

China is accepted as a modern country; in fact, China seems more modern in some areas than countries of the established developed world do. In a manner that is similar to how the world looked at Japan in the 1980s, China is seen as the cradle of future technologies. There is, however, an important difference. Fears of ever more intelligent technologies also serve our own justification for demonizing China's authoritarianism and Communism. This is a powerful mix: technology, the tool of the devil, in the hands of the archenemy—Communist China.

Yet technical advances that allow for comprehensive control and surveillance are not reserved for autocratic Communist regimes alone—despite all their real differences with democratic systems. Societies as a whole have become much more malleable, and governance is gradually shading into social engineering and opinion shaping. China is simply ahead of us in many of these areas, both positively and negatively.

All of this would of course not be all that serious if China had not also started to rise as a superpower. China's rise poses many threats to US hegemony and Western leadership more broadly in the international domain. Fears or misgivings about China are also heard from other parts of the world, particularly India, Southeast Asia, Eastern and Central Europe, and Africa, but in those places China is also seen as an opportunity. Western and US leadership is no longer self-evidently viable, and China presents an alternative that is attractive—or perhaps just inevitable—to many countries.

Hedging Chinese and US power and not picking a side have almost become the new normal, even in Western Europe. Beyond the opportunities for trade, investment, and development that it brings, China is often also seen as a chance to chart one's own course. To what extent this remains an option if the rivalry between the United States and China continues to deepen and escalate, is, of course, an open question.

What the world—and particularly the Western world—seems to face in China is in fact the insecurity about its own future: a technological and authoritarian dystopia coupled with the end of Western dominance. These fears are not infrequently projected onto China, regardless of what is actually happening there and what it does in the world. China is certainly no utopia, and it is easy to condemn the many flaws of its political system and what it does both domestically and abroad. But its rise is certainly not an existential threat to Western civilization: that would be something entirely of the West's own making.

The corona pandemic in 2020 has brought out these issues in even sharper relief. As a global "total event," the pandemic is a looking glass through which all kinds of issues are suddenly seen in different shapes and colours. The pandemic has revealed both the weaknesses and strengths of societies, serving as a global diagnostic whose lessons we are only beginning to learn. In the arena of international politics, the pandemic forces nations to take a hard, fresh look at their enemies and friends, and it is unlikely that they will ever seem the same again.

As the corona crisis in Western Europe and North America by mid-March threatened to spiral out of control, the US administration, followed by the

EU, a few individual Western European countries and Australia, responded not only by calling for an international inquiry but also framed both the initial mishandling of the corona virus outbreak and the subsequent harsh lockdown measures in Wuhan as symptomatic of China's authoritarianism and failing political system.

Since then, the United States and China have descended into a by now familiar but rapidly escalating pattern of weaponization of the issues that divide them. It seems likely that China will emerge from the corona crisis and its fallout stronger than the United States. This is more than just a matter of timing or of the number of victims or of the economic damage in each country. Trump's America First approach to the crisis has alienated US allies, especially those in Europe, impressing on them more than ever the need for a substantial and real strategic autonomy from Washington.

However, it is unlikely that China will be able to fully capitalize on the mistakes of its rival. The corona crisis has fed existing negative and threatening narratives about China, making it difficult for the Chinese authorities to present their handling of the crisis in a positive light. Because the virus originated in China, the easy tropes of authoritarian repression merged seamlessly with the nineteenth-century image of the Yellow Peril that cast a decaying China as the source of epidemic diseases like the plague or influenza. The victims of these suspicions included not only China, but also Chinese or Asians abroad who were denounced as carriers of disease, and in some cases were even physically molested.

But old stereotypes are only part of the story. After the 2003 SARS epidemic, scientists and popular writers alike suggested that the human race is "just one mutation away" from extinction, as a result of rampant globalization and the new, incomplete, and unpredictable modernities that emerged after the end of the Cold War, first and foremost in China, whose Communist dictatorship makes its modernity even more dangerous, inscrutable, and unpredictable (Lynteris 2018). The first corona outbreak at Wuhan's "wet market," associated with about half of the early cases in December 2019, fed seamlessly into this narrative. Dirty, contagious, and poorly regulated under opaque Communist rule, these markets are a source of exotic animal meat for China's nouveau riche to whet their increasingly decadent appetites. The wet market thus serves as an almost perfect metonym for everything reprehensible in imaginations about both traditional *and* contemporary China. Spawned right there, at the intersection of the traditional and the newly modern, the corona virus is not only dirty "matter out of place," in the sense of Mary Douglas, but also invisible matter that knows no boundaries, to be feared as much for what it tells us about the world that has emerged in the twenty-first century as about China itself.

REFERENCES AND FURTHER READING

European Commission High Representative of the Union for Foreign Affairs and Security Policy. "Joint Communication to the European Parliament, the European Council, and the Council EU-China—A Strategic Outlook." Accessed November 21, 2020. https://ec.europa.eu/commission/sites/beta-political/files/communication-eu-china-a-strategic-outlook.pdf.

Lai, Alessia, Annalisa Bergna, Carla Acciarri, Massimo Galli, and Gianguglielmo Zehender. 2020. "Early Phylogenetic Estimate of the Effective Reproduction Number of SARS-CoV-2." *Journal of Medical Virology* 92, no. 6 (February): 675–79. https://doi.org/10.1002/jmv.25723.

Lynteris, Christos. 2018. "Yellow Peril Epidemics: The Political Ontology of Degeneration and Emergence." In *Yellow Perils: China Narratives in the Contemporary World*, edited by Franck Billé and Sören Urbansk, 35–59. Honolulu: University of Hawai'i Press, 2018.

US Department of Defense. 2018. "Summary of the 2018 National Defense Strategy of The United States of America: Sharpening the American Military's Competitive Edge." Accessed November 21, 2020. https://dod.defense.gov/Portals/1/Documents/pubs/2018-National-Defense-Strategy-Summary.pdf.

TWENTY

Global China's Business Frontier

CHINESE ENTERPRISES AND THE
REACH OF THE STATE

Ruben Gonzalez-Vicente

CHINESE BUSINESSES HAVE EXPERIENCED a profound metamorphosis in the last four decades, transitioning from "work units" in a planned economy to profit-seeking enterprises in an environment dominated by market principles. The "contract management responsibility system" in the 1980s and the "modern enterprise system" in the 1990s represented key moments for the old work units to renounce their welfare and social security functions and focus solely on the "scientific management" of production and the quest for profits. These reforms were part of broader social changes, which caused the most extensive proletarianization in history and which were accomplished under an authoritarian regime that severely repressed labor rights and dissent.[1] At the same time, neoliberal norms came to reign in the international trade and production architectures, releasing vast amounts of capital from their national constraints. Soon enough, foreign direct investment (FDI) would gravitate toward China's shores, attracted by the country's cheap, disciplined, and increasingly productive labor force, as well as its unrelentingly upgraded infrastructures. As a result, China's international trade grew at an annual average of 18.6 percent between 1978 and 2017, a period during which the country also became the world's main destination for FDI.

In the latter half of the 1990s, the largest and most successful state-owned Chinese companies were consolidated and granted monopolies or oligopolies in strategic sectors of the booming Chinese economy. In parallel, some private and state-owned enterprises were successfully integrated into global value chains. Many of them became global giants, conquering international rankings, such as the Fortune Global 500. However, questions regarding the international competitiveness of Chinese firms emerged following the accession to the World Trade Organization in 2001, while overaccumulation started seri-ously threatening the country's economic success formula in the aftermath of the 2007–8 global financial crisis. These issues pressed many Chinese compa-nies to look abroad for investment opportunities. The central government contributed to this emerging trend with the inclusion of a "going out" strategy in China's tenth Five -Year Plan in 2001, having since then financed interna-tional business expansion with soft loans through two of the country's policy banks: the China Development Bank and the China Eximbank.

Chinese companies followed suit and acquired numerous projects and companies outside China, becoming the builders and managers of large mines, special economic zones, and major infrastructure works. Driven by the coercive laws of competition, their FDI strategies fit the classical types described by Dunning: opening new markets, increasing efficiency and cost-reduction, or gaining access to resources and strategic assets.[2] All these strate-gies are pursued, although some have been more prevalent than others in different periods. The early 2000s were characterized by a quest for competi-tiveness on account of China's accession to the World Trade Organization. A demand for natural resources drove many Chinese firms overseas during the natural resource boom (2003–13) and following the global financial crisis in particular. The contemporary period stands out for the efforts to open foreign markets for construction firms in response to a slowdown of the Chinese economy. As far as the central government is concerned, this imperative for continued accumulation is accompanied by "geoeconomic" considerations—that is, the belief that the expansion of commercial net-works is a key part of enhancing the country's international security and strength—as illustrated by the development of cross-border economic areas in China's border regions.

STATE AND BUSINESS INTERNATIONALIZATION

The close connection between Chinese firms and the Chinese state figures prominently in many accounts of Chinese business internationalization. Most of these characterizations are dominated by one of two positions. The first presents China's international campaigns as mere neocolonialism. This view is exemplified by the words of Donald Trump's former national security adviser, John Bolton, who recently cautioned about China's use of "bribes, opaque arrangements, and the strategic use of debt to hold states in Africa captive to Beijing's wishes and demands."[3] Another, more celebratory characterization emphasizes the Chinese state's unprecedented capacity to stimulate growth and promote win-win opportunities throughout the developing world.

These accounts have in common the assumption that the Chinese state plays a uniquely active role in the internationalization of Chinese capital. However, the Chinese state is far from the first to promote capitalist relations and business internationalization. Marx and Engels already described the modern capitalist state in nineteenth century Europe as a "committee for managing the common affairs of the whole bourgeoisie."[4] Likewise, the history of capitalist expansion beyond Europe was intimately tied to imperialism, and American hegemony in the twentieth century cannot be understood without considering the militarized support for an international liberal market order. More recently, national and multilateral development agencies, including the World Bank or the Organization for Economic Cooperation and Development (OECD), have increasingly focused on mitigating investment risks and on "escorting ... international capital into frontier and emerging market settings."[5]

Thus, when put in perspective, the way in which various Chinese state agencies or actors associated with the state (for instance, policy banks, embassies, and the Asian International Investment Bank) facilitate the entry of Chinese businesses into external markets may be distinctive in terms of format, but is by no means unprecedented. In essence, these state entities also "escort" businesses into frontier markets, facilitate credit, and derisk investment with large portfolios and through government-to-government agreements.

As Chinese enterprises make use of this support to set up shop in a variety of settings abroad, they encounter new types of legislation, civil societies, business cultures, and natural environments. This has entailed processes of adaptation, contestation, and indeed, both failures and successes. In what follows, I chart two modalities of outward investment that respond in great part to the characteristics of host countries. In some cases, the low level of development of a particular sector or country has required what I call *state-coordinated investment partnerships* that bring together Chinese firms and state actors. In other cases, the strength of already existing industry or the difficulties of navigating the relations with government agencies and civil society have prompted some businesses to rely heavily on local expertise via subcontracting, collaboration, and the hiring of local staff. I refer to these latter cases as *localized investments*.

The rapid development of the Chinese economy since the late 1970s has not followed a linear process of Washington Consensus-inspired orthodox liberalization and privatization. Instead, in China many key corporations have remained under different degrees of state ownership (from minority stakes to full ownership) and at different levels of governance (ranging from township to national ownership), while others that have been privatized have kept important formal and informal ties with the Party and its cadres, resulting in what Jonathan London describes as "market Leninism."[6] However, the weight and reach of the state in the Chinese economy does not imply that firms are predominantly motivated by nonmarket agendas. Quite the contrary, in its transition toward a capitalist state concerned with protecting the interests of capital over those of labor, the state in China has become infused with entrepreneurial practices and guided by growth and profit rationales.[7] In the process, complex networks of trust and power that link state entities with businesses have been developed, challenging clear demarcations between "the state" and "society," or between "public" and "private."

These domestic networks have also facilitated a certain degree of state-led coordination in international ventures through what I term "state-coordinated investment partnerships." This type of arrangement combines the financial muscle of a Chinese state-owned policy bank, the diplomatic networks of the state, and the specific expertise and interests of individual companies. An example can be found in the construction of the Bui Dam in Ghana. Ghana's fiscally constrained government sought recourse to a US$263 million concessional loan from the Chinese government, in addition to a buyers' credit of US$298 million from China's Eximbank.[8] While the dam itself was built by the Chinese company Sinohydro, the Ghanaian government committed itself to repay the debt with the sale of cocoa beans to another Chinese company, Genertec International Corporation. In order to make this happen, Chinese state institutions coordinated different actors and used diplomatic contacts to facilitate negotiations.

This unique investment modality has given Chinese businesses an edge in tapping into unexploited markets of countries that would otherwise not be able to undertake much infrastructural development, suggesting a *differential* impact. This capacity comes at the price of creating new forms of debt, which may undermine the long-term developmental aspirations of loan recipients, particularly when infrastructural investments turn out to be unproductive. In some instances, sovereign guarantees (i.e., a governmental commitment to meet all debt obligations) have resulted in the transfer of infrastructural projects to Chinese businesses, as was the case with the Hambantota port in Sri Lanka, which is now under a ninety-nine-year Chinese lease after the Sri Lankan government was unable to service its debt. In other cases, the valuation of the assets handed over to Chinese investors has been opaque or controversial. In Jamaica, for example, some NGO groups and politicians have protested the lease of 1,200 acres of prime land to Chinese companies as part of the compensation for the construction of the underutilized North-South Highway.[9] Yet, in many other cases, Chinese projects and finance have given a boost to local economic activity—while the ensuing economic benefits are not necessarily equally distributed, as in Cambodia, where vulnerable populations have often been displaced to make space for a tide of Chinese real estate and infrastructure investment.

A key feature of these investment partnerships is the limited linkages between Chinese enterprises and the local economy and society. In providing a "full package" arrangement for an infrastructural project, Chinese companies remain in a country only for a limited period of time, unless they are also contracted to manage the project. Such companies make only limited use of local suppliers or labor and are relatively isolated from local society and business. Interestingly, and also controversially, exceptional arrangements may be agreed on in order to facilitate quick and low-cost project delivery. In many of these cases, as the Jamaican one discussed above or the Ethiopian one discussed in the chapter by Driessen and Xiang in this volume, government-to-government deals include the management and control of Chinese labor on the basis of Chinese rather than local law. In this way, Chinese laborers embody a type of transnational Chinese sovereignty, as they are subject to Chinese regulations for taxation, salary and working conditions, as well as China's restrictions on independent labor unions.

LOCALIZED INVESTMENTS

Whereas state-coordinated partnerships have been instrumental to opening up new markets in countries otherwise unattractive to conventional forms of investment, Chinese businesses also operate in mature economies where they arrive as inexperienced players. The high-tech sector in California, the extractive sector in Australia or Peru, or the stock market in New York, to give just a few examples, require profound knowledge of existing regulations, practices, networks, and technologies. Moreover, when Chinese businesses arrive in these settings, they do not necessarily have a differential advantage that could allow them to negotiate exceptional conditions, as in the cases above; they can only add to existing trends and thus have an *incremental* impact. The embedding practices that these companies have to entertain necessarily rely—at least at an initial stage—on the assistance of local actors. In these cases, internationalization implies learning, while key elements of their background in the Chinese political economy also remain in place. Importantly, "learning" is a neutral process, as the new rationales internalized by Chinese investors can have both positive and negative impacts on the societies in which they operate.

There are plenty of examples of localization and learning. In trying to adapt to international standards, China's State Council hired teams of international advisors from the likes of KPMG and Price Waterhouse when they decided to float PetroChina on the New York Stock Exchange, something that fundamentally transformed the company's business practices.[10] Leading private technology firms such as Lenovo or Xiaomi recruited foreign CEOs in attempts to acquire market and management knowledge. In Australia, Chinese firms rely on the local talent pool for managerial positions in order to learn about the institutional context and leading practices in the mining sector.[11]

My own research on the engagement of Chinese firms in Peru found similar practices. The local offices of Chinese mining firms were filled with Peruvian, European, and American staff, while many key tasks were subcontracted to local or other foreign enterprises.[12] This resulted in behaviors that were quite familiar in the Peruvian context. Community management teams in charge of everyday relations with local communities used their training in American marketing strategies to promote participatory approaches to reach their goals. The adjunct general manager of corporate giant Shougang, in what would seem a clear breach of China's policy of noninterference, antagonized the Peruvian congress by threatening to stop Chinese investment in the country if an anticorruption investigation was to proceed any further. Public relations teams in the northern part of Peru attempted to discredit environmentalist NGOs critical of a Chinese state-owned company by depicting them—note the irony—as "Communists," indicating an important gulf between a company's headquarters and the practices of its local branches.[13]

However, it is important to note that while transformation can be profound, localized branches of Chinese enterprises remain linked to China in important ways. In particular, two elements stand out: financial links and the physical location of a firm's headquarters. The first of these two elements enables a longer-term perspective relative to other transnational firms thanks to the availability of Chinese state finance and a significant independence from shareholders concerned with short-term returns. This allows taking more time for particular phases of a project—for example, for trial and error in fixing strained relations with a local community affected by a mine. Perhaps more obviously, local branches of Chinese companies require approval from their headquarters for operations exceeding a certain threshold (in the case of a company in Peru the limit was set at US$5 million), guaranteeing the head office a certain degree of control. Finally, as I found in Peru, the physical location of headquarters within Chinese jurisdiction may preclude local activists from organizing campaigns or pursuing legal cases against Chinese companies by targeting the head company, which was a strategy often used by Latin American activist groups against European, Canadian, or American firms. Localization may significantly transform some practices, but it does not completely erase the national characteristics of a firm.

CONCLUSIONS

A mix of admiration and anxiety pervades most analyses of Chinese business internationalization. More often than not, Chinese enterprises are seen as the spearheads of an impeccable strategy carefully designed to "rejuvenate the Chinese nation," as President Xi Jinping put it, weaving an ever-growing network of economic activity that emanates from Beijing and seeks to capture resources and opportunities for accumulation throughout the world. This picture fails to grasp how the most recent wave of Chinese economic expansion responds to shrinking profit margins for infrastructural companies in the Chinese economy, how Chinese firms operate under similar competitive constraints as other firms in the global economy, or how it remains impossible to tightly control an extraordinary number of firms that pursue their own economic interests throughout diverse geographies around the world.

This chapter has charted two modalities of internationalization with distinct implications. State-coordinated investment partnerships require complex investment architectures and have a unique capacity to open up new markets closed to other businesses. Here, entities of the state coordinate— but do *not* control—several actors. Owing to the timeframes associated with these types of projects or the lack of local capacity, Chinese companies do not engage much with local actors and practices. By contrast, localized investments are common in consolidated markets and sectors. They are characterized by deep processes of learning and transformation that render Chinese firms similar to other transnationals. While in some cases this may cause tension between the interests of firms and those of Chinese state entities, Chinese officials have long upheld firm autonomy and the profit imperative as guiding principles to improve the allocation of resources and guarantee success in a competitive global economy. Very importantly, the continuing association between Chinese firms and the state does not come in the form of business capitulation to foreign policy objectives. Instead, the opposite seems to be true in most cases, as a number of state agencies devote public resources to create spaces for the international accumulation of firms that are driven by an eminently economic bottom line.

There is, however, some geographical variation. Overall, the state's control over financial means implies that a "geoeconomic" agenda may be more prominent with many investments within Asia, while in other regions, like Africa and Latin America, profit is the primary motive. This is of course not unlike the strategic priorities of other governments, which also flexibly align with the interests of capital at different places and junctures.

While new in some ways, the activities of Chinese businesses overseas with or without the direct support of the state have not disrupted the workings of world market capitalism. In adapting to a variety of capitalist settings throughout the world and the rules of global competitiveness, the need to localize business underpins a mix of local variation, mutual learning, and convergence. Rather than devising new rules of the game, the Chinese state and individual Chinese businesses envision and carve out a space for Global China at the center of a business-centric form of globalization, rather than aspiring to replace it with something altogether new.

NOTES

1. Walker and Buck 2007.
2. Dunning 1977.

3. John Bolton, "Remarks by National Security Advisor John R. Bolton on the Trump Administration's New Africa Strategy" (Heritage Foundation, Washington, DC, December 13, 2018). https://www.whitehouse.gov/briefings-statements/remarks-national-security-advisor-ambassador-john-r-bolton-trump-administrations-new-africa-strategy/.

4. Marx and Engels (1848) 1978, 475.

5. Carroll and Jarvis 2014, 538.

6. London 2014.

7. Gonzalez-Vicente 2011.

8. Odoom 2017.

9. Gonzalez-Vicente, 2019.

10. Lin 2016.

11. Huang and Austin 2011.

12. Gonzalez-Vicente 2012.

13. Gonzalez-Vicente 2012.

REFERENCES AND FURTHER READING

Carroll, Toby, and Darryl S. L. Jarvis. 2014. "Introduction: Financialisation and Development in Asia under Late Capitalism." *Asian Studies Review* 38, no. 4 (October): 533–43.

Dunning, John H. 1977. "Trade, Location of Economic Activity and MNE: A Search for an Eclectic Approach." In *The International Allocation of Economic Activity*, edited by Bertil Ohlin, Per Ove Hesselborn, and Per Magnus Wijkman, 395–418. London: Palgrave Macmillan.

Gonzalez-Vicente, Ruben. 2011. "The Internationalization of the Chinese State." *Political Geography* 30, no. 7 (September): 402–11.

———. 2012. "The Internationalization of China's Mining Industry: A Critical Political Economy of Chinese Mining Investment in Peru." PhD diss., University of Cambridge. ProQuest (AAT 10065129).

———. 2019. "Make Development Great Again? Accumulation Regimes, Spaces of Sovereign Exception and the Elite Development Paradigm of China's Belt and Road Initiative." *Business and Politics* 21, no. 4 (December): 487–513. https://doi.org/10.1017/bap.2019.20.

Huang, Xueli, and Ian Austin. 2011. *Chinese Investment in Australia: Unique Insights from the Mining Industry*. London: Palgrave Macmillan.

Lin, Kun-Chin. 2006. "Disembedding Socialist Firms as a Statist Project: Restructuring the Chinese Oil Industry, 1997–2002." *Enterprise & Society* 7, no. 1 (March): 59–97.

London, Jonathan. 2014. "Welfare Regimes in China and Vietnam." *Journal of Contemporary Asia* 44, no. 1: 84–107.

Marx, Karl, and Friedrich Engels. (1848) 1978. "The Manifesto of the Communist Party." In *The Marx-Engels Reader*, edited by Robert. C. Tucker, 469–500. 2nd. ed. New York: W. W. Norton.

Odoom, Isaac. 2017. "Dam in, Cocoa out; Pipes in, Oil out: China's Engagement in Ghana's Energy Sector." *Journal of Asian and African Studies* 52, no. 5 (August): 598–620.

Walker, Richard, and Daniel Buck. 2007. "The Chinese Road: Cities in the Transition to Capitalism." *New Left Review* 46 (July–August): 39–66.

TWENTY-ONE

Common Destiny in Cyberspace

CHINA'S CYBER DIPLOMACY

Rogier Creemers

ONE OF THE MOST CLOSELY observed elements of China's social and political transformation over the past decade has been the digital sphere. However, China's growing international footprint, its engagement with emerging regimes for global cyber governance, and its own diplomatic efforts have remained out of the academic limelight. Until around 2013, China did not play a role of great significance in global cyber-related processes and did not have a well-developed policy agenda of its own, nor dedicated institutions to support it. Between 2001 and 2009, China boycotted the Governmental Advisory Committee of the International Corporation for Assigned Names and Numbers (ICANN), the authority in charge of the internet's addressing system.[1] In some of the earliest iterations of the UN Group of Governmental Experts (GGE) on the Developments in the Field of Information and Telecommunications in the Context of International Security, China sent officials, who were less versed in the legal and security questions from its ministry of communication.[2]

Across a swathe of issue areas, China's foreign engagement remains limited. Together with Russia, it formed the core of a "coalition of the unwilling," a group of states united primarily in their rejection of what they perceived as an emerging American hegemony in cyberspace. Opposing US notions of a free and open internet governed by universal principles and values, they proposed sovereignty as the fundamental norm, and argued cyber affairs were a matter of national sovereignty. International coordination and cooperation between states should take place through UN channels, instead of using the multistakeholder model advocated by the West and practiced by institutions such as ICANN.

From 2013 onward, however, questions concerning cyber security and internet governance rapidly gained political prominence, as successive events demonstrated the severity of the challenge China faced. Many of these challenges, such as the proliferation of political activism on social media and online scamming, were primarily domestic in nature. Yet at the same time, incidents such as the Edward Snowden revelations and Microsoft's discontinuation of security support for Windows XP, as well as increasing tensions over cyber espionage, hacking, technology transfer, and intellectual property infringement, caused a new degree of awareness of risks from abroad, and particularly from the United States. In response, President Xi Jinping called for China to become a "cyber power."[3] To this end, both institutional and policy moves were made. A new top-level leadership organ, the Central Leading Group (later, Central Commission) for Cybersecurity and Informatization, came into being in 2014. Chaired by Xi personally, it included senior officials from propaganda, telecommunications, and technology ministries, as well as from the military. The State Internet Information Office, later renamed the Cyberspace Administration of China (CAC), grew in capacity and importance, serving, among other things, as the coordination body for the Central Commission. Numerous policy and legal documents saw the light of day, including comprehensive plans for the digital sector and the 2017 Cybersecurity Law. For the first time, international questions were addressed directly, specifically in the Strategy for International Cooperation in Cyberspace,[4] as well as through initiatives such as the Wuzhen World Internet Conference (WIC) and the Digital Silk Road (DSR). The latter provided a technological supplement to the flagship Belt Road Initiative.

CYBER GOVERNANCE AND CYBER SOVEREIGNTY

China's international cyber policies are predominantly shaped by its core domestic concerns: economic development and political stability. The prime international adversary is the United States, and the escalating tensions between these two countries concerning technology reflect growing opposition in the broader relationship. Put succinctly, China's leadership fears that the United States is determined to halt China's justified process of rejuvenation in its tracks, consigning the country to a permanent subordinate status. American positions and measures in cyberspace are usually interpreted in that light. Under the Obama administration, Secretary of State Hillary Clinton's open internet agenda, for instance, was portrayed as a direct challenge to China's ideological security. ICANN's past subordination to a US

Department of Commerce mandate was seen as giving the United States control over the strategic infrastructure of the internet. The Snowden revelations spurred anxiety about the extent to which China's reliance on foreign technologies created vulnerabilities.

Chinese policies have been largely reactive to these concerns, aiming to build "discursive power" in global cyber governance circles and to increase self-reliance in technology. In its search for discursive power, China's 2017 International Strategy of Cooperation on Cyberspace lists four fundamental principles: peace, sovereignty, shared governance, and mutual benefit. China rejects the use of cyberspace for military applications, even if it is currently developing defensive cyber forces. It also calls for collaboration in the fight against terrorists' use of the internet.

The most fundamental, yet controversial, principle is cyber sovereignty. Cyber sovereignty rejects the universality of political values and constitutional principles. Instead, China asserts that all countries have the right to govern the internet within their jurisdiction as they see fit, and to decide on their own technological development path. It assumes that borders exist in cyberspace as they do in real space. It is the prerogative of governments to police those borders and regulate the activities taking place within them. Sovereignty is primarily framed as noninterference and the right to self-determination: no fundamental values, such as free speech rights, outrank governmental power, nor should countries support the defense of such values outside their own borders. This assumption delineates what "shared governance" refers to in this context, as sovereignty also implies the supremacy of the state over nonstate actors.[5]

In contrast to the Western emphasis on multistakeholder governance of the internet, China proposes a "multiparty" model, in which governments and international governmental organizations take the lead, businesses, trade associations, and the technical community contribute specific expertise, and civil society is mentioned last.[6] Such cooperation should take place on the basis of mutual benefit—that is, efforts should be directed to making digital technology an engine for global growth and development. Together, according to Xi Jinping, the principles of cyber sovereignty, the multiparty model, and mutual benefit will combine to create a "community of common destiny in cyberspace."

These principles are important at the level of symbols and rhetoric: one of China's key objectives has been to insert these concepts into international normative documents on cyber governance and to persuade foreign actors, including governments, to adopt them. They have been accompanied by a push to expand China's footprint on the ground, most notably through growing the international market share of China's technology businesses, increasing the proportion of indigenous content in international technology standards, and incorporating technology cooperation in China's foreign development assistance.

DIGITAL SILK ROAD

China's "Silk Road Economic Belt" was announced in 2013. Later rebranded as "One Belt One Road," and still later as the "Belt and Road Initiative" (BRI), it was originally focused primarily on traditional forms of connectivity. Gradually, digital technologies entered into the plan. The 2016 thirteenth Five-Year Plan for National Informatization, for instance, contained a dedicated section on the "Online Silk Road." At the first BRI forum in Beijing in 2017, Xi Jinping underlined the importance of new forms of technology for innovation-driven development, including artificial intelligence, big data, cloud computing, and smart cities. As with the overall BRI scheme, goals of the Digital Silk Road include mitigating China's overcapacity problems, opening up new markets for national champions, and supporting the internationalization of the renminbi.[7] In some cases, digital technology is required for broader BRI objectives, such as satellite navigation for infrastructure construction. More specifically, the Digital Silk Road also contains elements intended to further China's cyber agenda, through building support in third countries and enhancing the clout and influence of its businesses. Like the BRI, the Digital Silk Road is not a sharply delineated project. Consequently, businesses, research institutions and governmental bodies regularly use the term as a politically convenient description for projects they are doing anyway, or to attract support and subsidies.

A first major Digital Silk Road element is the international adoption of Chinese technologies, ranging from telecommunications infrastructure and mobile handsets to satellite navigation and smart traffic control. This, it is hoped, will enable Chinese businesses not only to increase profitability but will also ensure that their technologies are incorporated in international standards and complex value chains. The highest profile effort is the attempt to include technologies developed by businesses such as ZTE and Huawei into standards for fifth-generation (5G) mobile telecommunications. Owing to rising national security concerns, both companies face increasing head-winds in developed markets. Intelligence agencies from the "Five Eyes" have reportedly decided to contain Huawei's growth.[8] The United States, Australia, and New Zealand have all banned Huawei from their market. The United Kingdom, Germany, and Belgium have launched security investigations into the potential risk posed by Huawei technologies but, as of May 2019, have as yet stopped short of an all-out ban. Huawei's chief financial officer, Meng Wanzhou, was arrested in Canada at the behest of the United States in December 2018. In subsequent months, tensions concerning Huawei escalated, leading to the US government imposing an export ban against Huawei in May 2019. China's cyber strategy is now at the core of the escalating conflict and the rivalry between China and the United States, as well as, increasingly and more broadly, with all major Western powers. A greater Chinese presence in third countries, such as Belt and Road nations, may mitigate China's exposure to further measures from Western powers and provide it with potential allies in future trade disputes.

In the area of satellite navigation, China has identified the Central Asian section of the BRI as the first major internationalization zone for its Beidou program, an alternative for the American Global Positioning System (GPS) and the European Galileo system. To this end, China has reached agreement with a number of countries on their military use of Beidou, while an industrial park for Sino-Arab satellite data services was established in Ningxia.[9] For recipient countries, Beidou may be attractive in order to hedge their reliance on GPS, even if only as a fallback option.

Secondly, China has used the Digital Silk Road as a platform for diplomatic engagement aimed at cooperation in the digital economy. At the 2017 Wuzhen conference, Saudi Arabia, Egypt, Turkey, Thailand, Laos, Serbia, and the UAE signed an agreement with China for an economically interconnected DSR.[10] The agreement included matters like expanding broadband connectivity and cooperation in international standardization. Perhaps more importantly, the countries also promised to work on the harmonization of e-commerce and data protection-related laws. Nonetheless, little fanfare accompanied this agreement. This, and the fact that it was circulated widely for several months, including among EU governments, suggest that the leadership had anticipated greater adoption. Foreign governments have remained doubtful about the business practices of Chinese companies and good governance issues where BRI and Digital Silk Road projects are concerned.

Given the relatively early stage of the Digital Silk Road, it currently remains largely speculative whether the project will contribute to Beijing's foreign policy goals in the short and long term. Moreover, Chinese actors have used the Digital Silk Road banner to tout projects and processes already underway. Kuala Lumpur, for instance, has purchased Alibaba's City Brain technology for urban management.[11] A major fiber-optic network has been completed in Afghanistan and will be run jointly by Afghan Telecom and China Telecom.[12] Chinese businesses have enjoyed considerable growth in e-commerce in South-East Asia and have established data centers along the Belt and Road. These projects do not necessarily require BRI support as they make commercial sense on their own. They have, however, provided opportunities to the businesses conducting them in order to get into Beijing's good books.

IMPLICATIONS

If the objective of China's foreign cyber policy has been to acquire greater acceptance of its stance, or at least a greater supporting coalition, there is little doubt that they have been largely unsuccessful so far. To a certain degree, this reflects the broader state of affairs in cyberspace, which is primarily caused by the continuing and deepening tensions between the United States and the "like-minded countries," on the one hand, and Russia and China, on the other. But even with countries farther removed from the US orbit, China is not faring very well, as the limited take-up of the Digital Silk Road initiative demonstrates. China has not yet managed the transition from a relatively small and insignificant player to a global leader. China's cyber policies have become slightly more elaborate but they remain largely programmatic and, to a certain degree, inconsistent. China may also have failed to generate sufficient trust among its potential foreign partners. Concerns about matters ranging from expanding surveillance and censorship to hacking and intellectual property rights infringement, to the real or perceived potential of espionage through China-backed infrastructure rapidly become more prominent in international discourse. To allay these fears, China would have to become more transparent about its policy mechanisms and intentions, and Chinese businesses would have to allow closer scrutiny.

Yet China's view of the world and policy approach may leave little space for foreign input. The Digital Silk Road is focused primarily on solving

Chinese domestic problems, even if it is packaged as a foreign aid and development project. With little room for target countries to develop their own tech industries, combined with the risks connected with indebtedness to China, the Digital Silk Road might therefore be less attractive than Beijing believes. The best—but unlikely—response would be for Beijing to relinquish absolute control over these processes and allow meaningful external participation in DSR-related decision-making.

These points raise two bigger questions. The first is to what extent Beijing will learn from its experiences in foreign affairs. The Chinese Communist Party prides itself on being a "learning party." With relatively little experience in leadership in complex geopolitical questions, a considerable amount of learning likely awaits. Together with climate change, the cyber domain is one of the most prominent issue areas in which China's newly found international assertiveness manifests itself. The extent to which Beijing digests, internalizes, and applies the lessons it learns through its policy experience will thus more broadly be a useful guide to China's evolving position in the global order. The second question is how the outside world will respond to China's ambitions. Increasing tensions between the United States and China have led to what some observers on both sides are already calling the "Sino-US Tech Cold War." If this trend continues, it may have major implications not just for the global internet but for global trade and geostrategic questions as well.

NOTES

1. Cheng 2017, 61.

2. Segal 2017.

3. Xi Jinping. "Ba woguo cong wangluo daguo jianshe chengwei wangluo qiang-guo" [Build our country from a large network country into a strong network country], Xinhua, February 27, 2014, http://www.xinhuanet.com//politics/2014-02/27 /c_119538788.htm.

4. Foreign Ministry of the People's Republic of China (FMPRC) 2017.

5. Schia and Gjesvik 2017.

6. Ministry of Foreign Affairs,, "International Strategy of Cooperation on Cyberspace," trans. Rogier Creemers, March 1, 2017, https://chinacopyrightandmedia .wordpress.com/2017/03/01/international-strategy-of-cooperation-on-cyberspace/.

7. Shen 2018.

8. The "Five Eyes" is an intelligence alliance comprising the United States, the United Kingdom, Canada, Australia, and New Zealand. See Chris Uhlmann and

Angus Grigg, "Secret Meeting Led to the International Effort to Stop China's Cyber Espionage," *Financial Review*, December 13, 2018. https://www.afr.com /world/asia/secret-meeting-led-to-the-international-effort-to-stop-chinas-cyber-espionage-20181213-h192ky.

9. Wu 2015.

10. Rogier Creemers, "Proposal for International Cooperation on the 'One Belt, One Road' Digital Economy" (proposed international agreement presented at the World Internet Conference, Wuzhen, Zheijiang, China, December 3, 2017).

11. Abigail Beall, "In China, Alibaba's Data-hungry AI Is Controlling (and Watching) Cities," *Wired*, May 30, 2018, https://www.wired.co.uk/article/alibaba-city-brain-artificial-intelligence-china-kuala-lumpur.

12. Rachel Brown, "Beijing's Silk Road Goes Digital," Council on Foreign Relations, June 6, 2017, https://www.cfr.org/blog/beijings-silk-road-goes-digital.

REFERENCES AND FURTHER READING

Cheng, Dean. 2017. *Cyber Dragon: Inside China's Information Warfare and Cyber Operations*. Santa Barbara, CA: Praeger International Security.

Foreign Ministry of the People's Republic of China. 2017. "Wangluo kongjian guoji hezuo zhanlüe" [International strategy of cooperation on cyberspace]. China Copyright and Media. March 1, 2017. https://chinacopyrightandmedia.wordpress .com/2017/03/01/international-strategy-of-cooperation-on-cyberspace/.

Schia, Niels Nagelhus, and Lars Gjesvik. 2017. "China's Cyber Sovereignty." Norwegian Institute of International Affairs. March 17, 2017. https://www.nupi.no/en /Publications/CRIStin-Pub/China-s-Cyber-Sovereignty.

Segal, Adam. 2017. "Chinese Cyber Diplomacy in a New Era of Uncertainty." Hoover Working Group on National Security, Technology, and Law. Aegis Paper Series, no. 1703. June 2, 2017. http://lawfareblog.com/chinese-cyber-diplomacy-new-era-uncertainty.

Shen, Hong. 2018. "Building a Digital Silk Road? Situating the Internet in China's Belt and Road Initiative." *International Journal of Communication* 12 (June): 2683–701.

Wu, Sike. 2015. "Constructing 'One Belt and One Road' and Enhancing the China-GCC Cooperation." *Journal of Middle Eastern and Islamic Studies (in Asia)* 9, no. 2: 1–15.

TWENTY-TWO

Chinese Correspondents around the World

Nyíri Pál

IN 2008, THE YEAR THAT THE GLOBAL RECESSION began, China's media also rapidly accelerated their global expansion. This included investment in, and joint ventures and content provision agreements with, foreign-based media organizations and film production companies. The globalization of China-based media involved online portals and mobile apps, the use of foreign social media platforms, such as Facebook, the export of telecommunications infrastructure, the launch of newspapers, television and radio channels directed at audiences abroad, and content provision agreements with foreign media in both Chinese and foreign languages.[1] This expansion has been driven both by the Chinese state's quest for "soft power" and by commercial interests, which are in most cases intertwined; it was facilitated by declining profits among media worldwide.

Most discussions of China's media expansion abroad focus on China's global influence. Opinions vary, but most analysts conclude that most important in influencing foreign audiences are content-sharing arrangements and the presence of Chinese satellite television and mobile providers, which, in Africa and elsewhere, offer low-cost satellite packages that include Chinese television channels.[2] The direct presence of Chinese journalists abroad has only a limited impact on the framing of world events in other countries. However, Chinese journalists' increasing engagement with the world does have a clear impact on media audiences in China itself, and this is the topic that this chapter will explore.

While most Western media are trimming their network of foreign correspondents, China's media have been building up theirs. Based on interviews with over seventy correspondents and editors from the People's Republic of China (PRC)-based media in Europe and Africa between 2011 and 2016, this chapter describes the diversity of correspondents' positions and experiences, their engagement with local societies, and the dynamics of their interactions with their media organizations.[3] It should be noted that foreign correspondents are not the only or even the main source of foreign news in China: social media platforms outside mainstream media sometimes have a wider reach.

THE EXPANSION OF CHINA'S CORRESPONDENT NETWORKS

China's state leaders have been calling for Chinese media to "go out" since at least 2004. The process accelerated spectacularly after 2008.[4] In that year, many Chinese students abroad reacted with outrage at what they saw as biased coverage of riots in Tibet and protests against the Olympic torch relay by activists abroad. This encouraged the Party's propaganda leaders to abandon their reactive tactics of silence and denial about inconvenient news and instead to embrace an approach of proactive, selective spin. Described as essential for China's "discursive power"—the ability to frame narratives of events—this objective required that journalists engage with foreign audiences and write with authority about world affairs. As Lu Wei, then deputy director of China's official Xinhua News Agency, wrote:

> The financial information in major global financial markets is often monopolized by Western information bodies, the data developing countries need is often imported or bought in. All policymaking analysis is built on second-hand data, and one can well imagine the results.[5]

The authorities allocated large sums to rectify the situation. The Central Propaganda Department (or "Publicity Department," as its name is officially translated into English) of the Chinese Communist Party (CCP) cofunded new master's programs in global journalism at five leading university media faculties. In 2012, the government declared the goal of training one hundred thousand "internationalized news media and publishing personnel" by 2015. In parallel, substantial funding was made available to expand Chinese media overseas.[6]

The lion's share of this funding has been going to so-called central media—that is, to media controlled by central state and Party departments: the Xinhua and China News Service (CNS) news agencies, China Central Television (CCTV), China Radio International (CRI), *People's Daily*, and the English-language *China Daily*. These media spent part of the money on establishing and expanding foreign bureaus and sending more correspondents and technical personnel abroad. By 2015, Xinhua reportedly had 180 offices outside mainland China, CCTV around seventy, and CRI and *People's Daily* some thirty each. In addition, CRI had 130 local radio stations overseas.[7]

Xinhua, *People's Daily*, and a few other central media had maintained foreign correspondent networks for many decades. These networks had undergone an earlier expansion in the 1980s, but their visibility and impact remained limited because, as *21st Century Business Herald* foreign desk editor Luo Xiaojun quipped, they had focused on the question "What do leaders like?" rather than "What do readers like?"[8] Now they were being told to think about readers, both foreign and Chinese. They had to find ways to become credible sources of information and opinion about the world, capable of setting agendas rather than merely reacting to those set by the West. They also had to compete with commercial media. In the words of a senior *People's Daily* foreign correspondent: "In the past, *People's Daily* followed the *New York Times* and other Western media too much. . . . On many issues, we . . . unconsciously reported the Western position. This is why people didn't take us seriously."[9]

Under director Li Congjun (2008–14), Xinhua made "professionalization" and global market share a priority, while undergoing what the director-general of Xinhua Europe, Wang Chaowen, described as a "strategic transformation" with the purpose of "getting closer to the reader," including a shift to more colloquial language and a presence in social media. The news doctrine of the "three getting-closers" (getting closer to reality, to the masses, and to life) announced by CCP Secretary-General Hu Jintao in 2003 acquired a new impetus after 2012, when his successor Xi Jinping said Party media should speak "human language." Having foreign correspondents on the ground was one of the ways to bolster credibility.

Meanwhile, beginning in 2007, some of the so-called financial media—papers and online portals focusing on the economy that catered to affluent urban audiences and decision-makers—began posting their own correspondents overseas. *21st Century Business Herald* was the first to do so, followed by *Caijing, Caixin*, and others. They received no state funding for their expansion and were not especially interested in projecting China's "voice." Their readers wanted accurate information about the foreign countries where they traveled, bought real estate, and sent their children to study. Moreover, editors saw international reporting—especially on economic issues—as an area in which they could produce distinctive content and thus build their brand without being subjected to the tight controls that apply to domestic reporting. As for-profit enterprises, they had more limited means to fund a network of correspondents; none had more than five or six full-time correspondents abroad, usually in the United States, Western Europe, Japan, and Hong Kong. After 2013, decline in advertising revenue owing to competition from social media platforms and increasing government pressure on journalists forced them to cut down again on their overseas staff.

WHO ARE THEY?

Ten years ago, the overseas bureaus of China's media were mostly staffed by senior journalists, usually men. Well-paid and stress-free foreign postings were a reward for years of service in China.

Today, most overseas correspondents are around thirty and often female. Because overseas postings are typically for about three years, Xinhua alone replaces two hundred to three hundred correspondents every year. At a time of rapid expansion, the international department fell far short of these numbers, offering an opportunity to journalists in other departments to be posted abroad. The same was true for CCTV and CRI. Yet not everyone was interested. Unlike earlier generations, today's young journalists have other opportunities to go abroad, and many have already been as students or tourists. Being away from headquarters may mean the risk of weakening important personal networks or worse, missing promotions. Furthermore, with the rise in living standards in China, overseas postings are no longer as attractive as they used to be. In the early 1990s, a *People's Daily* foreign correspondent's salary was ten times that of a domestic correspondent; today, it is only twice as much. Finally, for young, single journalists, being away from China often creates anxiety about finding a potential spouse.

The situation of commercial media correspondents is somewhat different. Because foreign correspondents working for these media are so few, they have a relatively high profile within their organizations and more personal freedom. On the other hand, their postings are often contingent on the financial position of the paper and shifts in editorial strategy; some have been transferred three times in as many years. With no prospect of job security and a heavy workload, many commercial media correspondents leave journalism for more lucrative jobs, not infrequently with a sense of burnout and frustration.

The strengthening of foreign correspondent networks has, therefore, ironically coincided with a weakening of foreign correspondence as a career path. This may be one reason why so many correspondents are unmarried women: they may be under less pressure to seek a stable, high-earning career than male journalists. As a correspondent for a leading financial daily commented, "Men who could be finance journalists usually prefer to be financial analysts, which pays better. They are more likely to have families."

WHAT DO THEY DO?

Wang Chaowen, the Xinhua director, said the agency's most important objectives were increasing localization, raising the share of original content, and being the first to break more news stories. This, too, is a major change compared to fifteen years ago. Back then, Xinhua correspondents spent most of their time at home, watching television, reading the local papers, and filing stories based on translating these. While there is still interest in China in stories taken from Western media, translations of these are now widely available online. Stories filed by foreign correspondents are now expected to have some original content, whether sound bites collected during an on-site report or quotations from an expert interview. Interviews with politicians whose names are recognized in China are particularly prized.

Apart from breaking news and exclusive interviews, the most important assignments for central media correspondents have to do with events related to China: visits by high-ranking Chinese delegations abroad or meetings of the CCP or the National People's Congress in China. Preparing for state visits from China begins months ahead of time, although foreign correspondents play second fiddle to the reporters accompanying the delegation. For Party congresses and plenums, correspondents are required to supply positive reactions from foreign experts and politicians. Every now and then, they are asked to participate in "global linkups" with correspondents in various countries on an issue usually connected to a current policy debate in China. Although individual contributors have little control over what happens with the material they supply, such assignments require a lot of work, and most central media correspondents have little time left to pursue longer stories. Commercial media correspondents are exempt from these obligations; they are expected to offer more in-depth economic analysis, but their workload is such that they, too, have few opportunities for longer stories.

Many journalists are interested in longer-format reporting, particularly on cultural and lifestyles issues. Such stories are less politically sensitive and are therefore less likely to encounter rejection or censorship; but owing to space limitations, they often end up in news magazines or online. Most central media operate several online platforms. For example, *People's Daily* journalists frequently contribute to the tabloid *Global Times*, the foreign news portal *Haiwaiwang*, or the *Global Times* online portal. Most readers access these by subscribing on the popular mobile application WeChat. According to Tencent, WeChat's owner, Haiwaiwang's posts are read 1.5 billion times on average.[10]

Except for *People's Daily*, the primary goal of expanding foreign correspondent networks for the central media is to increase China's influence in the global news market.[11] From this it follows that many correspondents have to file stories in both English and Chinese. Central media correspondents are frequently reminded that they are expected to serve both as professional reporters and broadcasters of "China's voice." Although some admit in interviews to being "confused" about this dual identity, most develop an intuition for when one role should prevail over the other. Explicit orders on foreign reporting are rare. Rather, reporters and editors exercise self-censorship based on general principles. They avoid reporting on antigovernment protests and on religion, overemphasizing reporting on elections and other forms of democratic participation, or direct criticism of foreign governments unless instructed to do so. Postpublication censorship is rare. Editors may cut passages deemed too risky, but their judgement varies considerably, as does correspondents' willingness and ability to exploit gray areas. In 2013, Xi Jinping told the Party's Propaganda Work Conference that China must create "new forms of foreign propaganda . . . to broadcast China's voice."[12] In the lobby of CRI's headquarters, a large slogan states "A Stand for China, An Eye for the World, A Concern for All Humanity." But the substance of a distinctive Chinese "voice" or "stand" remains elusive apart from representing the stance of the Chinese government in matters where such a stance exists. This contrasts with the clear positioning that Al Jazeera and, in particular, RT (Russia Today) have developed among international audiences. Ironically, it is in part because of the Chinese media's unwillingness to employ a confrontational, maverick tone that they have been less successful than RT in attracting an international following.

In practice, a "Chinese perspective" relates to the domestic interest in China in specific topics. As a commercial media correspondent put it:

Chinese correspondents in the US either want to show how good it is—and by contrast, how bad China is—or else they want to unmask US democracy as a fake. It looks like they send reporters with a very specific purpose, without caring much about what is really going on there.

A former Washington bureau chief of a central media organization observed that the station's leadership was mainly interested in using America as a reference point for China. What was the road quality like in the United States? What was the pension system like? Audiences, too, were uninterested in what counted as news in America and wanted instead to hear about the economy and Hollywood.

Audience figures are central to both commercial and central media. Although the latter are less vulnerable to the market and carry heavy doses of material that few people will read, they need ratings as a measure of how successful they have been in boosting their credibility. A correspondent for Sina, the largest Chinese news portal, lamented that since Sina's main readers were young men in second-tier cities who were "nationalistic, pro-Trump, pro-Putin, anti-Muslim and anti-refugee," the portal had to take into account their preferences when choosing stories. In other words, commercial media's need to cater to their audience's views may be as great a barrier to more factual and critical foreign reporting than government censors. When I asked a correspondent in Zimbabwe whether he reported on the opposition to then President Mugabe, an ally of China, he replied: "What's the point of reporting on the arrest of an opposition politician if no one reads it anyway? My most popular story was about a plane crash."

These circumstances make achieving a higher share of original and breaking content difficult. In 2014, when a Malaysian Airlines plane disappeared with 154 Chinese nationals on board, Chinese media dispatched unprecedented numbers of reporters to the region and yet failed to come up with any major leads. This failure resulted in considerable soul-searching within the profession. Why didn't Chinese correspondents do better? Some blamed China's media regime, which rewards "safe" stories and discourages journalists from going after scoops. Others pointed to foreigners' distrust of Chinese media. Yet others noted that Chinese correspondents tend to lack the kind of local networks or assistants that Western journalists cultivate.

Limited embedding in foreign societies, the conservative nature of media organizations, financial constraints, and correspondents' personal priorities have all restricted the impact of overseas correspondent networks on the globalization of PRC-based media. While the worldwide expansion of PRC-based online platforms and PRC-generated content in foreign media is indeed likely to have a greater impact on influencing global public opinion about China, the rise of Chinese "influencers" who live abroad and write about lifestyles and politics there for domestic audiences—subject to the usual censorship—in turn are shaping Chinese views of the world.

NOTES

1. Thussu 2017; Yang 2017.
2. See, e.g., Nelson 2013; Zhang, Wasserman, and Mano 2016.
3. The research for this chapter is described in more detail in Nyíri 2017.
4. Cf. Brady 2015.
5. Lu Wei, "National Discourse Power and Information Security against the Background of Economic Globalization," trans. Rogier Creemers, China Copyright and Media, December 21, 2014, https://chinacopyrightandmedia.wordpress .com/2014/12/21/national-discourse-power-and-information-security-against-the-background-of-economic-globalization/. Originally published as "Jingji quanqiuhua beijing xia de guojia huayuquan yu xinxi anquan," *People's Daily*, July 18, 2010. Cf. Yang 2017.
6. The extent of the funding is not known but it is estimated to be in the billions of dollars. See Nyíri 2017, 174.
7. Yang 2015; Wang 2016.
8. Interview in Shanghai, March 2014.
9. Interview in New York, June 2014.
10. 2016 data accessed by the author from Tencent's WeChat account.
11. See General Administration of News and Publications, "Guanyu jiakuai wo guo xinwen chuban ye de ruogan yijian" [Opinions on accelerating the international expansion of our country's news and publishing industry], January 10, 2012, https:// www.chinaxwcb.com/2012-01/10/content_236045.htm.
12. "Wang chuan Xi Jinping 8.19 jianghua quanwen: Yanlun fangmian yao gan zhua gan guan gan yu liang jian" [Xi Jinping's August 19 speech circulates on the net: In speech, we must dare to grasp, dare to regulate, dare to bare the sword], *China Digital Times*, November 4, 2013, https://chinadigitaltimes.net/chinese /2013/11/.

REFERENCES AND FURTHER READING

Brady, Anne-Marie. 2015. "China's Foreign Propaganda Machine." *Journal of Democracy* 26, no. 4 (October): 51–59.

Nelson, Anne. 2013. *CCTV's International Expansion: China's Grand Strategy for Media?* Washington, DC: Center for International Media Assistance.

Nyíri, Pál. 2017. *Reporting for China: How Chinese Correspondents Work with the World*. Seattle: University of Washington Press.

Thussu, Daya Kishan. 2017. "Globalization of Chinese Media: The Global Context." In *China's Media Go Global*, edited by Daya Kishan Thussu, Hugo de Burgh, and Anbin Shi, 17–33. London: Routledge.

Wang, Gengnian. 2016. "CRI 2016 Annual Report." *Journal of World Radio, Film and Television* 1: 3–12.

Yang, Suzanne Xiao. 2017. "Soft Power and the Strategic Context for China's 'Media Going Global' Policy." In *China's Media Go Global*, edited by Daya Kishan Thussu, Hugo de Burgh, and Anbin Shi, 79–100. London: Routledge.

Yang, Vivian. 2015. "How Chinese Media Is Going Global." World Economic Forum. Accessed November 21, 2020. https://www.weforum.org/agenda/2015/08/how-chinese-media-is-going-global/.

Zhang, Xiaoling, Herman Wasserman, and Winston Mano, eds. 2016. *China's Media and Soft Power in Africa: Promotion and Perceptions*. Basingstoke: Palgrave Macmillan.

TWENTY-THREE

Decoupling the US Economy

PREPARATIONS FOR A NEW COLD WAR?

Richard McGregor and Hervé Lemahieu

WASHINGTON'S NEW FOREIGN POLICY BUZZWORD, "decoupling," has a rather bland ring, especially given the momentous phenomenon it describes—of the world's two biggest economies, the United States and China, splitting apart. In the case of the White House, the phrase is short-hand for the administration's commitment, through tariffs, investment screening, sanctions, and other punitive measures, to disentangle its compa-nies and their technologies from China's supply chains. As Henry Paulson, the former Goldman Sachs chief and erstwhile US treasury secretary, said in a speech in November 2018: "I now see the prospect of an economic Iron Curtain, one that throws up new walls on each side and unmakes the global economy, as we have known it."[1]

But without a broader American economic strategy for the region, it's hard to see how a decoupling between the two countries will work out for the United States and friendly countries in Asia. Far from bringing business out of China, America might want to ensure that global supply chains remain anchored there after all.

For China, "decoupling" is both a gift and a curse. Beijing has been quietly pursuing a similar strategy for years, without articulating it in such an overtly political fashion. But China should be careful what it wishes for. Just as the United States would suffer from a world divided in two, so too would China, which still lags behind developed countries in key technologies.

Asia is home to the most important global supply chains—from electronics to textiles, from IT to cars—distributed across a vast range of countries. Owing to the nature of these cross-border links, and China's central role within them, a trade war with Beijing means a trade war with Asia. Given that context, if decoupling were to happen, the very model of Factory Asia, which has allowed developing countries to join the global age, starting with Japan in the 1950s, could be set on a path to extinction. This alone makes many countries and businesses nervous.

But with relations between the United States and China deteriorating on multiple fronts, decoupling has become about much more than just trade. Indeed, in the eyes of some officials and analysts in both countries, decoupling is seen not so much as a dangerous phenomenon that could unwind the economic benefits that flow to both countries from trade. Instead, it has become the natural and inevitable outcome of great power rivalry.

On the eve of a tense set of trade negotiations in Washington in early May 2019, one of China's best-known hawks, Dai Xu, a colonel in the People's Liberation Army, was frank about the best outcome for China. "I hope that the negotiations will break down," he said.[2] The idea that two sides will be driven to disentanglement from each other to position themselves for a long-term geopolitical and economic rivalry was also captured in a tweet by Hu Xijin, the hawkish editor of the *Global Times*—the tabloid mouthpiece of the Chinese Communist Party (CCP)—who wrote: "More and more Chinese now tend to believe the current US government is obsessed with comprehensively containing China. A trade deal, even if reached, will be limited in actual meaning and could be broken constantly." As a result, he added, "(many Chinese) support being tough on the US, giving up any illusion."[3]

The fact that breaking up global supply chains, or at least severing them in some products lines, is part of a wider political battle is now well accepted, and not just among attention-seeking commentators. Top government officials in both countries openly discuss the US-China rivalry in broad systemic terms. Li Ruogu, a former head of China's Ex-Im Bank, a position that gave him the rank of a minister in the Chinese system, has been frank about how the contest between the two countries goes far beyond trade. "For us, fighting an economic war, a financial war, a public opinion war, a science and technology war, an exchange student war, a sports war, and a cultural war with the

United States are all possible."[4] Donald Trump's national security adviser, John Bolton, struck a similar fin-de-siècle tone when talking about the reason for imposing tariffs on Chinese goods. "This is not just an economic issue. This is not just talking about tariffs and the terms of trade. This is a question of power."[5]

Another school of thought supports decoupling on quite different grounds: it could help stabilize the bilateral relationship. Much like separating combatants on a battlefield to create the conditions for a lasting peace, these scholars argue that by decoupling, the two countries will have a firmer basis on which to restore their relationship. Abigail Grace, at the Center for New American Security in Washington, DC, argued that the most likely outcome of decoupling was that the United States and China would end up protecting "high-value technology critical to their national interests, develop supply-chain redundancies, and continue economic networking with emerging middle powers in Southeast Asia and sub-Saharan Africa." As a result, she said, in the long term both the United States and China could "achieve a healthier diversification of economic connections that will forge a path to a distinctly new and more stable economic order."[6] Daniel Rosen of the Rhodium Group in New York advanced a similar argument. "In areas where advanced economies believe that the tide of statism in China does necessitate higher seawalls, the goal should be peaceful disengagement rather than bellicose threats to disrupt 40 years of global network building," he wrote. "There will be many areas in which previously encouraged activity may no longer be viewed as advisable, or may need to be curtailed."[7]

Most of the coverage of this issue has naturally focused on Washington, partly because of Trump's political pyrotechnics, and partly because the US system is so much more transparent than the Chinese. But it is also worth remembering that the impetus for decoupling is coming from both countries. There is ample evidence going back a number of years that China has long nurtured a policy of technological independence. In that respect, the US push simply mirrors longstanding Chinese policy.

US Vice President Mike Pence's speech articulating America's China policy reset in early October 2018 was spurred by the bipartisan conviction in Washington that engagement with Beijing had failed to alter the one-party state's determination to supplant the United States in Asia and compete in a hostile manner globally. Washington may be right on this point. As Beijing has integrated into the global system, it has displayed virtuosity in playing the power game beneath the threshold of out-and-out conflict with the United States. This is evidenced by everything from China's creeping takeover of the South China Sea to the theft of intellectual property and the protection and subsidies for swathes of its domestic economy to build national champions to take on the world.

The United States also argues, on that basis, that they are late to the decoupling game. Beijing's signature policies, such as Made in China 2025, which was issued in 2015, are all aimed at displacing foreign technology, especially from the United States, and climbing up the value chain. Almost from its inception, China's internet has been quarantined from the rest of the world through the Great Firewall. Global US companies like Facebook and Google are barred from China. In effect, America is playing catch-up, US officials say, to protect the technology, skills, and capabilities it needs for its national defense and economic independence. In the words of Vice President Pence, there is a direct line from Beijing's use of industrial policy to a more powerful military. "Through the 'Made in China 2025' plan, the Communist Party has set its sights on controlling 90 percent of the world's most advanced industries, including robotics, biotechnology, and artificial intelligence. To win the commanding heights of the 21st Century economy, Beijing has directed its bureaucrats and businesses to obtain American intellectual property—the foundation of our economic leadership—by any means necessary," he said. "And using that stolen technology, the Chinese Communist Party is turning ploughshares into swords on a massive scale."[8]

Beijing has its own popular terms for "decoupling," which are used by the more nationalistic elements in China's internal debate. At a forum attended by a number of outspoken conservative commentators in Beijing in May 2019, the participants referred regularly to "autonomous and controllable" systems,[9] buzzwords that underscore China's desire to develop its own technology and supply chains.[10] The phrase has been used by Xi himself, both in a speech in May 2018 at the nineteenth Meeting of the Academicians of the Chinese Academy of Sciences and at the fourteenth Meeting of the Academicians of the Chinese Academy of Engineering on May 28, 2018. "It is necessary to strengthen our 'four self-confidences,'" he said, citing the need for China to "strive to make key core technologies autonomous and controllable, and seize the initiative of innovation and development firmly in our own hands."[11]

Xi has begun to use the phrase "self-reliance" over the last year as well, a concept that had gone out of fashion in the reform period. The notion of self-reliance had become associated with autarkic states like North Korea.

But Xi has revived this old Maoist idea, including in his 2019 New Year speech.[12] Xi also discussed self-reliance during a high-profile tour of China's rustbelt in the northeastern part of the country in November 2018, invoking the term to urge industry to reduce China's dependence on imported technology. "Internationally, advanced technology and key technology is more and more difficult to obtain," he said in a speech to China First Heavy Industries. "Unilateralism and trade protectionism have risen, forcing us to travel the road of self-reliance."[13]

The immediate cause of Xi's concern was the dispute with the United States over sanctions against the Chinese telecommunications company, ZTE. In April 2018, Washington banned the Shenzhen company from buying US components for breaching an embargo on trade with Iran. The US ban threatened to send ZTE out of business, since it relies heavily on the United States for semiconductors as essential parts for its smartphones and other products. After nearly three months in July 2018, Trump reversed the ban as a favor to Xi following a conversation with the Chinese leader.[14] The realization that China was heavily dependent on imports for its semiconductors and indeed, that some large companies like ZTE could be bankrupted if they were withheld, was a wakeup call for China's hawks. "The dagger has been revealed; the real motive of the United States is crystal clear," wrote two scholars at the time.[15]

In a sign that China seeks proactively to turn the tables on the United States and maximize its leverage over the global economy, Beijing is reportedly establishing a mechanism for export control of its own emerging sensitive technologies. The mechanism—which the *Financial Times* reports was first proposed by the Ministry of Commerce in a May 2017 policy paper— will allow the National Development and Reform Commission (NDRC) to exercise control over manufacturing content of Chinese origin under the guidelines of China's national security law, which was passed in 2015.[16]

Beijing lags behind Washington's extensive financial, legal, and sanctioning powers abroad. Despite efforts to internationalize the renminbi, China does not yet have control over critical nodes in global financial architecture. Beijing's ability to make third countries and companies comply with so-called secondary sanctions is therefore limited. However, as an economic power responsible for 25 percent of global manufacturing output, China does have the capacity to exercise extended leverage through economic interdependencies exerted through supply chains. According to a 2018 PwC report on China's Proposed Export Control Law, China "appears to be implementing a longer-term strategy that recognizes its competitive advantage in manufacturing, while building towards competing for control over the real value in the modern supply chain—the intellectual property."[17]

WHICH SIDE HAS THE UPPER HAND?

The United States has many, often contradictory, reasons for taking a tougher line with China on trade. They range from accommodating protectionist sentiment at home and prizing open China's closed markets, to guarding core technologies and capabilities and restricting China's rise on national security grounds. One impulse looks to open China; the other to get it out of the market. It goes without saying that such conflicting reasons have produced policy with conflicting objectives. On the one hand, sections of the US policymaking establishment have been promoting decoupling. At the same time, US trade negotiators have been demanding greater access to the Chinese market and cuts in subsidies to industry in China, policies that would further enmesh the two countries rather than separate them.

These conflicting objectives were on display in the midst of the two countries' tense trade negotiations. On the day that US negotiators greeted Liu He in Washington in early May 2019 nearing one of the talk's many deadlines, the Federal Communications Commission blocked China Mobile on national security grounds from providing international phone services in the United States. China Mobile, a state-owned Chinese telecom company and "national champion," had filed its application in 2011. "There is a significant risk that the Chinese government would use China Mobile to conduct activities that would seriously jeopardize the national security, law enforcement, and economic interests of the United States," FCC Chairman Ajit Pai said.[18]

China's massive bilateral trade surplus with the United States would seem to indicate that Washington has great leverage over Beijing in this contest, something that Donald Trump has often cited as a reason the United States will win any trade war with China. But such views ignore a number of megatrends in the region, starting with the fact that China is becoming less reliant on the United States for its economic health, and more intertwined with Asia. Beijing's Belt and Road Initiative (BRI), which aims to harness Eurasia to China's economy, is cementing that trend, and may in fact be designed for that purpose. "Western countries have always been part of the international community; however, most countries are not Western countries," said Zhang Weiwei, a professor at Fudan University in Shanghai. "The international community also comprises countries from across the world. Now most of the world endorses the Belt and Road Initiative, meaning it is providing development opportunities for most countries."[19]

Today, bilateral trade with the United States accounts for 14 percent of China's trade flows. The United States' share of Chinese exports in trade in value-added terms actually declined from about 30 percent in 2002, just after China joined the World Trade Organization, to 20 percent in 2011. Since the global financial crisis, China has both overtaken the United States as the world's largest trading nation and seen its gross domestic product growth become less dependent on exports.

IMPACT ON THE UNITED STATES AND CHINA

Even in the most abrupt scenarios, decoupling is unlikely to existentially threaten the long-term health and growth trajectory of either of the of the world's two largest economies. In other words, the United States could slow but not reverse China's economic ascendancy.

Despite a slowing growth rate, in 2018 China's economy still grew by more than the total size of Australia's economy. At similar rates of absolute growth, its economy will have tripled in size in 2030 from 2015 levels. Under business-as-usual scenarios, China's economy is projected to level that of the United States at market exchange rates by that time as well.

According to research by the Lowy Institute, generalized tariffs and other punitive measures—including targeted US trade sanctions—could produce a hit of up to 3.5 percent of China's GDP, which is roughly the domestic value China gains from the exports it sends to the United States. This would also impact the United States. However, in a Trumpian beggar-thy-neighbor sense, China stands to lose out more, and there would be a continuing long-term growth hit. By 2030, China's economy would be approximately 8 percent—or US$2.7 trillion dollars—smaller than it is forecast to be under normal trends. The Unites States would be US$1.1 trillion dollars poorer too, with an economy more than 3 percent smaller than currently forecast for 2030.

Nevertheless, China's overall growth trajectory is unlikely to be fundamentally affected. The economy is much less vulnerable to escalating trade tensions than it would have been several decades ago. China may be the world's largest trading nation but, like the United States, its GDP is becoming less dependent on exports as it shifts to a domestic consumption model. The

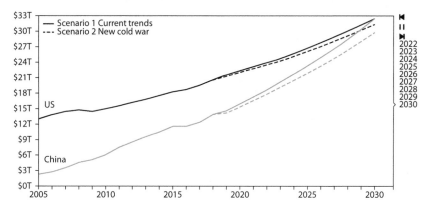

FIGURE 23.1. Global views of China. Source: 2018 Pew Global Attitudes and Trends Survey in 25 countries across the globe, in Pew Research Center, "International Publics Divided on China," October 1, 2018; and "5 Charts on Global Views of China," October 19, 2018.

country's trade-to-GDP ratio is around 38 percent. By comparison, Vietnam's trade to-GDP-ratio is over 200 percent. This suggest China's geoeconomic resilience is considerably higher than most other emerging economies.

At the same time, access to Western markets will likely prove increasingly marginal to the global ascendancy of Chinese tech. China's upper-middle-income consumer base is making large-scale implementation of new technologies such as 5G easier to achieve domestically before being rolled out to other emerging markets. It is significant, therefore, that Beijing has become the leading source of foreign investment flows into developing economies in the Asia-Pacific, even as the United States and Japan have remained the largest sources of foreign investment into the region at large in the past decade.

It remains to be seen whether China may at some point start to surpass the United States in terms of artificial intelligence, biotech, and information technology. However, China's success or failure might have less to do with its access to the United States market, and much more with how third countries, and developing markets in particular, react to secondary US sanctions.

In May 2019, the Trump administration blacklisted Chinese telecommunications equipment maker Huawei. As result, Google terminated its cooperation with Huawei, thereby depriving the Chinese smartphone maker of the license to use Google's Android software and related services in key growth markets far beyond the United States. For its part, Beijing has said it would retaliate against foreign companies that refuse to do business with Huawei, putting third countries and multinationals in the middle of a technological tug of war. So far, the countries that have banned Huawei, completely or fully, like Australia, Japan, and New Zealand, are all developed nations in the Pacific region that are allies or partners of the United States. Countries like the United Kingdom, Germany, France, and Brazil are so far taking a middle path. Most developing nations and Asian countries have put no obstacles in Huawei's path. With each action, both the United States and China continue to give the other, and the hardliners in their political systems, greater incentives to increase the pace of decoupling, rather than holding it back.

THIRD COUNTRIES' HEDGING

There is often a temptation to reduce the complexity of decoupling to a two-player zero-sum game between the United States and China. However, the global economy—bound by unprecedented levels of interdependence—is created and sustained by a much wider array of economic actors. China may be less susceptible to the downsides of a trade war with the United States than was first thought, but third countries in Asia, which, by and large, are strategically friendly to the United States, may be much more so. At the same time, third countries will play a deciding role between two gridlocked superpowers over which side dominates the next generation of technology and globalization.

This points to a more complex set of choices for third countries than the hegemonic trope of choosing sides suggests. Even if we are seeing a new Cold War between the United States and China, it is unlikely fixed blocks will emerge, defined in the sense of the last Cold War. Cases of choosing sides are likely to be issue-specific, diverse in scope, and reflect varying national interest calculations and negotiating leverage at different points in time. For most countries, globalization will fundamentally continue to involve the United States and China, while governments and businesses seek to manage the tradeoffs between them.

Certain countries will even be able to gain from decoupling by luring multinationals now based in China to relocate. There is already evidence that countries like Malaysia, Taiwan, Mexico, and Cambodia are doing just that. Taiwan's Foxconn Technology Group is considering assembling its phones in India, a potentially huge market. But many other investment decisions are a spillover of bilateral tensions. According to the *Wall Street Journal*, "trade flows once driven by cost, quality and proximity to customers increasingly reflect political priorities, whether it is Chinese purchases of US energy and agriculture or the location of manufacturing plants."[20]

Third countries will also be disproportionately affected by a paralysis in economic governance as result of the zero-sum politics between the two largest players. There were signs of that at the most recent G7 and APEC summits, where leaders were unable to come up with even a diplomatic communique at the end. With no lowest common denominator other than the agreement to disagree, things could get worse. By the end of 2019, the rules-based trading system built around the World Trade Organization (WTO) could wither—if not crack—under pressure owing to a refusal by the United States to approve new appointments on its Appellate Body. If the United States maintains its current policy, there will only be one judge left on the Appellate Body, which means appeals and trade law enforcement will go into limbo. That will affect a lot of trade-dependent countries, particularly smaller ones.

Large and more insulated and protectionist economies like India and Indonesia are better placed to withstand the erosion of the WTO trading system. Even so, the United States will be hard-pressed to find any regional friends—large or small—willing to join it in decoupling from China. But for most countries, including major industrialized US allies like the European Union, Japan, and South Korea, decoupling plus "America first" shape up as a toxic brew. For them, their economic ties with China are seen as a lifeline to be managed, not severed.

As things stand, China does 70 percent more trade with the Indo-Pacific region annually (US$2.5 trillion) than does the United States (US$1.4 trillion). Research by the Lowy Institute shows that the importance of the United States as an export destination for Asian countries is declining relative to an increasingly affluent China. The average export share in twenty-four Indo-Pacific countries to China is 23 percent, and just 12 percent for the United States. In other words, the economic leverage in Asia rests more with China as it does the United States.

AMERICA'S DISAPPEARING LEVERAGE

The United States will find it increasingly difficult to compete with China unilaterally. In geostrategic terms, it is the relativities that matter. In 1990, the US economy accounted for 21.8 percent of global GDP, based on purchasing-power-parity share of world total, compared to 4.1 percent for

China. By 2024, China will account for 21.4 percent of global economic output, well ahead of the United States at 13.7 percent.

Any sustainable comparative advantage that the United States holds over China will lie in taking a networked approach. Under such circumstances, middle powers in Asia, but also in Europe, become crucial in the overall balance of power. While Europeans are increasingly skeptical about the Chinese leadership's goals and methods, they do not share the Trump administration's determination to stem China's rise; and they do not want to find themselves trapped on one side of a new political-economic cold war.[21]

Similar sentiments are echoed in New Delhi. In January 2019, at the fourth Raisina Dialogue—India's flagship foreign policy conference—Retired US General David Petraeus insisted that India "has to decide, has to take a side in the new world order shaped by rising China."[22] India's former Foreign Secretary Subrahmanyam Jaishankar responded "India will take a side, its own side." More recently, in one of his first interviews as India's newly minted Minister of External Affairs, Jaishankar reiterated India would stay non-partisan in the Sino-US trade war: "Frankly, in every clash, there is an opportunity. There are risks also. My job will be to manage the risks and maximize the opportunity."[23]

The Trump administration's scatter-gun focus on balancing trade flows one country at a time has done little to mobilize broad-based support for decoupling. Far from containing China, forcing choices from third countries may ensure that global supply chains remain anchored in China after all. In 2000, the West still accounted for about 50 percent of all East Asian exports in value-added trade. Today, East Asia and other non-Western economies account for about two-thirds of that balance. Asia's economic transformation is resulting in a region becoming more self-reliant for its prosperity.

The United States could try a different approach, partnering with Asian allies and Europe on shared concerns like the abuse of intellectual property rights and nationalist technology ambitions. However, such an approach will require the United States to let go of its "America First" focus, and proactively sustain an environment where the combined strength and interests of its partners and allies are maximized—including by supporting the rules-based trading system that underpins the region's prosperity.

Setting regional standards and maintaining an inclusive multilateral architecture became a key organizing principle of Japan under the then prime ministership of Shinzo Abe. Tokyo successfully resuscitated the Trans-Pacific Partnership (TPP) in 2018, which became the TPP-11 of Japan together with ten other regional economies. Were Washington to be more strategic, it would embrace this trade pact that Trump left in one of his first decisions in office. Rejoining it would provide the region with a real, rules-based alternative to the emerging Chinese system.

There is no question of the need for enhanced resilience against China's exploitation of vulnerabilities in complex supply chains. Unfortunately, decoupling runs the risk of throwing the baby out with the bathwater. Poorly handled, wholesale decoupling will do little to advance Washington's goal to compete against an illiberal peer competitor on the world stage. To the contrary, it may only entrench China's growing gravitational pull. Much still depends on the trajectory of each country's political systems. For all their profound differences, and America's transparency and China's opacity, both countries have set off on unpredictable paths. Decoupling, and the unwinding of globalization more generally, will only restrict the ability of whomever is leading the two countries in coming decades to bridge the chasm between the world's two largest economies.

NOTES

1. Henry M. Paulson Jr., "Remarks by Henry M. Paulson, Jr. on the United States and China at a Crossroads," Paulson Institute, November 7, 2018, https://www.paulsoninstitute.org/press_release/remarks-by-henry-m-paulson-jr-on-the-united-states-and-china-at-a-crossroads/.

2. Yuan Yang and Nian Liu, "China's Industrial-Military Hawks Flex Their Anti-US Muscles," *Financial Times*, May 9, 2019, https://www.ft.com/content/eb36851c-7211-11e9-bbfb-5c68069fbd15.

3. Hu Xijin (@huxijin), "More and more Chinese now tend to believe the current US government is obsessed with comprehensively containing China," Twitter, May 9, 2019, 12:17 p.m., https://twitter.com/HuXijin_GT/status/1126536674106675200.

4. Li Ruogu, "Zhongmei guanxi fasheng le shizhixing bianhua" [US-China relations have experienced a substantive shift], *Jingji daokan* [Economic herald], January 19, 2019.

5. John Bolton, "John Bolton Previews Trump's United Nations Speech," interview, Fox News, September 23, 2018, https://www.foxnews.com/transcript/john-bolton-previews-trumps-united-nations-speech.

6. Abigail Grace, "China and America May Be Forging a New Economic Order," *Atlantic Monthly,* September 20, 2018.

7. Daniel Rosen, "Is a Trade War the Only Option? An Alternative Approach to Taking on China," *Foreign Affairs*, March 20, 2018, https://www.foreignaffairs.com/articles/china/2018-03-20/trade-war-only-option.

8. Mike Pence, "Vice President Mike Pence's Remarks on the Administration's Policy Towards China," October 4 Event, Hudson Institute, October 4, 2018, https://www.hudson.org/events/1610-vice-president-mike-pence-s-remarks-on-the-administration-s-policy-towards-china102018.

9. The phrase in Chinese is *zizhu kekong*.

10. Yuan Yang and Nian Liu, "China's Industrial-Military Hawks Flex Their Anti-US Muscles," *Financial Times*, May 9, 2019, https://www.ft.com/content/eb36851c-7211-11e9-bbfb-5c68069fbd15.

11. Xi Jinping, "Zai Zhongguo Kexueyuan di shijiu ci yuanshi dahui, Zhongguo Goncchengyuan di shisici yuanshi dahui shang de jianghua" [Speech at nineteenth Meeting of the Academicians of the Chinese Academy of Sciences and the four-teenth Meeting of the Academicians of the Chinese Academy of Engineering], Xinhuanet, May 28, 2018, http://www.xinhuanet.com/politics/leaders/2018–05/28/c_1122901308.htm.

12. Xi Jinping, "Guojia zhuxi Xi Jinping fabiao erlingyijiu nian xinnian heci" [President Xi delivers 2019 New Year's greetings], Xinhuanet, December 31, 2018, http://www.xinhuanet.com/politics/2018–12/31/c_1123931806.htm.

13. Gabriel Wildau, "China's Xi Jinping Revives Maoist Call for 'Self-reliance,'" *Financial Times*, November 12, 2018, https://www.ft.com/content/63430718-e3cb-11e8-a6e5-792428919cee.

14. Paul Mozur and Raymond Zhong, "In About-Face on Trade, Trump Vows to Protect ZTE Jobs in China," *New York Times*, May 13, 2018. https://www.nytimes.com/2018/05/13/business/trump-vows-to-save-jobs-at-chinas-zte-lost-after-us-sanctions.html.

15. Chen Ping and Shi Jian, "Zhong-Mei maoyizhan kong shengji bandaoti you cheng zhongzaiqu" [Fears of escalating US-China trade war, semiconductors again hit hardest], Mo'er xinwen, June 19, 2018, https://www.sohu.com/a/236618032_465984.

16. Lucy Hornby, "China to Roll out Export Controls on Sensitive Technology," *Financial Times*, June 9, 2019, https://www.ft.com/content/47562fd6–89f6–11e9-a1c1–51bf8f989972.

17. "Who's in Control? China's Proposed Export Control Law, Trade and Intelligence Asia Pacific," June–July, 2018, pwc Middle East, https://www.pwc.com/m1/en/services/tax/customs-international-trade/china-proposed-export-control-law-june-july-2018.html.

18. Sasha Ingber, "FCC Blocks Chinese Company's Bid for International Phone Services in the U.S.," NPR, May 9, 2019, https://www.npr.org/2019/05/09/721772856/fcc-blocks-chinese-companys-bid-for-international-phone-services-in-the-u-s.

19. "Weisheme shuo zhuazhu le 'Yidai Yilu', jiu zhuazhu le weilai?" [Why does seizing 'One Belt One Road' mean seizing the future?], Guanchazhe, April 24, 2019, https://www.guancha.cn/culture/2019_04_24_499001.shtml.

20. Greg Ip and Yoko Kobota, "Can This Marriage Be Saved? Chinese-U.S. Integration Frays," *Wall Street Journal*, May 9, 2019, https://www.wsj.com/articles/can-this-marriage-be-saved-chinese-u-s-integration-frays-11557414600.

21. Robin Niblett, "How Europe Will Try to Dodge the U.S.—China Standoff in 2019," Chatham House, December 21, 2018, https://www.chathamhouse.org/expert/comment/how-europe-will-try-dodge-us-china-standoff-2019.

22. Rashmee Roshan Lall, "A New Era of Pragmatic Foreign Policy Appears to Be Emerging in Modi's India 2.0," *National News*, June 11, 2019, https://www.thenationalnews.com/opinion/comment/a-new-era-of-pragmatic-foreign-policy-appears-to-be-emerging-in-modi-s-india-2-0-1.873121.

23. Dipanjan Roy Chaudhury, "Won't Pick Sides But Protect Interests, Says Jaishankar," *Economic Times*, June 7, 2019, https://economictimes.indiatimes.com/news/politics-and-nation/wont-pick-sides-but-protect-interests-says-jaishankar/articleshow/69684472.cms?from=mdr.

FURTHER READING

Asia Power Index. 2019. Lowy Institute. https://power.lowyinstitute.org/.

TWENTY-FOUR

State-Led Globalization, or How Hard Is China's Soft Power?

Ingrid d'Hooghe and Frank N. Pieke

CHINA'S RISE IS NOT JUST about the arrival of a newly developed country on the scene. It is about the rise of a new superpower and a concomitant power shift from the West toward the East as well as a changing international order. Moreover, China's rise, being that of a one-party-led authoritarian state, comes with state-driven globalization and the promotion of new approaches to global governance. The Chinese government seeks to reform the liberal international order to better align that order with China's needs and interests. It has taken the initiative to complement that order with alternative, Chinese-led institutions, with the establishment of the Asian Infrastructure and Investment Bank (AIIB) in 2015 as a clear turning point.

Many countries, principally those from the developed world, feel threatened and have started to push back against China's growing influence. They adopt policies to counter what they see as the negative consequences of China's rise, such as unfair trade practices, competition over technological leadership, the undermining of the rules-based international order, the erosion of US military superiority and global security leadership, and ultimately the challenges to the presumed superiority of democratic political systems. Since 2017, with a new, aggressively nationalist administration in power in the United States, the urgency of these worries has mounted. Telling examples of this are the China-US trade war, the "decoupling" of the US economy from, and the security measures against, China, and the European Union's toughened China policy, whereby China is not only referred to as a "partner" but also as a "strategic competitor" and a "systemic rival."

Many countries seek to stay away from publicly denouncing China's political system or its policies and prefer instead to maximize their interests by hedging the benefits and risks that the rivalry between China, the United

States, and (increasingly) the European Union present them with. Across the world, the rise of China has deepened divisions of interests and rattled old and created new alliances and rivalries. However, American calls to "pick a side" in what is becoming a hegemonic confrontation are largely falling on deaf ears, as it becomes clear that the United States has, in fact, less and less to offer beyond hard security and cannot be considered a trusted partner anymore.

China, in turn, is well aware that in order to sustain its rise and realize the Chinese Dream of becoming a world-leading country and reshaping the international order with Chinese norms, it needs to find new and better tools to deal with this pushback. It has to project its growing power and influence in ways that are attractive or at least acceptable to the world.

This chapter examines China's efforts to achieve that goal. It analyzes how China sells its ambition to become a leading power by mapping the country's extensive public diplomacy strategies and exploring its promotion of the Belt and Road Initiative. China develops these activities to help the country build and wield soft power, but one can well ask if the country's state-centered approach to soft power is really all that soft. As a result of China's growing economic and political weight and the increasing rivalry between China and the United States, Western audiences are looking at these messages with different and increasingly critical eyes. At the same time, the Chinese government progressively openly strengthens its efforts to get its messages across in soft as well as sharp ways that serve its hard power objectives.

SELLING CHINA'S GROWING POWER TO THE WORLD

In order to sell its rise and avoid a clash with other powers in the world, China develops extensive public diplomacy strategies aimed at promoting Chinese culture, values, and legitimate policies, as well as a positive domestic model, a successful economy, and even a capable military. China seeks to wield soft power—that is, "the ability to get what you want through attraction rather than coercion or payment."[1] Chinese policy makers and scholars embraced the concept of soft power—a term originally coined by American political scientist Joseph Nye—to an extent not often seen with political concepts from abroad.[2] They regard soft power as one of the four fundamental components of what they term China's "comprehensive national power," and it is on a par with economic, military, and political power. They believe that building soft power helps make China's rise palatable to the world and that it advances the

TABLE 24.1 Global views of China

Themes	2018 views in % (25 countries)
Having favorable views of China	45
Agreeing that China plays a more important role in the world than it did 10 years ago	70
Favoring a world in which China is the leading power	19
Having confidence in Chinese president Xi Jinping to do the right thing in world affairs	34
Agreeing that the Chinese government does not respect the personal freedoms of its people	66

SOURCE: 2018 Pew global attitudes and trends survey in twenty-five countries across the globe, Pew Research Center, "International Publics Divided on China," October 1, 2018; and "5 Charts on Global Views of China," October 19, 2018.

country's domestic and international agenda, wins friends and allies, and creates understanding, respect, and support for China's political model and policies.

In order to achieve these goals, the Chinese government invests heavily in developing public diplomacy instruments and narratives that paint a rosy picture of a future in which China and the Chinese model will be guiding the world. Chinese president Xi Jinping is urging his officials and the Chinese media to "tell China's stories well" by presenting "a true, multidimensional and panoramic view of China."[3] But China is doing more than just telling stories. Its narratives are complemented by concrete projects and ample funding, coupled with a diplomatic strategy aimed at keeping Chinese ideas and proposals for global governance on foreign governments' agendas and having them embraced by the international community.

But the harder China pushes its agenda, the stronger the pushback seems to be from countries that do not want to see China becoming a world leader. As table 24.1 illustrates, China's global image leaves much to be desired. Although majorities of the population in foreign countries see China playing an increasingly important role in the world, they neither favor a world that is led by China nor do they have much confidence in President Xi's global leadership.

The Chinese government is aware of the negative views of their country and keeps seeking a solution in expanding its efforts to build up soft power. It has been investing in public diplomacy since the 1990s, but under President Xi Jinping China's approach has seen important changes. The Chinese leadership has become more vocal and active on the diplomatic front; it has strengthened the role of the Communist Party in overseeing foreign relations; and it has developed new narratives to share with the world. Whereas in the past, China's stories were often defending Chinese political ideas, today Chinese leaders are proudly promoting Chinese policies, encouraging the world to learn from China's model. In the words of President Xi Jinping, "The world is too big, and challenges are too many, to go without the voice from China being heard, without solution ideas from China being shared, without the involvement of China being needed."[4] Indeed, in many of his speeches to foreign audiences, Xi is confidently spreading "Chinese wisdom," and advocating "Chinese solutions" to global problems.[5] As will be discussed further below, in the view of the Chinese government these Chinese solutions are not just an alternative to non-Chinese solutions; they are a *better* alternative.

China's policies and narratives are disseminated through a remarkable array of public diplomacy instruments, many of which are similar to those employed by Western countries in their public diplomacy strategies: the media; cultural institutions and activities; study tours for opinion-shapers such as journalists; politicians and young leaders; educational exchanges and aid policies. In addition, China employs unique instruments, such as the more than five hundred Confucian Institutes around the world,[6] and the communities in the Chinese diaspora, which the Chinese government actively engages to contribute to China's development and global image. Apart from these specific Chinese instruments, China's public diplomacy essentially differs from Western approaches in two respects. The first is the scale of China's efforts. There are no official figures available, but based on the investments in the international expansion of the Chinese media, Chinese cultural institutions and festivals, Confucius Institutes, and other public diplomacy instruments, the total amount must be in the billions of dollars per year, most likely much more than any other country.[7] The second and more important difference is that China's public diplomacy is strongly state-centered and state-controlled.[8] In China, the state "owns" public diplomacy: it is the state that develops the narratives, dominates and directs the actors involved, and attempts to control the flow of information as well as the content of media reporting. This approach enables China not only to develop long-term, well-coordinated, and comprehensive public diplomacy policies and unified messages. It also employs opaque, intrusive, and coercive methods that are considered part of the hard or sharp power rather than the soft power toolbox. *Hard power* refers to coercive approaches to convincing audiences to work with and not against a country; *sharp power* refers to activities aimed at "piercing, penetrating or perforating the political and information environments in targeted countries."[9] Although it is difficult to draw clear lines between these different types of power, public diplomacy and soft power reserve a big role for societal actors and build on the attractiveness of a country's culture, values, and policies, whereas hard and sharp power are state-driven, with sharp power seeking to exploit the openness and free flow of information in democratic countries in order to actively undermine the target country's values and policies. Needless to say, this carries a huge risk of backfiring, weakening the credibility of China's messages and confirming the authoritarian nature of the country.

Before looking into the case of China's selling of the BRI, the three most prominent public diplomacy instruments will be discussed in more detail. These are: the expansion of the Chinese media abroad; the proliferation of the Confucius Institutes; and the involvement of Chinese communities overseas.

The Media

Feeling that Chinese views on world affairs and the country's development are underrepresented in the global media and that Western media often deliberately creates a negative image of China, the Chinese government has decided to invest in the expansion and strengthening of Chinese media outlets both at home and abroad. It is their task to make the Chinese culture, language, policies, and narratives more visible and better heard in the world at large.

The enormous expansion of the Chinese media is reflected, first and foremost, in the growth of China's state news agency Xinhua abroad—as has been discussed in more detail by Pal Nyíri in his chapter on Chinese foreign correspondents in this volume. Xinhua provides most of the news items for Chinese media outlets, including major English language newspapers such as the *Global Times*, *People's Daily*, and *China Daily*, which are online available for free. Secondly, while most international broadcasters, including the Voice of America and the BBC World Service, have sized down over the past two decades, China Radio International (CRI or Voice of China) is sizing up and now broadcasts from dozens of overseas bureaus in sixty-five languages all over the world.[10] China Global Television Network (CGTN), too, has expanded to run international channels in six languages in 170 countries and regions.[11] Its programs may not appeal to large audiences in Europe and America, but they do reach overseas Chinese communities around the globe as well as broader audiences in both Asia and Africa. Chinese media outlets increasingly hire foreign reporters to write articles and present programs.

China also seeks to enlist the foreign media, including international social media and the newspapers of overseas Chinese communities. The government releases information to these media via the Chinese state news agency Xinhua, press conferences, and government websites. And while the Western social media apps Twitter and Facebook are banned inside China, Chinese media, government organizations, and Chinese diplomats abroad use them extensively to spread their messages to the global community, thereby exploiting international free flows of information that the Chinese government have blocked at home.

Chinese embassy staff work to have letters or opinion pieces from Chinese leaders and ambassadors published in the major newspapers of the countries they reside in, especially on the eve of foreign visits to the target country. The Chinese government also takes out political advertisements or paid-for inserts in foreign newspapers. In 2016, for example, the government placed an advertorial in a Canadian newspaper defending its territorial claims in the South China Sea. The headline read: "The South China Sea Arbitration Case Initiated by the Philippines Violates International Law." The official English-language newspaper *China Daily* allegedly made deals with dozens of foreign newspapers around the globe—including the *New York Times*, the *Telegraph*, *El País*, and—to carry four- to eight-page supplements prepared by Chinese state media called "China Watch."[12] A recent example of this is an insert in a local Iowa newspaper aimed at undermining Iowa farmers' support for Trump and his trade war against China by pointing out that China had started looking elsewhere for imports of agricultural products.[13] This action illustrates well how China's use of the foreign media may move beyond the domain of soft power.

Although it is difficult to assess the overall impact of China's media expansion, the country's growing presence in the global media environment has made Chinese news and views much more readily available to global audiences.

Confucius Institutes

Confucius Institutes and Confucius Classrooms have been established all over the world since 2004. They are regarded as an efficient way to promote soft power and appeal to students around the globe. In early 2019 there were more than 520 Confucius Institutes in more than one hundred countries. The institutes take the form of joint ventures with foreign-based educational institutes, often universities, which also have to participate financially. This approach encourages foreign partners to become directly engaged in developing ways to unlock China's culture for a local public. On the Chinese side, they are funded and directed by the Confucius Institute Headquarters or *Hanban* in Beijing, which is directly affiliated to the Chinese Ministry of Education and indirectly to various Chinese Communist Party organizations.[14]

The stated aim of the Confucius Institutes and Classrooms is to promote and teach Chinese language, culture, and history at schools and universities abroad and to strengthen understanding and friendship. In practice they are also an instrument to actively advance the Chinese government's political narratives in classrooms and at the seminars, conferences, and cultural events that they organize for broader audiences.

The jury is still out on the ultimate success of the Confucius Institutes. In recent years, a growing number of Confucius Institutes in the United States and Europe have closed their doors, not only because they have come under close political scrutiny but also because universities feel they do not belong in a university environment and have little to add to their academic cooperation with China. Despite these challenges, the Chinese government continues to expand their numbers.

Overseas Chinese

One of the most interesting aspects of Chinese public diplomacy is the engagement of tens of millions of Chinese people living overseas and throughout the world. This means Chinese citizens living abroad, including Chinese students, and foreign citizens of Chinese ancestry. As was discussed in Kwee Hui Kian's chapter in this book, the majority of such people live in Southeast Asia, but large number of Chinese people also reside in North America, Europe, Australia, and, more recently, Africa.

Ever since the establishment of the People's Republic of China, the Chinese government has maintained contact with pro-China associations among overseas Chinese communities around the world. In the 1980s, and especially in the 1990s, these efforts intensified, including the convening of regional conferences in a drive to form a united global network of such organizations. The Chinese government is also involved in the establishment and functioning of more than two thousand overseas Chinese scholars and students' associations and professional organizations.[15] Through these different types of associations, the Chinese government organizes or sponsors a great number of economic, educational, and cultural activities, such as the extensive Chinese New Year celebrations that are held all over the world. These are targeted at overseas Chinese but sometimes at broader audiences too.

Recently, the overseas Chinese have become much more directly enlisted in China's soft power strategy. Their nationalism has been connected not just to China or the People's Republic but also to the Communist Party and its mission to make China strong and respected again.[16] Overseas Chinese are both targets and vectors of China's public diplomacy. They are a target group because the Chinese government wants to keep the diaspora on its side. Yet they are also agents. Often taking pride in China's economic and political rise, they are willing to play a role in promoting Chinese culture and in lobbying for Chinese political interests. As He Yafei, former Deputy Director of the Overseas Chinese Affairs Office, pointed out, most of the overseas Chinese "care very much about China's image" and they are willing to help with China's public diplomacy work; they can act as go-betweens who can overcome cultural differences in communication with foreigners and whose China narrative "will not be considered ideological indoctrination."[17] In his address to the nineteenth National Congress of the Chinese Communist Party, President Xi declared that the Party would "maintain extensive contacts with overseas Chinese nationals, returned Chinese, and their relatives and [would] unite them so that they can join [the Party's] endeavors to rejuvenate the Chinese nation."[18]

The government also invests strongly in the expansion of overseas Chinese media. The state-run Xinhua news agency, for example, offers a special Chinese-language news service to overseas Chinese media for free and has established a "World Chinese Media Alliance," which organizes the World Chinese Media Forum and media workshops for Chinese people living overseas.[19] To emphasize the importance that the government attaches to the role of the diaspora, President Xi, Premier Li Keqiang, and other leaders regularly meet with overseas Chinese at conferences and cultural events specifically organized for such purposes. Representatives of overseas Chinese associations are also regularly invited to attend political events in China, so that they can explain China's economic and social policies to the people in their home countries. The diaspora was extensively engaged in defending China's image in the run-up to the 2008 Beijing Olympic Games and in promoting the 2010 Shanghai World Expo; they are again encouraged to support the Beijing Winter Olympic Games in 2022. Furthermore, overseas Chinese are encouraged or sometimes directly called on to participate in gatherings in their countries to cheer visiting Chinese leaders, to "drown out" protesters in anti-China demonstrations, and sometimes even to organize counter protests, activities that can no longer be considered just "soft."

THE BELT AND ROAD INITIATIVE

China's ambition to become a leading country is nowhere more pronounced than in China's efforts to win support for its Belt and Road Initiative (BRI). The BRI started as a largely economically driven strategy to enhance connectivity in and between Asia, Europe, and Africa with the aim of furthering China's economic development, but it has evolved into a comprehensive foreign policy strategy and vision of the world order. Noting that the current world order suffers from a "democratic deficit," a "governance deficit," an increasing wealth gap and other problems, China feels sufficiently confident and competent to "grasp the historic opportunity" to realize this vision.[20] The road to that leading position is paved by the BRI and the related, but more abstract. concept of the "Community of Shared Future of Mankind" (CSF).

Chinese leaders herald the BRI as the project of the century, a public good for the global community that will bring development and prosperity to mankind. Where the BRI can be understood as China's approach to development, its approach to global governance is centered around building a CSF. According to China's narrative, the CSF will make the global governance system fairer and more reasonable. China promotes the CSF as being inclusive and based on an equal sharing of responsibilities and prosperity among its member countries, opposing it to power politics and a Cold War mentality; China engages in cooperation for "win-win" results instead of rivalry; and China insists on peaceful coexistence instead of hegemony, transcending self-interest in international cooperation. The CSF is a comprehensive concept, referring to the political as well as the security realms. It is also an evolving concept: recently, the characteristics of treating nature with respect and treasuring the planet have also been added to the CSF. The CSF is considered to be the end goal of the BRI: a China-centered community that will cooperate on the basis of shared interests, while leaving differences in political systems and political views aside, thus transcending the prescriptive political norms of the current liberal world order.

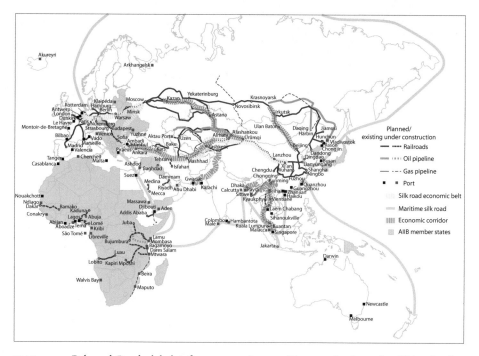

MAP 24.1. Belt and Road global infrastructure Source: Mercator Institute for China Studies (MERICS).

PROMOTING THE BELT AND ROAD INITIATIVE

The Chinese government is going all out in promoting the BRI and the CSF, using the experience it has gained with developing soft power and conducting public diplomacy since the mid-1990s. A major role is played by Chinese leaders and high-level officials who tirelessly explain the BRI and its benefits for the world in their speeches for international organizations, at regional and global summits, and during diplomatic visits abroad. In 2017, the Chinese government held the first Belt and Road Summit in Beijing to which world leaders were invited; in 2019 the second summit followed. In between the summits China used other high-level international meetings in China to ensure that the importance of the BRI w continuously highlighted.

The most important instrument in disseminating the BRI message is the Chinese media, including social media. As the government puts it, they need to be "the walkers, singers and ambassadors" of the Belt and Road, working diligently to spread, explain, and build support for the initiative.[21]

In addition, there are many government-run BRI-themed websites that offer information and news about BRI progress and success in several foreign languages.

The BRI is also promoted extensively through international higher education and research channels. In 2017, the government launched the Belt and Road Science, Technology, and Innovation Cooperation Action Plan, which aims to intensify international cooperation in the development of technological innovation and training of talent.[22] Many Chinese universities and research institutions push their own BRI projects. They organize BRI conferences and seminars and establish international BRI platforms or alliances.

Another important instrument for making audiences familiar with Chinese views on the benefits of the BRI are the Confucius Institutes. Particularly in Asia, the institutes are very active in promoting the BRI at academic forums and seminars. In Thailand, a Confucius Institute specifically devoted to supporting the BRI has even been established: The Maritime Silk Road Confucius Institute at the Dhurakij Pundit University.[23]

The overseas Chinese too have been called on to lend their talents and resources to BRI efforts. They are invited to develop and operate overseas cooperation, expand financial channels, conduct nongovernmental diplomacy, and promote information exchange and resource sharing. They are to organize BRI activities and exchanges in overseas Chinese cultural centers. Indeed, cultural activities are extensively used to familiarize broad audiences with the BRI and CSF. Here are a few examples: BRI photo exhibitions in all corners of the world; BRI essays and speech contests, sometimes held by the Confucius Institutes; a Belt and Road world choir festival; and Belt and Road concerts and ballets. China also produces films and documentaries, such as the documentary *Common Destiny,* which was shown at the Venice Film Festival and which tells the stories of ordinary people across five continents whose lives have been improved by the BRI. Other productions are targeted at children—for example, a *Sesame Street*-style clip of children of different nationalities singing an English song praising the BRI as "the future" and the way to "share goodness," or the video series *Bedtime Stories,* in which an American man explains the BRI to his young daughter with a world map, Lego, and camel toys, emphasizing how the world will benefit from the BRI.

The efforts are paying off, not in the sense that the BRI has been embraced around the globe but in the sense that the BRI is now widely known and, more importantly, is on the political and economic agenda of countries throughout the world. The CSF has not yet become a household term but it has made headway in the diplomatic realm: Chinese diplomats have even succeeded in including the concept in various UN documents.[24]

Although the number of countries joining the BRI is steadily growing, many countries, including the United States, Australia, India, and many EU members states, have so far not signed on, since they perceive BRI as primarily serving China's strategic goals. They complain about the lack of equal opportunities, the insufficient attention to sustainability, and the debt problems that BRI projects may cause. The more fundamental problem underlying the refusal to be drawn into China's BRI orbit, however, is the growing view, especially among developed countries, of China as what the European Commission terms a "systemic rival." At least some of these concerns are also shared by a number of countries that have signed up to the BRI purely for economic reasons.

GREAT POWER RIVALRY AND CHINESE STATE-LED GLOBALIZATION

According to President Xi's report to the nineteenth Party Congress in 2017, "China's international standing has risen as never before." The country's "cultural soft power and the international influence of Chinese culture have increased significantly" and, as a consequence of encouraging "the evolution of the global governance system," China has not only made great new contributions to global peace and development, but the world has also seen "a further rise in China's international influence, ability to inspire, and power to shape."[25]

However, doubts about China's rise in opinion polls, mounting suspicions of the Confucius Institutes, US and European measures to limit Chinese investments, and growing expressions of concern about the BRI in Asia all indicate quite the opposite. China's global stature is increasingly seen as problematic. Since 2017, China's soft-power strategy that we have discussed in this chapter has begun to be framed in a very different light—namely, as part of Chinese "influencing", "interference," "sharp power," or sometimes even "hybrid warfare." In this new perception, the Chinese Communist Party's long-standing united front tactics of enlisting non-Communist forces in support of the Party's policies and its newer public diplomacy tactics are being lumped together with more aggressive sharp power tactics and even simply illegal practices of political interference in democratic elections, bribery of politicians or opinion leaders, and even outright espionage.[26]

Clearly, there is much that is a threat to other countries in China's soft power strategy, which, as this chapter argues, increasingly includes sharp power approaches, and it is high time indeed that vigilance replace naïveté. The CCP leadership quite openly views its soft power as one pillar of its push to make China a world leader, complementing the strategies to further build Chinese economic and diplomatic clout, technological and scientific prowess, and military might. However, instead of blaming China for breaking the rules of a liberal game that exists in our mind, it might be more realistic and more productive to view China's deliberate attempts at gaining influence abroad as still just the first stages of a learning process of an emerging superpower that is beginning to flex its muscles abroad.

Like the Soviet Union and the United States before it, the new Chinese superpower does not seek to conform to the rules of the game but to set these rules, all the while always reserving the right to break or redefine them if it suits its purpose. As its interests expand across the globe and confront those of other powers, a superpower finds ways, both old and new, to mold the reality that it finds to serve its interests. The question to the ruling elites in other countries is therefore not how to expose, restrain, or even roll back Chinese influence. China can no longer be stopped or contained. Rather, other countries need to find ways to handle and live with the rising Chinese influence that safeguard their own interests as much as possible. China's rise should not so much be denounced as dealt with. This is true even for the United States: China is no Soviet Union that could only bring its military might to the table. China is part and parcel of every aspect of our globalized world, even in anti-globalizing times: a cold war with China will only produce losers.

NOTES

1. Nye 2004, x.
2. d'Hooghe 2015, 355.
3. Xi Jinping's speech at the National Propaganda and Ideology Work Conference, August 19, 2013. See "Xi Jinping's 19 August Speech Revealed?," trans. China Copyright and Media, December 22, 2014, https://chinacopyrightandmedia .wordpress.com/2013/11/12/xi-jinpings-19-august-speech-revealed-translation/; Xi

Jinping, "Secure a Decisive Victory in Building a Moderately Prosperous Society in All Respects and Strive for the Great Success of Socialism with Chinese Characteristics for a New Era," in *Report to the 19th National Congress of the Communist Party of China*, October 18, 2017, http://www.xinhuanet.com/english /download/Xi_Jinping's_report_at_19th_CPC_National_Congress.pdf.

4. Xi Jinping, New Year's Speech 2016, December 31, 2015, China Radio International, *People's Net*, January 1, 2016, http://en.people.cn/n3/2016/0101/c90000-8998156.html.

5. See "Xinhua Insight: From Hangzhou to Hamburg: Xi offers Chinese wisdom to G20," XinhuaNet, September 9, 2017, http://www.xinhuanet.com/english/2017–07/09/c_136429954.htm.

6. See "About Confucius Institute/Classroom," Confucius Institute/Classroom, accessed August 7, 2019, http://english.hanban.org/node_10971.htm.

7. d'Hooghe 2015, 180.

8. d'Hooghe 2015, "Conclusions."

9. Walker and Ludwig 2017, 13.

10. Koh Gui Qing and John Shiffman, "Beijing's Covert Radio Network Airs China-Friendly News across Washington, and the World," Reuters, November 2, 2015, https://www.reuters.com/investigates/special-report/china-radio/.

11. See, e.g., Lu 2018.

12. Louisa Lim and Julia Bergin, "Inside China's Audacious Global Propaganda Campaign," *Guardian,* December 7, 2018, https://www.theguardian.com/news/2018 /dec/07/china-plan-for-global-media-dominance-propaganda-xi-jinping.

13. Donnelle Eller, "Chinese-Backed Newspaper Insert Tries to Undermine Iowa Farm Support for Trump, Trade War," *Des Moines Register,* September 26, 2018, https://www.desmoinesregister.com/story/money/agriculture/2018/09/24 /china-daily-watch-advertisement-tries-sway-iowa-farm-support-trump-trade-war-tariffs/1412954002/.

14. Hughes 2014.

15. Brabantseva 2010, 125.

16. Wang Xiangwei, "The Question Facing Chinese Diaspora: For Love of Country or Party?" *South China Morning Post,* July 22, 2018, https://www.scmp.com /week-asia/politics/article/2155747/question-facing-chinese-diaspora-love-country-or-party.

17. He Yafei "Fahui qiaowu youshi, rang shijie liaojie yige zhenzheng de zhongguo" [To play overseas Chinese affairs advantage, let the world know a real China], *Gonggong waijiao jikan* [Public diplomacy quarterly], no. 12 (winter 2012), accessed November 25, 2020, http://www.cqvip.com/qk/88623x/2012004/50273633 .html.

18. Xi Jinping, "Secure a Decisive Victory," 36.

19. Xin 2012, 113–14.

20. Xi Jinping, "Secure a Decisive Victory," 25; "*People's Daily*: China Should 'Grasp Historic Opportunity,'" XinhuaNet, January 16, 2018, http://en.people.cn /n3/2018/0116/c90000-9315653.html.

21. Wang Chen, "Working Together to Build a Community of 'One Belt, One Road,'" State Council Information Office, July 27, 2016.

22. "Xi Jinping: China Launches Belt & Road STI Cooperation Action Plan," Ministry of Science and Technology, July 2017, accessed November 22, 2020, http://www.most.gov.cn/eng/eng/pressroom/201707/t20170713_134067.htm See also d'Hooghe at al. 2018.

23. Shuto 2018.

24. For example, in the resolution, "Social Dimensions of New Partnerships for Africa's Development" at the 55th Session of the Commission for Social Development, February 10, 2017 (with the wording, "to create a shared future, based upon our common humanity"); UN Security Council Resolution 2344 on Afghanistan ("to create a community of shared future for mankind"), http://unscr.com/en/resolutions/doc/2344. See also the two resolutions—"economic, social and cultural rights" and "the right to food"—at the 34th Session of the UN Human Rights Council, https://documents-dds-ny.un.org/doc/UNDOC/GEN/G17/085/33/PDF/G1708533.pdf?OpenElement.

25. Xi Jinping, "Secure a Decisive Victory," 4, 6, 9. and 22.

26. Benner et al. 2018; Brady 2017; Diamond and Schell 2018.

REFERENCES AND FURTHER READING

Barabantseva, Elena. 2010. *Overseas Chinese, Ethnic Minorities and Nationalism: De-centering China*. London: Routledge.

Benner, Thorsten, Jan Gaspers, Mareike Ohlberg, Lucrezia Poggetti, and Kristin Shi-Kupfer. 2018. *Authoritarian Advance: Responding to China's Growing Political Influence in Europe*. Berlin: MERICS and GPPI.

Brady, Anne-Marie. 2017. *Magic Weapons: China's Political Influence Activities under Xi Jinping*. Washington: Wilson Center.

Diamond, Larry and Orville Schell, eds. 2018. *China's Influence & American Interests: Promoting Constructive Vigilance*. Stanford, CA: Hoover Institution.

d'Hooghe, Ingrid. 2015. *China's Public Diplomacy*. Leiden: Brill.

d'Hooghe, Ingrid, Annemarie Montulet, Marijn de Wolff, and Frank N. Pieke. 2018. *Assessing Europe-China Collaboration in Higher Education and Research*. Leiden: Leiden Asia Centre.

Hughes, Christopher R. 2014. "Confucius Institutes and the University: Distinguishing the Political Mission from the Cultural." *Issues & Studies* 50, no. 4 (December): 45–83.

Jinping, Xi. 2017. "Secure a Decisive Victory in Building a Moderately Prosperous Society in All Respects and Strive for the Great Success of Socialism with Chinese Characteristics for a New Era." In *Report to the 19th National Congress of the Communist Party of China*. Beijing, October 18, 2017. http://www.xinhuanet.com/english/download/Xi_Jinping's_report_at_19th_CPC_National_Congress.pdf

Lu, Sun. 2018. "Developments and New Approaches of Internationalizing China's Media: A Case Study of China Global Television Network (CGTN) in Witness Perspective." *Global Media Journal* 16, no. 31 (August): 1–5.

Nye, Joseph S. 2004. *Soft Power: The Means to Success in World Politics*. Cambridge, MA: Perseus.

Shuto, Motoko. 2018. "Patterns and Views of China's Public Diplomacy in ASEAN Countries: Focusing on Confucius Institutes." *Journal of Contemporary East Asia Studies* 7, no. 2 (December): 124–48.

Walker, Christopher, and Jessica Ludwig. 2017. "From 'Soft Power' to 'Sharp Power': Rising Authoritarian Influence in the Democratic World." In *Sharp Power: Rising Authoritarian Influence*, 8–25. Washington, DC: National Endowment for Democracy.

Xin, Xin. 2012. *How the Market Is Changing China's News: The Case of Xinhua News Agency*. Lanham, MD: Lexington Books.

Afterword

EAST ASIA: BEING THERE AND
BEING ELSEWHERE

Ulf Hannerz

THE PRECEDING CHAPTERS IN THIS BOOK have together given a very rich overview of the ways East Asia is now at the center of the world stage. Asked to write an afterword, and not even being an Asianist, what could I possibly contribute? Perhaps with some reminiscences of the many ways this part of the world has claimed the attention of a veteran world watcher since the mid-twentieth century, through a number of visits, but also by being forever there on the horizon, even as I have been at home at my Stockholm address, or elsewhere, in yet some other place. As I zigzag in time and between places, my reflections may say something about what East Asia, in some of its parts, has come to mean over a period of recent history. It will undoubtedly be in some ways an idiosyncratic account—but then it is in the nature of the topic that it will look different to different people.

I learned to read in the late 1940s—the Second World War was just over, but I have no recollection of that. I was a child in Stockholm, where there had been no war. But soon enough I moved on to reading newspapers, and the Korean War had just broken out. On a map I could locate those places mentioned—Seoul, Pusan, Pyongyang... Then it took me a little over a third of a century to get there. It was 1987, the year before the Olympic Games in Seoul, and I was invited to a conference on "The Olympics and East/West and South/North Cultural Exchanges in the World System." After the conference, the sponsoring media conglomerate took the foreign participants on a bus tour through much of South Korea, and so I got to see a number of those places. We spent one night in the dormitory of a monastery, and even crossed the 38th parallel—the state border that used to be there had shifted slightly north at the end of the war. But Pyongyang was still a world away.

Back to the 1960s: while "globalization" really only became a keyword in the 1990s, decolonization in much of the world, and the Cold War, made at least the younger generation more aware of far-away places and the striking changes that seemed to go on there. I made my way to anthropology and became more involved with West Africa, but of my age-mates at Stockholm University a number became Maoists (although at much the same time, they might have gone to Cuba to help another revolutionary, Fidel Castro, with the sugar cane harvest). One of their more nearby heroes was Jan Myrdal, a young-ish writer who was one of the very few foreigners allowed to do something akin to field research in Maoist China. Originally published in Swedish, his book also became a bit of a bestseller in English translation as *Report from a Chinese Village* (1963). It was actually a people's commune he had been to, and it turned out that he had watched it through somewhat rose-tinted glasses.

Around the same time, he also had another book that probably had another set of readers. Jan Myrdal was in personal as well as political conflict with his parents, from whom he had already inherited considerable symbolic capital through the surname they shared. Gunnar and Alva Myrdal had both been government ministers, and both would individually become Nobel Prize winners. Gunnar Myrdal was also the author of *An American Dilemma,* an early 1940s study of race relations that would come to have a strong influence as the United States turned toward desegregation and racial justice. But their son would write a book about his troubled childhood, with two parents who were alternatively absent or absent-minded.

A late 1990s research project took me to more intense, although rather brief, engagements with East Asia. In a way it started in Hong Kong, and at the same time in Stockholm, at my breakfast table. There I was trying to really wake up, sipping my coffee, leafing through the morning newspaper, listening to the morning news on the radio. A familiar voice reported on what that new, obscure movement known as the Taliban was doing, reaching for power in Afghanistan . . . And then that voice signed off, with his name, and—"Hong Kong."

What? Reporting on Afghanistan from a metropolis in China? As an anthropologist, with a scholarly tradition of very local knowledge based on "being there," I may at first have been more outraged. Then, as I reflected on the fact that a rather small news organization like the Swedish public service radio would hardly have a specialized "Afghanistan correspondent," but instead would have a division of labor involving an "Asia correspondent," an "Africa correspondent," and a "Middle East correspondent," I wondered how those people would go about their work. That took me to a study of foreign news reporting in Jerusalem, Johannesburg, Tokyo, and indeed—staying on a little after a conference—Hong Kong. My prime research site in Hong Kong became the Foreign Correspondents Club, as one newsperson after another, from various countries, made appointments with me there. The Foreign Correspondents Club, especially the bar, seemed to have become their home away from home. For a long period, when most of China remained rather closed to the outside world after Mao's revolution, it had been from Hong Kong and the FCC that whatever China watching there could be took place.

Since then I have been back to Hong Kong a number of times, and I have seen it go through changes. I had first heard of Sha Tin, in a somewhat remote part of the New Territories, when one of my Stockholm anthropologist colleagues did field research there in the 1960s, among the small-scale, modest-income commercial horticulturalists whose gardens spread out over the fields. Now, as I got there, there were shopping centers, and a metro railway line connecting them to the major university campus two stops away. The long trains were crowded with people attending to their cellphones. In Tsimshatsui I could explore the labyrinthine lower floors of Chungking Mansions, on lower Nathan Road, with dirt cheap accommodation for refugees and young backpackers from everywhere, as well as other kinds of enterprises. I could see the female domestic workers from the Philippines and Indonesia, congregating on sidewalks during their weekend day off, sorting themselves by hometown origin, and I could take the Star Ferry across to Hong Kong Island, watching its skyline proclaim that this was one of the business and banking centers of the world.

Then, as the "Umbrella Movement" took to the streets in Hong Kong in 2014, I saw its struggles on my screen at home in Stockholm. In 2019, again on those streets, it was clear that many Hong Kongers were not so happy with the way "One Country, Two Systems" was really working out.

It would take me longer to get anywhere else in China, but eventually I made it to Kunming, in Yunnan, in the southwestern interior of the People's Republic, for a few days. It was late January, and in the center of the city there was a park with a small lake, where local people would enjoy feeding breadcrumbs to migratory birds, seasonal refugees from Siberia. In a bookstore I saw Michelle Obama's autobiography in Chinese translation. On the outskirts of the town I found an attractive museum devoted to celebrating China's cultural diversity. I could only reflect that, over time and in space, this has been an unevenly distributed enthusiasm.

Actually I should have gone to Kunming about a decade earlier. In 2008, a world conference of anthropologists was to have taken place there. But it was the year of the Beijing Olympics, and as the Olympic torch was carried from Athens to the upcoming site, it had been confronted by pro-Tibet protesters along the way. Evidently the organizers were apprehensive about the prospect of thousands of foreign scholars showing their sympathy with such protests, so the conference was—as it was explained—"postponed" for a year. And then the following year, this world conference drew mostly Chinese participants.

With Japan my engagements came rather late—in the 1990s and early in the twenty-first century. Long ago I had read the American anthropologist Ruth Benedict's *The Chrysanthemum and the Sword*, written as a "study of culture at a distance" when Japan was still a war adversary, but a book that eventually would become even more popular in Japan than in the United States, selling millions of copies. Then the time had already come, late in the twentieth century, when the Japanese economy was recognized as the second largest in the world. There was a certain nervousness, in North America and in Europe, with the scenario involving Japan as Number One: what was really behind its success? Getting around via an excellent subway system and on foot, sometimes with local guides and sometimes without, I was able to see a lot of Tokyo—the city's internal variations impressed me. I also made it to a number of other cities: Osaka, Kyoto, Beppu . . . And to Shikoku, that island of pilgrimage and hot springs, across an inland sea.

One New Year's Eve, I was in a Tokyo park watching the celebration of the arrival of a Year of the Monkey, seeing white balloons rising toward the dark sky. A few days later, another Tokyo park, with an old shrine, again became acutely controversial. The prime minister had visited there, in connection with the New Year—and this was the Yasukuni shrine that had become the recognized home of the spirits of war criminals from the Second World War—so the news of his visit had not been well received in China and Korea.

I was a visiting professor at the University of Tokyo when a young, female, Chinese student, from an anthropology class I had lectured to, came to see me in my office for a chat. She was from Shanghai, and she made regular visits home. But she intended to continue her life in the diaspora, in some kind of fashion work. She was of an age when the one-child policy was in effect in China, so she was an only child, and she did not envisage returning home to marry some young man in the same situation; that would be a future involving the two of them becoming responsible for taking care of four aging parents.

Yet my most intriguing contact in Tokyo may be one relating to my foreign correspondents study. I focused on European and American newsworkers there, and my entirely invaluable gatekeeper was the director of the Japanese government's international press center, who served me interviewees on a platter. Yet he was really even more interesting himself, with the long career he had previously had as a foreign correspondent with the *Yomiuri Shimbun*, a leading Tokyo newspaper that with time would build up one of the world's largest correspondent networks. In different placings and on different reporting tours, he had interviewed the Romanian dictator Ceaucescu, the South African apartheid prime minister P. W. Botha, and the Egyptian president Anwar Sadat. Among his strongest memories was the evening of November 19, 1977, when he had stood among the gathered world press at Tel Aviv airport. It was a dark and starred night, but a small dot of light was coming in from the Mediterranean; this was Anwar Sadat's plane, coming in for a daring opening of Egyptian-Israeli contacts. The Israeli military orchestra played the Egyptian national anthem more powerfully than this veteran Japanese correspondent had ever heard it performed in Cairo, and his eyes filled with tears.

When I met him again in Tokyo on a later visit, he had retired from his post at the press center, and he was now more engaged in an entity called "The English-Speaking Union of Japan." That may sound, in the early 2000s, with English as the world's single hyperlanguage, like an anomaly and an anachronism, but it seems that it was really a home ground for elderly but still active cosmopolitans who were still very much alive, and who still felt a certain need to formulate their views. He gave me his most recent business card, which included the website address of the organization; he wrote for it now and then.

My East Asian engagements have not all been in East Asia itself—in globalizing times, far from it. A Japanese American friend in New York turned out to be from one of those Japanese families who had been interned during the Second World War in a camp in inland United States, suspected on no other grounds than ethnicity of sympathizing with the enemy. That early experience surely played a part in leading her toward a lifetime of social activism. Early on, during my 1989 stay as a visiting professor in New York, Emperor Hirohito died in Tokyo, and so there was a demonstration march along 42nd Street, right below my office window. I was still in the United States in early June that year, watching the television news reporting on the Tiananmen Square massacre. Some twenty years later, spending a month or so as a visitor to a large state university in the American Midwest, I could see that its efforts to attract Chinese students had evidently been successful. They were very visible on campus—and, as they did not like to take all their meals in the university dining halls or at McDonald's, there were also a number of new low-cost Chinese restaurants just off-campus.

In the Museumsquartier of Vienna, some time early in the twenty-first century, I was impressed by an exhibition of new Chinese art. A little earlier, in Stockholm, I saw a striking Chinese dance performance, which turned out to be affiliated with the Falun Gong movement, a movement outlawed by its home government.

Spending much of the summer half of the year in a southern Swedish village where I have family roots, I have been happy to find a retired foreign news correspondent couple living not so far away. They spent much of their working lives reporting to Swedish newspapers from Beijing and Hong Kong, and I had first made contact with them at the Foreign Correspondents Club in the latter city. We now have a chance to keep discussing both China and local news when we get together—for instance, Chinese proposals for a small port, a little higher up on the west coast of Sweden. A few villages away in the opposite direction, the local grocery store of a national chain had been closed down. But the year after, the store was open again, run by a Chinese family. I was not really so surprised by this, as I had made my brief annual winter escape some months earlier to the Cape Verde islands, off the West African coast. There I had found that in the town I was staying, just about every small corner store with expatriate ownership was now referred to as a "boutica Chinesa." The Chinese government may have its own ways of engaging with other countries, top-down; but much of the Chinese presence in the world is bottom-up, through hardworking, small-scale entrepreneurs putting together a diaspora in their own way.

Now and then, moreover, I make my way to a Chinese novel, tipped off by a friend or colleague somewhere in the world, or after having read a review. It could be Jiang Rong's *Wolf Totem*, Yu Hua's *Brothers*, Mo Yan's *Red Sorghum*, or Ma Jian's *China Dream*. Or what is on my bedside table for late-evening reading may be Korean American Min Jin Lee's *Pachinko*. Or Amitav Ghosh's historical novel *Flood of Fire*, about the opium wars when Hong Kong became British. They offer me closeup insights into East Asian lives in fiction form—but, again and again, the stories are embedded in the contexts of wider conflicts and upheavals, national or regional, past or present. The dark shadows of history seem to be everywhere.

I can understand, at least to a degree, how East Asians, and particularly patriotic Chinese, can look with some favor on the achievements of Mao, and more recently on those of Xi Jinping, in first uniting their country, and then in putting it back at a central place on the world map, after decades or centuries of humiliation. But then, as I read these books, and as I follow the news stream and reflect on my own experiences, I see present and future uncertainties. A great many inhabitants of the region are obviously now at home in the world—I think of my old Tokyo journalist interlocutor as a wonderful example. Yet elsewhere in the region, the passage into a global ecumene, with a fairly free flow of ideas and expressive forms, is still troubled. For all its technological, economic, and political power, official China has hardly succeeded yet in reaching out with a soft power, a cultural power, of its own. And attempts to establish an arena for freedom of critical opinion and imagination may well lead to incarceration or exile. China's transnational voices may yet come from New York or London, or perhaps with some risk from Hong Kong. But this is, of course, in times when global interconnections, and opinions about them, keep changing elsewhere in the world, like in Europe and North America as well.

These, then, are some ways in which my own life's path has linked up with themes covered in the rich mosaic of earlier chapters in this book. I suspect that many of its readers will, like me, also connect in their personal ways to parts of the East Asian whole.

CONTRIBUTORS

EDITORS

FRANK N. PIEKE received his PhD in cultural anthropology from the University of California, Berkeley. After lectureships in Leiden and Oxford, he took up the Chair in Modern China studies at Leiden in 2010. Between 2018 and 2020 he was the Director of the Mercator Institute for China Studies in Berlin. His most recent books include *The Good Communist* (2009) and *Knowing China* (2016), both published by Cambridge University Press.

KOICHI IWABUCHI is Professor of Media and Cultural Studies at the School of Sociology of Kwansei Gakuin University in Japan. His recent English publications include *Resilient Borders and Cultural Diversity: Internationalism, Brand Nationalism, and Multiculturalism in Japan* (Lexington Books, 2015).

AUTHORS

ELENA BARABANTSEVA received her PhD in international relations at the University of Manchester in 2006. She was a British Inter-university China Centre Research Fellow before taking up the Lectureship in Chinese International Relations at the University of Manchester in 2011. She is the author of *Overseas Chinese, Ethnic Minorities, and Nationalism: De-Centering China* (Routledge, 2010).

ILDIKÓ BELLÉR-HANN is associate professor at the University of Copenhagen of Central Asian Studies and Turkish. She is the author of *Community Matters in Xinjiang, 1880–1949: Towards a Historical Anthropology of the Uyghur* (Brill, 2008) and *Negotiating Identities: Work, Religion, Gender, and the Mobilization of Tradition Among the Uyghur in the 1990s* (LIT Verlag, 2015).

LINDSAY O. BLACK received his PhD in the international relations of East Asia from the University of Sheffield. He has worked as a lecturer at the Leiden University Institute for Area Studies (LIAS) since 2007. He is author of *Japan's*

Maritime Security Strategy: The Japan Coast Guard and Maritime Outlaws (Palgrave Macmillan, 2014).

WILLIAM A. CALLAHAN is professor of international relations at the London School of Economics and Political Science. His most recent book is *Sensible Politics: Visualizing International Relations* (Oxford University Press, 2020). His other work includes *China: The Pessoptimist Nation* (Oxford University Press, 2010) and the documentary film *Great Walls* (2020), which asks why some people hate Trump's wall and love the Great Wall of China (https://vimeo.com/billcallahan).

SIDNEY C. H. CHEUNG is professor in the Department of Anthropology in the Chinese University of Hong Kong. He received his PhD in Osaka University in anthropology, writing on the study of cultural relations between the Ainu people and the Japanese. His research interests include visual anthropology, tourism, heritage studies, foodways, and scent.

LEE JIN CHOI is assistant professor in the Department of English Education at Hongik University, South Korea. Her research focuses on second-language acquisition and practice with an emphasis on sociolinguistic competence in language learning and use in South Korea. Her work has appeared in *Language in Society*, *Language & Education*, *Multilingua*, *International Journal of Bilingualism*, and *Gender & Language*.

ROGIER CREEMERS holds MA degrees in Chinese studies and international relations and a PhD in law. He is an assistant professor in the Law and Governance of China at Leiden University, after holding a lectureship at Oxford. His major research interests include China's technological ambitions in domestic governance, and its participation in global cyber affairs.

INGRID D'HOOGHE is a senior research fellow at the Leiden Asia Centre and the Clingendael Institute in The Hague. She combines academic research on China with a guest lectureship at Leiden University and China policy advice work for government organizations. Her research focuses on China's foreign policy and diplomacy, including science diplomacy. She is author of *China's Public Diplomacy* (Brill, 2015).

MIRIAM DRIESSEN received her doctoral degree in anthropology from the University of Oxford, where she still works. Her research examines migration in China and beyond. She is author of *Tales of Hope, Tastes of Bitterness: Chinese Road Builders in Ethiopia* (Hong Kong University Press, 2019).

JAMES FARRER is professor of sociology at Sophia University in Tokyo. His research focuses on the contact zones of global cities, including ethnographic studies of sexuality, nightlife, migration, and food. His recent publications include *International Migrants in China's Global City: The New Shanghailanders* (Routledge, 2019) and *Shanghai Nightscapes: A Nocturnal Biography of a Global City* (with Andrew Field, University of Chicago Press, 2015).

ANDREW DAVID FIELD earned a PhD in East Asian languages and cultures from Columbia University. He has since taught at universities in the United States,

Australia, Korea, and China. He currently serves as a professor and administrator at Duke Kunshan University. He is the author of *Shanghai's Dancing World: Cabaret Culture and Urban Politics, 1919–1954* (Chinese University of Hong Kong Press, 2010) and *Shanghai Nightscapes: A Nocturnal Biography of a Global City* (with James Farrer, University of Chicago Press, 2015).

RUBEN GONZALEZ-VICENTE received his PhD in geography from the University of Cambridge. He worked as an assistant professor in the City University of Hong Kong between 2012 and 2016. In 2017, he took up his current position at Leiden University as a university lecturer in global political economy.

CAROLINE GRILLOT is a social anthropologist and associated researcher at the Lyons Institute of East Asian Studies (France). Her research has focused on Chinese social margins, including underground musicians, folkorized ethnic communities, Sino-Vietnamese couples, and cross-border traders, and she has recently started a new project on transhumant beekeepers.

ULF HANNERZ is professor emeritus in social anthropology at Stockholm University. His research focuses on urban anthropology, media anthropology, and transnational cultural processes, with field studies in the United States, West Africa, and the Caribbean. A study of news media foreign correspondence included field research in four continents. His books include *Soulside* (Almqvist & Wiksell, 1969), *Exploring the City* (Columbia University Press, 1980), *Cultural Complexity* (Columbia University Press, 1992), *Transnational Connections* (Routledge, 1996), *Foreign News* (University of Chicago Press, 2004), *Writing Future Worlds* (Palgrave Macmillan, 2016), and *World Watching* (Routledge, 2019).

AKIKO HIRATSUKA-SASAKI is a research management officer at IDE-JETRO in Japan. Since 2019, she has been a visiting fellow at UNRISD in Geneva, Switzerland. After acquiring an MSc in spatial planning from the Royal Institute of Technology in Stockholm, she worked as a rural planning consultant in Japan between 2009 and 2013.

FUTAO HUANG is professor at the Research Institute for Higher Education, Hiroshima University. Before he came to Japan in 1999, he taught and conducted research at several Chinese universities. His research interests include the internationalization of higher education, the academic profession, and higher education in East Asia. He is editor of *Higher Education Forum*.

JEFF KINGSTON is director of Asian Studies and professor of history at Temple University Japan. Most recently he wrote *The Politics of Religion, Nationalism and Identity* (Rowman & Littlefield, 2019). His current research focuses on transitional justice and the politics of memory in Asia.

KWEE HUI KIAN is associate professor at National University of Singapore. Her research focuses on Southeast Asia and South China, where she has examined various themes relating to colonialism, political economy, and diasporic entrepreneurship, from the seventeenth century to the present.

HERVÉ LEMAHIEU is director of the Power and Diplomacy Program at the Lowy Institute, where he analyses the changing distribution of power in Asia. He was previously a research associate for political economy and security at the London-based International Institute for Strategic Studies.

JOHN LIE is C.K. Cho Professor of Sociology at the University of California, Berkeley. His main interests are social theory and the exploration of his Korean origins and Korean diasporic trajectories, studying the intersection of biography, history, and social structure. He is the author of numerous books, including *K-Pop: Popular Music, Cultural Amnesia, and Economic Innovation in South Korea* (University of California Press, 2014).

ADRIENNE LO is an associate professor in the Department of Anthropology, University of Waterloo. She is the coeditor of *Beyond Yellow English: Toward a Linguistic Anthropology of Asian Pacific America* (2009) and *South Korea's Education Exodus: The Life and Times of Study Abroad* (2015).

JULIA LOVELL is professor in modern Chinese history and literature at Birkbeck College, University of London. Her research has so far focused principally on the relationship between culture (specifically, literature, architecture, historiography, and sport) and modern Chinese nation-building. She is author of numerous books and translations, most recently *Maoism: A Global History* (Bodley Head, 2019).

RICHARD MCGREGOR is a senior fellow for East Asia at the Lowy Institute, Australia's premier foreign policy think tank, in Sydney. He is a former Beijing and Washington bureau chief for the *Financial Times* and the author of numerous books on East Asia.

PÁL NYÍRI is professor of global history from an anthropological perspective at the Free University in Amsterdam. His most recent books are *Reporting for China: How Chinese Journalists Work with the World* and *Chinese Encounters in Southeast Asia: How Money, People, and Ideas from China are Changing a Region* (edited with Danielle Tan). He is also editor of the *New Mobilities in Asia* series at Amsterdam University Press.

JUNG-SUN PARK received her PhD in cultural anthropology from Northwestern University. She is professor and coordinator of Asian-Pacific studies at California State University, Dominguez Hills. She was a visiting scholar at the Asia-Pacific Research Center at Stanford University (2003) and the Academy of Korean Studies in Korea (2010). She is coauthor of *After Hallyu: The Potential and Future Task.* (Academy of Korean Studies Press, 2015).

MICHAELA PELICAN completed her PhD at the Max Planck Institute of Social Anthropology in Halle/Saale. She was a senior lecturer at the University of Zurich, a guest professor at the Graduate School of Asian and African Area Studies in Kyoto, and she is now professor of social and cultural anthropology at the University of Cologne. She is the author of *Masks and Staffs: Identity Politics in the Cameroon Grassfields* (Berghahn, 2015).

HIROSHI KAN SATO is a chief senior researcher at IDE-JETRO in Japan. He served as a president of the Japan Society for International Development (JASID) from 2011 to 2014. With a specialization in development sociology, his research activities include development aid in developing countries and Japan. His BA was in sociology, from the University of Tokyo.

LOUISA SCHEIN teaches anthropology and women's, gender and sexuality studies at Rutgers University, New Jersey. She has worked on cultural politics with the Miao/Hmong in China and the United States for four decades. Author of *Minority Rules: The Miao and the Feminine in China's Cultural Politics* (Duke University Press, 2000), she coedited with Tim Oakes *Translocal China* (Routledge, 2006) and with Purnima Mankekar *Media, Erotics and Transnational Asia* (Duke University Press, 2013). She coproduced the documentary films *The Best Place to Live* (1981) and *Better Places* (2012) about Hmong Americans and she currently directs the international Chinese-English Keywords Project.

MARGARET SLEEBOOM-FAULKNER received her PhD in anthropology from the University of Amsterdam in 2001. After a research position in Leiden and a lectureship in Amsterdam, she moved to the University of Sussex in 2006, where she has been professor of medical and social anthropology since 2012. Her research concerns nationalism and education in East Asia, as well as the life sciences and society in Asia and beyond. She is the author of *Global Morality and Life Science Practices in Asia: Assemblages of Life* (Palgrave Macmillan, 2014).

TAKEYUKI TSUDA received his PhD in anthropology from the University of California at Berkeley and is professor of anthropology in the School of Human Evolution and Social Change at Arizona State University. He previously held academic positions at the University of Chicago and the University of California at San Diego. Tsuda is the author of *Japanese American Ethnicity: In Search of Heritage and Homeland Across Generations* (New York University Press, 2016)

CHIA YOUYEE VANG is professor of history at the University of Wisconsin-Milwaukee. She is the author of several books on the Hmong diaspora in the western hemisphere, including *Hmong America: Reconstructing Community in Diaspora* (University of Illinois Press, 2010) and *Fly Until You Die: An Oral History of Hmong Pilots in the Vietnam War* (Oxford University Press, 2019).

BIAO XIANG is professor of social anthropology at the University of Oxford and the director of Max Planck Institute for Social Anthropology in Germany. He has worked on various types of migration across Asia. He is the author of *Global "Body Shopping"* (Princeton University Press, 2007) and the lead editor of *Return: Nationalizing Transnational Mobility in Asia* (with Breda S. A. Yeoh and Miko Toyota, Duke University Press, 2013). His work has been translated into Japanese, French, Korean, Spanish, and Italian.

MEI ZHAN is an associate professor of anthropology at the University of California, Irvine. She is the author of *Other-Worldly: Making Chinese Medicine Through Transnational Frames* (Duke University Press, 2009). She is currently writing an ethnography titled *Bring Medicine Back To Life*, which examines the emergence of a new kind of classical medicine and cosmological practices in entrepreneurial China.

INDEX

Abe, Prime Minister Shinzo, 22–23, 27, 73–74, 290
Academic Ranking of World Universities, 124, 126
Academy of Korean Studies, 179. *See also* Korea
Acharya, Amitav, 72
acupuncture, 152–53, 156
Afghanistan, 73, 235, 237, 268, 308n24, 311
Africa, 4, 45, 249, 260; Chinese business internationalization in, 254–55; Chinese media in, 271; Chinese migrants in, 199–207, 300; emerging middle powers of sub-Saharan, 282; rural communities in, 60; West, 311
African Americans, 45. *See also* United States
Afro-Asian Solidarity Movement, 44
Ai Qing, 107
Ai Weiwei, 79, 104–13; *Fuck Off* (art exhibit), 105; *Human Flow* (film), 104, 107–12, 108*fig.*, 110*fig.*; *Remembering* (mosaic), 106; *S.A.C.R.E.D.* (art installation), 106; *Sunflower Seeds* (art exhibit), 104, 109; *Wall of Names* (artwork), 106, 109
Albania, 237
Al Jazeera, 276
Alliance for Regenerative Medicine (ARM), 148. *See also* United States
anticolonialism, 44–45; in Southeast Asia, 171

Anti-Imperialism Hospital, 153. *See also* China
antiterrorism, 55
Argentina, 186; Hmong in, 220; Japanese migration to, 189
Armstrong, Louis, 32
art: and activism, 79, 104–13; and politics, 104–13; traditional, 1
ASEAN Regional Forum (ARF), 68–72
Asia, 4, 45, 260; Chinese labor migrants in, 199–207; middle powers of, 290. *See also* Central Asia; East Asia; Northeast Asia; South Asia; Southeast Asia; Western Asia
Asian financial crisis (1997), 71
Asian International Investment Bank (AIIB), 255, 294
Asian Tigers, 71
Asia-Pacific Economic Cooperation (APEC), 68, 72
Association of Southeast Asian Nations (ASEAN), 66–68, 70–72. *See also* Southeast Asia
Australia, 4, 73, 130, 250, 257–58; banning of Huawei in, 267, 288; and the Belt and Road Initiative, 305; Chinese migrants in, 300; economy of, 286; education migration to, 136; Hmong in, 219–20
Azerbaijan, 235

Balkans, 235
Bangkok, 171–72. *See also* Thailand
BBC World Service, 298

Beidou program, 267. *See also* China

Beijing, 38, 44, 69, 79, 104, 107, 111, 130, 154; authorities in, 167; Confucius Institute Headquarters in, 300; economic power of, 246, 259; founding of the People's Republic of China in, 245; teachers in, 221. *See also* China

Beike Biotechnology, 145. *See also* China

Belgium, 267

Belt and Road Initiative (BRI), 67, 73–74, 162, 174, 235, 248, 264–68, 285–86, 298, 302–5; global infrastructure of the, 303*map*. *See also* Community of Shared Future of Mankind

Belt and Road Science, Technology, and Innovation Cooperation Action Plan, 304. *See also* Belt and Road Initiative

Benedict, Ruth: *The Chrysanthemum and the Sword*, 313

Berlin, 107. *See also* Germany

Bio-Vision 2016, 143. *See also* South Korea

Black, Lindsay, 13

Bolivia, 88

Bolton, John, 254–55, 282

Bo Xilai, 48

Brazil, 186, 288; Japanese migration to, 189

Brophy, David, 236

Brunei, 73

BTS (Bangtan Boys), 92, 99

Buddhism, 2, 234. *See also* religion

Burma, 2, 44. *See also* Myanmar

Bush, President George W., 70, 73, 141

Caijing, 273

Caixin, 273

Callahan, William, 67, 79

Cambodia, 45, 95, 288; Communist party of, 45; displacement of vulnerable populations of, 257

Cameroon, 212–13, 215–16

Canada, 73, 130, 267; education migration to, 133; Japanese migration to, 189

capitalism, 12, 41; authoritarian, 48; Chinese, 241, 256–60; modern European, 255; world market, 260. *See also* political economy

Carter, Jack, 32

Castro, Fidel, 311

Caucasus region, 235

Center for Democracy in Science and Technology, 143. *See also* South Korea

Center for New American Security, 282. *See also* United States

Central African Republic, 205

Central Asia, 3–4, 162, 234–40. *See also* Asia

Central Intelligence Agency (CIA), 26, 220. *See also* United States

Central Leading Group for Cybersecurity and Informatization, 264. *See also* China

Chaeho, Sin, 180

Chang Jiang Scholars Program (1998), 120

Chen, Jasmine, 31, 36, 38–39, 38*fig.*

Chen Quanguo, 237

Cheung, Sidney, 77

Chia-Bio, 144. *See also* South Korea

Chiang Kai-shek, 42, 68

Chiangmai, 226. *See also* Thailand

Chiang Mai Initiative, 71–72

Chicago, 32, 34. *See also* United States

Chile, 73

Chin, Peng, 44

China, 11–13; aid packages to the Third World from, 45; authoritarianism of, 248–50; business frontier of, 253–60; Chinese-foreign children's citizenship in, 209–17; citizenship in, 210–11; Communist regime of, 36, 41–49, 248–50; as a competitor of the United States, 246; conquest of, 3; cost of living in, 200–202; critique of the politics of, 104–13; cultural power of, 8; cyber diplomacy of, 263–69; diversity of, 233; dominance of, 2, 67; economy of, 121, 155, 174, 177, 217, 235, 245, 248, 253–60, 264, 280–91, 295; educational migration in, 133; expansion of social welfare in, 206, 207n5; food of, 82–83, 87–89; foreign direct investment in, 174; foreign policy of, 67, 248, 268–69; global public opinion about, 278; global views of, 287*fig.*, 296*fig.*; government of, 166–67; higher education of, 119–24; indebtedness to, 269; internal diversity of, 217; international students in, 123*fig.*; international trade of, 253; Japanese migration to, 189; medical science in, 142, 144–46; Miao people in, 219; migrants from, 159–61, 199–207; military power of, 1, 69, 248; ministry of education of, 120, 124; Muslims in, 236–38; National People's Congress of, 41; as the new center of the world, 245–51; non-Chinese people of, 233–41; policy of technological independence of, 282; rural communities in, 60, 161, 200, 205–6; strategic vulnerability of, 4; students from, 136, 315; subjugation by imperial powers of, 12; as superpower, 4, 121, 245, 249, 306; traditional medicine of, 117–25, 150–57; universities of, 119–24, 170; women of, 34, 209–17, 217n7. *See also* Beijing; Belt and Road Initiative; Chinese Civil War; Chinese Communist Party; Confucius Institutes; Hong Kong; Maoism; People's Liberation Army; Sinocentric world order; soft power; Tiananmen Square; trade war

China Central Television (CCTV), 272, 274. *See also* media

China Daily, 273, 298–99

China First Heavy Industries, 284. *See also* China

China Global Television Network (CGTN), 298

China Mobile, 285

China News Service (CNS), 272

China Radio International (CRI), 272, 274, 276, 298

China Scholarship Council, 123

Chinese Civil War, 68, 171, 173, 245. *See also* China

Chinese Communist Party (CCP), 42–49, 79, 107, 111–12, 171, 173, 245, 297, 301; Central Propaganda Department of the, 272; as a "learning party," 269; organizations of the, 300; Propaganda Work Conference of the, 276; united front tactics of the, 305–6. *See also* China; *Global Times*

Chinese Ministry of Education, 300

Chinese Ministry of Science and Technology (MoST), 144

Choi, Leejin, 116, 185

Chongqing, 48. *See also* China

Christianity, 52, 181; among the Hmong people, 226; of Korean Americans, 186; Nestorian, 234; orthodox, 203. *See also* religion

Christian Missionary Alliance (CMA), 226

Civil Rights Movement, 182. *See also* United States

Clayton, Buck, 34

climate change, 5, 269. *See also* environment

Clinton, Secretary of State Hillary, 264

Cold War, 3–5, 12, 18, 67–69, 171, 220, 288, 302; Anglo-American analyses of China in the, 43; dynamics of the, 70; end of the, 11, 69, 250; Maoism in the, 41–49

Colombo Plan, 53, 63n7

colonialism, 1, 3; era of, 62; of Europeans in Southeast Asia, 168–71; French, 220; Japanese, 9, 11, 160, 180–81; rebellion in Indonesia against Dutch, 169

Common Destiny (film, 2019), 304

Communism, 3–4, 12, 69; of China, 36, 41–49, 248–50; of Indonesia, 45, 172; leaders of Asian, 43–44; Peruvian, 258; of the Soviet Union, 42. *See also* Marxism; revolution; socialism

Communist Party of Nepal–Maoist (CPNM), 47–48. *See also* Nepal

Communist Party of Peru–Shining Path, 48. *See also* Peru

Community of Shared Future of Mankind (CSF), 302–5. *See also* Belt and Road Initiative

Confucianism, 2, 115

Confucius Institutes, 8, 174, 248, 297, 299–300, 304–5. *See also* China

Convention of Kanagawa (1854), 181

coronavirus crisis, 4, 249–51. *See also* global health

corruption: private, 105; state, 105

Council for Science and Technology Policy, 146. *See also* Japan

Crazy Rich Asians (film, 2018), 31, 38

Cuba, 311

cultural flows: inter-Asian, 34–36, 77–79; transnational, 78; trans-Pacific, 91–100

Human Flow (film, 2017), 104, 107–12, 108*fig.*, 110*fig.*
humanitarianism, 55
Hu Xijin, 281
Hwang, Woo-Suk, 142–43, 147
hypermobility, 200–202

identity politics: in China, 209; and Chinese migrants, 165–68; of Europeans in Southeast Asia, 168; growth of, 4; of Japanese Americans, 191; and Southeast Asian nationalism, 171. *See also* transnationality
Immigration Act (1924), 182, 190. *See also* United States
Immigration and Naturalization Act (1965), 160. *See also* United States
imperialism: American, 45–46, 181, 220; and capitalist expansion, 255; Japanese, 68; Soviet, 45
India, 13, 33, 44, 46–47, 249, 288–89; and the Belt and Road Initiative, 305; Communists of, 46–47
Indonesia, 45, 61, 165–67, 173, 289; anti-Chinese riots in, 160, 166, 176–77; ban against the use of Chinese languages in public in, 165; Chinese community in, 165–69, 175–77; Communists of, 45, 165–66, 173; Dutch administration of, 168–69; female domestic workers of, 312; food of, 88
Indonesian Communist Party, 45, 172. *See also* Indonesia
infrastructure, 56, 253–60; modern, 53. *See also* investments
International Conference on Hmong Studies, 227. *See also* Hmong people
international relations: of China, 12, 42; political economy and, 247; and trade, 6, 73. *See also* political economy
International Society of Stem Cell Research (ISSCR), 142
International Strategy of Cooperation on Cyberspace, 265. *See also* China
internet, 105, 224, 240; China in the, 263–69, 283; Great Firewall of China in the, 283. *See also* cyberspace; technology
intoku (hidden virtue), 53

investments: American, 287; of the Chinese Communist Party in the Communist Parties of Asia, 45; Chinese global, 246, 253–60, 305; Japanese, 287; localized, 255, 257–60; mitigation of risks of, 255; state-coordinated partnerships in, 255–60. *See also* development aid; foreign direct investment; infrastructure
Iran, 235, 284
Iraq, 73, 109
Islam: international, 240; politicization of, 238; Sunni, 236; and Uyghur ethnic identity, 236–38, 240. *See also* religion
Israel, 64n22
Italy, 19; Red Brigades in, 46

Jaishankar, Subrahmanyam, 290
Jaisohn, Philip, 180; *Hansu's Journey* of, 180
Jakarta, 32, 175–76. *See also* Indonesia
Jamaica, 257
Japan, 1–4, 9, 13, 22, 31, 70–73, 199, 289–90, 313; aggression in China in 1937 of, 171; banning of Huawei in, 288; comparison of conventional development method and "kaizen" method in, 59, 59*tab.*; cooking seminar in Aishima, 58*fig.*; cultural power of, 6–9; development aid of, 12–13, 52–63; earthquake in, 53; economy of, 1–2, 70–71, 190, 245, 281, 313; education in, 116; food of, 82–83, 86–89, 86*fig.*; higher education in, 121–22, 125–26; imperialist expansion of, 66–67, 171; international students in, 125*fig.*; and the Japanese diaspora, 189–97; jazz musicians of, 35; Korean migration to, 180–82, 185; mass media of, 9–10, 18; medical science in, 142, 146–47; military power of, 1–2; presence of the US military in, 28; rise of, 3; rural areas of, 58; stagnation of the economy of, 56; students from, 136; trade surplus of, 54; wartime, 16–17; women of, 34. *See also* Okinawa
Japan Business Federation (Keidanren), 56
Japanese Official Development Assistance (ODA), 52–57, 67; Revision of the Charter of the, 55, 55*tab.*; Trends in the, 54*fig.*, 56*fig.* *See also* Japan

Mao Zedong, 41–49, 68, 152, 234, 245; achievements of, 316; criticism of, 107; era of, 31. *See also* Maoism

marriages, 161–62; Chinese-Cameroonian, 212–13, 215–16; Chinese-Russian, 212, 214–16; Chinese-Vietnamese, 211, 213–14, 216; transnational, 225. *See also* women

Marx, Karl, 255

Marxism, 42, 46, 152, 156. *See also* Communism

Mass Line Campaign, 49. *See also* China

Mauritania, 152–53

media: American, 6–8, 135, 153; Canadian, 135; Chinese, 46, 49, 174, 210, 247–48, 271–78, 296–303; financial, 273; globalization of, 6–9, 77–79, 247, 271–78, 298–99; Korean, 91–100; print, 34; Western, 78, 271, 273, 275, 298–99. *See also* film; newspapers; radio; social media; soft power; television

medicine: Chinese, 117–25, 150–57; "integrative," 225–26; Japanese, 142, 146–47; preventive, 150, 155; regenerative, 117, 140–48; traditional Chinese, 150–57; Western, 225. *See also* science

Meiji Restoration, 2, 11, 52–53. *See also* Japan

Mei Zhan, 117

Meng Wanzhou, 267

Mexico, 73, 288

Miao people, 219–31; in China, 231n3. *See also* Hmong people

Microsoft, 264

Middle East, 168, 235–36

migration, 77, 85; and Chinese food, 87; Chinese labor, 199–207; Chinese overseas, 166–76; East Asian, 160; and education, 129–37; ethnic return, 190–91, 194–97; global age of, 169; globalization and, 134–37; permanent, 132; risks of, 206; short-term, 129; stratified form of, 133

Millennium Project, 146. *See also* Japan

Ministry of Agriculture (MOA), 57. *See also* Japan

Ministry of Foreign Affairs (MOFA), 54, 68. *See also* Japan

Ministry of International Trade and Industry (MITI), 54. *See also* Japan

Minnesota Center for Hmong Studies, 227. *See also* Hmong people

Miyazaki, Hayao, 7

modernity, 1, 6, 150; Chinese, 10; of East Asia, 77; unpredictable, 250; Western, 181

Mongolia, 2, 233, 235

Mo Yan: *Red Sorghum*, 315

multinational companies, 1, 11, 46–47, 71, 92

Munich, 106. *See also* Germany

music. *See* popular music

Myanmar, 2; migration to, 220. *See also* Burma

Myrdal, Gunnar: *An American Dilemma*, 311

Myrdal, Jan: *Report from a Chinese Village*, 311

Nanjing student uprisings, 213. *See also* China

National Development and Reform Commission (NDRC), 284. *See also* China

National Institute of Health, 147. *See also* Japan

nationalism, 4, 6, 8–9, 67–68, 220; American, 99, 294; anti-Chinese, 45–46; Chinese, 68, 171, 248, 277, 283, 301; criticism of, 107; Japanese, 68; Korean, 91, 180–81; Southeast Asian, 171

Nationalists (Kuomintang Party), 42, 68, 151, 173. *See also* China; Taiwan

National Security Council, 69. *See also* United States

National Stem Cell Advisory Committee, 145. *See also* China

Naxalbari, 46; Communist pantheon in, 47*fig*. *See also* India

neoliberalism, 253, 294, 302. *See also* political economy

Nepal, 47–48

New Delhi, 290. *See also* India

New Order, 165, 171–73. *See also* Indonesia

newspapers, 271; global correspondent networks of, 314; of overseas Chinese communities, 299. *See also* media

New York, 12, 39, 107, 135, 257, 314, 316. *See also* United States

New York Times, 153, 273, 299

New Zealand, 73, 133; banning of Huawei in, 267, 288; Hmong in, 219–20

NGO groups, 257; environmentalist, 258

Ningxia, 267. *See also* China

Nixon, President Richard, 153

Non-Proliferation Treaty (NPT), 69

North America, 4, 313, 316; Chinese migrants in, 170, 300; Japanese migrants in, 189; Hmong in, 219–20

Northeast Asia, 91, 181. *See also* Asia

North Korea, 4, 13, 45, 179–80; Communist party of, 45; in the Korean War, 69; nuclear arms of, 69–70; refugees from, 111; self-reliance of, 283; threats of, 15. *See also* Korea; Korean War

Nye, Joseph, 295

Obama, Michelle, 312

Obama, President Barack, 73, 264

Oh, David, 93

Okinawa, 11, 15–28; anti-base protests in, 20–21, 21*fig.*, 25–28; employment in, 24; governors of, 22; occupation by the United States of, 15–18; wartime, 15–16, 16*fig.*, 17*fig.*, 25. *See also* Japan

Olympic Games: in Beijing, 104, 272, 301, 313; in Seoul, 82, 310

One Hundred Talents Project (1994), 120

One Tambon One Product (OTOP), 61. *See also* Thailand

One Village One Product (OVOP), 52, 57–61, 60*fig. See also* Japan

Organisation for Economic Co-operation and Development (OECD), 13, 61–62, 255

Orientalism, 99, 101n17

Ottoman Empire, 236. *See also* Turkey

Overseas Chinese Affairs Bureau, 174, 301. *See also* China

Palau, 237

Pan-Asian ethnicity, 95–96

Park, Chung-hee, 183

Park, Jin-Young, 94

Park, Jung-sun, 78, 186

Paulson, Henry, 280

Pence, Vice President Mike, 282–83

People's Daily, 272–74, 276, 298

People's Liberation Army (PLA), 69, 281. *See also* China

Peru, 48, 73, 257; Chinese companies in, 258–59; food of, 87–88; Japanese migration to, 189

Petraeus, Retired US General David, 290

Pharmaceutical Affairs Act (2014), 146–47. *See also* Japan

Philippines, 22, 44, 61, 133, 299; female domestic workers of the, 312; jazz musicians of the, 31, 33*fig.*, 34–35; martial law imposed in the, 172

Pokémon, 7

political economy: Chinese, 173–74, 246–47, 253–60; of cultural inheritance, 81; and international relations, 247; of the world, 61, 253–60. *See also* capitalism; decoupling; global finance; international relations; neoliberalism; socialism

popular culture, 1, 9; export of, 85; Japanese, 96–98; Korean, 91–100, 101n16, 136. *See also* entertainment; popular music

popular music: Chinese, 32–33, 36–37; Japanese, 35, 96; Korean, 92–100, 186; media cultures and, 9. *See also* jazz; popular culture

pornography, 105

poverty: of the developing world, 225; elimination of, 56; reduction of, 55–57

protectionism, 4, 284–85. *See also* decoupling; trade war

Purnama, Basuki Tjahaja, 175–76

Pyongyang, 310. *See also* North Korea

Qing Dynasty, 2–3, 170, 181, 234. *See also* China

Qin Yaqing, 72

radio, 271. *See also* media

Raisina Dialogue, 290. *See also* India

Recruitment Program of Young Global Experts (2011), 120

refugees, 79, 104, 107–12; Hmong, 220–21, 223; North Korean, 161

Reischauer, Ambassador Edwin, 18

religion, 1–2; conversion of Chinese migrants in Southeast Asia to local, 168; of Ethiopians, 203; reporting on, 276; and Uyghur political discontent, 236–37. *See also* Buddhism, Christianity; Islam

Repeta, Lawrence, 25

Republic of China, 170, 234. *See also* China

Reston, James, 153

revolution: Chinese, 43–45, 171, 228, 245, 312; Laotian, 228; Russian, 34, 236; socialist, 221, 228; student, 183; Vietnamese, 228; world, 43–44. *See also* Communism; socialism

Revolution of Natural Life (RNL), 144. *See also* South Korea

Rhee, Syngman, 180, 182–83

Rhodium Group, 282

Rosen, Daniel, 282

Russia: as a competitor of the United States, 246; Federation of, 235; Tsarist, 2; women of, 34, 212, 214–15. *See also* Soviet Union

Russian Far East, 3. *See also* Russia

Russia Today (RT), 276

Sadat, Anwar, 314

Saigon, 220. *See also* Vietnam

San Diego, Obon Festival in, 194*fig.*, 195*fig.* *See also* United States

San Francisco, 31, 35, 150, 154. *See also* United States

SARS epidemic, 250. *See also* global health

Sasaki, Akiko, 12

Sato, Hiroshi Kan, 12

Saudi Arabia, 267

science, 1, 4, 150; Chinese, 145; global, 116, 147–48; stem cell, 140–48; Western, 116–17, 140–41, 148. *See also* medicine; technology

Second World War, 3, 12–13, 41, 67–69, 160; aftermath of the, 17, 28, 53, 72, 83, 180; atrocities of the, 4; end of the, 11, 70, 171, 181, 310; Japanese American concentration camps of the, 190–91, 314

Sen, Mohit, 44

Senaga, Kamejiro, 18

Seoul, 129–30, 133, 184. *See also* South Korea

Seoul National University, 143, 183

Serbia, 267

Shaanxi, 239. *See also* China

shamanism, 225, 234

Shanghai, 12, 31–39, 150–51, 154, 285, 313; wartime occupation by the Japanese of, 35. *See also* China

Shanghai Cooperation Organization, 239. *See also* Central Asia; China

Shufeldt Treaty (1882), 181

Silk Road Economic Belt. *See* Belt and Road Initiative

Sina, 277

Singapore, 12, 31–32, 36, 39, 71, 73, 167; Chinese labor migrants in, 199, 202; educational migration in, 133; immigration schemes of, 159; persecution of Chinese leftists in, 172. *See also* Malaya/Malaysia

Sinocentric world order, 67, 294–308. *See also* China

Sleeboom-Faulkner, Margaret, 117

Smith, Whitey, 31–32

Snow, Lavada, 32

Snow, Valaida, 32, 32*fig.*

Snowden, Edward, 264–65

socialism: construction of, 121; minority policies of, 238; period of, 12, 240; state, 161. *See also* Communism; political economy

social media, 248; and the globalization of Chinese media, 271–74, 299, 303; political activism on, 264. *See also* media

Social Networking Sites (SNS), 97

soft power, 7–9, 79; of China, 174, 248, 294–308, 316; competition of, 9; and sharp power, 248, 305–6. *See also* media

Son, Masayoshi, 185

South Africa: apartheid regime of, 314; gold mines of colonial, 199

South Asia, 46, 168. *See also* Asia

South China Sea, 67, 73, 248, 283, 299

Southeast Asia, 3–4, 33, 249; anticolonialism in, 171; Chinese migrants in, 159–60,

Turkey, 235, 239–40, 267. *See also* Ottoman Empire
Turkmenistan, 235
21st Century Business Herald, 273

United Arab Emirates (UAE), 267
United Kingdom, 104, 267, 288
United Nations, 107; and the Korean War, 69; refugee camps in Thailand of the, 220
United Nations Development Report (UNDP), 55
United Nations Group of Governmental Experts on the Developments in the Field of Information and Telecommunications in the Context of International Security, 263
United Nations Millennium Summit, 56
United States: aid to postwar Japan from the, 53; Asian migration to the, 190; banning of Huawei in the, 267; and the Belt and Road Initiative, 305; Chinese media on the, 277; Chinese migrant labor in the, 199; in the Cold War, 171, 220; control of the internet by the, 264–66; decoupling from China of the economy of the, 280–91; education migration to the, 130, 133, 136; flows of people to the, 160; hegemony of the, 245, 249; Hmong in the, 220–24, 227–28; Korean American communities of the, 92–100, 179–87; media industry of the, 6–8, 135, 153; military bases of the, 11, 17–26; military power of the, 1; policy toward East Asia of the, 66–74; political relations with South Korea of the, 81; Prohibition era of the, 39n1; racial justice in the, 311; as superpower, 4–5; technology companies of the, 283; triumph in the Second World War of the, 183–84, 245; unilateralism of the, 70; Uyghurs in the, 239. *See also* Cold War; Korean War; War on Terror
Urasaki, Akiko, 24–25
US Civil Administration (USCA), 18. *See also* United States
Uyghur people, 233–41; cultural traditions of the, 240; diaspora of the, 238–40;
politicization of the identity of the, 236–38. *See also* Xinjiang
Uzbekistan, 235, 239

Vancouver, 134. *See also* Canada
Vang, Mai Der, 227; "Your Mountain Lies Down with You," 222
Vietcong, 45. *See also* Vietnam
Vietnam, 2–3, 44–46, 73; Communist party of, 45; French colonial rule in, 220; Hmong people in, 220, 224; migration to, 220; persecution of ethnic Chinese in, 172–73; rebellion against French colonial armies in, 44; socialist, 172; students from, 136; trade-to-GDP-ratio of, 287; treaty of friendship with the Soviet Union of, 173; women of, 211–14. *See also* Vietnam War
Vietnam War, 20, 46, 66, 162, 219, 223. *See also* Vietnam
violence: of Korean Americans in Los Angeles, 135; of the Red Brigades, 46; of the Uyghurs, 234–38, 240. *See also* terrorism
Voice of America, 298

Wahid, President Abdurrahman, 165
Wall Street Journal, 288
Wang, Gary, 37
Wang Chaowen, 273, 275
Wang Jianlin, 38
Wang Sicong, 38
War on Terror, 236. *See also* terrorism; United States
Weatherford, Teddy, 32–35
Western Asia, 234. *See also* Asia
West Germany, Red Army faction in, 46. *See also* Germany
Widodo, President Joko, 175
women: Chinese, 34, 209–17, 217n7; empowerment of Japanese, 57; in Maoism, 43; in Thailand, 223. *See also* marriages
World Bank, 255
World Economic Forum (WEF), 156
World Summit for Social Development (Copenhagen, 1995), 55
World Trade Organization (WTO), 69, 254, 286, 289

Wuhan, 250. *See also* China
Wuzhen World Internet Conference
    (WIC), 264, 267. *See also* China

Xi Jinping, President, 41, 48–49, 73, 259,
    264–66, 273, 276, 283–84, 296–97, 301,
    305, 306n3, 316
Xinhua News Agency, 272–75, 298–99, 301.
    See also China
Xinjiang, 2, 112, 162–63; Chinese invest-
    ment in, 235, 237; Chinese treatment
    of, 233–41, 248; Communist takeover
    of, 239; Uyghur-Han tensions in,
    240–41. *See also* China; Uyghur
    people

Yamaguchi, Yoshiko (Li Xianglan), 35–36
Yamanaka, Shinya, 142, 146–47

Yang Jiechi, 67
Yan Xuetong, 67
Yeun, Steven, 185
Yeung, Thomas, 37
Yokohama, 83. *See also* Japan
Yomiuri Shimbun, 314
yuhaksaeng (students studying abroad), 94
Yu Hua: *Brothers*, 315
Yukio, Hatoyama, 22

Zhang Weiwei, 285
Zhang Xiao, 227
Zhao Tingyang, 67
Zhou Xuan, 33–34, 36
Zimbabwe, 277
Zimbabwe African National Union
    (ZANU), 45
ZTE, 203, 266, 284

Founded in 1893,
UNIVERSITY OF CALIFORNIA PRESS
publishes bold, progressive books and journals
on topics in the arts, humanities, social sciences,
and natural sciences—with a focus on social
justice issues—that inspire thought and action
among readers worldwide.

The UC PRESS FOUNDATION
raises funds to uphold the press's vital role
as an independent, nonprofit publisher, and
receives philanthropic support from a wide
range of individuals and institutions—and from
committed readers like you. To learn more, visit
ucpress.edu/supportus.

Made in the USA
Thornton, CO
12/28/22 18:08:46

f4f5ee6a-8f63-4b66-9eb9-d9d6ae913b93R01